D1165778

Majority Minority

Justin Gest

OXFORD

UNIVERSITY PRESS

OXFORD
UNIVERSITY PRESS

Oxford University Press is a department of the University of Oxford. It furthers
the University's objective of excellence in research, scholarship, and education
by publishing worldwide. Oxford is a registered trade mark of Oxford University
Press in the UK and certain other countries.

Published in the United States of America by Oxford University Press
198 Madison Avenue, New York, NY 10016, United States of America.

Library of Congress Control Number: 2021950971
ISBN 978–0–19–764179–8

DOI: 10.1093/oso/9780197641798.001.0001

1 3 5 7 9 8 6 4 2

Printed by Sheridan Books, Inc., United States of America

The difference between peace and mayhem is velocity.

—**Teju Cole,** *Blind Spot*

Contents

Acknowledgments

The seventeenth-century English poet John Donne, wrote, "No man is an island entire of itself; every man is a piece of the continent, a part of the main."

In pursuing this study of many islands—some on the periphery of the earth—in order to understand trends on the mainlands of today's politics, I was no exception to Donne's rule. Indeed, I was reliant on the support of so many dear colleagues and friends; they were each a bridge over the shifting sea.

Majority Minority was first conceived during my 2017 study leave at Henrietta Moore's Institute for Global Prosperity at University College London. Henrietta has always nourished my creativity and ambition, and I am forever in debt for her guidance. While in London, I had a fateful meeting with my other beloved mentor, David Held, at St. Pancras Station. David passed away before I ever saw him again, but his advice that August day was—as ever—so intelligent and pivotal to my formulation of this book.

Upon my return to Washington, DC, I was in frequent correspondence with Jack Goldstone, who always found time to read drafts of this book and its contents. His advice was sage, constructive, and so clarifying. In January 2021, Jack also masterfully chaired a two-day book workshop, during which I received invaluable feedback from brilliant thinkers, including Richard Alba, Johanna Birnir, Eve Fairbanks, Nancy Foner, Morris Levy, Noora Lori, Roger Waldinger, Min Zhou, and Daniel Ziblatt. Thank you, all.

In between the book's conception and completion, I learned an enormous amount from Mark Frost, Hidetaka Hirota, and Mariko Iijima, my collaborators in a special issue of the *Journal of Ethnic and Migration Studies*. Raymond Ramcharitar was another key contributor, indispensable to my fieldwork in Trinidad and Tobago and my general intellectual development these past few years. I am also grateful for the engagement of Amitava Choudhury, Jane Kinninmont, and Davianna Pōmaikaʻi McGregor, the last of whom was indispensable to my fieldwork in Hawaiʻi. I could not have covered so much ground without you all. My thanks also to the journal's editors, Paul Statham and James Hampshire.

In my fieldwork and case studies, I am profoundly grateful for the generosity of my many respondents. They trusted me, gave me their time, and opened their souls in a remarkably candid way. I am also indebted to various people whom I cannot thank publicly for the information and tips they provided off the record or on background. In the field, I was further aided by guidance from Hussain Al-Shabib, Betsy Cole, James Crabtree, and Justin Gengler, and research assistance from Justin Fraterman and Sally Kishi.

In my survey research, I appreciate the wisdom and friendship of my coauthors, Jeremy Ferwerda, Morris Levy, and Tyler Reny—wonderful partners and excellent scholars who have contributed so much to my understanding of political behavior and political psychology.

Different parts of the book benefited from a Social Science Research Council workshop led by Ira Katznelson, a special-issue partnership with Karen Alter and Michael Zürn, a journal workshop at George Mason University sponsored by Dean Mark Rozell, and personal feedback from Daphne Halikiopoulou and Steve Levitsky. I also want to thank Terri Givens, Eric Kaufmann, and the many anonymous colleagues who reviewed either the book manuscript or articles related to its contents over the last few years.

At Oxford University Press, I would like to thank my editors, Angela Chnapko, Dave McBride, and Niko Pfund for their balanced judgment, smart management, and faith in my work. Thanks also to Alexcee Bechthold, Richa Jobin, David Lampo, Mehmet Yildirim, and Alex Reeves for their work in preparing the book for publication.

Indirectly, this book benefited from my countless conversations with the unsung heroes of American civil society addressing the social challenges of demographic change and the political conflict it is generating. In particular, Wendy Feliz and Suzette Brooks Masters have been invaluable thought partners, and I also appreciate the impactful conversations I have had with luminaries like Samar Ali, Tom Davis, Josh Dickson, Mary Ellen Geiss, Jonathan Gruber, Zac Hill, Caroline Hopper, Katie Lauer, Maya MacGuineas, Andrew Mangino, Mike Murphy, Eboo Patel, Ashley Quarcoo, Stephen Noble Smith, Tim Shriver, Mike Van Haelewyn, and Eric Ward. If the United States is to surmount these challenges, it will be thanks in no small part to the tireless efforts of this motley group.

My fieldwork and survey experiments were made possible by research grants from the Alliance of Liberals and Democrats for Europe, Bloomberg Philanthropies' New American Economy, the Charles Koch Foundation, and the International Republican Institute. Thank you for your interest in the politics of immigration and demographic change and your generous support of my research agenda.

Subtly, silently, but substantially, this book has the fingerprints of my outstanding research assistant, Tim O'Shea. There was no task too daunting, too extraordinary, or too arduous for Tim. He rose to every occasion and supported the preparation of my manuscript despite his own scholarly pursuits and other commitments. And he did it all with charisma and a great sense of humor.

Finally, for their personal support, I would like to thank my friends, and especially my family—Max and Gail, Darren and Rebecca; Phillip and Franklin; György and Tanja; Ádám and George; Valentina and Hugo; and my dear Monika, who keeps everything in perspective for me and does so much to facilitate the work that brings me so much joy. As David Held wrote in one of his last messages to me, "Life is a joy. The rest will fall into place."

Justin Gest
Arlington, Virginia

PART I
DEMOGRAPHIC CHANGE AND THE NATION-STATE

1
Majority Minority

An Introduction

A Fortune Told

On March 3, 2015, the date for American social upheaval was set.

That day, the US Census Bureau published a report projecting that by 2044, the United States would become a "majority-minority" country—that is, a country where immigration and fertility rates lead one or more ethnic or religious minorities to outnumber the original ethnic or religious majority. In the United States, it has been understood as a scenario where non-Hispanic white people comprise less than 50 percent of the population.[1] The report's release spurred a string of news analyses—some gleeful, others anxious—about "the end of the white majority" just one generation away, a stunning forecast in a normally obscure government write-up.

The report's author never realized just how pivotal her projections would be to the course of American politics.

"No one's ever called my work 'historic,'" said Jennifer Ortman, chief of the Bureau's Population Projections Branch at the time of the report's publication, "but I suppose you get people's interest when you talk about where they are going. It's like a fortune teller, saying here's what our nation might look like in 10 or 20 years."[2]

Americans' reactions were swift and came from across the political spectrum. White nationalists fear-mongered about "white extinction," while Democrats in Washington, DC, declared that "demography is destiny" to herald their hoped-for future electoral victories with the decline of the Republicans' principal constituency. The predicted demographic decline of the majority racial group in a majoritarian democracy provoked equal parts anxiety and anticipation, and a large dose of hyperbole. Nearly all ignored the way that racial boundaries had historically shifted over the course of American history and how they might shift again.[3]

Demographic change has been driving wedges between Americans for decades, and these divides only deepened after the Census Bureau report's

Majority Minority. Justin Gest, Oxford University Press. © Justin Gest 2022. DOI: 10.1093/oso/9780197641798.003.0001

release. America's two political camps have hardened into those who embrace this projected future and those who resist it. On one side, leaders talk globalism, immigration, and reparation. On the other, they invoke nationalism, nativism, and nostalgia.

Studies have demonstrated the ways in which the most fearful Americans exaggerate the size of minority populations. However, even when their perceptions are corrected, such groups' attitudes toward immigration remain very restrictive.[4] Extensive evidence suggests that demographic change and the cultural threat that many Americans think it poses drove the 2016 election of Donald Trump and his overhaul of the Republican Party's approaches to immigration policy and global affairs.[5] There is a simultaneous sense of racial resentment and being left behind.[6]

The American experience has inspired fear in other multiethnic democracies that have also experienced changes in their immigration flows since the 1960s. Convinced that American demographic shifts presage their own futures, nativist movements and far-right political parties in other nations have grown in power. These groups advocate against further immigration and for the systematic assimilation or expulsion of ethnic and religious minorities already present. It doesn't matter that the demography of places like Britain, France, Germany, Denmark, the Netherlands, and Sweden bears little resemblance to that of the United States. The demographic anxieties, the racialization, the nationalism are the same.

Culture Wars

Across these American and European contexts, the sharp growth in the number of foreign-born people coincided with other major transformations in the late twentieth century. The decline of the manufacturing era stimulated the shift to a more service-oriented global market and a political realignment. This economic shift weakened the wealth, status, and political clout of millions of native-born white people and thousands of labor unions—which had long powered center-left and socialist parties across the transatlantic space. In the 1990s, Democrats, Liberals, and Labourites won a series of elections thanks to their incremental embrace of neoliberal economics. These "third way" politics brought the left into greater agreement with their center-right counterparts, leaving future elections to be contested much more on cultural grounds.

In the United States, debates raged over whether homosexual people should be permitted to serve in the military or marry, whether civilians have a right to own and carry automatic weapons, and the place of prayer and religion in schools. And as the Democratic Party became increasingly associated with immigrants and racial and religious minorities, Republicans also shifted debates to corner their counterparts into unpopular defenses of undocumented immigrants, refugees, asylum seekers, and Muslims.

This national discussion—oriented to mobilize voters to protect or rethink traditional American values—tested the extent of individual rights, tolerance, and empathy. Supporting further immigration or minority rights became associated with other cultural viewpoints about the prevalence of structural racism, the legality of recreational drug use, or what constitutes sexual assault. Each new value-driven debate suggested another dimension of American identity that was suddenly subject to demographic change and the shifts in cultural beliefs that accompanied it.

These debates and others moved into matters of moral conviction and lifestyle. Rather than ideological disagreements about how to pursue *shared* values, these culture wars implied the presence of vastly different value systems that attenuated the American social fabric. State and local governments began passing laws that created different legal environments where different parts of America endorsed different ways of life. Partisans moralized about the other side's constituents until it became conventional to perceive political counterparts to be fundamentally evil or depraved. As each new election posed a greater existential threat, Democrats and Republicans stepped up efforts to delegitimize electoral victories through impeachments, claims of election fraud and tampering, and conspiracy theories.

The result is an impasse—a political stalemate and legislative paralysis amid the racialization of American politics and the politicization of American culture.[7] Today, most Republican voters self-identify as white, vast majorities of nonwhite racial and religious minorities support Democrats, and American elections pivot on highly symbolic identity politics. Rather than broaden their outreach to rural or white working-class constituents, many on the left wait for demographic change to reach its righteous destiny. And rather than evolve with the demography of the country, many on the right trade in demonstrably false narratives and contort democratic institutions to sustain power. The imperative of culture wars is to narrow rather than broaden coalitions, purging those who compromise and question the moral orthodoxy.

How Individuals Respond to Demographic Change

Up until now, most of our knowledge about large-scale responses to demographic change extrapolates from social and psychological studies of individual people's reactions to different events or information. Much of this research has focused on the United States as a sort of laboratory in light of its remarkably diverse and diversifying population (see Figure 1.1). Between 1980 and 2015, the number of people of Hispanic origin has increased in every American state and 95 percent of all counties; in three states—California, New Mexico, and Texas—the population has reached majority minority status. A fourth state, Hawai'i, has been majority minority for some time.[8] In the same time period, the Asian American population increased in forty-nine states, the African American population increased in forty-six states, and there has been an across-the-board decline in the country's white population.[9]

According to this American-centered research, a principal obstacle to co-existence is that, even when native-born populations recognize the integration of ethnic minorities and immigrants, natives still perceive them to be different. In a 2016 survey, Washington University's Ariela Schachter showed respondents two profiles of individuals and asked which of the two they would rather have as a neighbor and how similar they rated the prospective neighbors to themselves. White Americans, she found, are generally open to relationships with immigrant-origin individuals, with the exception of Black immigrants, Black natives, and undocumented immigrants. At the same time,

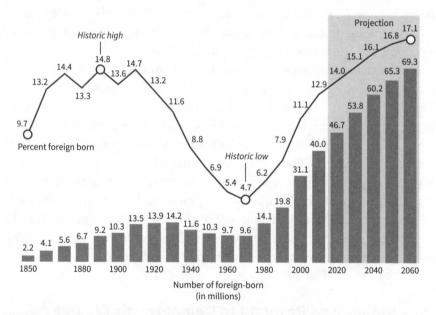

Figure 1.1 Foreign-born population of the United States between 1850 and 2010 and projected from 2020 to 2060 (unadjusted for the 2020 coronavirus pandemic).

Source: Jonathan Vespa, Lauren Medina, and David Armstrong, "Demographic Turning Points for the United States: Population Projections for 2020 to 2060," U.S. Census Bureau, March 2018.

white natives view all racial minorities, regardless of their citizenship status or other characteristics, as very dissimilar to themselves.[10] This disconnect suggests that, for nonwhite groups, even where assimilation occurs, cultural acceptance does not.

Researchers have also found that social relations are conditioned by the intensifying pressures of demographic change, intolerance, and tribalism. In a 2012 study, Trinity College's Robert Outten and his colleagues randomly assigned a sample of white American respondents to two scenarios: the first group viewed a graph of ethnicity-focused demographic data for 2003, while the second group viewed 2003 demographic figures as well as projections for 2060—the point at which white Americans were then estimated to become a minority. The researchers found that participants in the future white minority condition reported feeling greater sympathy for white people and significantly more anger toward and fear of ethnic minorities than participants exposed only to the 2003 information.[11]

When alerted to the growth of minority out-groups, white Americans attempt to protect and enhance their social position. In a 2015 study, Columbia University's Maria Abascal randomly exposed American respondents to information about Hispanic population growth and then tested the effect of the information on their redistributive generosity. White people who received this information contributed significantly more to white recipients than to Black recipients; they were also significantly more likely to define their identity as "white" rather than as "American."[12] New York University's Maureen Craig and Yale's Jennifer Richeson found that white participants who read about future American racial demographics expressed a greater relative preference to be in settings and interactions with other white people than with racial minorities, when compared to those who did not receive the treatment.[13] Like Abascal, they found that such implicit bias emerged even in reference to minority groups that are not primarily responsible for the dramatic increases in the nonwhite share of the total US population.

Other researchers have used different techniques to simulate demographic change in order to test its effects on public attitudes. In a 2014 study, Harvard University's Ryan Enos assigned a small number of Spanish-speaking individuals to board particular commuter trains at stations in homogeneously white communities in the Boston metropolitan area at the same time each day for two weeks to repeatedly expose the same commuters to a diversifying population. Enos found that respondents who waited on platforms with "non-invasive Spanish-speaking people" favored more exclusionary policies, indicating that threatening behavior is "not a necessary component for the stimulation of exclusionary attitudes."[14] Notably, Enos recorded opinions after both three days and ten days. While opinions on both days were more exclusionary for the Spanish-exposed group, opinions on Day 3 were more exclusionary than those on Day 10, indicating that longer exposure to an outgroup may moderate negative reactions and ultimately lead to more comfortable coexistence.

Of course, the process of becoming a majority-minority society is one that lasts far more than ten days; it is a multidecade, if not multicentury, process. And in the groundbreaking studies I've highlighted, people are alerted to demographic change suddenly and asked for their swift reactions. In contrast, demographic change is experienced far more gradually or through interpersonal exposure,[15] and there is time for people's sentiments to be influenced and shaped by the adaptations of institutions, businesses, and civil society.

How Societies Respond to Demographic Change

Alas, we know much less about how societies respond when the majority status of the native group is threatened. In a well-known study of such a phenomenon, Massachusetts Institute of Technology's Myron Weiner examined the consequences of internal migration between Indian states and regions, particularly cases in which opportunistic migrants clash with natives unnerved by the subsequent alteration of social, economic, and political hierarchies. In conclusion, Weiner wrote, "The challenge of a political leadership is to find a way of assisting those who are falling behind in the development process, without adopting policies that constrict the innovative, ambitious, creative elements of a society whose talents are essential if the entire country is to move forward."[16]

As explored in the fledgling field of political demography, finding this balance is highly subject to the actions of states and their political institutions.[17] While governance by ethnic or religious minorities was common in earlier history, the modern spread of democracy and popular sovereignty has produced a pervasive expectation that majority ethnicities should hold power.[18] These expectations have led to violent conflict in states confronting political matters related to multiple indigenous ethnic groups, but also social conflict in states confronting political matters related to ethnic minorities of foreign origins that ascend to power, such as those considered in this book.[19] The conclusions from these studies show the extent to which the state is both an actor and a stage and how the majority itself is a subjective entity—a nation whose boundaries are constructed by the state.[20]

In sum, social scientists have come to understand human habits in the face of demographic change; they are largely competitive and untrusting.

Despite decades in each other's presence, significant divisions between ethnoreligious groups still characterize most diverse societies today, dimming hopes that simple repeated exposure to other ethnoreligious groups promotes coexistence. Worse, the state—with its power over popular conceptions of national identity and membership—frequently uses rhetoric about national culture to reinforce social divisions and fortify the status of one subgroup at the expense of others. However, we know little about why and how these bad habits are sometimes tempered to promote greater coexistence. Filling this gap in our knowledge requires a long-term and cross-national examination to understand the ways social and psychological habits may be affected by differences in institutions and leadership in different countries. To anticipate future responses to demographic change, this book begins by looking to the past.

Island Nations

The evidence I collect in this book shows that America's contentious standoff is predictable but also preventable. To anticipate the American future and those of other diversifying multiethnic states, I study the experiences of other sovereign societies that reached earlier majority-minority milestones similarly driven by foreigners' immigration.

Majority-minority transitions are rare, but they are not unique.[21] In modern history, not even a dozen societies qualify, and all those that do emerge as the residual demographics of the British Empire's pursuit of free-flowing capital, commerce, and labor between its dominions, where the arrival of settlers brought wars or epidemics, then slavery, and then migrants to fill labor needs. The path of the various countries currently facing a majority minority future is not so different. While this sequence of events within a century transformed the populations of the small societies I study here, it will end up taking another generation before the same milestone is reached in the United States, and a couple more in Canada and Australia, if present trends continue. Still, we can learn from the experiences of other countries—their successes, their struggles.

The societies that I study—first historically and then with contemporary fieldwork—represent the full range of circumstances across the world's majority-minority milestones. They feature different original populations, sources of labor, regime types, and histories of slavery, immigration, enfranchisement, and identity politics, all across disparate historical periods and geographic regions (see Figure 1.2). But despite these differences, I discern

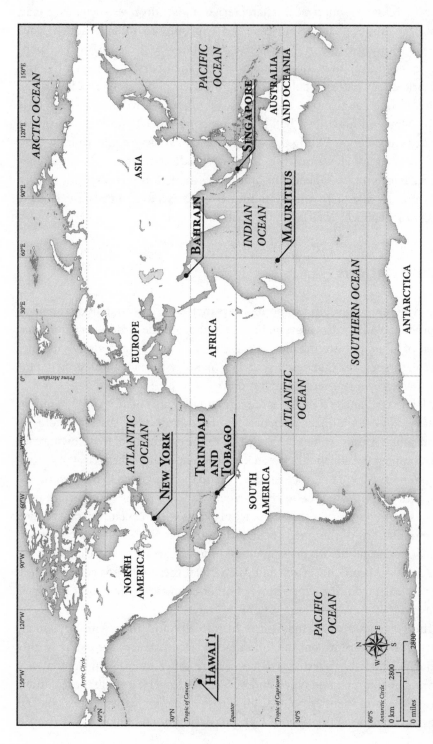

Map of case societies.

similar patterns of segregation, identity politics, and backlash that produce specific classes of social outcomes, each an alternative political response.

My cases center on six sets of small islands: Bahrain, Hawai'i, Mauritius, Singapore, Trinidad and Tobago, and the islands comprising New York City. Islands' separation from the world's mainlands and their fragile population distributions make them acutely sensitive to demographic change. This separation is also what makes them especially exposed to demographic change: historically, they were accessible from all sides and often relied on their links with the rest of the world for commerce and the exchange of social and economic resources. Moreover, for the purposes of this study, islands act as a sort of social scientific laboratory—microcosms that simulate a range of human reactions to transformational social change to better anticipate responses to such transformations on a larger scale.

In **Singapore**, the regime uses meticulous administrative laws, immigration admissions, and public narratives to secure Chinese hegemony over a city-state that was a small, though important, part of the Malay Federation until August 9, 1965. Its majority-minority milestone came overnight, when the island came under the control of a Chinese-origin head of state, Lee Kuan Yew, overseeing a large Chinese-ethnic majority.

Bahrain's Royal Court and Sunni minority rule a predominantly Shia citizenry, but all are outnumbered by a mix of low-skilled guest workers recruited principally from South Asia and high-skilled Western and Arab expats—none of whom has access to Bahraini nationality and the generous state subsidies it guarantees. But the island country's population imbalance—and social stability—has been shaken by the regime's strategic naturalization of thousands of Sunni Arab immigrants recruited for its police and security services over the past two decades.

Trinidad and Tobago reached its majority-minority milestone around 1995, when the islands, long ruled by an Afro-Caribbean majority, elected their first Indian-origin prime minister, Basdeo Panday. The political parties have since been bitterly split into factions of predominantly African and Indian origin. Since then, every debate, no matter how small, has become a proxy battle in the existential war for racial and cultural preeminence on these southeastern Caribbean islands.

In **Mauritius**, parties are similarly divided by religion and ethnicity. There, the Catholic African Creole population was the Indian Ocean island's majority twice—once when Dutch colonizers abandoned Mauritius and left their slaves behind, and again when slavery was abolished in 1835. But the majority-minority milestone came three decades after the British Empire began importing indentured laborers from India, who took control with independence in 1968, leaving Creoles consumed by a nostalgic politics that seeks to reinstitute a sovereignty they never fully held.

The state of **New York**, which controlled its immigration admissions and removals until US immigration laws were federalized in 1882, was subject to virulent ethnic politics after the arrival and enfranchisement of Irish Catholic migrants fleeing the Potato Famine. Its majority-minority milestone was postponed with the changing definitions of whiteness in nineteenth- and twentieth-century America, but its politics were irreversibly altered when the weight of Irish bloc voting drove Democratic electoral victories in the 1840s.

The native population of the **Hawaiian Kingdom** was decimated by Western disease after contact was first made in 1778 and was outnumbered within a few decades of immigrants' recruitment to sugar plantations established by American entrepreneurs after 1840. Before an 1893 coup by the United States, the native population contested foreigners' power and landownership with a wave of nationalism that pressured the monarchy to pass laws that privileged the status of Native Hawaiians.

While all these societies that confronted a majority-minority milestone inevitably experienced a wave of nativism—and sometimes quite intense backlash—Singapore and Bahrain resisted demographic change through co-optation or *suppression*; Trinidad and Mauritius suffer from racialized political parties and endured irresolvable social *tension*; and New York and Hawai'i eventually reconciled through a *redefinition* of the nation. To inform a better approach in the United States and other countries confronting demographic transformations today, this book's motivating question is: What drives majority- minority states to these different outcomes?

Nation-Building

Many observers of social relations would have us believe that the answer lies in individuals' ability to cope with social change. The implication of the many political and psychological studies of human reactions to demographic shifts—as sophisticated as they are—is that social progress is principally held back by persistent human tendencies toward racism and xenophobia. Even historical studies of immigration emphasize the outsize role played by popular backlash and discontent.[22] Indeed, the scourge of social exclusion and prejudice is unquestionably pervasive. However, individuals tend to perceive their identities as primordial and static; consequently, any approach that relies upon individuals' self-realized enlightenment as the vehicle for successful coexistence discounts the constructed nature of national identity and the power of the state to manage the process of demographic change through its *institutions* and *rhetoric*.

This book reveals the way that majority-minority relations are neither primordially conflictive nor derived solely from uncontrollable popular sentiment; they are the product of leaders' political and rhetorical choices. Majority-Minority milestones are governed.

The state has always had a subtle hand and a strong interest in the process of unifying diverse peoples sufficiently to govern them. National anthems solemnly croon of glory from centuries-old battlefields; national flowers symbolize the nation's indigeneity; national museums assemble artifacts to crystallize narratives about the origin, tragedies, and victories of an indomitable people. The state is ultimately responsible for defining and regulating many of the practices in which people can partake, the spaces in which they are permitted to move, and—through broadcast media, education, and environmental measures—provides a framework for daily life.[23]

Identity and unity, while individualized and always evolving, are also something we construct and commit to as a society, and if government doesn't have a hand in coordinating these efforts and bringing them to scale, it will be left to markets, algorithms, and opportunistic politicians—which is where the world finds itself right now.

The essential challenge that diversifying states face is the evolution of their identity. For so long, states have been built on the idea of an inviolable nation, implicitly or explicitly united by a common ethnicity, race, or religion. Large-scale, persistent migration fundamentally alters the composition of that nation, and therefore many of the political conflicts we witness today can be understood as attempts to reconcile a desire to maintain antecedent understandings of who "we" are with who "we" have become. Much like any individual, societies are composed of dual, countervailing inclinations: to honor our heritage and preserve the traditions of the past and simultaneously to acknowledge, adapt to, and progress into the future. Just as any state that abandons its heritage risks losing the people's continuing allegiance, any state that fails to adapt risks paralysis.

I find that these dueling tendencies express themselves in the politics of inclusion and exclusion, particularly at two critical junctures in their development. First, states must decide if all peoples will be recognized and treated equally as citizens before the law, and also represented equally in its institutions. Second, states must decide whether the construction of the nation and its identity is one that reflects the diversity of the people or one that seeks to promote one group over others. While inclusive redefinitions overrode historic inequities (e.g., Hawai'i and New York), governments that pursued exclusive identities were confronted by either suppressed social tension in states with structurally unequal constituencies (e.g., Bahrain and Singapore) or overt contestation in states with equally recognized constituencies (e.g., Mauritius and Trinidad).

More specifically, I identify a variety of ways that states build inclusive or exclusive nations through their institutions. These focus on the following:

1. The orientation of state ideologies.
2. The education of young people.
3. The curation of national culture and tradition.
4. The governance of commerce.
5. The identification of threats.

Grounded in a rich variety of examples that arise over the histories of my six case countries, these five pivots apply to any society grappling with identity politics. And just as no society will pivot only to coexistence, no society will pivot only to inflamed social tensions. Indeed, in most societies, there will be coinciding examples of inclusive and exclusive actions in different regions or among different subgroups. It's a matter of where the national balance lies.

As the final part of this book will emphasize and explore, the scales are often tipped by government rhetoric. My surveys of contemporary public opinion show how anti-immigrant nativists may be persuaded to liberalize their views if they are approached by leaders with whom they co-identify and if they are presented with justifications for immigration that relate to the survival of their nation. In the context of demographic changes, these findings reveal the strategic political importance of "meeting people where they are." They also provide new evidence that emotionally charged attitudes toward immigration, identity, and demographic change—long thought to be rooted in prejudice and therefore resistant to change—are actually subject to leadership.

Overview

The late historian Eric Hobsbawm wrote that nations are constructed from above but cannot be understood unless examined from below, in "the assumptions, hopes, needs, longings, and interests of ordinary people."[24] In the spirit of this dialogue between states and their citizens, I triangulate the subject matter by examining it from different angles and with different methods: secondary historical research, contemporary interview-based fieldwork, and survey experiments.

Part I: Demographic Change and the Nation-State

Chapter 2 considers the relationship between nationalism and demographic change. I argue that states undergoing transformational demographic change have struggled to escape the pull of nationalism because they have failed to evolve the concept of their respective nations and peoples. Instead, they have sought to institutionalize the understanding of the current (and perhaps temporary) majority as the boundaries of an enduring people—which has made the definition of the nation and its public identity a primary source of conflict.

Chapter 3 introduces the book's comparative historical analysis of six societies in which the indigenous or native-born majority lost its numerical advantage—Bahrain, Hawai'i, Mauritius, New York, Singapore, and Trinidad and Tobago—with the goal of understanding what drives divergent reactions to such demographic transformation. With a majority minority transition imminent, these societies pursued one of three different paths: (1) resist demographic change through co-optation or suppression, (2) endure racialized politics and persistent social tension, or (3) reconcile through a redefinition of the nation. Aligning their histories reveals parallels across disparate majority-minority countries but also the ways in which they diverge. I pause the analysis after the first point of divergence in order to contextualize our historical understanding in contemporary social outcomes, based on fieldwork in each region.

Part II: Island Nations

Chapters 4 through 9 report the results of my fieldwork in the six case countries. This research centers on the primary venues of identity and heritage politics—the cultural spaces subject to demographic change. In Singapore, I study the government's portrayals of national history in museums, textbooks, and other formal media. In Bahrain, I examine the kingdom's use of citizenship as a political instrument. In Trinidad and Tobago, I study the latent power relations of the annual Carnival. In Mauritius, I study the symbolic politics of ancient maroon villages. In New York, I scrutinize the century-long hold of Irish Americans on New York City's Police Department (NYPD). And in Hawai'i, I study land reclamation initiatives pursuing a semblance of Native Hawaiian sovereignty.

Each case is motivated by the same existential questions that vex societies undergoing rapid demographic change today: Who are the legitimate people entitled to rule? What is the source of nationhood that binds a people together? I explore the origins of these questions with extensive secondary historical research and then study how they manifest in today's cultural politics by conducting over one hundred face-to-face, unstructured interviews. My subjects range from former prime ministers and sitting ministerial-level officials to local activists, each selected for their unique perspective on the cultural and political phenomena I examine in each venue. I supplement this interview content with observations from full-immersion fieldwork that lasted about eight weeks across the venues. These detailed examinations not only tell the discrete stories of troubled island nations; they also reveal alternative futures for today's multiethnic democracies.

Part III: Redefining the People

Chapter 10 resumes the comparative historical analysis with these contemporary contexts in mind. In all six of the majority minority cases, demographic change led to calls for greater power-sharing by once-subjugated social groups and subsequent backlash against them. Surveying the six cases, I find that states employ a variety of techniques to slow down or mitigate the impact of demographic change. I classify these instruments by the outcomes they seek to achieve: who comes; who counts; and to a much more limited effect, who connects. "Who comes" refers to the number and attributes of immigrants admitted and the state's monopoly on border control. "Who counts" focuses on the distribution of electoral power among people already present and the state's attempts to alter it. Finally, "who connects" refers to the extent to which different population subgroups meaningfully interact with one another.
While demographic change destabilizes the elementary components of a nation, it is not alone a sufficient condition that predicts social conflict. Rather, I find that social conflict is contingent on whether the state equally enfranchises the newcomer population and whether its subsequent redefinition of the national identity is inclusive or exclusive—according to the combination of state institutions and rhetoric.

Because the historical and field research demonstrates the critical power of rhetorical leadership on political relations, chapter 11 considers the effect of strategic "messages" on public opinion about migration and demographic change. Using nationally representative surveys across nineteen European countries, the chapter explores how public attitudes liberalize when citizens are presented with information that frames demographic change not as a threat to the nation but as a tool for national survival. Are people more resistant to cultural threat frames once they understand the way immigration allows their nation to maintain current population levels?

As messages can be lost or weakened in a cacophonous public sphere, chapter 11 applies similar logic to the selection of messengers. Emerging evidence suggests that exposure to messages from elites who share in-group identities with citizens can change those citizens' attitudes on divisive issues, particularly if the message is counter-stereotypical but believable.[25] If elites can mollify immigration concerns, this may open strategies for promoting acceptance of demographic change among those otherwise inclined toward nativism. In the second part of chapter 11, I report the results of an experiment testing the extent to which white Republicans in the United States update their attitudes on immigration policy when exposed to messages from in-group (white Republican) elites who provide counter-stereotypical cues on immigration by advocating a moderate perspective.

In chapter 12, I examine the way that debates over national identity are often played out at the level of individual identity choices. A majority-minority milestone in the nineteenth-century United States was co-opted when the government admitted European-origin ethnic minorities into the American concept of whiteness. In this chapter, I report the results of survey research that evaluates the likelihood that this might happen again. Indeed, a century later, American society is becoming more ethnically mixed than it has ever been,[26] and today's melting pot reflects the growing embrace of identity choice, fluidity, and multiplicity.[27] Does a rhetorical environment that excludes people of foreign origins or minority backgrounds deter borderline white Americans from adopting multiple identities that bridge different groups or pressure them to "drift" toward whiteness?

In scope, the choices of governments affect population trends but also frame identities at the most personal level. Based on the sum of the book's research findings, chapter 13 concludes by clarifying the goal of any multiethnic society confronting swift demographic change: expand the sense of who "we" are. This goes far beyond who holds citizenship; it is a matter of reimagining the boundaries of the nation—the people with whom we perceive sharing a common experience, such that we may identify them as an extension of ourselves, that we may empathize with their plight, and that we may expect them to listen to our own. At its core, this reimagining and unification of disparate groups must become a criterion for governance—a multidecade endeavor, the greatest social challenge of our times.

2
Escape Velocity

The Pull of Nationalism amid Demographic Change

The Indispensable Nation

The US Census Bureau's 2015 announcement of the country's approaching majority-minority milestone only made tangible what observers of democracy have long known: precisely because the government is subject to the will of its people, the country is subject to its demographic composition. When the composition of the people changes, therefore, the governance and character of the country change too.

This volatility, however, runs counter to the static national images that countries work hard to cultivate. Governments have historically constructed the idea of their country—no matter how new it is—as primordial in origin and long enduring, even if in different, unrecognizable forms. Governments may change, but the people and their culture are thought to remain steadfast.

These static national images, even those with the most historically accurate origins, are often exaggerated and cleansed of complications. The boundaries between nations of people have always been blurry. All peoples are the product of cross-national influences to some degree. And primordial stories often justify nefarious, false hierarchies of moral worth: colonialism, slavery, eugenics, and genocide. Such details are inconvenient for the assembly of a purified, virtuous national myth.

This chapter focuses on the relationship between nationalism and demographic change in democracies because the contemporary states most acutely affected by demographic change are largely democracies, particularly those advancing toward a majority-minority milestone. However, the image of the nation as a rock is vital to any regime's survival. All nation-building projects anchor their future in the unity of some popular collective will. Independent of constitutional rules and decision-making processes, this concept of the nation is indispensable to the state.

Nationalism starts as a political justification for a nation's—a people's— claim to territory, a claim that the people and the state are inextricable.

Majority Minority. Justin Gest, Oxford University Press. © Justin Gest 2022. DOI: 10.1093/oso/9780197641798.003.0002

But once the claim to the territory is no longer in question, nationalism becomes a popular instrument to define and defend the political community in times of change. This popular form of nationalism is inflamed by war and conflict, but more conventionally today by the settlement of immigrants, by the investments of foreign companies, by the creep of global mass culture. Popular nationalism has been seized by political leaders and manipulated to serve political purposes by framing their adversaries or certain phenomena as threats to "the people." It is this form of nationalism—practiced by both the state and average people—that concerns this book.

All countries periodically argue about and update their definition of "the people" in the vigorous, sometimes divisive debates that characterize a robust public sphere.[1] Each debate requires "the people" to build new political coalitions, adapt to new ideas, and accommodate demographic change. These national discussions always alienate certain subgroups, those who may be excluded from ruling majorities but who remain in the political community. That underlying sense of inclusion is essential for a nation to survive these passing debates, so democracies need to offer their constituents a "thick" sense of collective meaning, a sense of civic status, and material well-being.[2]

Still, identifying "the people" necessarily entails exclusion. In what has recently been called the "boundary problem," the question of how "the people" can rule can be answered only after the boundaries identifying "the people" are determined.[3] The problem is that, precisely because "the people" are thought to precede the state and transcend its different governments, "the people" are identified according to very undemocratic principles that are not necessarily reflective of the current population. Even the world's most democratic states are rooted in ethnoreligious, antecedent understandings of "the people" and routinely contest their peoplehood.

Sometimes, it's simple: the Swedish people have historically been Scandinavian, Protestant, and until recently, rather homogeneous. It gets complex when states are federations of nations, like Spain, which is centered on Castilians but surrounded by the irredentist nations of Cataluña and the Basque Country. It is even complicated in secular states like France, which is still awkwardly subject to its postcolonial and Catholic heritage. But it is especially thorny in multiethnic settler states like Australia, Canada, and the United States, which were founded on the basis of white racial dominance to justify their early self-governance and now feature some of the most ethnically and religiously diverse populations in the world. Of course, in the era of global migration, even the Swedes have had to rethink their identity; many of the world's most advanced democracies are now multi-ethnic spaces.

Because different interests vie for power by claiming that they represent the collective will, attempts to define the people never really end in these environments. The practices of democratic politics, political scientist David Bateman writes, "constantly reopen the question of 'who are the people,' creating a fundamental tension and perhaps intractable dilemma between the requisites of stable democratic regimes, the types of politics these are likely to produce, and the questions that need to be answered by those looking to build or consolidate a democracy."[4]

Demographic change injects enormous uncertainty into political communities because it challenges nations that have long explained and identified their persistence with the creed of a specific ethnoreligious people to endure when their ethnoreligious composition changes and includes people they once excluded. Such complications are commonplace throughout history but wiped clean from national memories to reify the nation and consolidate its identity.

Some of today's nations are challenged to endure despite the incorporation of people once identified as existential threats. The patron saint of Spain, where Moroccans make up the largest share of all foreign nationals today, is St. James the Moor-Slayer. The southwestern United States, which was acquired in a war against Mexico, is now populated by more than 30 million people of Mexican origin who were specifically targeted by American immigration rules for a century after the Treaty of Guadalupe Hidalgo. One of Japan's largest immigrant minorities originates from Korea, which Japan has fought on and off since at least the seventh century.

The construction of nations as static and indigenous, therefore, has served to unify disparate subgroups into a unified "people" but also ossified concepts of "the people" in ways detrimental to its inevitable evolution. In the remainder of this chapter, I argue that states undergoing transformational demographic change have struggled to escape the gravitational pull of nationalism precisely because they have failed to evolve the concept of their respective nations and peoples. Instead of achieving this escape velocity away from the tug of ethnic and religious affinities, they have sought to institutionalize the boundaries of the current (and perhaps temporary) ethnic or religious majority as the boundaries of the enduring "people"—which has made the definition of the nation and its public identity a primary source of conflict.

The Gravitational Pull of Ethnicity and Religion

Amid the globalization of the post–Cold War world, ethnic and religious ties were dismissed as a bygone basis for political community, more relevant to the turn of the twentieth century than to our contemporary, cosmopolitan times. Absent the need for liberation from empire, national identities were thought to have run their course. In 1990, Eric Hobsbawm wrote that nationalism was not the historical force it once was: "No longer a major vector in historical development," nationalism now "rarely pretends to be more than a cry of anguish or fury."[5] Anticipating backlash against international migration, he concluded, "The call of ethnicity or language provides no guidance to the future at all. It is merely a protest against the status quo or, more precisely, against 'the others' who threaten the ethnically defined group."[6]

Today, this "mere protest" is realigning party coalitions, paralyzing legislatures, and shredding the social fabric of the world's most advanced countries. Why has it proven to be so difficult for governments to establish escape velocity from the gravitational pull of ethnic and religious politics? Why, across both the developing and advanced world, do ethnic and religious identities continue to mobilize political coalitions and conflict?

Part of the explanation is often thought to be biological: humans are wired to identify with and defend their kin. As much as we yearn for freedom, we crave security—not only physical security but also the security that comes from a connection to family, tribe, ethnicity, religion, and culture.[7] The instinct to focus on preserving those who look like us is one degree of separation from the ethnic nepotism that underlies ethnopolitical disputes.[8] Ethnic change in societies or regions can evoke and trigger these instincts: when individuals believe they are losing control and their world suddenly looks less familiar, defense mechanisms are activated.[9] Differences in ethnic group size and growth then drive the threat perceptions that sow the seeds of conflict. Tracking news articles from the nineteenth into the twenty-first century, there were far more mentions of the phrase "population decline" linked with "nation" or "power" during the decade from 2000 to 2010 than in any earlier decade on record,[10] even though human biology was no different in 1910 than it was in 2010. But racism and interethnic conflict is not genetically coded; it is inflamed by politics.

During the intervening years, the fall of authoritarian regimes and the global diffusion of democracy suddenly increased the salience of ethnic and religious boundaries as a means of political mobilization.[11] Many regions have engaged in interethnic and interreligious disputes, justified as righteous struggles to wrest control of homelands, such as those in the Balkans, the Caucasus, and the Middle East.[12] The differential power of ethnic factions has driven similar conflicts in Lebanon, Pakistan, Iraq, Malaysia, and throughout sub-Saharan Africa.[13] After wars, there has often been an inclination to create coherent territorial states, each inhabited by a separate ethnically and linguistically homogeneous population.[14]

These prominent examples all come from multiethnic or multireligious societies where each of the warring subgroups has some claim to territorial indigeneity or a long-standing presence on the land. The tensions emerging in many of the world's more advanced, democratic societies today are between those with a sense of indigeneity or nativity and those derived from later immigrant arrivals. Democratic participatory institutions allow citizens—by birthright or by naturalization, and of all backgrounds—to compete for their own interests on equal footing. As a result, the racialization of politics is common in all multiethnic democracies, and institutionalized political conflict is considerably more common and stable than violent conflict.[15]

But blaming frayed political relations on liberal democracy is simplistic. By following majoritarian logic and offering short-term electoral rewards to divisive leaders, liberal democratic institutions tempt such leaders to appeal to the worst human instincts when governing multiethnic or multireligious societies. However, liberal democracy does not inherently entail or produce ethnic conflict.

The problem is that governments and their leaders have failed to evolve the concept of their respective nations and peoples sufficiently to establish this metaphorical escape velocity, a national solidarity that is free from or cuts across ethnic and religious affinities. They have struggled to innovate sufficient social and political institutions that bring together the interests of changing ethnic and religious groups. They have barely tried to break down ethnic and religious hierarchies that appropriate social, economic, and political advantages to certain identities, even when this is precisely what demographic change demands. Instead, they have sought to institutionalize the boundaries of the temporary majority as the boundaries of the enduring "people."

Thin Nationalisms

For democracies that admit large numbers of immigrants, defining who "we" are has been challenging because it necessarily entails exclusion in liberal countries with constitutions protecting individual rights. In the resulting cultural debates, scholars and governments have struggled to make both immigrants and native-born people feel included as part of "the people."

At the same time as the Culture Wars of the 1990s and 2000s, a wave of political philosophers set out to craft a concept of "civic" or "inclusive" nationalism grounded in a set of principles *thick* enough to foster a sense of social solidarity but *thin* enough to sustain their countries' liberal foundations.[16] Proposed as a middle ground between the warring ethnoreligious fundamentalism and global cosmopolitanism of the era, this concept sought to balance the reinforcing virtues and illiberal excesses of nationalism.[17] "The idea of a deep attachment to a thin cultural identity is not a paradox of liberal nationalism," Will Kymlicka wrote, "but rather is part of the very definition of liberal nationalism. If such a thing as liberal nationalism exists, it can only be in this form of a deep attachment to a thin identity."[18]

Scholars like Kymlicka inspired a number of governments to attempt to broaden their national identities to incorporate diversifying citizenries into concepts like "Britishness."[19] Founded on universal liberal values, however, these identities were so broad and vague that they lacked any distinct meaning. Indeed, liberalism is inherently averse to such distinctions and traditional values; rather, it is concerned with protecting the fundamental equality of individuals *across* distinctions. To promote the rights of the individual is to supersede the collective will of any majority, the order of any hierarchy, and the authority of any church.[20]

In March 2000, British prime minister Tony Blair sought to unite his country amid a diversifying population, Scottish separatism, and Euro-skepticism by articulating a cohesive British identity centered on "qualities of creativity built on tolerance, openness and adaptability, work and self-improvement, strong communities and families and fair play, rights and responsibilities and an outward looking approach to the world."[21]

But "tolerance," "openness," and "adaptability" are not values that were or are specific to Britain in the way that national identities are expected to be. Indeed, the atmosphere around the 2016 Brexit referendum suggests that these values may not even have been British at all. Blair preceded his proposed principles by stating, "Few would disagree with the qualities that go towards that British identity." And that was the problem. Strong and effective national identities require a mix of inclusivity *and* exclusivity—a tall order.

Ultimately, Blair and other liberals also underestimated the affinity that many of their countrymen held for their ethnicity and/or religious distinctions. Indeed, many people—particularly those of working-class backgrounds—derived their self-worth from their heritage and the privileged status historically associated with being a native-born national. When the value of such heritage began to be replaced with an emphasis on intangible "shared values," their status was threatened with nothing in return.

So far, in nearly every case in which states have sought to develop national or cosmopolitan identities to transcend the tensions of ethnic differences, they have eventually regressed to ethnic appeals and politics.[22] And globalization—which inspired many to rise above ethnic and religious affinities— has intensified resource disparities and inspired backlash among people yearning for a renewed connection to more traditional forms of belonging and heritage-based status.

At Home

In a keynote address to a Princeton University symposium titled "After the Backlash" in May 2019, the communitarian thinker Michael Walzer sought to address liberalism's failure to unite multiethnic societies. To an auditorium full of liberals from different parts of the world, he argued that nativism is not unreasonable and could be accommodated.

"People have a right to be at home in their homeland, where they have shaped the landscape and contributed," he said, "and this is a right that Leftists should acknowledge. It is not the only right. They have a right to hope their grandchildren will grow up there. Open borders over time would abolish homelands, and cosmopolitans would welcome that. . . . But good homelands have staying power because of assimilation and integration. This should be a point of pride, that we can make foreigners into home folks." To clarify that he was not advocating for draconian assimilation programs, he added, "Most immigrants [to the United States] did so without adopting Anglo customs and in many cases without learning English."

For a moment, let's accept this right to be "at home" as just. The problem remains how such a right is understood and protected. What does it mean to feel "at home"? Does it mean native-born people should have special access? Or be granted special treatment? Or be allocated greater power? Or be given greater resources? Do immigrants relinquish the right to be "at home" when they move to a new country? Walzer did not elaborate, but even the most conservative thinkers would bristle at the notion that certain citizens be endowed with special treatment, power, and resources beyond those of other duly recognized citizens, simply owing to their nativity.[23] And Walzer is a socialist.

Perhaps Walzer's idea of being "at home" is best interpreted as having a sense of familiarity? Or feeling a greater sense of belonging? As you might literally feel inside of your own home. But what are the attributes of a society that make native-born people with extended heritage feel more or less at home? Don't these attributes change across time, regions, and people? And are we prepared to grant the native-born the right to preserve such attributes in the public sphere?

One attribute that most agree should be preserved is the use of the predominant national language, but this is as much a matter of heritage as it is of logistics. In a similar vein, one might ask that newcomers drive on the right side of the road, use the national currency, and abide by the Gregorian calendar and Western workweek. Whatever sentimental attachment there may be to speaking English and these other norms, governments do not mandate adherence to make natives feel "at home" so much as to ensure that newcomers can communicate, coordinate, and participate fully in the society and marketplace.

No, being "at home" is about sentimental comfort, and the discomfort driving the politics of popular nationalism relates to the physical and cultural attributes of newcomers—their religions, their norms, their beliefs, their ethnicity, their race. Here there is no defensible argument about logistics or communication. Once an agreement to abide by the rule of law and democratic principles is met, societies do not logistically struggle because their people come from more diverse ethnic, religious, or normative backgrounds. Quite the opposite: societies draw social and material benefits from such diversity.

And as we have seen, home is precisely where many of these battles over identity are waged. Residents have engaged in housing discrimination and residential segregation where they live, employment discrimination where they work, voter suppression in their home electoral districts, and efforts to prohibit the establishment of foreign religious institutions or cultural symbols in their neighborhoods. These are the ways nativists have sought to be "at home," and they are grounded in nationalism, the most fundamental components of which demographic change disrupts.

Nationalism Disrupted

While nations are portrayed as primordial peoples, they actually have been the basis of modern states only since the late eighteenth century, when leaders sought to unify diverse peoples of a given territory. Indeed, they rely on modern technology in order to forge and communicate a national identity against evidence of earlier social and cultural fractures. While in most countries the national identity is defined explicitly in ethnic and religious terms with an implicit civic foundation, oneime settler countries like the United

States explicitly define the national identity in civic terms but also have an implicit ethnic and religious foundation.

Despite being constructed by their elites, nations must mobilize a certain sense of collective belonging among common people to be effective.[24] Today's nativism is an expression of marginality among people who derive their sense of belonging from various ethnic and religious components.[25] With the presence and growing power of minorities with foreign origins, nativists feel alienated in the countries they once defined. This is because immigration-driven demographic change disrupts two fundamental components of nationalism.

1. The first is the classic entitlement of the nation to the state. In and of themselves, immigrants from foreign countries with different cultural traditions, religions, and norms do not violate the congruence between the nation and the state. Even when the immigrant population grows to comprise a larger proportion of the state, the state may still be defined by the founding nation so long as immigrants do not have the right to representation. The disruption occurs when immigrants make claims for representation or when democratic institutions mandate that the state be a reflection of the people that comprise it. There can be a democratic nation-state, but there cannot be a democratic, multiethnic nation-state unless the nation is redefined on explicitly and implicitly nonethnic and nonreligious terms.

2. The second component of nationalism that is disrupted by demographic change is the dominance of the nation. Historically, the founding nation managed to sustain its preeminence in its state because it leveraged the advantages of incumbency to subordinate newcomers or pressure their assimilation into the founding nation's creed and culture. Thereafter, early immigrants often enforced the same assimilation on future waves of arrivals as surrogates and naturalized nationals. However, contemporary immigration brings in many high-status foreigners with greater resources and status than some natives. Further, because states no longer hold monopolies on media that once communicated dominant norms, traditions, and language, contemporary immigrants can more easily maintain their own norms, traditions, and language. Indeed, they may carry their own sense of nationalism from their country of origin.

Through this lens, nativism is an attempt to salvage the nation—in some original conception—by reasserting its dominance inside the territorial state. Natives' disengagement from attempts to forge cultural consensus with newcomers threatens to devolve social and political relations back to the warring, irredentist subcultures that the original nationalists sought to reconcile into coexistence.

The ultimate conclusion may be that modern political communities cannot look past ethnic and religious differences. Indeed, as sociologist Andreas Wimmer has found, history is filled with examples where the main promises of modernity—political participation, equal treatment before the law and protection from the arbitrariness of state power, dignity for the weak and poor, and social justice and security—were fully realized only for those who came to be regarded as "true members of the nation."[26] True throughout history, this remains true today given the modern state's interest in elevating nationals over foreigners.

It is not surprising, then, that so many battles have been waged over the identity of the "nation." So long as membership in the central, dominant nation is in dispute and consequential, ethnic communities may always feel the need to defend their interests and demand recognition.[27] So perhaps it is in the definition of "we"—the people, the nation—that a resolution resides.

Who Are "We"?

Sociologist Craig Calhoun has asked whether there are "attractive forms of collective identity that offer nationalism's potential to integrate large populations and produce mutual commitment—without assuming its tendencies of external exclusion and the rejection of internal difference?"

For the past several decades, many conservative parties thought they had the answer. As detailed by political scientist Daniel Ziblatt, conservatives have designed strategic campaigns that divided along lines of race, nationality, ethnicity, language, or religion to remain competitive amid the expansion of the electorate to immigrants and minorities, but only so long as this strategy was contained by professionalized political parties and continued to affirm the democratic regime.[28] This strategy, it turns out, reinforced social divisions, emboldened nationalist ideologies, and whetted the popular appetite for ever more muscular assertions of the national character as a fixed, primordial entity. In short, it softened the ground for far-right identity politics and today's hardcore nationalism and nativism.

Numerous analyses suggest that the 2016 election of Donald Trump, the Brexit referendum, and the ascendance of far-right politicians across Europe represent a backlash to demographic change, but also to milquetoast and "thin" definitions of the nation. Support for Trump's nativist agenda is strongest among voters characterized by resentment toward racial and religious minorities[29] and ethnocentrism and intolerance.[30] His 2016 swing voters were principally motivated by a desire to preserve the Christian faith, deport undocumented immigrants, and reduce immigration.[31] Both American and British support for radical right candidates and groups is driven by a sense of lost political status and power. The far right's muscular nationalism leverages nostalgia and asserts control over a seemingly uncontrollable set of circumstances.

In nearly all European states, far-right parties seek to reduce immigration and counter the accommodation of Islam in the public sphere, a reaction to three decades of immigration liberalization.[32] And this phenomenon is not limited to the West. In Japan in 2019, the government of Prime Minister Shinzo Abe finally increased immigration to relieve severe labor shortages in one of the world's most aged societies, but he openly assured his citizens that the newcomers would not stay long. In Israel, advocates of a Jewish state openly strategize how to maintain a numerical majority of Jewish citizens. The specter of demographic change, in fact, looms over contemporary politics in all immigrant-receiving countries.

"Take back control," exhorted the Leave campaign during Britain's 2016 Brexit referendum.

"Nippon o Torimodosu" (Take back Japan) was long the slogan of Japan's centrist but nationalist Prime Minister Abe.

"Wir sind das volk!" (We are the people) declared Germany's far-right Alternative für Deutschland.

"Au nom du peuple" (In the name of the people) proclaimed Marine Le Pen's far-right National Rally party in France.

"We are the silent majority," Trump often called his followers, a reference to their enduring numerical power amid evidence of social change.

However, these slogans beg the question: Which people? From whom are we taking back control? Who are "we," anyway? Such questions always go unanswered, for it is far easier for such movements to define the "other" than to define the nation purportedly entitled to power. "We may not know who we are, but we know who we are not," today's nativists seem to be shouting in their backlash to immigration, Muslims, and the emergence of an increasingly globalized culture.

But despite the ambiguity in the far right's vision of national identity, their opponents are even less specific in their response. Stung by their earlier struggles, socialists, progressives, and liberal globalists generally eschew attempts to define the people. Some are disinterested in engaging in such a vulgar exercise that distracts from universal matters of social justice. Others, despite recognizing that there is a collective human need for a sense of who "we" are, are still unable to synthesize the diversity of their constituents. They are not sure how to build a national identity that honors heritage but also respects differences, a fellowship of people that is universally open but locally distinct.

Great rewards await the leaders and movements that can strike this elusive balance between a broad identity and tight cohesion.[33] Social solidarity certainly streamlines governance and fosters compromises over the distribution of resources and moral disputes. And as this book will exhibit, great risks raise the stakes of failure. Majority minority societies with unresolved demographic politics are condemned to undemocratic acts of suppression or social tension. Many have been subject to violence or always seem to be on the brink of civil conflict.

The Limits of State Control

The reason the effects of unresolved demographic politics linger is that the social dynamics are otherwise unlikely to change. Demography is difficult to control.[34] While states have great rhetorical and institutional power to affirm national identity, demographic change entails a variety of interconnected phenomena that are largely beyond the reach of these powers.

One such phenomenon is fertility—the rate at which people reproduce. Wary of overpopulation, for example, China instituted birth control programs like the so-called one-child policy between 1979 and 2015. Other states with aging populations have attempted to encourage procreation with "baby bonus" financial incentives, public service announcements, and even public holidays and events geared around reproduction. Ultimately, however, this is a hands-off matter; there is only so much government can do to encourage population growth.

A second phenomenon is life expectancy, or mortality—the rate at which people die. Again, while governments can provide healthcare services, enforce health and safety regulations, and encourage healthy behavior, there is only so much they can do to control the private health choices that citizens make.

A third phenomenon is emigration, which reduces the national population. While all states assert control over the admission of people from other countries into their sovereign territory, only the most totalitarian governments restrict the departure of their citizens.[35] It is notable that some governments actually encourage poorer citizens and political dissidents to leave, but when people decide to leave for another state voluntarily, there is very little governments can do.

A fourth fundamental demographic phenomenon is marriage and inter-ethnic or interreligious marriage. While marriage is associated with fertility, intermarriage affects population size when citizens marry foreigners, and it affects a state's ethnic composition when citizens marry people from different ethnic backgrounds and have children. While strong social norms and rules once governed the choice of a spouse or partner, that choice is now largely out of parents' and governments' control.

Despite being beyond the state's reach, fertility, mortality, trends that shape the composition of a nation's people, the definition of whis at the center of today's demographic politics. For this reason, states have sought ways they *can* control the composition of their people, or at least the extent to which certain subgroups gain and exert political power. The next eight chapters examine these attempts in a variety of majority minority societies, and the way that many attempts are exclusive, divisive, and oppressive. They all face the same question of how the state can counter the worst human instincts and innovate symbolic and practical institutions that resolve social tensions and reconstitute the national identity—how the state achieves escape velocity.

Connectedness

That people seek out and wish to connect with a national community is not in question. That states require this sense of community is also beyond doubt. Allegiance to a national community motivates people to sacrifice a share of their wealth, a share of their land, a share of their time. In extreme cases, people sacrifice their lives to protect their nation. These sacrifices are more readily justifiable when they are made in the name of a distinct and recognizable community—a community that has heretofore been constructed as an ethnic or religious group.[36]

The challenge is that national communities are evolving into multiethnic, multireligious unions. On the one hand, insistence on outdated ethnic or religious definitions of "the people" will not only leave out large shares of the national community but threaten its viability. On the other hand, insistence on ignoring traditional definitions of "the people" in favor of abstract forms of moral agreement jeopardizes the sense of allegiance citizens have maintained to their countrymen, their government, and its institutions. It also underestimates the extent to which immigrants assimilate to a national creed and culture.[37] Nationalism should be neither too thick nor too thin.

But striking this balance and achieving a progressive redefinition of the nation may take generations. And so for states currently undergoing demographic transformation that are eager to resolve social tensions, the expectation cannot be an immediate shift to uniform moral agreement. At least in the short run, the aim must be far more modest and incremental. The aim should just be connectedness.

Connectedness[38] takes place when people who identify in many different ways and are subject to some divisions bridge these social boundaries to bond over a shared national purpose. It is the critical sense of "we" that allows people to see themselves in the eyes of their countrymen, to at least listen to each other's perspectives, and eventually to empathize. It is the "bridging capital" that precedes more ambitious social goals like intermarriage or the reconciliation of differences.

This book does not develop an empirical way to measure connectedness. It is approximated by the various metrics that capture social solidarity, social cohesion, and social capital. And even if there was a consensus metric, historical calculations would not be available in the cases I study. However, the concept of connectedness helps to clarify a basic social outcome toward which a state or society can work: the breaking down of barriers between citizens to broaden the sense of "we." And over the course of this book, I frequently evaluate institutions and rhetoric according to whether or not they do so, whether the state reinforces or dissolves the ethnic and religious boundaries that prevent the evolution of a more inclusive nation.

Connectedness is something that many citizens believe should be second nature to their society. This is because they perceive their national identity to be primordial and static in nature, and therefore a connection to it is something persistent that one may inherit but also bestow on others. My historical research and fieldwork show the way that public officials tend to reinforce this perception. However, national identities evolve and, as chapters 10, 11, and 12 will conclude, public perceptions about immigration and the majority minority milestone are subject to the moral leadership of elites and the inclusive acts of leaders in cultural and commercial spheres.

We see when examining the historical record that connectedness tends to require time to achieve. It can be expedited when newcomers or different ethnoreligious groups share attributes, such as a common language, religion, or race. It can be expedited in the presence of an external threat or with the arrival of an even more different, foreign outgroup. However, per chapter 10, it can also be expedited when the state takes action in ways that seek to include disparate subgroups in the national story, in the marketplace, in the pursuit of national culture. The next chapter's comparative historical analysis is, in part, a study of state efforts to preserve antecedent sources of connectedness or pursue new forms of solidarity in the face of demographic change. In the same way majority minority relations are governed, connectedness is cultivated.

In sum, for a political community to reach escape velocity away from the pull of ethnic and religious nationalism, connectedness is the accelerant. States and societies must foster a sense of linked fate across disparities that were once grounds for division. They must instill the shared sense of purpose in every institution and at every opportunity. In doing so, they must reinvent who "we" are. The historian Benedict Anderson famously wrote that "nationalism is not the awakening of nations to self-consciousness; it invents nations where they do not exist."[39] In the face of transformational demographic change, the nation must be invented anew.

3

Pathways of Majority-Minority Societies

A Comparative Historical Analysis

Critical Junctures

Recent commentaries suggest that the nativist backlash in the United States and Europe represents a reaction to a level of demographic change never before seen. In a *Washington Post* commentary, political theorist Danielle Allen wrote:

> The simple fact of the matter is that the world has never built a multiethnic democracy in which no particular ethnic group is in the majority and where political equality, social equality and economies that empower all have been achieved. . . . This fight is different than our earlier ones because this time everyone begins from the psychological position of fearing to be a member of a vulnerable minority.[1]

This idea—that majority-minority demographics, due to declining native fertility rates and rising immigration, represent uncharted waters for social and political relations—is commonplace. It underpins a transatlantic search for pathways toward democratic coexistence and away from authoritarianism. The discussion, however, has been unmoored from historical study.

In fact, a majority-minority milestone is rare, but it is not unique. There have been multiple cases where one group of people—usually defined by race, ethnicity, or religion—lost its numerical advantage in the territory of a sovereign state, and the historical record offers significant evidence about how such societies and their governments responded. In this chapter, I offer a comparative historical analysis of six case studies, in which the indigenous or native-born majority lost its numerical advantage—Bahrain, Hawai'i, Mauritius, New York, Singapore, and Trinidad and Tobago—with the goal of understanding what drives divergent reactions to such demographic transformation. I will draw conclusions from this analysis in chapter 10, after reporting the results of contemporary qualitative research in each of these six societies in chapters 4 through 9.

Majority Minority. Justin Gest, Oxford University Press. © Justin Gest 2022. DOI: 10.1093/oso/9780197641798.003.0003

With a majority minority transition imminent, these societies pursued three different paths in response to the transition: (1) resist demographic change through co-optation or suppression, (2) endure racialized politics and irresolvable social tension, or (3) redefine the nation. In my review of these countries' histories, I find that these outcomes were contingent on whether the state equally enfranchised the newcomer population by granting them equal rights as citizens and whether its subsequent redefinition of the national identity was inclusive or exclusive. While inclusive redefinitions overrode historic inequities (e.g., Hawai'i and New York), governments that pursued exclusive identities were confronted by either suppressed social tension in states with structurally unequal constituencies (e.g., Bahrain and Singapore) or overt contestation in states with equally enfranchised constituencies (e.g., Mauritius and Trinidad). (See Figure 3.1).

Put another way, I ultimately find the state has two sequential choices when responding to transformational demographic change: First, political leaders must decide whether they will:

A. Emphasize ethnic divisions and seek to establish the predominance of one constituency (whether it is a majority or a minority).

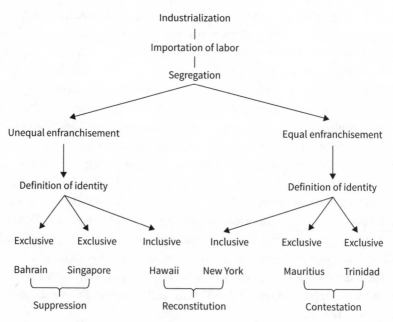

Figure 3.1 Pathways of majority minority societies and the case venues.

Or

B. Minimize the salience of such social boundaries and try to construct an inclusive polity that provides equal opportunities for leadership and influence (e.g., Hawai'i and New York).

Should political leaders elect to emphasize social divisions in the interest of one group's supremacy, a second choice is whether they will:

C. Formalize the marginalization of subordinate groups by enacting discriminatory laws that, while affording the subordinated groups an economic role, reduce or remove the prospects for their political power (e.g., Bahrain and Singapore).

Or

D. Sustain the veneer of equal opportunity and equal power while relying on more subtle and informal discrimination to reduce the prospects for the empowerment of one group or another (e.g., Mauritius and Trinidad).

While these findings may appear intuitive at first glance, the role of government responses to demographic change plays a subordinate role in the existing scholarship, which has largely been pursued by political psychologists and public opinion researchers who focus primarily on contemporary public attitudes. Immigration historians have studied the power of government institutions in the management of demographic change, but many analysts suggest instead that popular discontent, racism, and xenophobia may be more important than government policy and rhetoric in determining the outcomes of demographic change.[2] These findings contextualize contemporary developments in the course of the history of majority minority states and provide a roadmap of the critical junctures where social conflict may be averted.

A Comparative Historical Approach

As I underscored earlier, there have been very few majority minority milestones in modern history. In my review of societies with sovereign control over their immigration policy, not even a dozen qualify: plantation societies like Fiji, Guyana, the Hawaiian Kingdom, Mauritius, Suriname, and Trinidad and Tobago, which received large numbers of indentured laborers from South and East Asia; Gulf emirates like Bahrain, Kuwait, Qatar, and the United Arab Emirates, onetime pearling hubs that eventually recruited enormous numbers of South Asian laborers and Western and Arab professionals; and the unique circumstances of Singapore, a Chinese-majority island that was expelled from the Malay Federation. In this book, I also include the American state of New York, which held sovereign control over its immigration admissions and removals until 1882—and therefore agency in the demographic change.

All of these majority-minority societies emerged as the residual demographics of the British Empire's pursuit of free-flowing capital, commerce, and labor between its dominions, where the arrival of settlers brought wars and epidemics that decimated indigenous populations.[3] The trafficking of African slaves then brought self-sufficiency and prosperity to colonial settlements with fewer local interdependencies. In parts of the Americas and Oceania, this process solidified white majorities in a number of self-governing settler states and African-origin majorities across British territories in the Caribbean Sea and Indian Ocean. It was the postslavery innovation of alternatives to forced migration, however—indentured servitude, penal contracts, and "assisted migration"—that brought large numbers of South Asians, East Asians, and others to every corner of the earth, forever altering the delicate demography of these small societies. And it was the British Empire's reification and exploitation of racial and religious divisions that ensured these boundaries would be so challenging to transcend forever after.

Six Cases

The six cases I study are the island societies of Bahrain, Hawai'i, Mauritius, New York, Singapore, and Trinidad and Tobago (Table 3.1). While New York was subject to mainland governance, the demographic change was acutely concentrated on the islands comprising New York City. In each, the immigrant-origin newcomers were all from rather populous homelands with strong diasporas but also histories of subjugation in light of indentured servitude or poverty. And compared to the resident populations they displaced, they had different racial, ethnic, and/or religious backgrounds and were characterized by composite understandings of these backgrounds that broad-brushed them into monolithic stereotypes (e.g., Indian Hindus or Irish Catholics).

These six cases are a subset that represents the full range of circumstances observed in majority-minority shifts. Per Table 3.1, they feature distinct original populations, sources of labor, regime types, and histories of slavery, immigration, enfranchisement, and identity politics—all across different historical

Table 3.1 Variables, Controls, and the Three Principal Outcomes

Controls						Independent Variables					Outcome
Societies	Colonial Rule	majority minority Milestone	Independence Milestone	Original Population	Labor Source	Slavery	Regime Type at Milestone	Immigration	Equality	Identity	Social Relation
Bahrain	British	~2008	1971	Shia and Sunni Arab	South Asia, Sunni Arab	Limited	Constitutional Monarchy	Continuous	Unequal	Exclusive	Suppressed
Singapore	British	~1965	1965	Malay	China, South Asia	Limited	Uncompetitive Republic	Continuous	Unequal	Exclusive	Suppressed
Hawai'i	American, British	~1890	1949 (statehood)	Hawaiian	China, Japan, Philippines	No	Constitutional Monarchy	Concentrated	Unequal	Inclusive	Reconstituted
New York	British, Dutch	~1880	1776	English, Protestant	Catholic Europe	Limited	Presidential Republic	Continuous	Equal	Inclusive	Reconstituted
Mauritius	British, French	1861	1968	Afro-Creole	India	Yes	Crown Colony	Concentrated	Equal	Exclusive	Contested
Trinidad	British, Spanish	1995	1962	Afro-Creole	India	Yes	Parliamentary Democracy	Concentrated	Equal	Exclusive	Contested

periods. The six cases also represent the full range of social outcomes observable across majority-minority societies in modern history. These include societies that:

1. Resist the implications of demographic change through co-optation or *suppression*.
2. Endure racialized politics and irresolvable social *tension*.
3. Reconcile demographic change to some degree through a *redefinition* of the nation.

The six cases can be classed according to these three outcomes.

Suppression

Singapore: Singapore is a Chinese-majority city-state that was created when it was expelled from the Malay Federation in 1965, instantly making a minority of its resident Malay population. After a series of minor racial disturbances around the same time as its independence, Singapore's exclusively Chinese prime ministers and predominantly Chinese leadership have been careful to construct an explicitly civic (and not ethnic or religious) national identity. While rhetorically insisting that the city-state sustain racial harmony and "balance," the government has pursued this balance by freezing its percentages of different racial groups at levels recorded early in the twentieth century. To do so, the city-state has used highly selective immigration admissions policies to compensate for declining fertility rates and aging among the Chinese-origin community in the face of the growing Indian and Malay population. This de facto race-based selection squarely contradicts the country's official meritocratic, race-blind doctrine. While Singapore has managed to resist both demographic pressures and significant social conflict, the government's awkward contortions to preserve Chinese hegemony have begun to foment the very anxieties and competition they were designed to prevent.[4]

Bahrain: The demography of Bahrain, long a crossroads for the pearl trade, has for decades reflected tensions between the Shias, who comprise a majority of its nationals, and the Sunnis, who have historically ruled the island with the backing of the British as a bulwark against the Persian Empire. Since the 1970s oil boom, as elsewhere in the Gulf region, vast numbers of temporary labor migrants have grown to outnumber both sects of the national population and complicate the preexisting tensions. Driven by these new immigrants, the population of Bahrain nearly tripled between 1995 and 2017, from 559,000 to 1.5 million.[5] On one hand, this demographic transformation has discomforted Bahrainis of all religious backgrounds, and the kingdom has severely restricted access to citizenship to ensure that migrants do not receive access to the country's subsidies to and benefits from the country's oil industry. On the other hand, unlike elsewhere in the Gulf, the government has selectively wielded these same citizenship laws to naturalize Sunni Arab migrants as a buffer against the sectarian tensions that flared during the 2011 Arab Spring. The result is a society characterized by social tension, suppressed by a powerful state that placates Shia nationals with government subsidies, and subordinates immigrants as a second-class constituency with limited rights and freedoms.

Tension

Trinidad and Tobago: The 1807 abolition of slavery and subsequent emancipation of African-origin slaves in 1838 led the British Empire to import indentured labor from India to Trinidad and Tobago's plantations, forever altering the two Caribbean islands' demography. Placed together as an unintended consequence of British mercantilism, these two ethnic communities would evolve quite separately for a century, until the colony's 1962 independence left them to govern one another as coequals. Afro-Trinidadian Creoles ruled for the country's first thirty years of sovereignty and made fervent claims to the islands' cultural heritage. Indo-Trinidadians, however, have prospered economically, challenged Creole claims to authenticity, and grown in numerical share and power thanks to the emigration of many Afro-Trinidadians to Britain, Canada, and the United States. With the two communities now comprising near-equal, nonmajority shares of the national population and a growing minority of mixed-race Trinidadians, many political matters have been interpreted through the narrow lens of ethnic supremacy with very slim margins. Suddenly, mundane issues such as immigration admissions, and even calypso and Carnival, assume symbolic meaning for the balance of power. The result is a society openly concerned with ethnic differences.[6]

Mauritius: A small island off the coast of southeastern Africa, Mauritius became inhabited when Dutch, French, and then British settlers imported slaves from Madagascar and eastern Africa. In 1834, Mauritius became the earliest territory to introduce Indian indentured laborers in the world, the so-called "Great Experiment." Within thirty years, Indians outnumbered the African freedmen and had completely displaced them on the sugar plantations. Many Indians received land at the conclusion of their indenture—a reward unavailable to the former slaves upon their emancipation—which set the Indian community up for economic advantage in the decades thereafter when Indians and largely African-origin Catholic Creoles were given the right to vote. As tensions between the two communities deepened into the twentieth century, Indian Hindus increasingly appealed to emerging Indian and Hindu nationalism and sustained diaspora links to their country of origin rather than reconcile with their African-origin countrymen. Hindu schools, missions, and associations reinforced their status and asserted their dominance in a country they quickly defined and controlled.

Redefinition

New York: US immigration admissions and removals were federalized only in 1882. In the preceding years, states like New York managed their own policies of selection and deportation the same way a sovereign state might do so. This left the New York commissioners of emigration responsible for the unprecedented number Irish people who entered New York between 1845 and 1854—an influx that outnumbered immigrants from all other countries since 1776 combined.[7] At the time, the state and city of New York were largely of English and Dutch origins, and the United States was being swept by a wave of support for the xenophobic Know Nothing movement and its nativist American Party, which scored election victories in many mid-nineteenth-century gubernatorial, congressional, and mayoral races. The backlash focused on the predominantly Catholic Irish, many of whom arrived as paupers and public charges. While there was a great deal of saber rattling, there was very little action by the government to actually prevent immigrants' arrival or deport them. New York's immigrant population was by then a well-organized voting bloc that was courted by political candidates, as well as a labor force that was valued by powerful business interests—a model for future waves of newcomers. Beginning with this incorporation into the political system, the Irish (along with Italians and other once-discriminated-against groups) were incorporated into the American fraternity of whiteness by the 1960s, which both cemented their higher status and distinguished them from future waves of excluded non-European immigrants.[8]

Hawai'i: Before their annexation by the United States in 1898, the Hawaiian Islands were a multiethnic kingdom with a prosperous economy centered on its sugar plantations and mid-Pacific harbor. Both to position the islands geopolitically and to ensure their crops were harvested, Hawaiian monarchs pursued relations with foreign governments by populating their cabinets and cane fields with foreigners. After the introduction of continental diseases killed two-thirds of the Hawaiian population by 1823,[9] their share of the population was further reduced by the arrival of Chinese, Japanese,

Filipino, Portuguese, British, and American immigrants, most of whom were recruited by the kingdom to work in its predominantly American-run sugar industry. From 1840 to 1898, the Native Hawaiian population declined from a 97 percent majority to a 36 percent minority. While some intermarriage (particularly with Chinese laborers) and relatively generous treatment of foreigners produced more harmonious interethnic relations during this period, it also produced an 1893 American-backed coup that was opposed by Native Hawaiians, who—by this point—were without sufficient popular or military power to resist. One result of the American annexation was the segregation and suppression of Native Hawaiian culture. This part-Hawaiian, multiracial, and "nonwhite" underclass quietly preserved Native Hawaiian culture until a 1960s revival that is carried on today by a multiethnic coalition of advocates in the face of American hegemony.[10]

It may be tempting to dismiss majority minority societies as an anomalous artifact of British imperial history that emerged in a number of small island states with uniquely fragile population distributions. That conclusion would be wrong for two reasons.

First, it is not that majority minority demographics emerge only in these unique social ecosystems; it is that they emerged there *first*. Countries like Australia, Canada, and the United States have arguably already passed the majority minority threshold if one thinks of the original majority in early-nineteenth-century terms, as Anglo Protestants. Today's "white" majorities in these countries include numerous ethnicities that were excluded from earlier conceptions of whiteness, including the Irish, Italians, Portuguese, Greeks, Jews, Turks, Iranians, and Arabs, among others (see chapter 12). The same is increasingly true in Belgium, France, and the Netherlands, which already have indigenous religious minorities and have experienced great influxes of people from their former colonial territories and the European Union.

While forced immigrants are no longer imposed on the societies that today face similar demographic futures (except with asylum seekers), there are parallels in the intensity of popular discontent with immigration currently expressed in the United States and Europe. Views about immigration, once considered a peripheral social issue, have become the litmus test for conservative politics.[11] In 2018, one in four Americans and Europeans independently selected immigration as the most salient political issue for them,[12] and political entrepreneurs around the world have seized that fervor to transform electoral coalitions and energize far-right parties that blame liberal elites for the imposition of immigrants. Global migration, the product of liberal and democratic institutions in the modern era, has produced an environment that puts these institutions to the test.

Second, dismissing the study of majority minority societies also ignores important evidence about the constructed nature of national identity. If national identities are formed based on those who comprise the nation, changing the composition of the nation, by definition, changes the national identity. Just as Trinidadian cuisine has embraced curry, Britain's national dish today is chicken tikka masala. Just as non-Chinese Singaporeans commonly understand expressions in Mandarin, Americans casually employ expressions in Spanish, Yiddish, and Italian. Just as the Hawaiian Kingdom created space for Buddhist temples and Christian missions, Canada has made provisions for sharia councils. While this does not necessarily mean that the popular conceptions of what it means to be a Briton, American, or Canadian changes, it does mean that the state will accommodate new norms and tolerate new expressions of difference. Adjustments and the incremental alteration of social boundaries lay bare the evolution of purportedly static national myths and symbols.

The state-level studies that follow not only clarify the connections that link cases of majority minority transitions but also reveal the unique local conditions that inform different governments' ultimate responses to disorienting demographic change. These nuances matter because they exhibit the way that local factors moderate or amplify global trends. These comparative histories are especially useful for their cross-national connections, which alert us in the present to the echoes in time.

A Path Analysis

The small selection of majority-minority cases under consideration, and the small number of cases quite generally, prohibits statistical analysis of the causal factors that might drive the different outcomes across the states. Contemporary public opinion polling research can gauge individuals' reactions in today's world, but how preferences translate into institutional behavior requires a long-term view. When considering processes that require decades or centuries to gestate, a comparative historical approach provides a view of the pathways that different societies take and the critical junctures when certain events or actions alter the trajectory of social relations. To more reliably identify those critical events and actions, I study multiple cases of each outcome.

In the remainder of this chapter, I examine the history of each selected society and undertake a structured comparison of these narratives to identify these critical junctures and the range of intervening variables that combine to produce different outcomes. Ultimately, I distinguish a chronological sequence of six stages in majority-minority states' path toward this demographic milestone:

Stage 1:　Industrialization of the British Empire
Stage 2:　Importation of Labor
Stage 3:　Segregation and Segmentation
Stage 4:　Enfranchisement and Equality
Stage 5:　Nativism and the Reconstruction of Identity
Stage 6:　Political Backlash

All six societies proceed in parallel through Stages 1, 2, and 3. In each of these case studies, the industrialization of the British Empire galvanized the first steps toward majority minority societies. To accommodate new demand for agricultural and mineral commodities, the empire found the labor in colonies inadequate and began to import it from elsewhere. To control the natives and newcomers who together outnumbered them, the British (often with their national government partners) then segregated different ethnic groups and segmented the labor market. Eventually, the newcomers settled, and questions arose about the structural equality of immigrants in the eyes of the state.

It is at this juncture, Stage 4, that the cases diverge. While some minorities were granted formal equality and the right to vote, others elsewhere remained subject to discriminatory institutions. While the democracies were inclined toward enfranchisement, their "one person, one vote" elections made them prone to ethnic or religious conflict amid demographic change. Once we arrive at this point of divergence, I will pause the comparative historical analysis until chapter 10, where I resume my analysis of Stages 5 and 6 on nativism and backlash, which emerge independent of regime type.

On the Ground

In the intervening chapters, 4 through 9, I deepen the comparative historical analysis by reporting my findings from contemporary fieldwork. In each case society, I trace the fuller course of each society's history and study today's expressions of each majority minority transformation, some of which are more recent than others. While Trinidad and Tobago reached the majority minority milestone in only the past few decades, it has been more than a century and a half for Mauritius. But a scratch to the surface of the Indian Ocean community that advertises itself as a harmonious "Rainbow Nation" reveals unresolved identity politics at the center of current affairs and racial tension as raw as Trinidad and Tobago's.

Because of these different timelines and the unique components of each case, my field research centers on different venues where the identity politics associated with each majority minority milestone endure. More specifically, I focus on cultural spaces that continue to express the politics of demographic change. In Singapore (chapter 4), I study the government's portrayals of national history in museums, textbooks, and the public record. In Bahrain (chapter 5), I study the kingdom's use of nationality as a political instrument. In Trinidad and Tobago (chapter 6), I study the latent power relations of the annual Carnival. In Mauritius (chapter 7), I study the nostalgic politics of ancient maroon villages. In New York (chapter 8), I study the century-long hold of Irish Americans on the New York Police Department. And in Hawai'i (chapter 9), I study land reclamation initiatives pursuing a semblance of Native Hawaiian sovereignty. The politics in each of these different expressions are motivated by the same existential questions that vex societies undergoing rapid demographic change today: Who are the legitimate people entitled to rule? What is the source of nationhood that binds a country together?

Using secondary historical research and over one hundred face-to-face, unstructured, elite interviews, I explore these questions and study how they emerge in today's cultural politics. Selected for their unique perspective on the cultural and political phenomena I examine, my subjects are a mix of high-ranking public officials, social movement leaders, and community elders—prime ministers down to a village witchdoctor. While I challenge my interview subjects to defend and elaborate their ideas, in order to reflect the most realistic version of social affairs, I do not censor their most divisive thoughts. I supplement these interviews with my observations from eight weeks of fieldwork.

Contextualized by the comparative historical analysis that follows, this field research not only tells the discrete stories of troubled island nations; it reveals a set of alternative futures for today's countries confronting rapid demographic change. The research also shows how so much of the politics associated with demographic change is contested on cultural grounds—in the rhetorical definition of the nation, the telling of its history, the practice of its pastimes, and the expression of its traditional art forms. In exploring these cultural spheres, the case studies illustrate and elaborate politics summarized in each of the stages I identify in the remainder of this chapter.

Stage 1: Industrialization of the British Empire

Over the course of the eighteenth century, a series of mutually reinforcing trends took place. In Britain and elsewhere in Europe, labor markets were shifting from nonspecialized, seasonal work to more specialized occupations in single, full-time, year-round industries facilitated by the development of new production technologies. Meanwhile, the British Empire was frequently at war—principally with the French—as the rival colonizers sought overseas territories in Africa, the Americas, and around the Indian Ocean. The colonies provided venues for trade and access to tropical agricultural goods like cotton, tobacco, and sugar to meet the demand of a rapidly growing British population, principally at home but also in some of the British colonies. Though heavily dependent on slave labor, the empire had assembled an efficient system of trade and transport within an insular, protectionist economy, the philosophy of which had changed little since Britain founded its first settlement in Jamestown in 1607.

Beginning in the early nineteenth century, the British Empire began to industrialize and shift its orientation to supplying a new global economy of free trade. The superiority of the Royal Navy led to the acquisition of new territories. Markets once oriented to serve Britain were scaled up to meet new demand from the hundreds of thousands of British colonists around the world, as well as others outside the British Empire. This led the empire's administrators in the resource-rich colonies to further commoditize agricultural and mineral products, which were of value both as raw materials and in the finished products of Britain's burgeoning textile, metalwork, and hardware industries. In Europe, these phenomena reoriented domestic economies, specializing labor markets and displacing millions of subsistence farmers into rapidly urbanizing cities.

Many of the case countries took on new value during this period. The British had only recently acquired Mauritius and Trinidad (Tobago was ceded by the French in the 1815 Treaty of Vienna but became a ward of Trinidad in 1889). Until this time, Mauritius had a rather diverse agricultural economy that produced coffee, timber, and rice, and wooded land in Trinidad was still being converted to farming. Trinidad's economy was highly underdeveloped as the island's colonization had only begun in the late eighteenth century, but soon sugar production would take over in Mauritius and Trinidad, while planters in Tobago dedicated themselves to cotton.

The xenophobic and isolationist Hawaiian Islands repelled the British and most other foreigners with unfriendly landholding and trade laws until 1843, when the Hawaiian monarchy made concessions to obviate threats from Western powers eager to access its whaling and sugar industries. Initially, the kingdom agreed to adopt a Western-style constitutional monarchy and appointed more Westerners than Native Hawaiians to cabinet positions. From these posts, the foreigners began to enact laws to transform the Hawaiian communitarian social system into a capitalist commercial market. Subsequently, the king and the Council of Chiefs would grant foreigners the right to naturalize, to hold government office, and, in 1847, to own land.[13] These amendments would open land to American missionaries and planters, who received land grants and discounted sales. A lucrative market for Hawaiian sugar opened and grew exponentially when the 1875 Reciprocity Treaty removed American tariffs in exchange for control of Keawalau O Pu'uloa (Pearl Harbor).

The industrialization of the British Empire touched Singapore and Bahrain around the same period. Singapore's position on a strait between the Indian Ocean and South China Sea made it critical for British control of sea routes to East Asia when it was first acquired from the Johor Sultanate in 1819. And while it would become a critical crossroads for imperial commerce, its settlement grew with its agricultural production of pepper, gambier, and the discovery of tin in Malaya in the 1840s.

In Bahrain, the British gained jurisdiction over all resident British subjects in 1861 and over all foreign subjects by 1906, as the island became a de facto protectorate of the empire. At the time, there was a pearling boom, and Bahrain became a source of lucrative customs revenue that the British did not want to yield to the Persians or Ottomans. However, the island's true industrialization came with the 1929 discovery of oil and its bonanza in the 1970s.

New York is very much integrated into the industrial history of the British Empire in the nineteenth century, but as a consumer rather than a producer. By then an independent republic, the United States was a major importer of British manufactured products, and New York was a primary port of trade. The state's demography was most affected by the exportation of *people* from Europe, however, not goods. Most Irish immigrants left voluntarily, but European governments and landlords also routinely paid the passage of paupers to North America as a means of addressing poverty and reducing public charges. The British government and officials in Irish workhouses conducted this "assisted emigration" of the Irish poor with more intensity during the Irish famine between 1845 and 1852.[14] Still, despite its unusual circumstances, the immigration of the Irish and other Europeans satisfied the United States' nineteenth-century need for labor—in cities and the hinterland—so that America could also compete in the new world of manufacturing and free trade.

Stage 2: Importation of Labor

At just around the time the British Empire would require more labor, it cut off its most precious source of manpower: slavery. After slavery's abolition in 1807, British colonies emancipated millions of predominantly African-origin people over the course of the next thirty years. Before abolition, there were attempts to improve working conditions to make the practice of slavery more palatable in the face of new global norms of universal humanity. Many planters converted slaves into "apprentices" to obscure the exploitation of the arrangement, but ultimately most freed slaves in the 1830s fled the sites of their bondage. Rather than offer them fair wages, however, planters scrambled for an alternative source of cheap labor.[15]

A more voluntary, exploitative system called indenture replaced the overt exploitation of slavery. It capitalized on innovations in communication and transportation from one corner of the empire to the other. Imperial bureaucrats in London now controlled a global web of local agents, recruiters, and colonial protectors who promised land and freedom to those "indentured servants" once they completed their contractual term. By this point, planters and imperial bureaucrats were dismissive of African labor and worried that even indentured Africans would attract the skepticism of antislavery activists. Consequently, they pursued non-African people, some from Europe, others from Southeast Asia, but ultimately most of them came from India, with a smaller number from China.[16]

Some of the newcomers were political exiles, others on penal contracts, but the vast remainder were laborers who sought new opportunities. Upon their arrival, they were almost instantly situated in opposition to indigenous peoples (in the case of Singapore and Hawai'i) or to the former slaves they replaced (in the case of Mauritius and Trinidad). While some of the contractors would return to their countries of origin at the end of their term and re-indenture elsewhere, many would settle in their original destinations. They were offered marginally better labor standards by the plantation administrators, who considered "Asiatics" to be more docile and manageable and perhaps higher than Blacks in the nineteenth-century hierarchy of races—setting the tone for future social tensions.

Mauritius and Trinidad and Tobago were two of the largest importers of indentured labor. Mauritius was the earliest British colony to do so when a ship of indentured servants arrived from India in 1834, a year before slaves were emancipated. A small number of Indians had already been employed on the island, and within thirty years Indians would outnumber the resident African Creole population. In Trinidad, Indians did not alter demographics quite so swiftly, but nearly 150,000 Indians immigrated between 1845 and 1917, about a third of the total number who came to the Caribbean during this period. Their presence alarmed African Creoles, who used nascent political associations to organize against them. Ultimately, the arrival of Indians was a concentrated shock to the two countries' demographics. The number of immigrants grew in a relatively short period, and while the influx was sufficient to alter Mauritius's population distribution within mere decades, Trinidad's would be altered over a longer period of time thanks to Indian fertility and the emigration of African Creoles to the United States, United Kingdom, and Canada from the 1950s onward.

Chinese indentured labor in Singapore and elsewhere was preceded by long-enduring Chinese mercantile relationships with Britain and the other European empires.[17] China partnered with colonizers throughout South and East Asia to construct port cities like Jakarta and Manila, and it was already an important source of resident labor on the Malacca Peninsula when the British took Singapore. Many Malaccan Chinese followed Maj. Gen. William Farquhar when he departed Malacca to serve as Singapore's first British Resident, or governor. Historically, the networks of Chinese merchants around the region had provided Europeans with desired goods, acted as multilingual intermediaries with local suppliers, and employed the logic of capital investments. With a preexisting system of Chinese *towkay* labor recruiters, it was natural for the British to engage Chinese contractors—and not Malays—to build up Singapore and harvest the agricultural plantations and expanding tin mines in the Malaya countryside.[18] This predisposition was only reinforced when John Crawfurd, Singapore's second British Resident, undertook and published an empirical study of labor productivity and declared the Chinese of greater value than Indians or Malays.[19] While each group would sustain their residence in and immigration into Singapore, the Chinese quickly became the favored nationality.

Hawai'i's monarchy was far less discriminatory about its laborers. With the signing of the Reciprocity Treaty in 1875, sugar production grew more than sevenfold thanks to open access to the American market.[20] With a native population depleted by earlier epidemics and resentful of Americans' imperialist impositions, the kingdom offered labor contracts to thousands of Chinese, as well as migrants from the Philippines and Portugal. In 1872, prior to the Reciprocity Treaty, 3,299 Hawaiian laborers comprised 85 percent of the plantation workforce, and 526 Chinese contract workers comprised 14 percent. By 1882, 2,575 Native Hawaiian laborers comprised only 25 percent of the plantation workforce, while 5,037 Chinese immigrant contract workers comprised 49 percent. In 1884, in anticipation of the renewal of the Reciprocity Treaty, the Hawaiian government signed a labor agreement with the Japanese government not only to contract Japanese laborers but also to counterbalance American influence. By 1892, there were 13,019 Japanese employees on Hawai'i's sugar plantations, comprising 63 percent of the workforce. A mere 1,717 Native Hawaiians remained in the fields.[21]

While Bahrain had admitted traveling merchants and seasonal labor migrants for pearl harvesting earlier in its history, the 1929 discovery of oil created what would become a voracious appetite for foreign labor. At each stage, there were strong incentives to ensure that expatriates returned to their countries of origin. When the state oil company, BAPCO, recruited a large number of Iranians to support increased production during World War II, the British encouraged their immediate repatriation at the conclusion of their construction work as a hedge against Persian encroachment. Later, the Bahraini government would bring in thousands of laborers from Egypt, Iraq, Jordan, Lebanon, Oman, and Palestine, only to ensure their repatriation to prevent the rise of pan-Arab political ideologies and avert any claims to state entitlements. It was only after the oil price escalations of the 1970s, however, that unprecedented numbers of immigrants—initially from the Arab world but ultimately from South Asia—flocked to the Gulf region, and the local kingdoms and emirates developed institutions to facilitate their arrival and mandate their return after they completed their work.

Stage 3: Segregation and Segmentation

The residential segregation of migrants from natives and the segmentation of labor markets that placed migrants and natives in separate industries or jobs reinforced social boundaries and prevented the two constituencies from unifying to produce coalitions of solidarity. In the dominions of the British Empire, this was done overtly as a matter of economic and social policy. Separation was often justified by eugenicist logic that classified different ethnic groups according to racist judgments of civilization and moral character. But it also was instrumental in fostering resentment among different classes of laborers and competition for the Crown's favor. This blinded each constituency from understanding the circumstances of the other and subverted broad attempts to co-organize or rebel. The nefarious legacies of these divisions would endure for many generations and, in many cases, never fade across the cases under study.

In Mauritius, the seeds of division were planted when Africans fled the sugar cane fields and were replaced wholesale by indentured Indians, setting the two constituencies onto different paths. By the 1840s, Africans had gradually populated Port Louis and became an urban labor force of petty laborers, craftsmen, hucksters, artisans, and mechanics; a smaller share squatted on Crown land and took on freeholds.[22] Unlike the African Creole population, the Indians received land grants when their indentures concluded. On a rather small island, British administrators reinforced their separation by prohibiting the mobility of Indians and their children during and well after the end of their indentures, effectively enacting a quarantine. The segmentation of the Mauritian labor market therefore entailed the concomitant residential segregation of the two constituencies—one more densely concentrated and urban; the other dispersed, agrarian, and landed.

Similar residual rural-urban ethnic divisions emerged in Trinidad and Tobago, but demographic change was not as swift. The arrival of indentured Indians did not occur as quickly, and the African-origin Creole population increased when others immigrated from neighboring islands in the eastern Caribbean. As late as 1901, Indo-Trinidadians comprised a mere 34 percent of the population.[23] Over the course of the twentieth century, African Creoles' numbers and urban geography set some up for postslavery incorporation into the professional classes and British imperial oversight, which eventually offered cross-ethnic voting rights. Each ethnic constituency had representation in the colonial legislature, and in the interwar years a labor-socialist movement for the first time advocated a multiracial platform.[24] Concurrently, Europeans caucused with influential middle-class African Creoles seeking to distinguish themselves from the Creole underclass and an underclass of newcomers from smaller Caribbean islands.

This period was complicated, however, by the global invigoration of anti-colonial Pan-Africanism and Indian nationalism, which swept up members of the African and Indian diasporas everywhere. These ideologies were reinforced in popular literature, cinema, and, ultimately, politics.[25] By the time Trinidad received independence in 1962, its party caucuses were effectively distinguished by racial differences. The Creole group collapsed into a single ethnic-political structure with permeable boundaries, maintained only because of the need for votes from the Black proletariat. Nationalism was an especially powerful political force in Mauritius because of its proximity to India, and the ready availability of language, educational, and religious institutions that nourished Indian diasporic identity. Trinidadian Indians, a visible minority and already defined as Orientalist by colonial epistemology, relied on a thinner stream of visiting missionaries, religious rituals, and domestic and communal social practices. Their social institutions were modeled after Creole and British institutions, and they developed a minority psychology. Ethnic competition for power and status became a permanent part of the social landscape into which the Indians integrated. Over the course of the twentieth century in Trinidad, African Creoles were socialized into the British class system and internalized the idea of progress through education and personal attainment.[26] The Creoles' numbers, urban geography, and social organizations—modeled on British society—created routes into various strata of the professional classes, like civil service clerks and schoolteachers. This mobility fed anticipation for the inevitable transfer of power to African Creoles—self-government.

Immigrants likewise displaced the native workforce in Hawai'i's sugar cane farms, just as they did in Trinidad and Mauritius, but American and European pressures on the Hawaiian Kingdom ultimately divided Hawaiian society by race, not nativity. When King Kamehameha III succumbed to European and American pressure to establish a constitutional monarchy in 1840, the government gradually granted foreigners selected rights, such as intermarriage, trial by a jury of peers, and public officeholding. However, foreigners were initially unable to access the full rights of citizenship, particularly the right to own land.[27] The ownership of land—which so divided other societies—was considered the privilege of the Hawaiian people and the chiefs in common.[28] The natives' collective entitlement was compromised with the passage of new laws that allowed foreigners to acquire a freehold estate in 1847 and full ownership rights in 1850.[29] This opened the door to the government's ceding of large plantations and territories to white investors and missionaries, who would ultimately establish a racialized system of contract labor that subordinated people of Chinese, Filipino, Japanese, and Portuguese descent.

Employing the same techniques as observed in Mauritius and Trinidad, planters residentially segregated the different ethnic groups. Some even tried to revive US southern-style plantations on O'ahu, where foreign laborers were whipped, stripped of their names, and referred to only *by their "bango" name tags*.[30] *These boundaries were* frequently crossed thanks to union membership and intermarriage, however, and with the American-led coup in 1893, a clear boundary emerged between white business interests and Hawai'i's mix of natives and "colored" immigrants. This bifurcation forged new bonds between Hawaiians and immigrants, who were indiscriminately subject to American pressures to "assimilate."

From its original settlement by the British, colonial Singapore was designed to be a segregated settlement. From the time Sir Stamford Raffles established an East Indian Company factory in 1819, the original plan for the settlement featured urban enclaves for its different ethnic groups.[31] These enclaves and their residents were governed according to the Dutch *kapitan* system, which identified community leaders and rendered them significant autonomy to rule their populations. This ensured that the different ethnic groups would be able to interact in mundane commercial dealings but paralyzed collective political action. While Singapore's postcolonial government promoted a "multi-racial" society characterized by "racial balance," its continued recognition of ethnic boundaries in every aspect of governance from housing to education has reinforced their salience in everyday life.

While the Irish in New York City were subject to residential segregation and extensive discrimination for both their Catholicism and their economic status, it was perhaps their political segregation that held the greatest consequences. As their numbers swelled in the first half of the nineteenth century, the Democratic Party cultivated their political support as a fledgling growing bloc by defending immigration and the foreign born and channeling the American tradition of welcoming newcomers.[32] While the period between 1840 and 1880 was characterized by virulent nativism throughout the United States, the party recognized the value of Irish and other immigrant voters and restrained its use of anti-immigrant slogans. On the one hand, the Democrats' embrace of the Irish was a triumph of political integration. On the other hand, this racialized the party system in New York and elsewhere.[33]

The historic experience of Irish Americans provides stark contrasts with that of immigrants in Bahrain, who were simply cut out from political deliberation. The Bahraini labor market and living arrangements are severely segregated according to nationality. The public sector nearly exclusively employs Bahraini citizens, while the private sector largely employs foreign nationals. The unique *kafala* system of employer-sponsored, temporary labor contracts ensures that migrants are closely controlled—often in segregated employer-owned dormitories—and without any political rights or legal protections or any expectation of permanent residence. As early as 1982, Fred Halliday underscored the "systematic segregation of the migrants from the political and social lives of the countries where they work." With the enormous state subsidies endowed to Bahraini nationals, there are strong incentives keep this system in place and preclude paths to naturalization or any other source of political empowerment like free speech or trade unions. Consequently, there was little cooperation between Shia protesters in 2011 and the mostly

Sunni migrants, who could otherwise also make rights claims against the government.

Stage 4: Divergence over Equality and Enfranchisement

It is at this point that the trajectories of the six cases diverge. The realization of immigrants' enfranchisement—equal voting rights to the majority population—and formal equality before the law signaled to natives a change in the status of the migrant population. It signaled that they would be permanent, recognized as fellow nationals, and, in some cases, granted exceptional, even advantageous treatment. Equal recognition is therefore a pivotal step in the course of majority minority social relations. Naturally, this took place in the three regions governed by democracies—Mauritius, New York, and Trinidad and Tobago—in which each state eventually mandated people's incorporation independent of their ethnic background. Even in cases in which the immigrant-origin newcomers did not benefit from special treatment, their enfranchisement challenged the status of native communities, who placed value in their heritage and authenticity. Where democratic governments resisted the recognition of equal status, systems of stratification emerged that preserved such values.

In Mauritius, there has been formal equality between people of Indian and African origin effectively since emancipation freed Africans in 1835 and the end of indentured contracts in the late nineteenth century. Literate, property-holding men could vote as early as 1790, while universal suffrage was introduced in 1959. Africans were initially granted their freedom at a time when people of Indian origin were still largely subject to contractual obligations and restrictions in mobility. However, indentured servants were set up for economic and political advantage in what remained an agrarian economy when they were granted land of their own. Many of these allotments were located on planters' property with arable soil that yielded sugar cane, which Indians could then sell to the larger estates. Some Indian families were able to amass multiple and larger farms that elevated them to bourgeois status mere decades after their arrival. Meanwhile, most Africans fled to cities and towns to work in menial jobs, separating them from their islands' principal source of prosperity and impoverishing them for generations thereafter. Reinforced by their access to land provisions but also by incipient nationalism, Indians sought to distinguish themselves as racially superior under nineteenth-century theories of civilization and grow closer to the British government. The British did little to facilitate interethnic harmony or bolster African Creoles. They were wary of African Creole loyalties to the Roman Catholic French and also sought to protect their relationship with India, their most populous and prosperous colonial possession.

In Trinidad, where many Indians accessed land in lieu of return passage to their native land and successful Indian merchants have been visible since the late nineteenth century, landownership was not commonplace and certainly did not translate into social and political organization. Indians' relatively late arrival and the clustering of the Creole population in the urban centers allowed Creoles to dominate control of civic and educational institutions. This outsized place in the public sector continued after independence but was eventually challenged. Indo-Trinidadians established their own institutions—news publications, religious organizations, political parties, and social associations—over the course of the twentieth century. During an oil boom from 1973 to 1983, Indians with small businesses began to acquire wealth, and using this new wealth to access education, they began to enter the professions (medicine, engineering, law, accountancy) in large numbers. By the 1990s, Indo-Trinidadians were also gaining more representation in government and law enforcement, once the exclusive domain of Creoles. Apart from the cultural, no other sphere of Trinidadian society was out of bounds.[34] The political sphere, once guarded through gerrymandering, changed so much that by 1995, the Indian-led party came into power through a coalition.

In Hawai'i, integration and, eventually, intermarriage signaled the ultimate equality of foreigners and the dissolution of any sense of pure indigeneity. When immigrant Chinese, Filipino, and Japanese laborers completed their indenture contracts, many settled in rural Hawaiian communities. While some were able to lease farms they dedicated to taro, rice, poi, and sugar cane, others acted as buyers, middlemen, and merchants. A significant number married Native Hawaiian women, who inherited ancestral lands. White people from the United States and Europe also began intermarrying and serving in the Hawaiian government. From 1842 to 1880, white people comprised 28 percent of the legislature despite making up only 7 percent of the population.[35] By 1910, intermarriage was so common that census representatives included the ethnic classifications "Asiatic-Hawaiian" and "Caucasian-Hawaiian" alongside "Hawaiian." While this hybridity transcended the social boundaries that plagued other majority minority societies, it also structured American policies of assimilation that sought to eliminate the Native Hawaiian language and culture. Americans secured advantages for the white planter class and grouped Hawai'i's mixed population into an undifferentiated "colored" underclass that was to be reeducated and civilized. While the Hawaiian kingdom was pressured into granting foreigners formal equality, American colonizers felt no such reciprocal pressure and offered few concessions.[36]

Since independence, the Singaporean government too had sought to assimilate its population—but into a civic rather than ethnic or racial identity—in the interest of assuaging social tension and creating the veneer of equality. After race riots in 1964 by Malay and Chinese residents, the government justified authoritarian control over the press, freedom of assembly, and freedom of speech as necessary measures to prevent an unraveling balkanization. The ruling People's Action Party soon dedicated itself to breaking up ethnic enclaves and recalibrating ethnic distribution in schools, electoral districts, and housing to reflect the country's Chinese-majority demographic "balance." Critics have argued that such measures simply diluted dissent and cemented the party's rule by extending the Chinese majority to all constituencies and sectors of the city-state. In the 2011 general election, opposition members of Parliament attracted nearly 40 percent of the popular vote—their largest share since independence—but won a mere six seats (6.9 percent) in the Singapore Parliament.[37] Political inequality became plain for all to see.[38]

No such veneer belies the Bahraini political context. The *kafala* system overtly and systematically uses citizenship to distinguish and disenfranchise foreigners, which is why recent upsurges in naturalization have raised so many eyebrows. While naturalization rates are near zero in every other member state of the Gulf Cooperation Council, Bahrain offered citizenship to 1.5 percent of its foreign-born population as recently as 2011.[39] The selective grants of citizenship not only offered equal access to the state's generous subsidies and entitlements but also suggested the equal status of people whom nationals came to believe were subordinate. It is arguable whether this loss of national distinction has irked Bahraini Shias more than the government's thinly veiled objective to alter the country's sectarian demography. Though the vast majority of foreigners remain highly precarious and subject to contingent labor contracts, the exceptions have undermined social stability.

Again, the experience of the Irish in New York offers a contrast. Without any such constraints on their numbers and integration in a still-growing country, the Irish wasted no time pursuing equal status. Even before the potato famine induced large-scale immigration, the Irish comprised half the priests in the diocese and a majority of New York City's parishes.[40] During this period, Archbishop John Hughes helped establish a relationship with the Democratic Party such that when thousands more Irish arrived between 1845 and 1854, a powerful political bloc was created to counter the tide of xenophobia then sweeping through the United States. During this period, the Irish pushed for the founding of the Commissioners of Emigration and incentivized Democratic leaders to pursue pro-immigrant policies to solicit their votes, or at least avoid their ire.[41] As new immigrants of Italian, Jewish, and Chinese backgrounds entered the United States later that century, the Irish had already established a number of institutions that protected immigrant interests and facilitated their equal enfranchisement.[42] They were also deeply entrenched into a New York political machine that worked off an elaborate, overt system of patronage.[43]

Institutions and Culture

The provision of immigrants' equality—or its denial—was more than just an institutional choice by governments. It was laden with meaning. Governments can ratify into law the acceptance of a group that has already achieved pervasive social acceptance. Braver governments can assert the acceptance of a group otherwise subject to social rejection and threat. And in their denials, governments can reinforce the boundaries that keep a group excluded in a lower status position. But all such decisions take place in a cultural context that, to some extent, affirms or contradicts them.

The state plays a role in the affirmation or formalization of national culture. Political candidates and officials identify the common denominators that connect distinct groups and cull them into a viable people. In its regulation of the workplace, the media, the environment, and schools, the state enforces and prioritizes specific norms and behavior.[44] And as it allocates funding and arbitrates the wishes of different advocates for education, art, and festivals, it ranks the tastes of particular classes, regions, and ethnic groups—all against the imaginary of the nation as a composite of many equal communities.[45]

The state's hand notwithstanding, culture is ultimately created from interactions between people. And it is through these interactions that they derive meaning about the world around them. Unlike institutions, which are usually more accessible to the established ethnic or religious majority, the cultural sphere is accessible to all and may be influenced more equally. For this reason, a population is often first alerted to demographic change when established cultural traditions like sports, music, or food are altered by minority groups. And so it is on these accessible cultural grounds—where the state is but one voice among many—that peoplehood is often debated, defined, and symbolized before government catches up and takes a stand.

Institutions and culture thus evolve in opposing and complementing duality. Culture is inherently deceptive. The pretense of frivolity veils the communication of participants' most incisive understandings about the world around them. Poetic verses and musical lyrics appear innocuous next to the candor of everyday prose. Museum artifacts and public performance distract the senses. Humor and charisma reduce tension. Indeed, inside culture's fantastic escapism, we may view the deepest truths of a given reality. Much as negative space defines the positive, culture's hiatus frames the everyday life it suspends. Simulating the struggle for power, culture is politics at its most subtle.

Despite a more level playing field, even cultural grounds are initially tilted toward the majority, much like the government and business sectors. If the continued existence of a national identity is subject to what French philosopher Ernest Renan called "a daily plebiscite,"[46] the majority retains a first-mover advantage, because each subsequent generation of immigrants adapts to the original cultural context, reinforcing its primacy even as society diversifies. Eventually, immigrants themselves demand such adaptations by newcomers that follow them to a context they inherited and only partially created.[47] But this first-mover advantage in the cultural sphere cannot be institutionalized forever through gerrymandering, lifetime appointments, or financial inheritances. Short of political and financial capital, minorities accumulate cultural capital and leverage their connection to the public to communicate their grievances, beliefs, and critiques in different forms.

Amid institutional change and resistance, the next six chapters' case studies focus heavily on the culture of national definition. The accessibility and relative egalitarianism of this cultural sphere make it ideal to demonstrate how multiethnic countries pivot toward either conflict or coexistence. Once policy options are exhausted, culture is the place where contestation happens.

PART II
ISLAND NATIONS

4

"An Unnatural Country"

Singapore's Quest to Control the Uncontrollable

A cloud forest is among the world's rarest and most vulnerable ecosystems. It requires consistently cool temperatures and regular misting typically found only at high elevations in the tropics. And yet this fragile environment survives at sea level, on reclaimed land, no less, in the withering afternoon heat of Singapore's Gardens by the Bay. Encased in an asymmetric lattice of steel and glass that undulates from the city's southern marina, the Cloud Forest's elaborate vines and orchids envelop a thirty-five-meter-tall indoor waterfall—the earth's tallest. It is a gratuitous, artificial attraction that ostentatiously asserts Singapore's status as a global economic power and humanistic triumph, but one that is publicly advertised as a monument to the perils of climate change. Like the Cloud Forest, Singapore is also a feat of human ingenuity, strategic engineering, and disciplined maintenance, shrouded in beautiful, tropical vegetation. And like the Cloud Forest, Singapore's carefully preserved utopia is publicly justified by the noblest aims. It has been written that Singapore's creation of an orderly society "symbolises the human manipulation of nature,"[1] but in this instance, the human manipulation of nature symbolizes the maintenance of an orderly society.

The Constant Gardeners

Throughout Singapore, evidence abounds that—separate from the wild jungles that surround it—this is a society under close control. Queues form at designated taxi stands. Public spitting incurs a stiff fine, and vandalizing brings corporal punishment. The pristinely clean streets are lined with gardens of aromatic flowers and colorful foliage, pruned to ensure that their ferns and fronds do not impede rights of way. After all, there is business to be done. And business, according to the country's founding prime minister, Lee Kuan Yew, requires high levels of discipline, stability, proactivity, and air-conditioning.

Majority Minority. Justin Gest, Oxford University Press. © Justin Gest 2022. DOI: 10.1093/oso/9780197641798.003.0004

Covering a mere 278 square miles (the United States governs 3.7 million), Singapore's adept management and global commerce have made it a prized port for two centuries and, today, one of the world's economic wonders. Its high per capita income and development is unique among nondemocratic countries without oil resources—or any other natural resources, for that matter. Its principal resources are human: highly educated professionals who populate Fortune 500 satellites and the honeycomb of government offices that closely regulate and monitor seemingly every dimension of daily life. Few aspects of society are exempted from the Singaporean government's surveillance and micromanagement.

The government owns or controls 85 percent of all real estate in Singapore. This facilitates the massive, coordinated building projects that would elsewhere be delayed by lawsuits, bureaucracy, and consultancy periods. Inside public housing—where most Singaporeans reside—the distribution of ethnic groups is regulated by the state to ensure each building's ethnic composition matches that of the country at large. The thousands of temporary immigrants who enter the country each year to address labor gaps in everything from construction to healthcare are subject to regular checks to ensure they are not pregnant or infected with disease—grounds for swift deportation. The government is constantly evaluating, reevaluating, and tinkering, on the unending march toward progress and efficiency.

But socially Singapore is a hall of mirrors. It has deep roots in Malay Southeast Asia and yet seems distant from its indigeneity. It is run by a Chinese-origin elite that champions race-blind meritocracy but has acted to secure the Chinese tilt of Singapore's labor force and leadership. A city of global diasporas, its languages, traditions, and cultures are all subject to countervailing influences and interpretations. While residents seem to mix these elements fluidly, the state imposes structural boundaries between the different ethnic constituencies and has nationalized children's education. While English is the official language, most Singaporeans—multiple generations removed from their respective countries of origin—continue to speak those native tongues first.

In justifying this state of affairs and assembling a national story that brings Singapore's assorted peoples together, government ministers are grandmasters of paradox. They appeal to common human virtue but govern in ways that undermine it. They recognize the whimsical nature of humanity and yet go to great *lengths* to control it. They acknowledge the impossibility of forcing a singular national identity, but they do so anyway. Amid a history and the specter of demographic change, how does Singapore understand itself?

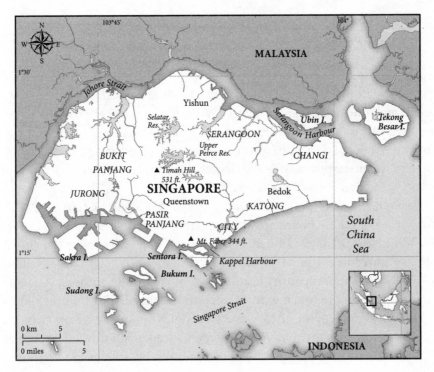

Figure 4.1 Map of Singapore.

In other countries under study here, such meaning-making emerges through the organic expression of cultural performance—through ritual and commemoration. In Singapore, like everything else, even culture is state-owned, carefully scripted, and dictated by the regime. Speaking to a Japanese diplomat, a Singaporean official once explained the anxiety that underpins its governance, that the state's success rests on the fact that it "worries about potential conflicts daily" and that "the day we stop worrying the problem may get out of control."[2] He likened the government's approach to that of a gardener constantly tending to his plants, and said that the reason Singapore is beautiful is because it is "all the time being interfered with."[3]

As a result, Singapore offers a window into what a state—ethnocentrically Chinese and with the luxury of vast resources devoted to all-consuming control—does to sustain and justify its power to a diverse and highly educated citizenry. Whereas elsewhere in the world the mechanisms of social control are often veiled by their expression through the subtleties of art, custom, and ceremony, the Singaporean government's propensity to interfere in the most trivial affairs betrays its intentions.

From these interventions, we can discern three steps used to achieve Singapore's social control in the aftermath of its demographic transformation. First, the state pursues *population control*, the strict regulation of immigrants' admission, integration, and removal. While Singapore may do so more aggressively than other countries, its interest in engineering an enduring majority is not out of the ordinary. Where Singapore diverges is in its realization that, to sustain its power with and despite this population control, its control must extend to other social spheres.

Second, the state pursues *identity control*, the construction and reinforcement of ethnic boundaries. Segregating its people into crude classes of "Chinese," "Malay," "Indian," and "Other" that determine the provision of government services, the state sustains the racial consciousness of a Chinese-origin majority that has assimilated into Southeast Asia and may otherwise lose touch with its ancestral heritage. This both invokes a Chinese-origin people's history as a sometimes oppressed minority in the region and primes them to view Singapore's leadership through an ethnic lens, hindering the development of cross-ethnic solidarities that may threaten its authority.

Third, to justify its overt racialization of Singaporean social relations, the state pursues *narrative control*. Asserting the primordial nature of ethnoreligious affinities, the government creates the impression that Singapore teeters on the edge of imminent racial conflict. In this representation, only the regime can be trusted to unify its cacophonous masses and secure order for the sake of mutual prosperity. In the face of contradictory historical details, narrative control begs information control— the designation of official storytellers and the absolute discrediting of dissenters.

This chapter will explore each of these three steps but will also ultimately interrogate the storytellers—the national museums and the politicians who oversee them, naturalize them, and fiercely protect the perceived veracity of the national story. The realm of information is thus the venue where the legacy of demographic change continues to be contested in Singapore and, correspondingly, the site of both overt and covert subversion. Analyzing the mechanics of the government's control reveals a human tendency to both derive authority from ethnic boundaries and somehow transcend them.

"An Unnatural Country"

The sheer diversity of its citizens aside, Singapore's understanding of its nation is complicated because there was no nation until 1965. Before that, the island was always a nodal hub, something useful to a world larger than itself: the Malacca sultanate, the Johor sultanate, the British Empire, the Japanese Empire.[4] Both small and occupied by the business of global commerce, its orientation had been to these other, larger entities with their own civilizational and national histories from which to draw. At its birth, Singapore was not the inheritor of these rooted narratives but rather the orphan of the failed Malay Federation.[5] Its story had yet to be written, because its story had yet to begin.

On August 9, 1965, Lee Kuan Yew wept as he announced the separation of Chinese-majority Singapore from Malaysia. "I have believed in the Malaysia merger and the unity of these two territories," he said that day. "A people connected by geography, economics, empires of Asia." Until that time, Singapore was for all intents and purposes an integral part of the Malay Peninsula, serving as its primary staple port and linked by deeply integrated economic hierarchies and commercial arrangements.[6] Singapore's affinity for greater Malaya suited British colonials who were skeptical of the city's Chinese, who they suspected would seek to turn the island into a Chinese homeland, like Zionists in Israel. The dissolution of the Malay Federation, for Singapore, was both the end and the beginning of its history.

At the time, Singapore had a population of atomized ethnic enclaves organized to support an economy, not a state. As historians Michael Barr and Zlatko Skrbis have written, the parting provided opportunities that few imagined or wanted: "The Singaporeans were left to construct a nation on weakened social, political and economic infrastructures and a scarcity of historical and cultural resources. There were no idealized histories to recount, no indigenous heroic figures to mobilize the populace, and no autochthonous literary works that would lend themselves to nation-building. Furthermore the only ethno-nationalist impulse offering itself as a basis for nation-building—'Chineseness'— was out of bounds."[7] Wary of the sensitivities of a resident Malay population that was abruptly severed from the mainland, and distrustful of a population that had flirted with Communism and leftism in the years since independence, the government was tasked with finding something stable to unite all.

One of the principal individuals tasked with drafting this new narrative over the past few decades is historian Tan Tai Yong. Currently the president of Yale-NUS College, he serves on the boards of multiple government committees tasked with chronicling and displaying Singapore's history and is the former chair of the National Museum Board and the country's Bicentennial Committee. In telling the national story, the organizations he has led have worked to portray a rather natural trajectory from a Malay fishing village to colonialism to statehood. "But it was all very unexpected; it is an unnatural country," Tan told me in an interview in his spacious campus office.

Peering out the window toward the college's terraced garden, he continued: "Placing the last fifty years in seven hundred years of history, this is a blip, and it's not solidified. We don't have a civilizational core. We are so heterogeneous, there is no indigenous core either. The whole idea of belonging to Singapore is relatively new. It had to make itself into a nation-state, but even as it does so, it goes back to its old role as a global node. So the tensions between an open global city and a nation-state are felt. One third [of the population] are foreigners, a shrinking local population; you'll always have the tension between local citizenries and the members of the global city-state. It has to keep telling its story because it has to make sense of this history and convince its people that they are part of it without turning them inwards."

To survive, Singapore and Prime Minister Lee leaned on education. As it was executed, Singapore's educational system created advanced human resources to compensate for the lack of inherited or natural resources, but it also assimilated multiple diasporic populations into a people integrated enough to carry out business but segregated enough to control. Curricula fostered citizenship values that emphasized obedience to the state rather than knowledge of democratic principles and conveyed ethics, especially purportedly pan-Asian values of family, filial duties, and loyalty.[8] The product of this uncompromising focus on human capital has been the formation of a ruling and administrative elite tasked with perpetuating this vision of the nation.[9] It is an Anglo-imperial vision that "leapfrogs" its local region to engage the world beyond its immediate environs—a global city-state that, at its core, has remained an economic entity.[10]

In these exceptional circumstances and in an effort to preserve them, the administrative elite serve a system that has been called a "stable semi-democracy,"[11] a "façade electoral regime,"[12] and a form of "tyranny"[13] subject to "soft authoritarianism."[14] As the dominant party since 1965, the People's Action Party (PAP) has tolerated token opposition in Parliament and government-vetted critics offering "constructive dissent."[15] Until the 1980s, the Chinese-led party went out of its way to fashion an image as a fair arbiter between Singapore's ethnic and religious groups. However, as the memory of the Malay Federation dimmed and the population became middle class, the government recognized that the people would be more prone to exploring and interrogating Singapore's national history and heritage. They responded by investing in a national education and textbook program that institutionalized a national story but also engaged in more overt Chinese ethnocentrism.

Since the end of the Cold War—which had given the government cover to justify more violent, draconian measures to silence critics—Singapore has ruled more subtly, with legislation giving the state maximum control over land, media, and information. Punitive defamation laws controlled internal criticism of the government, while external criticism of the state in the foreign media was regulated by the Newspaper and Printing Presses Act of 1986.[16] The Housing Development Board undertook massive building projects, such that it now accommodates more than three-quarters of Singapore's population on ninety-nine-year leases, an arrangement that allowed the state to organize the racial composition of the electorate, enhance its surveillance, and discriminate in the dispensing of state infrastructure against constituencies voting for opposition parties.[17] As a result, the ruling elite can micromanage Singaporeans' economic advancement, domestic life, and access to information—sufficient to monopolize the construction of a national identity. Sparing no effort to proactively control even mere nuances in the city-state, the government appears to strive for omniscience, if not omnipotence.[18]

The churning, fiery core underneath the cool, polished veneer of Singapore's leadership is ultimately its own insecurity. "The sense of vulnerability is still there," says Tan, the historian. "Precisely because we are very physically small without hinterlands, the whole idea of a national identity—this place, if not properly run, is easily divided and will collapse quickly. There is no buffer. What drives the government is to make sure it works economically and [is] socially united. There is always this fear that there are fault lines underneath the surface."

"Do you agree?" I asked him.

"I think the fault lines are there," he replied in a way that seemed to channel others. "If these are not carefully managed, they can surface and rupture Singapore. You cannot leave it to chance. If things go awry, you can't put the genie back."

"But if divisions across social boundaries are the top concern, why does the government reinforce them?" I asked.

"I think [recognizing the different racial groups] was necessary at one part of Singapore history, and it remains debatable now," he said. "Lee once described himself not as a 'racist,' but as a 'racialist.' While he doesn't make judgments on the basis of people's race, he accepts that racial identities are a reality that he has to deal with in policymaking. . . . But it does predominate views of identity. They don't adopt a melting pot kind of policy; it's a kaleidoscope, where each

Table 4.1 Key Factors in Singapore

(Majority Minority in ~1830, but as a State in 1965)			
Immigration	Equality	Identity	Social Relations
Continuous: Chinese, South Asian, and European immigrants enter regularly for 150 years, during its affiliation with British Malaya. Since 1965, state preference for Chinese-origin entries through "population control."	*Unequal:* Strict system of racial classification drives racial corporatist state that gerrymanders to secure PAP control and dilute residential concentrations of Malay and Indian minorities. No free dissent or fair elections.	*Exclusive:* Despite state cultivation of a uniform civic identity, state subtly ensures Chinese predominance—historically by fostering Chinese values and Sinicization campaigns, and today through immigration policy and "identity control."	*Suppressed:* Called "multiculturalism stuck in neutral," division and racialization persists in social relations. Though peaceful, state actors insist that racial conflict lurks just beneath the surface at all times in order to sustain power.

part has the right to function on their terms in peace. That's all right in the first two or three decades, but after fifty years of nation-building, are these categories still valid? With intermarriage, cosmopolitanism, those complexities are coming in.

"The degree of paranoia is very high. They always think we are this unfinished product. As a nongovernment person, it's easy for me to say it's time to review this policy. But government is concerned that they're making the wrong decision. But you have to do something to see if it's producing the right results. Instead, they're keeping to the same old playbook of racialist policies."

After half a century, this racialization and the division that persists in Singapore's management of social relations contrast with the uniformity demanded by its government elites behind their vision for social identity. Indeed, the government strives to create authentically Singaporean institutions and an authentically Singaporean identity, but their appeal is limited by their investment in a single, valid perspective of Singapore's history.[19] In the remainder of this chapter, I explore the tensions challenging this elite quest for control.

Population Control

As Singapore's livelihood relied on its cultivation of human capital, immigration was an early strategy for economic development. Even as the country built an advanced educational infrastructure, immigrants were required to fulfill a persistent demand for high- and low-skilled labor to stimulate and sustain economic growth and satisfy new consumption habits. Today, Singapore maintains recruitment offices in Australia, China, Europe, India, and North America to attract talent, and its government provides clear, easy, and quick employment pass applications, tax incentives, and often a path to naturalization or permanent residence to highly skilled migrants.[20] Temporary migrants represent the vast majority of all annual migration flows, however, and since the 1970s the low-skilled laborers who constructed the city-state's infrastructure have been regulated by a system of dependency ceilings and fees[21] imposed on employers to ensure that local workers are not replaced by migrant workers, meaning that such migrants are present only for a short period.[22]

Unlike highly skilled workers entering Singapore, workers in semi-skilled and unskilled temporary positions are limited to shorter stays and caps on their overall periods of employment.[23] Benefits such as visa renewal, family reunification, and paths to citizenship are reserved for higher-skilled and higher-income visa holders.[24] Under the terms of temporary work permits, low-skilled immigrants to Singapore must repatriate to their native country if their employment is terminated or they become pregnant. If they wish to marry a Singaporean national, they must receive special government approval.[25] Immigrants are subject to regular medical tests,[26] and their employers must post sizable bonds and purchase insurance policies in case of accidents or illness.[27]

Sinocentrism

Despite this emphasis on immigrants' ability to contribute to Singapore's development, the selection of immigrants has always been subject to Lee's elite, Sinocentric vision and his "concern that there was a shrinking pool of talent from which elite cadres could be recruited."[28] In his imagination, Singapore's Chinese are naturally inclined to absorb and reproduce "Confucian values" because they are descended from tough, resourceful, and industrious immigrant stock.[29] And so he sought to address low fertility rates among Chinese women, both in light of the inherent virtue of Chinese workers and also to prevent social conflict by recruiting more Chinese-origin people to fill the ranks.[30] Accordingly, the government has manipulated both the flows of immigrants admitted to Singapore and the ethnic composition of those immigrants granted Singaporean citizenship. Unsurprisingly, the population of immigrants from the People's Republic of China (PRC) has grown significantly, from only "several thousands" in the 1990s to "close to 1 million" twenty years later, making them one of the largest and most visible communities in Singapore.[31]

While the importation of mainland Chinese labor appears to reinforce the Chinese-origin majority in Singapore, this underestimates the differences between the Chinese-born immigrants and the Singaporean Chinese. The latter are largely Peranakan, a class of people with Chinese ancestries but who spent many generations in the part of Southeast Asia—Nanhai to the Chinese, later known as Nanyang, or "South Seas"—that had seen vibrant Chinese trade in luxury goods and other artifacts for almost two centuries under British rule but since as early as the second century BC.[32] Among Peranakan Chinese, those with any strong affinities for mainland China have likely already returned to the mainland to defend China in its various twentieth-century wars or since its economy began developing. This reduced the number of Peranakan Chinese even further to those committed to life in Malaya—a life that has been thoroughly adapted to local culture and environments.

Consequently, "PRC immigrants," as they are called, have not seamlessly blended into Singapore. Shared heritage aside, their status has been undercut by their "unskilled" labor classification, which not only denies them residency rights but also subjects them to the grid of rules, checks, and regulations that ensure their presence in Singapore is transient.[33] It is uncertain how many of Singapore's approximately 1 million temporary work permit holders are from China, but most are not top-paid expatriates or transnational elites elsewhere in Singapore.[34] This has complicated Lee's vision of the Chinese as both intrinsically (biologically) and extrinsically (materially) desirable.

"Social Stability"

Frustration with the persistent flow of PRC immigrants into the city-state drove the government's embarrassing loss of vote share in the 2011 election (which, thanks to gerrymandering, barely affected parliamentary representation). Just before the election, the release of a government white paper recommending further intake of PRC immigrants spurred five thousand locals to protest in the streets—a rare event. Nonresidents make up 1.11 million of Singapore's 3.11-million-person workforce, the highest proportion of foreign workers among all Asian countries east of Oman (see Table 4.2).[35] They are often associated with the "3D"—dirty, dangerous, and demeaning—jobs, while wealthy

Table 4.2 The Foreign-Born Share of Singapore's National Population between 1990 and 2015

1990	1995	2000	2005	2010	2015
24.1%	28.5%	33.6%	35.0%	40.7%	45.4%

Sources: United Nations Population Division, "International Migration Stock 2013: Migrants by Destination and Origin," 2013, https://www.un.org/en/development/desa/population/migration/data/estimates2/estimatesorigin.asp; United Nations Population Division, "Trends in International Migration Stock: The 2015 Revision," December 2015, https://reliefweb.int/sites/reliefweb.int/files/resources/MigrationStockDocumentation_2015.pdf; Singapore Department of Statistics, "Census of Population 2010 Advance Census Release," accessed 15 March 2021, https://www.singstat.gov.sg/-/media/files/publications/cop2010/census_2010_advance_census_release/c2010acr.pdf.

Chinese expats are thought to be ostentatious, arrogant, and reckless.[36] Both have led to a gradual "Sinicization" of the public face of Singapore.[37] Many complain that migrants have increased housing costs,[38] overwhelmed public transport,[39] and overcrowded an already congested city.[40]

Government officials have shifted away from Lee's "racialist" rhetoric about the industry of Chinese-origin people but in interviews still openly discuss their preference for maintaining a 73 percent Chinese majority. And because of low Chinese fertility rates, doing so requires further migration.

I interviewed Shawn Loh, the deputy director for population policy and planning for the prime minister. A model of Singaporean meritocracy, he was educated in multiracial state schools before graduating from Oxford and the University of Chicago on government scholarships, and he has since worked at the ministries of manpower and education. We met at a café inside the St. Regis Hotel, an opulent high-rise adorned with vermillion velvet and gold drapes in the Orchard Street neighborhood. He ordered char kway teow, a classic Southeast Asian noodle dish ubiquitous in Singapore's hawker markets.

"If our immigration framework stopped looking at ethnicity, at what point would it be sustainable?" he asked me rhetorically. "At what pace would each community accept it? There are not many sources of Malay immigrants; there are more sources of Indian and Chinese. So the pace of change would need to be managed very carefully."

"But isn't it likely that fewer Malay people apply because the bias against their applications is well known?" I asked. "You don't know who would apply if there weren't quotas."

"If you exclude the Middle Eastern [Gulf] countries, we don't have another country to learn from," Loh said. "We don't know the best way to think about integrating the foreign-born population. Is there a tipping point beyond which openness to foreigners decreases and you can't come back? We are a bit worried that we will face that situation in the future."

He continued, "There is a concept of absorptive capacity—the population's ability to absorb demographic change. And there is a tendency to assimilate and accept people who look like you and have your norms. The question is whether [ethnic selection] as a model is sufficient to address that. An immigrant from PRC is now very different from Singaporean Chinese. But because of [lower Chinese] fertility rates, it means we [admit] more immigrants from the PRC, and that has changed the way Singaporeans look at the model. They see a PRC Chinese as PRC, not Singaporean. . . . I guess the counterfactual is: What if we didn't use [racial classification] as the model, and focused on family ties, economic contributions, human capital? Would that support better economic outcomes, and at what cost to social stability?"

"But we need to make a distinction between stability and a complete lack of change," I suggested. "You can imagine a stable change over time that society can accept and absorb across generations."

"We've only been a country for fifty years," he responded, "and prior to that, a lot of people were not locally born, and we still managed to integrate. So to some extent, the sentiments that we see are a function of our success in building a national identity. You don't feel strongly about the out-group unless your sense of an in-group is strong. Now immigrants are needing more time to integrate into Singaporean society."

Foreshadowing my conversations with other officials, Loh claims in one breath that Singapore is at once divided and unified—its citizenry so fractious that they are prone to conflict at any time and yet dubiously united in their xenophobia. For Loh, population control is required not only to ensure the competitiveness of Singapore in a global marketplace but also, more important, to ensure that Singapore's purportedly neutral identity survives. In this understanding, population control is pointless without identity control.

Identity Control

Identity control was not the objective of the Singaporean state alone. It has been a part of Singapore's governance since Sir Stamford Raffles first established a British settlement at the southern tip of the Malay Peninsula. Inspired by the Dutch *kapitan* system, the colonial government appointed liaisons to represent each of the diverse ethnic communities, communicate requests, and execute government policies throughout their first century of rule. The organization of the different groups was best described by Barr and Skrbis:

Colonial Singapore [had] a racial division of labour. All the various people met in the economic sphere, the market place; but they lived apart and continually tended to fall apart unless held together by the British Government.[41] Colonial ideology ranked the myriad of races under its jurisdiction according to stereotypes of racial attributes. Racial groups were distinguished one from the other and included in colonial society in distinctive ways that minimised inter-communal interaction. The role of the colonizer was seen to be one of an umpire, arbitrating the relationships and conflicts between the various communities. The division of colonial society into ethnic silos facilitated the generation of stereotypes that persist to today. The Malays were viewed by both the Chinese and the colonial administration as being "endowed with traits of complacency, indolence, apathy, infused with a love of leisure and an absence of motivation and discipline"[42] while Indians were stereotyped as being dirty, argumentative and troublesome.[43]

The overarching categories of "Chinese," Malay," and "Indian" were first used in the 1891 Straits Settlements.[44] However, as evidence of their socially constructed nature, the labels were not recognized by Singapore's residents. Colonial officials regularly complained about how the "difficulty of achieving anything with a scientific or logically consistent classification is enhanced by the fact that most Oriental peoples themselves have no clear conceptions of race."[45] Singaporeans did not organically develop the artificial boundaries that came to define their society; these boundaries were learned. Though they segregated Singapore's diverse constituencies, the British were ultimately interested in connecting all Malayan people with British identity so that they would enact pro-British laws and policies. This and all future understandings of Singapore's multiracialism were based on the presumption that the city-state's commercial future lay in assimilating its various ethnic cultures into a dominant hegemonic culture.[46]

However, inspired by the global waves of unionism, socialism, and nationalist pushback against racial and colonial ideologies, Singaporeans—particularly those of Chinese origin—began to mobilize against their rulers. Fearful that the Chinese sought to turn Singapore into a Chinese homeland, the British responded by crushing protests with violence, starving Chinese-language schools of funding, and indoctrinating Singaporean children with an English-speaking curriculum that focused on British and Malayan history, ignoring any Chinese or Indian contributions. By 1950, there were twice as many Chinese schools as English schools, but 80 percent of all British educational funding went to English schools and only 5.8 percent to Chinese schools.[47] Chinese textbooks were banned, schools were prohibited from being used as meeting places to spread unlawful ideologies, and police raided

Chinese schools seeking evidence of subversion. In a remarkable act of protest in 1953, a grassroots Chinese movement raised money to found Nanyang University (now Nanyang Technological University, NTU) to raise educational standards among Chinese who were unable to access higher education institutions because of discriminatory admissions policies. Its success emboldened further Chinese resistance. Long a minority in Malaya, the Chinese began to wield their majority in Singapore.

CMIO

The future founders of a sovereign Singapore came of age in this highly politicized environment, and despite their anticolonial spirit, they channeled British propensities to exert control over public identity and quash subversive elements. Between 1959 and 1965, in order to persuade Malaysia to sustain their federation with Singapore, the Singapore government gave primacy to Malay culture and language. It is for this reason that Singapore's national motto and anthem are in Malay, despite the fact that Malays have historically made up only about a seventh of the population. After separation with Malaysia in 1965, the Singaporean government pivoted away from Malay consciousness, but it remained concerned that a civic Singaporean identity would not be strong enough to supersede ethnonational affinities and possibly separatism. Indeed, in the initial decades of PAP rule, Singapore's government even suppressed Chinese nationalist sentiment and cultural expression in order to establish a purportedly race-blind meritocracy and quash "Chinese chauvinism."[48] To quell ethnic tensions, the Chinese have consistently been treated as just one of the country's ethnic groups, and English has been employed as a universal language. All this has perpetuated the veneer that the Chinese are not dominant and allowed Chinese elites to meet challenges to power from their high ground as neutral umpire.[49]

As with so many other postcolonial states, the post-1965 Singaporean government pursued nation-building strategies for modernization to promote the development of their society and justify the power transferred from the empire. But despite the break they sought to create from colonial rule, they allowed inherited racial classifications to seep into new forms of governance. These antecedent, British-generated understandings of race then became the meme[50] through which Lee and the postcolonial state sought to build their nation atop a hierarchy of races. As recently as the 1990s, Lee confidently stated:

When doing a project [the British] would put the Chinese in the middle and put the Indians on the side, and the Indians were expected to keep the pace of the Chinese. And there was a hell of a problem, because one Chinese would carry one pole with two wicker baskets of earth, whereas two Indians would carry one pole with one wicker basket between them. So it's one quarter. Now that's culture. Maybe it has to do with genetic characteristics. I'm not sure.[51]

This is a primordialist conception of society—rooted in colonialism and appropriated by the Singaporean state—for which ethnic characteristics are inborn, unchanging, and unchangeable.[52]

Singapore's nation-building project may be based on transcendent values, but the government has never intended to transcend ethnic differences to construct an amalgamated Singaporean ethnic identity. Quite to the contrary, the state has reinforced the racial composites invented by the British: "Chinese," which encompasses the Mandarin language, Confucianism and Buddhism, and Chinese culture; "Malay," which encompasses the Malay language, Islam, and Malay culture; "Indian," which encompasses the Tamil language, Hinduism, and Indian subcontinental culture; and "Other," a residual category that has historically included Arabs and Western "Eurasians." Conventionally called CMIO, this *quadrature* is the fulcrum around which Singapore rotates. Each label is a factor in determining the schools children may attend, what languages they learn at school, where people may live, how they access welfare and public services, and their ability to join "group representation constituencies" that run for office—mechanisms of control that would otherwise be hard to justify. This "race" is the only demographic data on the front of a Singaporean identity card apart from date of birth and sex, and it defines the way government statistics offices present data on matters like graduation rates and university results.

Sinicization

After the initial suppression of Chinese nationalism, Lee and the PAP began a program of Sinicization that promoted Chinese attributes to create a Mandarin- and English-speaking elite that would populate the state bureaucracy and manage everyday life. Launched in 1979, this program instituted an annual Speak Mandarin Campaign and developed a collection of Chinese Special Assistance Plan schools.[53] During the 1980s, the government led campaigns to teach and promote Confucianism, both to make Singapore's Chinese community more self-consciously "Chinese"[54] and to pressure

Malays and Indians to adopt Chinese virtues, which were marketed to be commercially and socially advantageous.[55]

Confucianism helped produce a degree of social conformism and paternalism. Under such an ideology, it was thought that the values and ideals of the majority race "may form the basis of the national values . . . [and] the minority group or race would seek to integrate their values."[56] In May 1991, Lee expressed his satisfaction that the physical interspersion of the Malays throughout Chinese-dominated housing estates had "helped increase competitiveness in the Malay community by example and interaction."[57] He once described a Malay who was doing well in business as "acting just like a Chinese. You know he's bouncing, running around, to-ing and fro-ing."[58] Behind the façade of even-handed multiracialism and meritocracy thus lurked a methodical and pervasive racial sensitivity that asserts the Chinese character of Singapore's multiracialism.[59]

The system of racial corporatism also created a politics of patronage that provides work for many non-Chinese Singaporeans and a comfort with race-specific institutions.

Mohamed Imran, a Malay Singaporean, is the director of the Centre for Interfaith Understanding, an independent consultancy that advises private- and public-sector clients about interfaith and interethnic relations. "Managing [race relations]—for the state—meant creating racial structures," he told me. "But that was a short-term, immediate concern."

"How long is short term?" I asked. "It's been fifty years."

"Sometimes along the way, you think it's benefited you," he answered.

"Have you benefited?" I asked.

"People who are socially mobile and have privileged access to resources may feel like they have the capital to transcend social boundaries," he explained, "but lower-class people are dependent on them. Let's take a low-income Malay family seeking help. They will feel comfortable going to a Malay welfare organization to seek help—psychologically—from my own circle, rather than a Chinese organization that may not understand their language or everyday habits and relate to them better. If you go to a Christian organization, they may fear pressure to convert."

"But the alternative is not a Chinese welfare organization, but rather a new welfare organization that has no affinities at all," I sought to clarify.

"But that is an extra burden for the state," said Imran. "We do have [non-denominational] Family Service Centres that disperse financial assistance to needy families. But I have heard Malays go there, and they try to find Malay counselors and case officers."

"Is that not better?"

"Well, there is efficiency, but those efficiencies may eliminate jobs for Malays."

"Multiculturalism in Neutral"

The government's close management of cultural production and change allows it to strike a calibrated balance that cautiously acknowledges the country's diversity but sustains structural inequality—a system of equal recognition without equal rights or equal representation. Recognition and the accommodation of ethnic distinctions are hallmarks of multiculturalism. And Singapore has presented the image of a multiracial and multireligious community in official publications,[60] public relations,[61] public media,[62] and even performances at the annual National Day Parade.[63] However, multiculturalism as it is practiced in Canada or Australia is designed to ease the integration of ethnic minorities in the short run to promote long-run adaptation and harmony. Immigrants don't remain in second-language schools forever or rely on organizations with ethnic affinities after the first generation. And whereas multiculturalism conventionally accommodates all forms of difference, the Singaporean variety accommodates only the three major composite categories—ignoring common exceptions like Indian Muslims or Sikhs, Chinese Christians, and Chinese Cantonese speakers. This is "multiculturalism in neutral," as it has been called.[64]

In Singapore—forever the "child of diaspora"[65]—so long as current ethnic boundaries endure, the government may orient immigration admissions, residential distribution, and electoral constituencies around them to engineer a Chinese majority. The indefinite maintenance, rather than the dissolution, of ethnic differences therefore ultimately preserves PAP control. In such primordialist visions of ethnicity, according to anthropologist Clifford Geertz, the "congruities of blood, speech, custom, and so on, are seen to have an ineffable, and at times, overpowering, coerciveness in and of themselves."[66] And so Singapore divides to conquer in a matter inspired by but nevertheless distinct from its old British governors.

The ossified distinctions and hierarchy of Singapore's corporatist multiracialism is at odds with the meritocracy on which the national myth is founded. This myth functions to cut across ethnic communalism but also to reassure Singaporeans that their government is comprised of the best and the brightest independent of their racial background and upbringing. When critics question the meritocracy and the balanced treatment of Singapore's racial groups, they implicitly question the legitimacy of the state itself.

In 2015, Singaporean researcher Sangeetha Thanapal coined the term "Chinese privilege," a derivative of the "white privilege" being acknowledged in racial justice movements in the United States and elsewhere at the time. In a series of blogs and social media posts, Thanapal wrote, "[T]he Chinese supremacist state of Singapore constantly tells us that the Chinese are what makes Singapore successful, that Malays are lazy, that Indians are violent and that only Chinese people can save Singapore."[67] Calling Singapore a "a terribly racist country," she has alleged that the government "embarked on a form of eugenics in the 1980s meant to displace its indigenous population and replace it with settler colonial Chinese people." After Singapore's government warned and subsequently detained her, Thanapal moved to Melbourne out of fear for her safety and liberty. Singapore, she says, is "a country that is unsafe for activists, intellectuals, writers and a whole host of anyone who dares to think and speak differently." Whether one regards Thanapal's ideas as accurate or hyperbolic, the tempest she stirred revealed the way state identity control has necessitated equal control over the flow and interpretation of information.

Narrative Control

The approach of the PAP and Singapore's elite bureaucracy cannot be understood without an appreciation for *kiasu*, a Hokkien word that means "afraid to fail" but extends to an all-consuming fear of missing out. *Kiasu* underpins the ambition of the state to accumulate educational credentials, talent, and material success, but also its obsessive micromanagement of public life and information. In this spirit, there is no platform too minor to monitor, no inaccuracy too petty to be corrected, and very little space for interpretation of art, history, or data. Indeed, *kiasu* instills the sense that there is constantly something else that can be done to achieve set goals—a feeling that mobilizes an insecure bureaucracy, constant gardeners, to protect an insecure state. However, to justify the racial corporatism that ensures the Chinese majority, the fragility of state failure is now equated with the fragility of social relations.

Equally important as the national narrative of meritocracy is the national narrative of Singapore's fractious racial "balance." In this telling, Singapore is understood to have always been on the verge of racial conflict. While British governance was characterized by both ethnic tension and harmonious mixing, the national story has underscored the tumultuous period immediately after independence as a test drive of an open society. Largely overlooking the pan-ethnic coalition that elected the leftist reformer David Marshall in

1955, history books often focus on the last months of the doomed Federation of Malaya.

After the PAP decided to contest Malaysian elections outside of Singapore in 1964, tensions rose between them and the United Malay National Organization (UMNO). Amid a variety of political disagreements, the PAP portrayed Malays as backward and rural, while the UMNO accused the PAP of "Chinese bias" and new "colonialism." On July 21, 1964, the Prophet Muhammad's birthday, during a parade on Kalang Road in Singapore, fights broke out and spread island-wide for a week, killing twenty-two people. The instigator of the violence remains contested even today, and while there were multiple sources of political tension at the time, the PAP has characterized the riot as a "racial" conflict ever since—evidence that social relations must be contained by the state. In the absence of state control over Singapore's population and identity construction, it warned, more riots would surely start.

This idea, that Singapore is always on the verge of racial conflict, pervades popular discourse around CMIO practices and has a chilling effect on discourse around de-emphasizing racial identity and crossing social boundaries. In almost every interview I conducted, respondents from government and civil society made reference to the delicate fragility of Singapore's social harmony. Some examples:

"The reality is that it is fragile. We don't take things for granted. There is some separation."

"These things can easily come apart. We can't be complacent."

"When you look at what's happening in our region, it's a stark reminder that we can't take things for granted. Social media reveals a lot of hate and fault lines. More work needs to be done."

"Ethnocentrism. It's a bit more insidious. The reminder of what can happen during the riots is in every history book, and every permanent exhibition."

"It's about distress, small things, discrimination. Singaporeans are detail-oriented. They don't want daily life disrupted. The idea is that social relationships would be strained and then it takes just one thing."

"They are fragile in the sense that the forces that swirl around us are moving in the wrong direction and we face a very real risk."

"That cautionary tale of 1964 is still the modus operandi for how race needs to be spoken about in Singapore."

The 1964 riots were the first and only instance of racial violence ever instigated in Singapore, and despite its hand in stirring racial tension in advance of the conflict, the PAP has asserted that they and their system of racial corporatism are the only things standing between the country and a total breakdown of order.

Fragility in Question

Counterevidence abounds. Setting aside debates about PAP policies and the historical accuracy of depictions of the 1964 riots, there are many indications that—despite Singapore's reinforcement of racial boundaries—an immense amount of boundary-crossing has taken place since 1965. Singapore has unique cultural references and norms, its own dialect of English—colloquially called "Singlish"—and a hybridized Southeast Asian cuisine featuring elements from Malaysia, India, and China. When a viral Facebook post publicized a PRC migrant's complaint about the smell from curry cooked by their Singaporean Indian neighbors, citizens retaliated by cooking curry "en masse" the weekend before the 2011 election.[68] Without a hinterland to anchor Singapore to anachronistic forms of heritage, Singaporeans across racial backgrounds are uninhibited cosmopolitans.[69] These attributes defy the state's primordial approach to ethnic identity. Indeed, anecdotally, when I asked interviewees (including government officials) whether they felt closer to Singaporeans of other ethnicities or to immigrants of the same ethnic background, everyone chose the former. The rate of interracial marriage rose every year from 2010 to 2018, when 22 percent of all marriages registered in Singapore were interracial[70]—an act that Lee once portrayed as a transgressive adventure.[71]

These are the green shoots of a pan-racial Singaporean ethnic identity rather than a society on the verge of civil war, but Loh, the official from the prime minister's office, pooh-poohed such bridging.

"Unless you're saying that the creation of the Singaporean identity is so strong that people identify with it more than their race or religion," he said, "that could be one of the reasons why we reexamine CMIO. But the way we see things, the affinity with C, M, and I is very strong. If your assumption is that human nature creates in-groups based on immutable traits—as the state does—the argument is that you need to lean against this by putting mechanisms in place. We can all agree that the ultimate goal is social cohesion, and [the] CMIO model helped us over time."

"You've said 'over time' two dozen times," I intervened. "When does the short term end? When is it time to reevaluate whether this is working?"

"One of the indicators could be whether people are identifying by anything other than their race," Loh replied.

"But what other options do they have right now?" I asked. "Look at your identity cards."

"When you interact with government, this is what we use for administrative purposes," Loh said, pulling his card from his wallet. He was labeled "Chinese," naturally. "I understand that CMI reinforces these markers, but . . . the downside of getting this wrong is you only have one chance to get social stability right. If we could find out what's the pace of change we could get away with, I would be interested. But we don't know what that is. I think we define stability in a few ways. One way is how people feel about immigrants, the attitudes of people toward each other. It's a measure of resilience. I don't see a situation where you have a big anti-immigrant backlash and society can be stable."

Imran, the interfaith leader, is sensitive to this backlash. In many ways, his revenue depends on racial tension.

"So how fragile are race relations in Singapore?" I asked him.

"I don't think they are that fragile," he said. "Certainly, there are issues that might have a negative impact on race relations, but we are much more resilient than our leaders would like to think. We're certainly not immune to problems and racial tensions, especially when they have to do with events outside Singapore. But I think we have enough resources and ties to stem unforeseen issues."

"The government has always been cautious," he continued. "Reinforcing the danger of racial conflicts benefits them by making people more vigilant. They want to maintain the structures in place that they've built. The business of every government is to maintain their power, especially for a political party that has been in power since independence. Why would they give that up, and cede space to groups that may undermine their power? . . . And that is something they will always be wary of.

"If poverty suddenly became a concern beyond Malays, the disgruntlement would spread. Now they can blame a cultural deficit or attitudes. That segments the problem, blinding people to the structures creating poverty. And that structure doesn't only affect Malays. And if there were a groundswell of people unhappy with inequality, that would pose a problem to the government. The British did it with 'divide and conquer.' It makes it easier to govern, while defusing a groundswell that might undermine your power base."

When confronted with these trends, Singaporean officials cite them as evidence that CMIO separation is working to ensure a fair meritocracy, as if division is the path to unity. In conversation after conversation, officials simultaneously cast images of a people hesitant about racial progress but at the same time insistent that racial progress is taking place. The dog chases its tail.

The Tharman Premiership

Never have the contradictions of Singapore's meritocracy come together so publicly and poignantly as when Deputy Prime Minister Tharman Shamugaratnam was being considered as the next prime minister of Singapore in 2019. Tharman, as he is ubiquitously known, was chairman of the Monetary Authority of Singapore, coordinating minister for social policies, and deputy chairman of the GIC, Singapore's sovereign wealth fund. He also chaired the Group of Thirty (G30), the independent council of economic and financial leaders, and in 2019 he was on the short list to be head of the International Monetary Fund. Previously, he had served as Singapore's minister of education (2003–2008), minister of finance (2007–2015), and minister of manpower (2011–2012). He holds degrees from the London School of Economics, Cambridge, and Harvard. And while he is a member of Parliament representing the Jurong constituency, he is immensely popular all over Singapore, praised by taxi drivers, shopkeepers, and the intelligentsia alike for his sober judgment and charisma. He also happens to be of Sri Lankan Tamil ethnicity—in Singapore, an "Indian."

Among intense speculation and loud public calls for him to be named the next prime minister of Singapore after Lee Hsien Loong steps down, a March 2019 cabinet reshuffle "promoted" Tharman to senior minister, a post previously held by Lee Kuan Yew and other Singaporean officials before their retirement. Instead, Deputy Prime Minister Heng Swee Keat was named first assistant secretary-general of the PAP, aligning him to become prime minister that May. Amid public disappointment and unofficial polling that revealed Singaporeans' preference for Tharman, Heng was asked by NTU professor Walid Jumblatt Abdullah, "Is it Singapore who is not ready for a non-Chinese prime minister, or is it the PAP who is not ready for a non-Chinese prime minister?"[72]

Heng disputed the notion that Singapore is ready for a non-Chinese prime minister because the older generation is not prepared to accept a minority prime minister. Noting that many students might be happy to have a non-Chinese prime minister, Heng said that his "own experience in walking the ground, in working with different people from all walks of life, is that the views—if you go by age and by life experience—would be very different."

He reassured the NTU audience that the government's position is "not contradictory" to its race-blind, meritocratic values given that it reserved the Singaporean presidency, a figurehead post, for minority candidates. He added, "It is precisely because we need to place this emphasis institutionally that we recognize that we have not arrived. It is important for us to ensure that we have that safeguard. . . . I can tell you that it is not easy because it triggers all the feelings about race, which are not obvious. But when it comes to an election, it becomes an issue."

The widely reported remarks echoed an earlier statement by Lee Kuan Yew, who said that he had considered Minister for National Development Suppiah Dhanabalan to be the prime minister in the 1980s but decided that the country was not ready for an Indian head of government. Singapore historians Barr and Skrbis have written that the only way to understand such clearly contradictory statements "as anything other than cynical duplicity is to accept that contemporary multi-racialism in Singapore is at heart a Chinese construction and that the minority communities are not being asked to accommodate themselves to an ethnically neutral hegemony, but a Chinese-generated and Chinese-dominated hegemony."[73]

Tharman has played this game well though. He learned Chinese calligraphy and has given karaoke performances in Mandarin.[74] His children are some of the few non-Chinese Singaporean youths who attend a Chinese school and study Mandarin as their "mother tongue." Such efforts to adopt Chinese culture and values would have pleased Lee, who in 2001 said doing so helps "increase competitiveness" in the Malay and Indian communities "by example and integration."[75] And when he was denied the premiership, Tharman—ever the party man—handled the injustice with grace. "Swee Keat is the best person to move up to become DPM and take over as PM during the next term of government," he wrote on his Facebook page.

> He has exceptional ability, mettle and the confidence of the 4G [fourth generation] team. We have avoided sudden change. It may be unexciting and predictable, but it works for Singapore. We will have a strong crew in Cabinet. . . . We each have our strengths and individual characters, but none of us is perfect. Our system of political renewal in Government only succeeds if we complement each other and play as a team, work with Singaporeans, and never let success get to our heads or assume that all that worked in the past will work in the future. It is how the Singapore story keeps going.

I met Tharman in a mod, airy Italian restaurant in the Clarke Quay district of the city's financial center on his last day as deputy prime minister. When he arrived, another customer shook his hand in admiration. Conversant in subjects from populism and finance to sports and foreign affairs, his intellect ranges and he speaks in cogent paragraphs—a rehearsed paragon of the party line, and ultimately an apologist for Chinese dominance.

I began, "There is no small amount of irony that Singapore—a country that will tinker and micromanage everything, ever under construction—has left the construction of national identity effectively unchanged for over fifty years. Has the country achieved perfection?"

"It is very hard to understand Singapore's model of multiracial, national, and civic identity without understanding that the Chinese community was a minority in Southeast Asia for a very long period of time" he said. "And that cultural antecedent is so obvious to me, when I compare it to fresh PRC immigrants or post-1999 Hong Kong migrants. This is a community that came as a minority into urban towns and cities in Malaya, Borneo, Singapore, and the Philippines. In Thailand, they immersed themselves in Thai culture, so it's much more integrated. But the point I'm making is that the unusual feature of the majority Chinese community in Singapore being willing to be part of a multiracial society where no one is up or down, is a matter of formal status. That you have to extend civil courtesies is actually a product of that long cultural antecedent of having to defend yourself and survive, if not for the fact that you're well regarded by your Malay neighbors. That history of Nanyang Chinese that emigrated out of poverty and chaos is fascinating, but they didn't come with the majority mindset. And then suddenly you have this accident of history and Singapore is formed, and they are the majority. But we have the fabulous advantage of having a majority community with a minority mindset."

It is unclear to me whether having a "minority mindset" makes a majority population more understanding of the plight of other minorities or more defensive of their gains. Certainly, in other majority minority cases, empathy is rare. Singapore's purported racial "neutrality" has nodded to Malays' and Indians' wariness of Chinese dominance but also secured Chinese dominance—socially, economically, politically, and demographically. "Our stance on demography is one of caution rather than one defined in stone," Tharman added.

"Is it paralyzing?" I asked.

"You just have to have a sense of how unsettling it can be to have significant change," Tharman said. "It's a very young nation, and it's had to make tough decisions on language and education. If you think about what the Chinese community went through, it was major changes in cultural identity, and I don't think in that context it would be wise to include a sudden change of demographic composition. I say it as a conjecture. You cannot have too many changes in cultural identity at the same time."

"But what you're saying could have been said in [the] 1970s or 1980s."

"I'm a retail politician. I spend a lot of time on the ground in my constituency. Those in their fifties and beyond came out of a very different set of experiences. The Chinese really are Chinese, very Chinese. So it's just not true that Singapore has changed that dramatically. Children are growing up in those families."

"That Chinese Singaporeans feel that way, does that suggest that CMIO has failed in its integration mission?" I asked.

"It's not a lack of progress," he replied. "It's a reflection of how society evolves. It's not simply an integration model. Values and sense of sameness through shared experiences . . . Every one of us who grew up in the 1960s and beyond knows how dramatically Singapore has changed. Race was thick in the air everywhere, and I grew up with it, but in a very accommodating society." He recalled discrimination by Chinese bus drivers, bus riders, and judgment about being in an interracial marriage; his wife is Japanese. Invoking Lee, he said, "It was not a racist society, but a racialist society. And those things just don't happen now. We haven't arrived in nirvana, but we are making progress, and it comes out of mixing people in education and housing."

"But if such progress has been made and the country is truly multicultural, why does the government insist on freezing the Chinese share of the population at 73 percent?"

"The decision for it to be a meritocratic, multiracial country was a political decision. For the majority community, they had a sense of themselves in Singapore just like Malacca and Penang. These were cities where they were predominant. So it's not that they thought of themselves as a minority, but their culture and values had been shaped by their experience in the diaspora on the Southeast Asian archipelago. Singapore was their town. Penang was their town. So it's not a contradiction."

"You're implying that there is a need to reassure them that it remains their town."

"That was not the conscious basis for the decision. When you make major changes in housing and education, you don't want to change everything at the same time."

And yet that is Singaporean style in every other matter—to embrace evolutionary change at the speed required for survival. "I'm wary of creating a straw man," I said. "Just because you alter demographic distribution doesn't mean that you go from seventy-three percent Chinese to forty-three percent Chinese. There is a gradient here."

"People don't have a formal sense of the demography as who they're meeting in society," he said. "We cannot have a policy that keeps percentages unchanged forever. You have to survive economically and you need talent. They are changing de facto because of intermarriage. CMIO boundaries are blurring. Realistically, the supply of immigrants from China and India vastly outstrip the demand, compared to Malays. If you look at the composition of the expatriate community, it is very diverse. And if you look at intermarriage, a significant share is with Westerners."

"Is there a timeline for this evolution?" I pressed.

"There is a sense of caution about changing something you inherit. It doesn't mean you don't change by one percent here and see what it's like, but we're not scrambling to get Chinese and Indian immigrants. At any point in time, we're having to control the number of Chinese and Indian immigrants. In fact, we would be very happy to get more Malays who qualify according to [our standards] to come to Singapore. Historically, we didn't need to control the population, but now it's a practical issue to control the big bulge of Chinese and Indian immigrants. Suddenly, you'd see seventy-three [percent] become eighty-three and eighty-five, and Indians grow [from eight percent] to sixteen percent. That's the new reality of immigration in Asia."

The deputy prime minister was rambling, in my view. Singapore did not "inherit" a hard racial distribution from the British; the PAP froze the distribution and likely benefited from the migration of some Malays to Malaysia after the federation broke off. Since then, it is impossible to know if Malays' disinterest in immigrating to Singapore is not due to entrenched Chinese dominance; there is no counterfactual. The immigration policy likely deters immigration applications. And if there is such a surplus of Indians as well as Chinese immigrants, why not accept more Indian-origin workers rather than Chinese-origin workers? This story was flimsy.

"In light of all the social progress you cite, and intermarriage, are social relations in Singapore really all that fragile?" I asked.

"We're much more vulnerable," he said. "In practice the policy thinking is coming from a different direction than what you think. Because of intermarriage and global forces, how do you avoid a significant reduction in the number of Malay Muslims in our society? If the Indians were to catch up, that would be a significant change to the Malay psyche."

Of course, it is not the Malay psyche that needs protection, nor is the Malay psyche the one that Tharman has most analyzed. The marginality of Malays was deepened when Islamophobia intensified in reaction to the September 11, 2001, terrorist attack and the emergence of Southeast Asian extremist group Jemaah Islamiyah, which allowed the Singaporean government to justify Malays' detention without trial because the United States was doing the same.[76] And indeed, were the Malay population to shrink, the government could always recruit Malay immigrants to fill any shortages, as it recruits highly skilled Western expats.

"We are just a city," Tharman said. "We are only New York. Only San Francisco. We don't have a white majority in the mid-country [to anchor the ethnic identity]. When you're just a city, you need policies—a little strange to some—that are sensitive to people's social identities. . . . [Relations are] not fragile in the way you'd see it in other parts of the world. But they are fragile in the sense that the forces that swirl around us are moving in the wrong direction and we face a very real risk. . . . We feel we need to address this by doubling up on being proactive—being open about the problem, being straight about it."

CMIO is proactive, but it is not straight. Its objective is not to temper Chinese dominance but rather to secure it while making other ethnic groups feel as if they are equal. In this way, Tharman is the ideal Singaporean minority but also a national tragedy. He is a true overachiever, a patriot who has unquestioningly served his country, and when his crowning moment arose, he accepted his status as second class. The society is just too "fragile"; Tharman was never going to be Chinese enough to lead. He claims to feel confident in the "fourth-generation" leaders in his party. If only his party were confident enough to have faith in his first-generation profile.

Information Control

Just as the Singapore government strives to create the veneer of equality, it also strives to create the veneer of openness in an otherwise heavily monitored and managed public sphere. The general strategy is to pass laws that criminalize a wide range of behavior and make the definitions of that behavior vague enough to selectively target dissidents while insisting that the country abides by impartial rule of law. The Public Order Act effectively criminalizes all public activity by one or more people. To protest, a citizen needs a permit from a licensing regime overseen by political officials, the Media Regulatory Agency, and the police. The Films Act criminalizes a wide range of films, including undefined "political films."

Most recently, the government enacted the Protection Against Online Falsehoods and Misinformation Act, also known as the "fake news law." It states that an assertion is false if it is false and misleading—a tautology. Ultimately, a statement is deemed false if a minister decides it is false, or it causes people to lose confidence in government institutions. The government can then compel the perpetrator to make a dictated admission and publicize a correction. In this way, even if the government cannot censor the internet, it hovers over its users and vets all information—monopolizing the nation-building narrative by monopolizing truth itself.[77]

The People vs. PJ Thum

This is why the work of Ping Tijn "PJ" Thum has been taken so seriously. In another world, Thum would be celebrated as a national treasure. From a well-to-do Singaporean Chinese family, Thum was admitted as an undergraduate at Harvard University when he was just sixteen, competed in the 1996 Olympics butterfly and relay swimming heats under the Singaporean flag, and received a doctorate in Southeast Asian history from Oxford University as a Rhodes Scholar. However, he is an activist who has persistently criticized the Singaporean government for its crackdown on dissent via his blog and website New Narratif. But perhaps most menacingly, he has published revisionist accounts of Singaporean history that question the pillars of government power—the meritocracy and the fragility of social relations.

Through his writing and an epic, fifty-episode podcast authoritatively titled *The History of Singapore*, Thum focused his research on the period between independence and the breakup of the Malay Federation in 1965, a critical time when the PAP was consolidating power, but also a tumultuous time the party has frequently referenced to justify its political choices ever since. Among hours and hours of monologue, Thum contends that the 1955 election of the leftist Marshall—who won with a multiracial coalition of voters in Singapore's "first and only free and fair election"—is evidence that Singaporeans are not as conservative as the PAP suggests and that ethnic divisions are constructed by the PAP to maintain power. He contends that the 1964 riots were propelled by politicians and not as racially motivated as they have been portrayed. And he paints the legendary Lee Kuan Yew as a duplicitous opportunist who detained many people without trial and betrayed his colleagues and country to consolidate personal power. In so doing, Thum crafts a new national story founded upon a democratic, racially harmonious, and progressive Singapore that could have been and still could be.

The Singaporean state's response was to make a public example of something that may have otherwise been largely dismissed as esoteric, academic quibbling. In response to a call for submissions from the Singapore Parliament's Select Committee on Deliberate Online Falsehoods, Thum submitted a paper arguing that any legislation by the Singapore Parliament against online falsehoods must also apply to the Singapore government, which, he asserted, detained dissidents without trial between 1963 and 1988.

On March 29, 2019, Thum was called in for questioning by Kasiviswanathan "K." Shanmugam, Singapore's minister of law since 2008 and minister of home affairs since 2015. During a six-hour testimony that made doctoral thesis defenses look like tea parties, Shanmugam cross-examined Thum about his academic credentials and a paper he published in 2013 regarding the formation of Malaysia.

Shanmugam concluded that Thum, who holds a nominal, unpaid position at Oxford in addition to his commentary work, falls short of the standards of an objective historian, and that his research "ignores evidence which you don't like, you ignore and suppress what is inconvenient, and in your writings you present quite an untrue picture." For his part, Thum countered that his paper had been peer-reviewed and had not been contested by any other historian. The next morning, the state-controlled *Straits Times* and Channel NewsAsia reported that Thum conceded there were parts of the paper he could have worded better, that some of his statements were misleading, and that he had not consulted the accounts of some historical figures he deemed to be unreliable. The government claimed victory; the truth had been preserved. But the scene looked as if the state had chased off a fruit fly with a sledgehammer, and then flexed its muscles.

I met Thum at the National Museum of Singapore, the country's official showcase of the national story. Now forty years old, Thum remains in good shape. He is eloquent but verbose, passionate but reserved, with a propensity to neurotically nudge his spectacles up the bridge of his nose in the best academic tradition. Sitting at a café in the atrium outside the historical gallery that ignores many of the nuances he brings to light, I asked Thum, "How are you not in prison right now?"

"Singapore is way more sophisticated than that," he laughed. "The government has over time pursued a strategy of carefully calibrated coercion. It is reliant upon foreign investment and goodwill from major creditor nations and markets. It wants to be seen as a good place to do business and a reliable ally. During the Cold War, it was easier to oppress because they just needed to be less oppressive than others. But they had to scale back on direct oppression in the 1990s, and instead shifted to control the environment in which we operated. They passed laws to suggest a rules-based, objective environment, which is just not true. But it co-opted language about human rights and fit oppression within global dialogues about liberty and security. . . . Basically, they're saying that 'we get to decide what the truth is.' And that's how they can control Singapore.

"But why am I not in jail?" he asked. "The government is really careful about how it uses and justifies oppression. Because it is so responsive to international capital, it is more cautious with people who can mobilize international public opinion. Last year, my lawyer was confident they were going to come after me, but I was able to rally two hundred academics and publicity for my case. So the government shifted from accusations of lying to accusations of initiating a conspiracy. I've also been very careful to focus on writing, research, but I don't generally take part in protests. I organize letter-writing and citizen groups, but the government accused us of being agents of foreign influence seeking to destabilize Singapore."

"Why is what you're doing so dangerous in the eyes of the state?" I asked.

"It's complicated," Thum said. "First, the government asserts a monopoly on information. Everything produced by the government is automatically a state secret; there is no Freedom of Information Act; there is only an Official Secrets Act. It hangs over retired civil servants as well. They also assert a monopoly on expertise. They are proud of how they can bring in or co-opt the best and brightest through the scholarship system and the education system. Using their rigorous system of testing, they can find the smartest people here and get them to work for the government. . . . It's really important, when you're an authoritarian country, to monopolize the understanding of history. You need to create a monoculture—a specific idea of the nation. And by monopolizing its definition, you can tar anyone who disagrees with you as an anti-national threat to the people. It justifies a range of powerful oppression, and people respond to that. A lot of my work undermines their definition of the nation and identity, and through that, undermines their policy, oppression, and monopoly of power.

"We are challenging their fundamental assumptions about the world," he further explained. "This is their religion, their values. So when you're a party in power for sixty years, you have a lot of baggage, a worldview based on these myths. If someone nudges one of the pillars, the whole thing comes falling down. If development is not a universal good, what has the PAP been doing for sixty years? If we're not the best and brightest, why have we been in charge? If we are not vulnerable, our oppression makes us the bad guys. The PAP is strong and powerful . . . but they are paranoid that they are fragile. And this derives from Lee Kuan Yew's sensitivity to any threat or dissent. . . . The PAP and Singapore is built in his image."

Minister Shanmugam

Several days later, I sat down with Minister Shanmugam. He asked that we meet in a basement tandoori restaurant, underneath a Holiday Inn. Rather than speak in the dining room, the minister's staff reserved a remote, window-less salon that was part of the hotel's conference center. The door was manned by multiple members of staff, wearing leather utility belts with oversized two-way radios on their hips. The restaurant staff was on pins and needles and communicated with one another in whispers. The table was dressed in a satin crimson cloth and ornate plates, and the room's walls were lined with panels of richly stained beech wood, but it had the feel of a gilded int-errogation room.

"I watched excerpts from the Select Committee Hearing on Fake News with testimony by Thum Ping Tjin," I opened. "Why is it so important that Singapore's history is gotten right?"

Minister Shanmugam chuckled triumphantly. "There are two levels to this answer. One, there is a crisis of trust across countries in the world. What do I mean? People don't believe in institutions, experts, politicians. They don't believe doctors, lawyers, and that crisis of confidence—you need to believe in an infrastructure of fact to have meaningful public discourse in a democracy. . . . Trust remains high in Singapore, but that requires the government to be up front but also maintain its integrity. People have to see you as being so. Government has to make sure that when they [make statements and release data] it has to be accurate. So that if it is announced, it must be true. When people question the truth, it's a problem.

"At a second level, this was a serious process," he continued. "People take an oath. . . . PJ put forward a five-page note, which said that Lee Kuan Yew was the biggest creator of falsehoods in the last fifty years. Clearly this is not by any stretch an academic work; it was designed to cock a snook—to treat the matter much less seriously. If we left it alone, we might be seen to be agreeing with him. If we don't ask him questions, we're accepting what he says. If you want to be puerile and juvenile about it, let's go through your research. And I got him to admit that his research papers are inaccurate about the under-lying notes he refers to. And he refers to this as his seminal work. And it was important for me and the historical record to establish that.

"You cannot have one understanding of history. Different people will take different understandings. We should strive to put out the facts, and present as objectively as possible the interpretation of those facts. But it would be difficult to say that there can only be one understanding." He gave an example about whether Raffles actually founded Singapore. "It's not so much to get the historical narrative in a single picture; it's about making sure that what you say is accurate."

"I know that you are leading the charge for a new law regulating the publication of false information online, particularly false information about the Singaporean government, its institutions, and its legitimacy," I said.

"Obviously, fake news is a problem globally. Is Singapore more vulnerable than other governments?"

"The answer is yes at three levels," he began. "We have seen the effect it has had in the US, the UK, and the complications of Brexit and others in France and Germany, country after country. One, our identity as a nation, is still very new. We have been in existence since 1965. Second, it's the fact that we have very deep, strong ethnic and religious identities. Race and religion continue to be very strong factors in individual identity. And three, Singapore is tiny, and therefore it takes the position that we will have to defend ourselves. It has constantly built up its military capabilities. . . . Because of this, it is more vulnerable to softening up through online falsehoods by foreign agencies, because starting a conventional war with Singapore doesn't make sense."

Like so often before, a state official leverages the diversity and fragility of Singapore's society to justify tactics that preserve PAP power. I decided to pursue this line of inquiry further and asked, "Would the state and its identity be stronger if the ethnic boundaries were not so reinforced by state policy?"

"It's not for the government to interfere," Shanmugam said, citing data from a recent report. "We would exceed our mandate."

"The government interferes all the time," I interjected.

"You're not wrong on the facts," he answered, "but let's look at the reasons. Can you remove references to race on all these documents and yet have the benefits that target the needs of different racial groups? . . . We can try to avoid it. But it matters to the community, and I don't think it's because of our parties."

"Does this not mean that the national identity strategy has failed?"

"It hasn't failed," he countered. "It's not perfect. It simply means that in today's world, with the internet and racial and ethnic identities becoming more important, our attempt to create a national identity is working but constantly challenged. . . . This is not a government that seeks to divide people. But there are limits to what can be achieved. Left alone, we could have moved further, but it has never been the government's policy to suggest that one day the individual identities will never be there."

"Quite the opposite," I said. "The government seems to be ensuring that individual identities remain. Why is there a need to freeze the share of Chinese people at seventy-three percent?"

"[Indians and Malays] don't want to go below where they are [in terms of population share]; that's their concern," Shanmugam said. "A separate point is the nature of immigration and where you take them from. We take [immigrants] from everywhere, but we favor immigrants from countries where people are racially or ethnically more assimilable. If the complexion changes fast, people will not accept it."

This is practically the same argument for why Shanmugam's fellow Tamil-origin minister Tharman was not recently promoted to prime minister. Assuming the population is as close-minded as they are portrayed, I asked, doesn't the government have an obligation to lead public opinion and attitudes toward racial tolerance rather than pander to them? Wouldn't an "Indian" prime minister serve as the hallmark of a race-blind meritocracy?

"I don't deny the point you make. Mine is different," he responded. "The Indian prime minister will start with a discount more than the Chinese prime minister. And if you go to members of Parliament, the cadres who select the executive committee and prime minister . . . they'll know that an Indian will bring them less in terms of popular support. How much less? We can argue. But there will be a difference. It's possible that there is an individual who can overcome these natural factors of race by sheer personality and character, and we're hoping that someday we'll arrive at that point. But second, the average member of Parliament will ask, for battle, why should I take a discount? Could we lose a few more seats? The answer is more open. Will you take that chance?"

"I think it depends on how devoted you are to the national identity that you said it so central to Singapore," I said. "If you are, what better symbol of a unified national identity than a Sri Lankan prime minister?"

"That is important," he agreed, "but winning the election is important."

"You said you would lose a few seats," I recalled.

"It will only be doable when the MPs and party cadres believe that the Malay and Indian candidates will not stand at a disadvantage to a Chinese candidate."

"Won't they always stand at a disadvantage given the frozen demographics?"

"Well, the older generation has very strong views."

"So it's about waiting for people to die?"

"You can't quote me on that," he said, chuckling. "But it's a matter of education, and people sixty and above were born before independence, and people under thirty only know a multicultural, prosperous Singapore. There will always be a discount but maybe not a thirty-eight-point discount. Maybe a ten-percent discount."

Shanmugam then summoned data from one of his assistants. Digging into a labeled file folder thick with paper, the assistant quickly produced a

Table 4.3 Acceptability of Prime Ministers of Different Races by Racial Group

Acceptability by race	... to be Prime Minister of Singapore		
	Singaporean Chinese PM	Singaporean Malay PM	Singaporean Indian PM
Chinese respondents	98%	53%	60%
Malay respondents	86%	93%	75%
Indian respondents	88%	70%	89%
Other respondents	87%	81%	68%

Source: Matthew Mathews, "CNA-IPS Survey on Race Relations," Institute of Policy Studies and Channel NewsAsia, August 2016.

report from the Institute for Policy Studies that polled Singaporeans about whether they would find politicians of different races acceptable to serve as prime minister (see Table 4.3). There was indeed a 38-point drop in Chinese Singaporeans' support for a Singaporean Indian premier, but quickly aggregating the results of the table, it became abundantly clear to me that more than 60 percent of the population—better than 63 percent upon later calculation—would find an Indian prime minister acceptable. In any country, this is a resounding majority. I pointed this out to Shanmugam.

"I personally think it's [a matter of losing] a few seats, but other people think it's a whole election," he said. As always, the government produced the information, and the government determined how to understand it.

The Singapore Story

The Singapore story, or at least the components that the government wishes to emphasize, is told over and over in government rhetoric. But the officially sanctioned understanding of who Singaporeans are emerges from the materials created to educate the population. Education has always been the cornerstone of the Singaporean nation, because its land yielded neither material resources nor a common legacy of memories[78] from which its people could build an economy or identity; it needed to be constructed and then taught. These stories are inherently prescriptive[79] and are as significant for the information they include as for the information they omit. As this chapter has demonstrated, the free realm of information is a site of government power and, correspondingly, a site of both overt and covert subversion.

National Education

Throughout the world, school history textbooks routinely establish and maintain the existence of nations in the personal and public imagination in order to sustain the political reality of a nation-state.[80] Addressing the Historical Society of Nanyang University in 1978, Lee Kuan Yew urged students to "retain a key sense of our inheritance," which would "inoculate" them against "foreign attitudes to life."[81] In a nationally televised broadcast later that year, he encouraged Singaporeans to "know something of [their] past . . . to identify [themselves]."[82] Thereafter, Singapore incrementally centralized the planning of its curriculum and published the first state-authored textbook in 1984. By then, Singapore's leaders saw the children's history curriculum as integral to education's nation-building objectives, or, in Prime Minister Goh Chok Tong's words, as nothing less than "education for citizenship."[83] Correspondingly, the classroom experience of the official narrative became "hegemonic and totalising," rendering "alternative memories . . . irrelevant, inaccurate, and even illegitimate."[84]

As fears of shifting political loyalties arose in 1996, Prime Minister Goh attributed younger Singaporeans' desire for parliamentary opposition to their "lack of knowledge of Singapore's history."[85] While their parents had "voted solidly" for the PAP, youths had "no personal experience of Singapore's struggle," and hence undervalued his party's "strong leadership." To remedy this, he argued, history teaching should emphasize "the constraints we face, how we have overcome them, and what we must do to thrive"—a narrative he referred to as "national education" (NE).[86] The following year, NE was launched as a curricular campaign by the Ministry of Education, with an accompanying NE exhibition that all students and many other Singaporeans attended.[87] It was titled "The Singapore Story," as were the memoirs of Lee Kuan Yew published in 1998.

A principal focus of the 1980s curriculum was to adopt a monolithic, stereotypical understanding of the officially recognized racial groups. Authors like Koun Chin Kok asserted that "each race wanted to preserve its own customs," and supported this with anecdotal evidence.[88] After NE was established, British colonialism was increasingly depicted as a benevolent force exercising enlightened stewardship over a multiracial colony, in which pluralism resolved competing racial allegiances.[89] Textbooks presented racial differences as latent sources of communal tension, and hence threats to social stability. This could be seen in consistent portrayals of the 1964 riots as a predominantly racial affair, national in scale, and fundamentally antagonistic, even while popular accounts suggest a more nuanced historical reality.[90]

The Museums

The artifactual companions to school textbooks are the various museums controlled by the National Heritage Board. In the way they collect, display, but also deactivate and remove recovered materials from their original purpose, museums suggest a supreme control over the narratives of the past. With their glass cases and explanatory placards, they also assign value to the objects and stories they present and imply the power of the state to assign such value.[91] The museums are born from the recognition that controlling population demographics is insufficient without asserting equal control over the national identity and national narrative. Their goal is to naturalize and authenticate an otherwise wholly constructed and artificial story put forward by the Singaporean government.

Independent of their collections, Singapore's museums are physical embodiments of the corporatist national identity the state hopes to sustain. There are "cultural centers"—one for each major racial group—as well as the National Museum of Singapore and the National Gallery, which aim to assemble the ethnic lineages into a common legacy. The Asian Civilisations Museum similarly contextualizes Singapore as representative of the diverse South and East Asian cultures that surround it.

Curators and administrators execute the visions of the state but—as with all cultural forms of expression—have enough space to subvert them. In each of the four exhibitions I consulted during my visit, there are nods to the authority of the Singapore story and subtle attempts to undermine it. In the words of one former museum official, "They can't censor us. We cite sources. We show the truth. We provide the evidence without the angst."

First, the Malay Heritage Centre is housed in a large, stately villa near the Sultan Mosque in Kampong Glam, surrounded by a manicured garden of coconut palms, mango, tamarind, and breadfruit trees. It was previously the residence of the sultan of Singapore and his family until they were evicted in 1999. They were in severe debt, housed dozens of squatters, and it had fallen into disrepair. Makeshift walls subdivided grand corridors and halls into cubicled living quarters for extended members of the sultan's family. The government reclaimed the building, restored the original walls and garden, and renovated the entire facility to house its permanent collection. To simulate the experience of entering a Malay home, visitors are asked to remove their shoes at the entrance.

Filled with antique tapestries, ledgers, and photographs, the museum subtly pieces together the unrecognized past and legacy of Singapore before and during British colonialism—as a commercial hub of Southeast Asia and as the region's principal conduit to Mecca. The curator of the Malay Heritage Centre, Suhaili Osman, told me, "There is a tendency to refer to everything that existed before 1819 as legend and irrelevant to the city that Singapore became; hence the perspective of 'how far we've come.' In a sense, we are challenging the publicly accepted notion of who are Malays. We're not asking who we are, or what our name is, but rather what type of Malay are we. We take offense to the thought that we are another one of Singapore's diasporas. The question is: What has Singapore made of us? We were never a sleepy fishing village. It's not that we're trying to be subversive. We understand the need to build a nation, but it should not sacrifice nuance. And the textbooks tend to oversimplify."

Second, the Asian Civilisations Museum sparked controversy and a national debate with its 2019 exhibition "Raffles in Southeast Asia" to mark Singapore's Bicentennial, a milestone that celebrates the moment of British contact. The exhibition, which used artistic and cultural artifacts to present a multilayered picture of Raffles in the years leading up to his arrival in Singapore, benefited from a provocative advertising campaign in which a cut-off portrait of him asked, "Scholar or Scoundrel?" It is hard to overstate how ubiquitous and unquestioned Raffles's legacy is in Singapore; the Raffles name is everywhere. The Raffles Hotel. Raffles City Mall. Raffles Hospital. Raffles College of Music. Raffles College of Design. The list goes on. In scrutinizing this legacy, the museum scrutinized the Singaporean state as its custodian, as its meme.

The museum director, Kennie Ting, told me, "We were rather critical, because we were criticizing the fundamental philosophy of colonialism. And if people got that right, they would have seen that Raffles collected all [these artifacts] for the purpose of subjugation. And so in many ways, we were being very critical, but subtle about how it was communicated. . . . If you look at these pieces of regalia, you would know that they could only have been created by a sophisticated cosmopolitan civilization—not a sleepy fishing village. We've designed the regalia, as a memorial to the Johor sultanate, to remind people that when something new is created, something else is lost. So there are multiple layers of messaging. It can't be read like a textbook. . . . Out of necessity, there's a narrative we learn in school, but there just hasn't been an interest in diving deeper into our identity. I think the shift to explore a richer narrative has been driven by a groundswell of deepening interest in our heritage and identity."

Third, the National Museum of Singapore embodies the authoritative edition of the Singapore story in its main historical gallery—a vast maze that presents dioramas, portraits, and curiosities depicting life in Singapore for a thousand years. Given its prominence, the National Museum is a more conservative venue, subject to state visits and scrutiny from the Ministry of Culture, Communication, Youth, and Sports. All children must visit the museum once before they complete their formal compulsory education—200,000 unique domestic and international students a year.

The historical gallery's longtime curator, Iskander Mydin, recalled when Lee Kuan Yew once visited. "You could hear a pin drop. When he came here, it was quite stressful. Each of us had to be stationed at different sections. And after I explained the contents of a letter from Stamford Raffles, he asked me in an interrogative way, 'How do you know this is genuine and not a fake?' He asked [the director] where these paintings were before their display here. He questioned me about a film about a Shinto shrine here, and . . . said that, besides the troops, there were no Japanese young children in Singapore. He said, 'I'm prepared to wager with you.' My boss gave me body language to shut up. So I said, 'You're right, sir.' He wanted to make sure you did your homework, very particular about the accuracy of facts and historical information."

Conspicuously, the main historical gallery makes effectively no mention of the 1964 riots, apart from a single newspaper clipping printed on a wall of hundreds of such clippings from the 1961 to 1965 period. Given its centrality in textbooks and rhetoric, I raised this curious omission with the museum director, Angelita Teo.

"I don't think we did it on purpose," she said. "We were looking for milestone events, and based on them, we found examples of stories that represent people from all races. But I don't think we're going to overtly address it. It was just not something that we felt—it's hard to showcase as a museum. The presentation has to be collection-driven, and it's not easy to talk about these issues with our collection."

But the gallery's curator, Mydin—who lived through the riots and said their racialization was divisive, even as a child—had a different response. "If you look at it in historical context, the riots are an exception rather than the norm in the scope of Singapore's history," he said. "It was tied to the developments arising from the merger and separation. Much work has been written about the riots, but the number of deaths was way below the traffic deaths that same year. It just reveals the fault lines in the social fabric. . . . The riots were engineered by extremist factions of the Malaysian ruling party, which wanted a Malay Malaysia. It was a political riot, expressed in racial terms."

"Why do racial lines endure, despite the emergence of a civic Singaporean identity?" I asked Teo, the museum director.

"It is so ingrained into every aspect of everything that we do," she explained. "It goes back to Lee Kuan Yew's [1965] separation speech. He stated it very clearly: it's not just a Chinese country; it's a Malay country, an Indian country. He named each group. The lines are artificially maintained to be consistent over the last fifty years through immigration policies. It's still being done."

"Do people still need that assurance?" I asked.

"I think they think this is a nice balance."

"Balance suggests that it is a balance."

"It's not really a balance; it's more a consistency. I don't think regular Singaporeans question all these things."

Fourth, in 2019, the National Gallery opened a four-hundred-piece exhibit, "Siapa Nama Kamu? Art in Singapore since the 19th Century," which featured a "catalogue that stands on the shoulders of giants to present a survey of Singapore art," according to the official description. As one might expect, its earliest works were deferential to the colonial governors and featured British depictions of a dangerous, untamed wilderness. Along with a portrait of a popular colonial governor, there was a print of a tiger attack on a pith-hatted colonial administrator, botanicals of exotic, indigenous flora, and British renderings of the port—all with Government Hill, the seat of colonial authority, in the background. By implying the British civilizing mission, this collection dramatized how far the city-state had come.

From there until the mid-twentieth century, the artists were nearly exclusively of Chinese origin, each depicting different components of life in Nanyang. A seated Malay man. A Balinese fête. A Thai temple. Multiple portraits of topless indigenous women. These idealized renderings comprise Singapore and its region as seen through Chinese eyes—Chinese attempts to capture and make sense of a new land and their place in it. Essentializing the components of life in turbulent times renders a sense of control, but it also keeps the respective communities of Singapore in their place within social hierarchies—revealing Chinese people's complicated sense of estrangement and embeddedness in local Malay life.

After independence, mid-twentieth-century art shifted away from these ideal types to search for a collective consciousness—an identity that crossed racial boundaries as Singaporeans sought to found a nation. Portrayals of protest movements and recalcitrant street hawkers reflected the insurgency and organization that forged a civic sense of "who are we." It reflected the pan-Malay sentiment that made Singapore's birth so unlikely and ironic, but also the multiracial leftism that the PAP regime has often ignored in their rhetoric and storytelling. The locally famous portrait *National Language Class* depicts Chinese and Indians coming together to learn a common language, Malay, during the federation years.

The title "Siapa Nama Kamu?" is Malay for "What is your name?"—an existential question more appropriately addressed to the Chinese Singaporean majority than any Malay. The prompt peers deep into the Chinese soul.

"The Chinese majority are looking for who they are because they are less able to perform Chinese," one curator told me. "They speak less and less Mandarin, and they are distanced from their original culture."

In many ways, it is this identity crisis that is at the center of majority minority politics. The constructed boundaries of ethnicity and race are sustained because—and so long as—it is so challenging to form a new understanding, a new identity, a new name for who "we" are together.

What Is Your Name?

Paradoxical to the end, Singapore offers countervailing lessons for the societies that today confront majority minority milestones. On the one hand, the Singaporean state is an exemplar of how a multiethnic and multireligious society may pursue a civic, national identity. Aiming for a race-blind meritocracy, the government has leveraged its supreme power to cultivate a singular people through residential integration, national service programs, inclusive public information campaigns, and its careful oversight of cultural heritage. These are advanced, coordinated programs that many liberal democracies are not yet capable of executing.

On the other hand, the state has employed these same levers to sustain subtle Chinese supremacy. Its leaders and policies implicitly and, if prompted, explicitly invoke a primordial understanding of ethnicity and religion that no civic identity could ever supersede. Repeated references to the city-state's precious racial "balance" relate to the maintenance of Chinese predominance rather than any calibration of equal power among population groups entitled to equal treatment and representation. Their actions straddle the lines of coercion, co-optation, and propaganda that no liberal democracy would ever approach.

Singapore, whose government is not subject to free dissent or fair elections, therefore reveals the power of an uninhibited state over demographic change. It is highly unlikely that any future society will possess the same degree of control over the nuances of daily life. Control requires not only a certain type of regime and level of resources but also the logistical advantages of a tiny island. As this extreme case shows, though, Singapore is an experiment in the capacity of human social engineering. While maintaining the veneer of free dialogue and enterprise, what can the state do to sustain the power of one social group over others?

This chapter reveals all that the state can control. First, it can control the composition of the population; second, its identity construction; and third, the national narrative—the story of the country that justifies its policies and tactics. It is Singapore's story of inherent ethnic conflict in a fragile meritocracy that continues to legitimize the government's colonial-style racial corporatism. But ultimately, at its core, all of this requires some control over information itself. And here, the Singaporean state reveals another extreme, the limit of state control over popular understandings of history, heritage, and culture.

It therefore excites little surprise that subversion is taking place here, where state power ends. PJ Thum knows that the state could control the newspapers, but it could not control the internet. Museum curators know that the state could control the exhibitions, but not their interpretation. And at the street level, Singaporeans know that the state can control racial classifications, but it cannot place boundaries on love. It is in these loosely regulated spaces and in the subtleties of art and culture that the many paradoxes of modern Singapore emerge into the daylight.

The Chinese-run state is beginning to harvest some unexpected fruits of their constant gardening: increasing intermarriage, demands for free speech, and an "Indian" as the favored candidate for prime minister. In a liberal democracy, these would be triumphs of meritocracy and social integration, but for Chinese elites in the Singaporean government, they are equally a threat to social stability. This is because, as Tharman told me, "The Chinese are a majority with a minority mentality." In seeking to preserve Chinese dominance, the PAP has engaged the Chinese population's defensiveness and insecurity and largely wasted their empathy and adaptability.

However, this is not unique to the Singaporean Chinese. As political theorist Danielle Allen foresaw in the United States and elsewhere, when facing a majority minority milestone "everyone begins from the psychological position of fearing to be a member of a vulnerable minority."[92] The challenge for all minorities and majorities is to concern themselves less with the future of their population subgroup, and more with the collective future of their nation. But to the introspective question of "What is your name?" Singapore's PAP officials—ever the developers—have yet to develop a satisfying answer.

5

None for All

Citizenship and Peoplehood in Bahrain

Beneath the shimmering peaks of Manama's ever-evolving skyline of steel and glass, the sands of Bu Mahir seashore have sat largely undisturbed for over a century. For millennia before, however, these banks at the southernmost tip of Bahrain's Muharraq Island were a crossroads of *al-khaleej*, the Gulf region. At the beginning of each summer, people would gather for *al-rakbah*, the first day of the pearling season, when a fleet of dhow ships would depart for months at sea to collect one of the world's most precious jewels. Attracting divers, haulers, and boat captains from Persia, India, East Africa, and all over Arabia, pearling brought together crews who worked grueling hours on and under the water for their shared prosperity. As they heaved their boats to the sea and set sail, the men were cheered by the families and community they left behind to the rhythm of traditional songs chanted every year. Dhows were extremely crowded and reeked of dead and rotting oysters, and the diverse crews lived without comfort or privacy.[1] They regularly suffered from ear infections, burst eardrums, scurvy, and decompression sickness and had to fend off sharks and jellyfish. The sailors slept on the deck or, for greater support, atop piles of shucked shells. After diving, washing, and anointing the lesions on their skin, many would stand naked, shivering as they dried in the arid breeze off the Arabian Desert.[2] On the same Bu Mahir beach in September or October, women and children would assemble again at the first sight of the fleet's return, watching in trepidation for the black flags that indicated a death at sea.[3] In these moments, Bahrain—in all its diversity—chanted as one, praying for the safe return of their loved ones. These are the travails that forge disparate tribes into a unified people, but, by design, Bahrain's people were never unified.

A Society Off-Balance

Bahrain's strategic harbor and proximity to the Gulf's best oyster beds long made the island desirable to the powerful interests swirling through its

Majority Minority. Justin Gest, Oxford University Press. © Justin Gest 2022. DOI: 10.1093/oso/9780197641798.003.0005

surrounding seas (Figure 5.1). As regional empires in Persia and Muscat struggled to dominate Arab tribes from the Gulf's coastline, and all parties fought European and Ottoman agents who coveted commerce via the Strait of Hormuz, the eighteenth century was a turbulent one in Bahrain. As 'Utub tribes, the Omanis, the Persian Safavids, and the Huwala all traded control over its pearl fisheries in this political vacuum, merchants and sailors migrated between Bahrain and pearling settlements on the Gulf littoral. Eventually, in 1783, the Al-Khalifas' 'Utub tribe from Zubara—encircled by Saudi forces at the time—invaded Bahrain, killed the representatives of Iran's Zand dynasty, and have ruled the island ever since.

As they had in Zubara, the Al-Khalifas suspended all custom duties, and Muharraq and Manama quickly grew into the most important pearling towns in the Gulf. While the Persians had applied an ancient, hierarchical system of formal legal governance of the pearling economy, the Arabs employed an egalitarian, free-market ethos that was regulated by customary practice. Likely an extension of earlier tribal systems, the Arab way allowed boats to fish outside

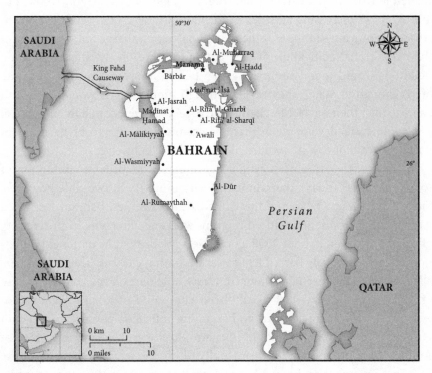

Figure 5.1 Map of Bahrain.

state control, initially untaxed, with profits divided into shares among the crew.[4] Amid growing global demand for pearls in the nineteenth century, a British-enforced 1820 truce along the Gulf coast facilitated booming profits and consolidated power among the sheikh signatories in Bahrain, Kuwait, Qatar, and the Trucial States (today the United Arab Emirates).

Acknowledging that their tribal feuding was inhibiting the pearl fishery, a series of nineteenth-century treaties prohibited plunder, piracy and slavery, endowed protectorate status upon the emirates, and established borders that have effectively endured for two centuries. Bahrain held a near-monopoly on pearling in the 1820s, but its market share dropped precipitously amid a leadership contest inside the Al-Khalifa family in the late 1830s. Near anarchy cut annual trade in half and dropped house rents to an eighth of their value. Many of the island's inhabitants migrated elsewhere before Isa ibn Ali Al-Khalifa assumed power and reestablished order in the 1860s.[5]

The rapid expansion and sudden abandonment of pearl towns was as much a product of shifting power alliances as it was a quality of the mobile populations the settlements attracted. During the boom years, migrant labor rushed in from India, Baluchistan, Iran, Iraq, Dhofar, Aden, and Somalia to join Arabs crisscrossing all sides of the Gulf. Many divers were slaves from Africa. Significant numbers of the island's pastoral Baharna Shias broke from their traditional cultivation of date palms to serve on the ships, and even Bedouins would spend summers at sea before returning to their nomadic lifestyle inland.[6] When they earned enough money, some would settle and come to own their boats. Merchants' and divers' transience in light of political and commercial developments placed a premium on intergroup harmony in Bahrain's growing towns, as much as on the ships themselves.

In a sense, the Al-Khalifa family never ceased its delicate calibration of social relations. Today's Bahrain is majority minority in two different ways. First, like Kuwait, Qatar, and the United Arab Emirates, Bahrain features a large number of disenfranchised migrant workers who come from a variety of origins and, since about 2008, comprise a majority of its national population but are effectively barred from ever becoming citizens. They lead a parallel existence that excludes them from any influence on the country's sense of "people," which has historically been composed of a Sunni population associated with the royal court and an indigenous Shia population. Second, uniquely, the regime has continuously naturalized a growing number of Sunni Arabs, whose numbers are incrementally tilting the sectarian balance of the citizenry. Though there has not been a formal census since 1941, the Shia population is thought to be larger, but this advantage is likely dwindling due to Shia expulsions and Sunni naturalizations.

Whereas other multiethnic and multireligious states have wielded primordial and constructed forms of nationalism to unify diverse publics, Bahrain has sustained a more instrumental and transactional approach to citizenship and residency. Whether it was oysters or oil being pulled from the surrounding seabeds, the royal family offered the same bargain: stable prosperity in exchange for dutiful allegiance or labor. This approach, and similar approaches that have persisted in other Arab emirates of the Gulf, remains unique in the world but suppresses a set of universal questions that concern all the case societies: Who are its people? Who belongs? What is the source of identity that binds their country's people together?

In other societies, such questions are addressed by state institutions and popular culture alike. But unlike even other suppressive states like Singapore, which veils Chinese supremacy in the language of multiculturalism and an ostensible meritocracy, Bahrain overtly privileges the status of different groups for different political purposes. The result is a state without a nation, where conceptions of "the people" and its culture become irrelevant because all exist in service to the Crown.

Given this book's concern with the power of culture, Bahrain's experience is instructive in further ways. Manama is a liberal hive of cultural expressions from different religious, ethnic, and national groups, but none really purports to represent, define, or speak to a common Bahraini identity. Rather, Manama's many cultural expressions are symbolic representations of smaller, more specific identities, each subsumed under the transaction that all Bahrainis make with the regime. This is because the state does not recognize the heritage or customs that give meaning to would-be forms of national culture; it recognizes only its own power, to give and take identity away. Culture without recognition is just noise.

Based on secondary research, a series of interviews with exiles, and a number of off-the-record interviews that protect the identity of sources fearful of retribution, this chapter reviews the history of Bahrain's governance of social relations and its extraordinary model of citizenship acquisition in the context of contemporary immigration patterns. In light of the state's selective naturalization and denaturalization, I explore not only the contemporary ethnic and sectarian political tensions that seem to keep everyone off-balance but also the way these disparate groups of Bahrainis make sense of their nationality. Without a clear sense of peoplehood and common ends, the regime's instrumental bargain replaces the need for social cohesion, for cultural exchange. Under these circumstances, the regime becomes the end itself.

Tribal History

In recent years, dissidents in Bahrain's Shia community have contended that people's sectarian identity should take precedence over their national identity. Some allege that the Al-Khalifas have been illegitimate "occupiers of Bahrain for over two hundred years."[7] When the Al-Khalifa family first arrived in 1783, however, it was already unclear who Bahrain's people were. While the original Baharna remained, the volatility of eighteenth-century political alliances and commercial markets drove people to bounce around the maritime societies on both sides of the Gulf thanks to a tight web of family, commercial, and religious networks that intersected the region.[8]

These sometimes spontaneous migrations inextricably intermingled the region's tribes and religious groups in the pearl trade, just as it did across Ottoman cities of the same era. The agriculturally oriented Baharna Shias are thought to be indigenous to the island, but they were also more marginal to the pearling economy that developed on the northern archipelago and attracted a mixture of regional peoples. The nonindigenous Persian Shias long ruled Bahrain but were evicted by the island's Huwala sailors in a 1740 mutiny. When the Persian Nader Shah was assassinated in 1747, Bahrain was contested by multiple Sunni and Shia groups. The Al-Khalifas finally took power, and ever since, they have accommodated rather than replaced these tribal divisions.[9]

Since the peacetime pearling boom of the late eighteenth century, the port towns of Manama, Dubai, and Kuwait transformed from smaller outposts into full-fledged migrant cities. In just the last quarter of the nineteenth century, the number of residents in Manama nearly tripled,[10] with much of the growth driven by the arrival of foreign mercantile communities, particularly Indians, Persians, and Jews, all of whom played an increasingly important role in the import of essential foodstuffs that supported growing urban populations.[11] These disproportionately young, elite newcomers remained linked to their towns and regions of origin and built networks of clients among immigrant groups by virtue of family, business, and social connections. While offering employment and often housing, they also sponsored independent institutions, including schools, mosques, synagogues, Hindu temples, and—among the Shia population—*husayniyyah* hall for the commemoration rituals of Ashura.[12] British political agents, concerned with the protection of trade and public order in the Gulf ports, safeguarded the position of the non-Muslim, immigrant communities (many of whom were British subjects), often acting as intermediaries between them and the royal court.[13]

The global pearl market collapsed with the beginning of the First World War and the Great Depression, but when oil was discovered beside Jebel al-Dukhan in 1929, the Bahraini government recruited familiar peoples to build and operate the rigs. Many experienced engineers, mechanics, and drillers came from Iran, where oil was discovered in 1908. Reza Shah's reforms after the First World War drove Persian Sunnis with Arab heritage to "return" to Arabia, but a number of Shias were recruited as well. In the first decades of its existence, the Bahrain Petroleum Company (BAPCO) relied primarily on Iranian laborers, a significant share of whom already resided in Bahrain.[14] The British government resisted the contracting of non-British subjects, but while BAPCO did recruit some Indians and Iraqis, the company had weaker links with India, and complications frequently arose with Mumbai's Protector of Emigrants.[15] Beyond oil production, a number of Indian communities remained in Bahrain, including Gujarati gold dealers, Bohra merchants, and Dhobi laundrymen, while other Indians and Baluchistanis were in government police forces—a legacy of the early days of British Trucial governance.[16]

Across the fluctuating waves of immigrants and sojourners, Bahrain maintained a system of de facto indentured servitude that grew more formal with time. As far back as the fourteenth century, wealthy sheikhs provided loans to the pearl divers' and haulers' families through the summer diving season to tide them over, or through the off-season if there had been a poor return. Under this *amil* system, money was advanced at no interest, but the financier—who sometimes captained or sponsored the entire dhow—bought pearls at a certain percentage lower than the market rate.[17] Rather than being clients of the upper echelons of the pearling establishment, these laborers were subordinate and trapped in a vicious cycle of debt that was often inherited by their children. Their subjugation led some European observers to view the pearl industry as a system of migrant "enslavement."[18] As Manama expanded at the beginning of the twentieth century, this migrant underclass was pushed into shanty towns on the city's periphery.[19]

The administrative apparatus of Gulf towns centered on the ruler's *majlis*, a personal council that served as a forum for consultation with merchants, tribal leaders, and the population, and *alfi dawiyyah*, militias organized along tribal lines that controlled public security.[20] Tribal quarters segregated the peoples of Manama but allowed for a form of feudal governance sanctioned by tribal customs rather than Islamic law or imperial legislation. An early, albeit extreme form of multiculturalism, the *majlis* and segregation of Bahrain's diverse population rendered a sense of order and representation that endures in contemporary times.[21] The ruling families (*al-dirah*) retained ultimate ownership of properties, people, and resources, while state patronage usually took the form of trade concessions, land allocation, and the distribution of merchants' access to pearl banks.[22] These networks of patronage were formalized into modern institutions of governance only when Manama evolved into a centrally managed municipality in the 1920s.

Consolidating the state's provision of services related to jobs, water, food, and public events, the new institutions also modernized earlier tribal forms of administration by issuing nationality certificates, identity cards, and passports. These documents created new political and legal distinctions between nationals and nonnationals and gave the state the supreme power to delineate political identities and grant access to labor markets.[23] The new means of state control contrasted with the old desert world dominated by tribes, merchants, and British political agents—the primary regulators of immigration prior to the discovery of oil.[24] The new system of surveillance worked to the advantage of seafarers and commercial classes, but it was opposed by Shia and Sunni clerics who considered nationality a shameful and illicit "innovation" (*bida*) that fragmented the transnational ummah.[25]

As British agents from Mumbai pressed for further administrative reforms that would create a more orderly bureaucracy in the 1920s, the Al-Khalifa regime wielded the concept of nationality to rally the allegiance of their subjects against imperial "intrusion."[26] They championed the interests of the "true patriots" (*al-wataniyyun*) of Manama against its "foreigner" population (*al-ajanib*), particularly the Persians who retained links to Iran's Pahlavi regime and, like many immigrants, benefited from British protection.[27] However, the British reforms were also favored by agrarian Shia Baharna, who advocated for a full British takeover and leveraged their ancestral indigeneity against the Al-Khalifas' rhetoric of nationality. While Bahrain's Shia and Sunni Arabs were automatically entitled to citizenship, the government conditioned other people's nationality on residence and property ownership. Legislation in 1929 and 1937 disqualified Bahrain's laboring underclasses but also aimed to transform Manama's wealthy Persian property owners into loyal citizens when the government threatened to confiscate their assets if they refused to apply for Bahraini passports.[28] At least until the Second World War, however, many of these Persians continued to own both Bahraini property and Iranian travel documents.[29] The Al-Khalifas remained wary.

The *Kafala* System

The midcentury rise of labor socialism and, later, pan-Arabism set the stage for contemporary approaches to immigration policy. Bahrain has a long history of labor unrest. Organized movements and strikes had recurred since the 1920s, so a principal reason for the regime's reliance on expatriate labor was to weaken the leverage of the local population and limit the likelihood of strikes.[30] The regime's fears were realized in 1938, when a movement of Bahraini Sunnis and Shias demanded a democratic government, a modernized bureaucracy, and the appointment of Bahraini citizens at BAPCO. The regime promptly refused these demands, suppressed the movement by force, and—following a strike at the petroleum company—began a deliberate policy of hiring more compliant Indian and Iranian workers who accepted lower wages than Bahrainis and other Arabs.[31] Not surprisingly, the foreign-born population more than doubled between 1950 and 1971.

Arab migrants to Bahrain brought their politics with their manpower. Many were Omani laborers, but educated Egyptian schoolteachers and others from the Mashriq spread Arab nationalism and fomented further labor protests and demonstrations against British imperialism and the Al-Khalifa autocracy.[32] In 1953, a number of Sunni men, including at least one member of the Al-Khalifa family, insulted the annual Ashura procession that Shias organize to commemorate the martyrdom of Imam Hussein. Violence and intermittent clashes ensued and continued in villages and on BAPCO grounds through 1954.[33]

In October 1955, these events prompted Bahraini merchants, petroleum workers, and labor movement leaders to put an end to the sectarian conflict and form a trade union with six thousand members, the Bahrain Labor Federation. Reviving demands from 1938, they submitted similarly progressive legislation to the Al-Khalifas, but the union was weakened by the exclusion of noncitizens—including fellow Arabs—whose membership in the union was out of the question because of their immigrant status. The labor movement thought all foreigners impeded Bahrainis' professional promotion by monopolizing coveted intermediary positions.[34] While this divide characterized labor relations forever after, it also informed the regime's approach to labor recruitment and its management of national politics.

In 1971, Britain ended its nineteenth-century treaties with the Gulf states and withdrew its military, and Bahrain declared its independence. Bahrain's 1972 National Assembly elections were decided on sectarian lines: predominantly Sunni constituencies voted overwhelmingly for Sunni candidates, and predominantly Shia constituencies cast ballots for Shia candidates.[35] The chamber did not pass a single piece of legislation for eighteen months before the emir dissolved it when representatives refused to pass an internal security law in 1973. Many of the legislators were exiled and their supporters detained and tortured.[36] The Public Security Law was quickly enacted, which enabled detention without trial for three years and suspended many constitutional protections related to civil and political rights, including freedom of speech.[37] Free of British oversight, the Al-Khalifa regime consolidated its power and soon Bahrain's treasury.

Later in 1973, Middle Eastern oil producers limited supply to the global market in response to the Yom Kippur War between Egypt and Israel, and the "first oil crisis" quadrupled Bahrain's petroleum income overnight.[38] Instantly wealthy, the Al-Khalifas and their Gulf counterparts expedited and broadened the development projects that had begun in the 1960s. Bahrain established a variety of modernization plans, including infrastructure projects to build new highways, bridges, buildings, museums, universities, and mosques.[39] The government also expanded the capacity of its bureaucracy and created new welfare systems for its citizens, increasing state expenditures tenfold by 1980.[40] To execute these projects and fill the bureaucracies, immigration flows reached unprecedented highs: between 1971 and 1981, the population of non-Bahrainis jumped from 37,885 to 112,378, most of whom were not highly skilled. While one out of every five individuals in Bahrain was a noncitizen foreigner in 1971, one out of every three individuals on the island was a foreign worker a decade later.[41]

The coinciding political, institutional, and demographic developments of the 1970s were not independent of one another. Oil rents concentrated an enormous amount of resources into the Al-Khalifas' hands. As pearling revenues were once spread to ruling families and members of the *majlis*, the Al-Khalifas were prepared to distribute the newfound wealth in exchange for their continued hegemony.[42] However, Bahrain was no longer a feudal pearling society. The Al-Khalifas were already wary of labor unrest and Arab nationalism, and the 1972 elections laid bare the extent of Shia resistance. To secure their allegiance, the Al-Khalifas, like other Gulf monarchies, assembled a comprehensive package of state subsidies that guaranteed their citizens access to free housing, education, healthcare, and comfortable public-sector employment[43] just as the regime stripped them of their civil and political rights.

This rentier state was and is contingent on Bahrain's ability to attract large numbers of nonnationals to fill private-sector labor demand without further distributing state subsidies—a challenge not unlike the kind presented by a volatile pearling economy in the nineteenth century. The *kafala* system of transient labor that emerged therefore cannot be understood in historical isolation. Under this approach, employer-sponsors (the *kafeel*) take full responsibility for unskilled foreign workers, leading to a "structural dependence" in which workers rely upon their employers to live and work.[44] Foreign workers

Table 5.1 Key Factors in Bahrain (Majority Minority in ~2008)

Immigration	Equality	Identity	Social Relations
Continuous: Temporary labor migrants from South Asia, present on two-year, renewable visas, who comprise a majority but lack citizenship; a number of Western and Arab expat professionals; selected naturalized Arabs largely recruited for the security services.	*Unequal:* With the exception of the naturalized, immigrants are exclusively temporary in nature and prohibited from accessing legal status. Among citizens, Shia nationals are excluded from many government jobs, particularly those in police and security services.	*Exclusive:* The key in-group is the royal court itself, and national identity is oriented around allegiance to the regime. While the royal family is Sunni and there have been allegations of sectarian favoritism, Sunnis' status has been undermined by the arrival of the naturalized.	*Suppressed:* The royal court maintains separate relationships with different ethnic and sectarian constituencies bilaterally and mutually exclusively, to keep order over all of them at once. Sectarian and immigrant groups lead parallel lives.

are required to work for the same employer throughout the tenure of short-term (usually two-year) renewable contracts; if they choose to break their contract, they are expected to pay their own return ticket to their country of origin.[45] Rules also severely restrict workers' rights of marriage, family reunification, education for children, and labor conditions.[46] Many unskilled laborers are paid a poverty wage and dispossessed of their passports.[47] Large businesses and employers justify the wages by providing housing in remote labor camps, so that most of the little money earned can be remitted to families in Bangladesh, India, Nepal, Pakistan, and elsewhere.

Skilled professionals are subject to the *kafala* system's contingencies but benefit from its economic liberalism and Bahrain's social liberalism. They are paid a globally competitive wage and incentivized by tax exemptions on income earned—reminiscent of the duty-free pearling from eighteenth-century Zubara and Muharraq. And much like the pearling towns of old, and more so than its counterpart capitals in the Gulf region, Bahrain has remained a liberal nexus of international communities given the freedom to live as they wish in their own cultural quarters. Expats can worship at one of the churches, temples, or synagogues discreetly tucked around Manama, consume alcohol in one of the many bars around the island, and dress as they wish without fear of the Mutaween, the religious police of Saudi Arabia.[48] Its cosmopolitan nationals listen to *bhangra* and hip-hop music, watch movies from Hollywood and Bollywood, and tolerate the millions of tourists—many from the Gulf's more conservative Sunni states—who flock to the island on weekends.

However, the genealogy of this economic and social liberalism explains its persistence: inside a rigid social hierarchy, Bahrain has given space to a diverse populace within the boundaries of an enduring political understanding between the royal court and its people—whoever they may be.

A Most Precious Gift

In the Al-Khalifas' mode of governance, citizenship is provided less as a conventional entitlement of the country's people and more as a precious gift that is bestowed and rescinded at their discretion. In 1963, a new nationality law made this explicitly clear. It stipulated that the emir could grant citizenship to anyone regardless of whether they met the usual residency, property, and language requirements for nationality, and noted in particular that the emir could give citizenship to any Arab who had "rendered Bahrain great services."[49] It also laid out several scenarios in which Bahraini nationality could be revoked, including if nationality had been obtained by fraud, if the person served an enemy country, or "if he causes harm to the interests of the state."[50] This was the basis for the exile of some dissidents around 1973 and after.

The 1973 design of the rentier state persisted in relative stability for two decades. However, beginning in the early 1990s, opposition groups filed a series of petitions demanding the reinstatement of the Parliament, the Constitution, and the amnesty of political prisoners and exiles. In 1993, the emir, Sheikh Isa, responded by forming a thirty-member consultative Shura Council appointed to share its opinions on Bahrain's general affairs and bills issued by the emir. The council held no formal authority, nor did it contain a single member of an opposition group. In response, a number of young leftists, liberals, and Islamists led an intifada of sporadic rioting against security forces and migrant workers from 1994 until Sheikh Isa's death in 1999.[51] Shortly after his succession, the new emir, Hamad, began a process of national dialogue with former exiles, journalists, civil society representatives, and religious leaders of Sunni and Shia backgrounds to hear their concerns.[52] He then pardoned all political opponents who were detained or exiled for their role in the 1990s unrest, abolished the State Security Law, reestablished a Parliament, and pronounced himself king of a new "constitutional monarchy" in 2001.

However, the ruling family's wariness of Shia disloyalty became a self-fulfilling prophecy. During a decade of government concessions to the Shia opposition and victims of torture, symbolic appointments of women and minorities, and a 2006 election that put Shia representatives in 40 percent of Parliament's seats, the regime's suspicions never wavered. In the run-up to the

2010 elections, the government arrested and accused twenty Shia opposition leaders of plotting to overthrow the monarchy by promoting violent protests and sabotage. The primary opposition group, the Islamic National Accord Association, gained only a few seats in an election on sectarian lines,[53] and any goodwill King Hamad had built with the Shias dissipated.

When massive uprisings erupted across the Arab world in 2011 and inspired Shia and some Sunni dissidents in Bahrain, the unarmed protestors were crushed by government forces reinforced by Saudi troops that rolled in via the King Fahd Causeway. Opponents outwardly questioned the king's legitimacy, and antiroyal opinion proliferated in more subtle ways. In the years since, the regime has moved to suppress opposition parties by suspending their participation in Parliament, arresting their leaders, and prohibiting former members from seeking election. As in the past, it also wielded its citizenship laws. Amendments in 2014 gave the interior minister the power to revoke nationality based on a variety of new justifications.[54]

Since then, according to the dissident-led Bahrain Institute of Human Rights and Democracy, Bahrain has revoked a national's citizenship an average of once every two days—several hundred per year, per Figure 5.2.[55] Put into comparative perspective, the United Kingdom, which expanded the grounds for revocation related to Islamic State accomplices after 2012, has never rescinded the citizenship of more than twenty-three people per year, despite a national population over forty times larger than Bahrain's.[56] Shia

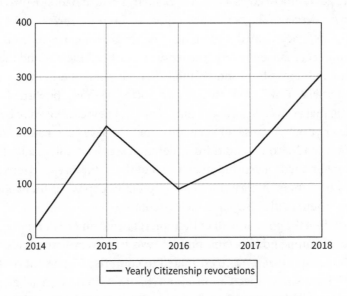

Figure 5.2 Citizenship revocations in Bahrain between 2014 and 2018.

citizens comprise the vast majority of the revocations, despite some Sunni involvement in opposition activities and protests. In 2016, the government revoked the citizenship of Ayatollah Sheikh Isa Qassim, widely regarded as the spiritual leader of Bahrain's Shia population, for using his position to "serve foreign interests" and promote "sectarianism and violence."[57] The move was perceived to be an attack on all Bahraini Shias.

By revoking the citizenship of individuals considered to pose a political threat, Bahrain aligns the political behavior of its subjects with citizenship.[58] In a 2015 *Foreign Policy* article, Mohammed Altajer, a Bahraini human rights lawyer who represents many of the country's stateless people, said, "When the Bahraini government publishes these lists of revoked nationalities, they are a mix of innocent people and actual Daesh [Islamic State] terrorists. The majority of the people on the list are just regular Shiite academics, human rights activists, lawyers, clerics and businesspeople. But by placing them on a list with actual terrorists, the government hopes to discredit those who have done nothing wrong." Political dissent is thus equated with sectarianism, terrorism, and national betrayal.[59]

The gift of citizenship is equally powerful when it is awarded. Elsewhere in the Gulf region, citizenship is closely guarded to limit the distribution of oil rents. In many years, Kuwait, Qatar, and the United Arab Emirates grant citizenship to fewer people than Bahrain revokes.[60] Since the democratic reforms of 2001, however, Bahrain has granted citizenship to tens of thousands. This "political naturalization" program was first suggested in a 2006 report released by former government adviser Salah al-Bandar, a British Bahraini dual national of Sudanese descent. The bombshell report accused the government of organizing a "conspiracy" aimed at marginalizing Shias by rigging elections, spying, and stirring sectarian animosity. The report made headlines around the region, infuriating Bahrain's Shias. Shortly thereafter, Ebrahim Sharif, the Sunni head of the leftist National Democratic Action Society (Wa'ad), published a report calculating that an average of about nine thousand new citizens were being naturalized per year.[61] Because no Shias are known to have been naturalized since several thousand second- and third-generation stateless individuals of Persian origin were granted citizenship in 2001, all of the naturalized citizens are presumed to be Sunnis. A clear attempt to tip demographic scales exposed, the royal court then scuttled parliamentary attempts to investigate.[62]

The last time the government of Bahrain reported official demographic statistics on its Sunni and Shia communities was in its very first census in 1941. At the time, Shia citizens were estimated to comprise 53 percent of the population.[63] Ever since, speculation about Bahrain's Sunni-Shia balance has been a subject of intense debate and government evasion. A wide range of disparate estimates puts Bahraini Shias at between 55 and 75 percent of the current population, reflecting conflicting anecdotal impressions about the relative birth and immigration rates. Forbidden from using state entities to administer a properly sampled national survey, Qatar-based researcher Justin Gengler undertook his own poll. Published in 2015, his research showed that Shia respondents made up only 57.6 percent of those surveyed, corresponding to an estimated range (based on 95 percent confidence intervals) of between around 53.0 percent and 62.3 percent of the population.[64] To the extent one accepts the general view that Shias' population growth outstripped that of Sunnis over the half-century following 1941, Gengler wrote, this survey finding would seem to call attention to "the pace and scope of Bahrain's modern program of Sunni naturalization." Gengler has been barred from returning to the island.

The politically naturalized—or, as they are known in Bahrain, *mutajaniseen*—are exclusively Sunni, largely originating from Arab countries such as Iraq, Jordan, Syria, and Yemen. Extending the British tradition that began with Indians and Baluchis, they are given jobs with the police, military, and security services, which some posit makes them more likely to remain loyal to the ruling family that admitted them.[65] These jobs—which were all previously held by Sunnis—also require law enforcement against the native-born population, who consider them "mercenaries."[66] Rarely, the Bahraini government has also granted citizenship to prominent foreign businessmen with long-standing ties in the kingdom. The de jure requirements include twenty-five years of residence (fifteen years for those of Arab descent), fluency in Arabic demonstrated in interviews, and high fees that can reach hundreds of thousands of dollars.[67]

Not all the *mutajaniseen* are police and military officers. As early as 2002, the Bahraini government is known to have awarded citizenship to unknown thousands of Saudis affiliated with the Dawasir tribe that at one time lived in Bahrain but has long resided in eastern Saudi Arabia. The naturalized Saudis were said to have been transported to voting booths at the midpoint of the causeway linking the two countries to allow them to vote in October 2002.[68] A decade later, the Bahraini government reportedly naturalized more than five thousand Sunni Syrian refugees living in the Zaatari refugee camp in Jordan, where it established a cultural center to acquaint refugees with Bahraini culture.[69] With the participation of Saudi security officers and Jordanian security coverage, the Bahrainis reportedly taught the refugees the names of areas, streets, villages, and other historical geographic information about the kingdom and trained them to be loyal to the regime.[70]

Opposition figures estimate that 95,000 foreigners were naturalized by 2010 in a country with only about 600,000 citizens.[71] With the increases in the number of Bahraini citizens, new job sectors have become "Bahrainized" and allocated to the nationals displaced by the arrival of the *mutajaniseen*, including taxi drivers, gas station personnel, and guards at shopping malls.[72] To no avail, opposition leaders have demanded that the government halt the entire program; some have even exhorted Bahrainis to give birth to more native-born children.[73] Ali al-Fayez, a rights activist based in Manama who was later imprisoned, told one journalist, "It is ethnic cleansing, there is no other way to describe such demographic remapping."[74]

Lost in the debate around the *mutajaniseen* is the effect of naturalization and revocation on the very concept of citizenship in Bahrain. With so many foreigners present and such great benefits associated with nationality, citizenship is held in high regard but subject to significant ambiguity. Ethnic and sectarian divisions are far more salient than national identity. Simultaneously, many nationals feel a sense of estrangement from the labor market—a source of cross-boundary interaction elsewhere—because of the saturation and sectarian segregation of the public sector, their mismatched skills, and the reluctance of private-sector employers to hire them.[75] Despite sharing such a small island, Bahrain's citizens are separated into sectarian enclaves, maintain competing histories, are employed in different sectors of the economy, tend to have wildly divergent political orientations, and are readily distinguishable to fellow nationals by their names, dress, and a number of other outward cues.[76] They don't even speak the same Arabic dialect. Therefore, the gift of nationality is not a bond of equality with one another; rather, it is a personal relationship between the citizen and the ruling family that should not be betrayed.

Guests Uninvited

Jawad Fairooz so betrayed the ruling family. And on Wednesday, November 7, 2012, he was stripped of his citizenship and made stateless in a brief written announcement by Bahrain's Interior Ministry. Citing a clause within the country's Citizenship Law that "permits re-evaluation of nationality when a holder of Bahraini citizenship causes damage to state security," the kingdom simultaneously revoked the nationality of thirty other activists that day, including Said al-Shihabi, head of the Freemen of Bahrain movement; Ali Hassan Mushaima, the son of the leader of the Al-Haq Movement for Liberty and Democracy; three Shia clerics, Hussein Mirza, Khaled Mansour Sanad, and Alawi Sharaf; and Fairooz's brother, Jalal.

The Fairooz brothers were distinguished members of Parliament and leaders in the opposition, Shia-linked Al-Wefaq Party. But according to a BBC report at the time, the Fairooz brothers "represent the more moderate wing of the opposition. They are a far cry from the masked petrol bomb–hurling activists who are terrorising neighbourhoods and clashing with police almost every night in the villages west of the capital Manama."[77] They had been campaigning peacefully for a more equal distribution of power and wealth in the country but, "suited and eloquent, these former MPs are adamant they do not want to overthrow the ruling family. They just want a constitutional monarchy with an elected executive."[78]

Between 2002 and 2006, Jawad Fairooz served as an elected representative in the Northern Municipality Council, and between 2006 and 2011 as one of seventeen Al-Wefaq representatives elected to the forty-seat Majlis an-Nuwab, the elected half of Bahrain's eighty-seat National Assembly. When the king dissolved Parliament in the wake of the 2011 uprising, Fairooz was chairing its Public Utilities and Environment Committee. By mid-2012, he was imprisoned, interrogated, and tortured for three months and seven days before the Interior Ministry's announcement. Born to a Bahraini father and an Iranian-born mother who naturalized in Bahrain, Fairooz possessed no other nationality and fled to Lebanon before resettling with his immediate family as asylum seekers in the United Kingdom.

While in state custody, Fairooz observed with awe the security infrastructure derived from the naturalization program he previously criticized. Most of the guards, the interrogators, the torturers, the caterers, even the judges were foreign-born. Once, when he was being transferred by car to one of four different prisons where he was detained, an officer asked him why, as a member of Parliament, he did not support the naturalization of foreigners in Bahrain. "All of us, including you," said the officer, "are guests in the House of the King. So he has full right to receive us and to tell us when we must leave. We should be thankful that he allows us to remain."

Fairooz now lives in the West London neighborhood of Yeading, in the Borough of Hillingdon, where he runs a small nonprofit organization that advocates for democracy in Bahrain and the Middle East. Now sixty-one years old, he speaks in a stately manner that belies his passion for the country that exiled him.

"This country started the day the Al-Khalifa family arrived," he told me cynically. "Naturalization is the exclusive concern of the Royal Family, and crucial to the country's security. Throughout the Al-Kahlifa family's history, they viewed demography as either supportive [of] or threatening to their ruling power. So after independence, they had full power to engineer the demography to reduce the threat and increase the ruling family's sovereignty.

"For example, in the seventies, when the threat of Jamal Abdel Nasser as leader of the Arab national identity [arose], the ruling family preferred to bring up certain types of citizens to balance these politics. So they naturalized certain Shia from Iran or Basra [Iraq]. Because during that time, the threat was from leftists and nationalists. But that was on a smaller scale.

"After the [1979] Iranian Revolution and the rise of Shia power in the area, they began to look at Shia as a threat, the Shia identity became more salient, and avoided naturalizing any Shia—as many Shia began expressing opposition to the regime and demanded political rights. It became clear as certain groups, particularly those supporting the Iranian Revolution in public and advocating for an Islamic Republic, that this was a threat. So there became a speedier process to alter demography to tilt toward Sunnis—naturalizing some with less education and a tribal background from [Saudi Arabia] and some Yemenis. Their main objective was to change the demography, engage them in institutions dedicated to defense and security, and establish a population loyal to the family. That way, in case there was a challenge to their power, they could maintain support. This is three decades in the making.

"We, in Parliament, we realized that a huge number of these political naturalizations were happening—and not for business reasons. Many of those naturalized were illiterate. When we examined who was eligible to vote between 2002 and 2006, we found a huge increase in the percentage, beyond the bounds of natural demographic increases—one hundred twenty thousand people in ten years, between 2000 to 2010. The chairman of Al-Wefaq inquired with the Statistics Bureau, and they offered no answer. It was so clear that the king's court was controlling this process.

"The Al-Dawasir [Bedouin] tribe consists of twenty-five thousand Sunni individuals from Saudi Arabia, and all received Bahraini passports. It is said that they backed the Al-Khalifas in nineteenth-century conflict with [the indigenous Shia] Baharna. The British demanded that they leave Bahrain, and they settled in eastern Saudi Arabia. In a video, they admitted that they are being used as a means of balancing voting. Buses transport them across the King Fahd Causeway, and they vote and return. Their addresses were falsified. The pace has increased substantially since 2011. The door has opened to Syrians, Baathist Iraqis, Pakistanis, Indians, and fewer Yemenis because of suspicions derived from the war with Saudi Arabia. It is an assurance that any future democratic process will support the monarchy.

"My naturalization was revoked. And it was so speedy, so easily. Just as easily, they naturalize others. Beyond the law, beyond the judiciary, and without justification. And any inquiries are unanswered. . . . The criteri[on] is not nationality or legitimacy, but loyalty."

Fairooz paused, and I asked, "But were loyalty to cease to be the singular criterion of membership in Bahrain, who are the Bahraini people? Is there a sense of shared identity?"

"We know that Bahrain consists of multicultural Muslim communities by sect and religion, very few Christians, and a countable number of Jews," he said. "Bahrain was a trading center historically for goods from Iran, Saudi, [Iraq]—with very few tribes indigenous to the region. Bahrain's people's backgrounds are often from the southern part of Iran and Iraq, the eastern part of Saudi, or the southern part of Syria. So besides the native Baharna, the country's citizens have always originated from settlers who came from elsewhere. In this process, it is understandable that the country is a mix. . . .

"But I can assure you that divide-and-rule was always the main approach of the ruling family, not just as a policy, but as an identity. Just as easily they could use the same powers to bring people together.

"I remember, during the 1990s, a mix of Shia and Sunnis submitted a petition to the late emir [Isa bin Salman Al-Khalifa]. But [the emir] refused because he wanted them to approach the Crown separately. It is an atmosphere designed to raise barriers.

"The original Bahraini identity has been dissolved, along with Shia slang and Shia history. Any culture that reinforces the Shia or Baharna heritage and roots, it is ignored or destroyed. There are two days off for [the Shia holiday] Ashura, but the cultural celebrations are ignored by the media, which are government controlled.

"So the country is not one, because they do not want it to be one. If the country were to be one, it would not be in the ruling family's favor."

None for All

Ostensibly—as it is conventionally reported by journalists and other observers—the sectarian and ethnic tensions inside Bahrain make the island unwieldy for the Al-Khalifas to govern. In reality, the distrust between Bahrain's different communities is the ruling family's greatest political advantage. As long as the Sunnis, Shias, *mutajaniseen*, and foreign workers are unable to consolidate their interests, there is no coalition large enough to overpower the monarchy. According to this logic, the naturalization of the *mutajaniseen* is designed not only to tilt the Sunni-Shia distribution but also, more important, to incentivize any disgruntled Sunnis to keep competing for the royal court's favor. If all are not for one, then no one will be for all.

Because Shia citizens have made it clear that their political allegiance can never be purchased with the promise of material benefits, the Al-Khalifas have distrusted them and ensured their marginality.[79] This is primarily done by excluding Shias from sensitive government positions. Shia citizens have been disproportionately excluded from sovereign ministries and are altogether disqualified from police and military service.[80] The Bahrain Defense Force, a voluntary force of some 2,700, is strictly Sunni; Shia applicants are not even considered. Officers are recruited from the ruling family and from those families considered traditional allies of the Al-Khalifas.[81] Gengler's 2009 survey found that whereas 17 percent of all employed Sunni males reported being employed in the police or armed forces, not a single Shia from the 117 working males randomly sampled indicated the same. The sectarian screening is generally accomplished via requirements for certificates of "good history and conduct" issued by the police to verify that an individual has no prior record of arrest or detention, including for political reasons.[82] A Sunni Bahraini is 56 percent more likely to be employed in the public sector than a Shia of identical employment-relevant attributes.[83]

The government has also subtly excluded Shia representation in the Parliament and in public expressions of national culture. As part of the 2001 electoral reforms approved by King Hamad, the government gerrymandered parliamentary electoral districts to ensure majority Sunni representation. The sparsely populated but largely Sunni southern governorate was allocated extra seats, while the heavily populated and overwhelmingly Shia northern governorate was allocated fewer.[84] More symbolically, the Bahrain National Museum's sprawling dioramas depicting pre–oil industry livelihoods give a prominent place to the Sunni-dominated activity of pearl fishing while neglecting the quintessentially Shia agricultural sector and the date palms that were the basis of the Baharna's early existence.[85] Even characters in government-sponsored television shows speak a Sunni Arab dialect and largely omit the dialects of the Baharna and Persian-origin 'Ajam.[86]

Sunnis' estrangement from Shias has also become more important to regime stability as Bahraini Sunnis have recently cast aside traditional political parties like Al-Asalah and Al-Manbar in favor of more populist coalitions.[87] Nominally pro-government, parties such as the Gathering of National Unity and its more youth-oriented offshoots maintain a more ambivalent relationship with the state, pressing for a tougher security crackdown on the opposition and a more generous economic distribution.[88] No longer content to be mere obstructionists, these new Sunni factions demand their own seats at the negotiating table and demonstrate that Bahrain's reform movement is not limited to Shia activists.[89]

This continued splintering is as attributable to changes to the country's electoral institutions as public opinion trends. In 2014, Bahrain held its first national election since the 2011 uprising. With its leaders either exiled or imprisoned and having secured no meaningful concessions, opposition Shia parties vowed to boycott the polls. Concerned to legitimize a process that much of its majority-Shia citizenry was sitting out, the monarchy's electoral officials threatened to penalize citizens who did not cast a ballot by making them ineligible for government jobs.[90] Because Shias were practically disqualified from many such jobs, the result was an influx of new less-informed, Sunni voters—motivated by the threat of consequences more than any political agenda. They supported a slate of candidates unaffiliated with any Sunni political movement, weakening the Sunni political establishment and hindering their coordination of legislative priorities and solidarity.

While Shias have condemned the naturalization of Bahrain's *mutajaniseen* as a thinly veiled attempt to tilt the island's demography, native-born Sunnis have not greeted the new nationals with open arms either. Rather, they have fled when the *mutajaniseen* arrivals were settled near their communities. Between 2006 and 2010, in a district in historic Muharraq, the number of eligible voters fell by more than 40 percent.[91] However, when the government has allocated new housing units built as part of Manama's sprawl southward, Sunnis have complained that the *mutajaniseen* are receiving housing to which native-born citizens should be entitled. While native-born Bahrainis have also fled neighborhoods with growing numbers of other (usually highly skilled) foreign workers, there are far fewer calls to mitigate their numbers given their private-sector economic contributions and lack of access to state resources. It is the *mutajaniseen*, who have instant access to state subsidies and have taken jobs once reserved for Sunnis, who are stirring resentment.

In discourse that quickly slips into xenophobia, Bahrainis opposed to naturalization of these migrants emphasize that "new Bahrainis" do not "belong."[92] In a widely read commentary for the privately owned newspaper *Akhbar Al-Khaleej*, the Bahraini Sunni journalist Ibrahim Al-Sheikh wrote, "The state has not succeeded in integrating some of the newly naturalized groups into society and its culture. . . . Nationality has conditions, entitlements and obligations, and those who abuse them should be progressively punished until they are withdrawn if necessary. These are dangerous in a country undergoing significant demographic change, and the subject cannot be left as such without genuine and responsible integration governed by rights and duties."[93] Revealing the extent of distrust, during the 2011 uprising a number of Pakistani expatriates were attacked, seemingly because mobs of protestors assumed they were intelligence agents.[94]

It is therefore not surprising that there has been no joint political movement between the country's traditional Shia opposition and either Bahraini Sunnis or the *mutajaniseen* newcomers. The secretary general of Bahrain's UNESCO National Commission, Lubna Selaibeekh, has written that until the sprawl and new housing of Manama altered neighborhood compositions in the 1990s, "there was an almost total residential separation of Sunni and Shi'a." She goes on to describe how this physical separation has produced parallel lives with few opportunities for meaningful interaction between them:

> Until very recently there was no intermarriage between the Sunni and Shi'a communities, and it is still relatively rare, even in the more liberal atmosphere of Manama. Each sect maintains its mosques, its own religious courts and, in the Shi'a case, *mawatim* (funeral houses), which serve not only as centres for mourning of Shi'a during Muharram (first month of the Islamic calendar), but also as places for the Shi'a religious education which [was] not provided by the government school system [until] the establishment of the Jaffari Institute in 2002.[95]

And despite outnumbering all three groups combined, the community of foreign workers is powerless and as estranged from Bahraini citizens as all three groups are from each other. Referring to South Asian immigrants specifically, Andrew Gardner explained the extent of the diaspora's segregation from Bahraini citizens:

> South Asians forge lives largely separate from the host society: in Bahrain, for example, the transnational proletariat dwell in decrepit apartment buildings in the central urban slums now largely abandoned by the citizenry, or bunk in labor camps on the semi-industrial periphery of the city. Families of the diasporic elite send their children to separate schools (e.g., the Indian School, the New Indian School, the Pakistani School) and join social clubs specific to their home nations or regions (e.g., the Young Goans Club, the Pakistani Club). Intermarriage between citizens and noncitizens is uncommon, and many of the elite Indian families I spoke with—families that, in some cases, have been in Bahrain for several generations— had never been invited to a Bahraini house.[96]

Citizenship does little to alter the lived experience of the *mutajaniseen*. One of Gardner's wealthier subjects told him, "If I take a Bahraini passport, my face says that I'm an Indian. The people will still not take me as a Bahraini. They will treat me as an Indian."[97] The children of these well-established foreigners feel utterly between, if not without, national allegiances.[98] All communities in Bahrain are therefore kept off-balance and—at the national level—unaligned.

National Culture

The old pearling towns of Bahrain were subdivided into quarters for the different tribal communities. Each quarter was a microcosm, with rich and poor living alongside one another and sharing mosques, fountains, hammams, ovens, markets, and workspaces.[99] Each with its own council and headman, the quarters were traditionally considered by the state authorities as administrative and taxation units that could be managed via a single liaison who approached the ruling family and sought to sustain its favor. Even though the urban development of Bahrain has mixed together the old quarters and the people who once resided in them, the Al-Khalifas have organized social and political relations in such a way as to maintain a variety of distinct communities of people who live separate lives and compete with one another for power. Bahrain's national culture, however, is not subject to the same contestation.

Through their preservation efforts and museum exhibitions, the Al-Khalifas have historically recognized a version of Bahraini culture that anthropologist Thomas Fibiger has called "globalized heritage."[100] The "global" here relates to those lost Bahraini traditions and other secular artifacts that connect Bahrain to broader civilizational trends, and it rebukes demands for the government to honor "local" Islamic values. Both, of course, entail selective readings of Bahrain's past. And according to Fibiger, the state has strategically chosen to promote and preserve some forms of Bahraini heritage while neglecting or completely erasing others.[101]

By way of example, according to Fibiger, the state has long prioritized the preservation of the Dilmun burial grounds, an enormous four-thousand-year-old necropolis. After each new discovery, the state has provided full access to foreign archaeologists to excavate the mounds and featured many of the findings in exhibitions. In the National Museum, the government also prominently exhibits a letter, written by the Prophet Muhammad to the governor of Bahrain, inviting the people of Bahrain to join Islam. The letter dates to the year 7 in the Hijri calendar (629 in the Gregorian), three years before Prophet's death. This letter is proudly displayed in the museum and is regarded with pride by most Bahrainis, as it shows that Bahrain was incorporated into the Islamic world as one of its earliest territories outside Mecca and Medina, during the lifetime of the Prophet Muhammad himself.[102]

This contrasts with the state's historic treatment of numerous graves and shrines to saints venerated by the Shia community. Many of these saints can be found in Bahrain's well-documented theological history or they are well-known figures from the early days of Islam.[103] Most interesting, the grave of Sheikh Abdel Aziz, while small and belonging to a lesser-known Shia scholar, attracted a great deal of attention after it managed to withstand multiple attempts by the state to remove it as part of a new road construction project. As a result, the shrine sits in the middle of a traffic junction and has become one of Bahrain's most visited Shia landmarks.[104] Other places of Shia gatherings have been demolished as part of the state's post–Arab Spring crackdowns, despite Shia protests that these shrines are just as much a part of Bahrain's heritage as the Dilmun mounds.

The difference between these regime priorities is not as simplistic as favoring Sunni over Shia heritage; it is a broader approach to culture that seeks to circumvent divisive sectarian traditions altogether and link Bahrain to milestones of greater human civilization. The Dilmun necropolis is prehistoric compared to the Shia shrines, and the letter from the Prophet predates the Battle of Karbala, after which the ummah was forever split into Sunni and Shia factions.

This was also the cosmopolitan spirit behind the erection of the Pearl Monument. Built in honor of the 1982 meeting of the Gulf Cooperation Council (GCC) in Manama, its six curved spires represented dhow sails and each of the six member states, hoisting up a single pearl—honoring the Gulf-wide tradition of pearling and its reliance on a multireligious, multiethnic community of divers, sailors, and merchants. There was thus no shortage of irony when the Bahraini government demolished the monument in 2011 shortly after it was the staging site of Arab Spring demonstrations, which its military had put down with help from the very GCC states the monument honored. Suddenly a symbol for democracy, the meaning of the monument became contested, and contested culture could not be recognized.

And yet culture is meant to be contested. In other settings, different individuals and groups make claims to their authenticity as the "true people," complete with their music, food, dialects, literature, traditions, and pastimes. As we will see in coming chapters, the state may favor one heritage and promote one perspective, but ultimately culture is subject to mass consumption and a vigorous exchange. In Singapore, the Chinese eat Malay food and seamlessly use Malay phrases in conversation. In Trinidad and Tobago, Indians make soca music and participate in the annual Carnival. In New York, the entire city drapes itself in Kelly green and pauses for St. Patrick's Day. But in Bahrain, there is one principal arbiter that may recognize culture as national, just as there is only one arbiter that may recognize *a person* as national.

National Identity

So what does it mean to be a Bahraini national?

"This a dangerous subject," says Abbas Al-Morshed, an exiled Shia activist and historian. He was granted asylum by the United Kingdom in 2014 after a two-month prison sentence in 2011 and repeated threats from security service personnel thereafter. Agents followed him on his commute between home and work on a regular basis. He says he was in a "cat-and-mouse game" with them and the Bahraini court system for a two-year period before he left with his family, fearing for his life. He worked as a teacher and social worker for Bahrain's Ministry of Education for eighteen years, and now finds work as a freelance report writer and journalist.

He took a drag from a cigarette as he walked around Golder's Green, a northern suburb of London, where he now resides in exile. "The first class of people are actually the Shia Baharna," he said. "We think we're the original, the old people of Bahrain—that Bahrain is ours. The second class of people are Arabs from Jedda or Saudi [Arabia]. They think they represent the identity because they are close with the government. The third class of Bahrainis come from outside Arab countries like Syria or Yemen. I don't know how they feel now, but after ten or twenty years they start to feel authentic too. Meanwhile, my family's history goes back over two hundred years. But this is the Al-Khalifa family's plan: in their minds, it is the Royal Family first, then Sunnis, the *mutajaniseen*, the migrants, and after everyone else, then we can talk about the Baharna.

"Most of the Baharna, they are the Other. Not 'one of us,' not 'from our country.' This is how people look at me now. Because they think we are working with Iran. They think we are always plotting a political movement."

Al-Morshed is the half-brother of Sheikh Ali Salman, a Bahraini Shia cleric and the secretary-general of the Al-Wefaq political society, currently serving a life sentence in prison. Long before Al-Morshed's exile, the Bahraini government forcibly exiled Salman to Dubai in 1995 for leading a campaign demanding the reinstatement of the 1973 Constitution and the restoration of Parliament. After receiving asylum in London, Salman returned to Bahrain in 2001 as part of the slate of pardons made by King Hamad at the time of his coronation. Al-Morshed still hopes he will one day be welcomed to return as well.

"The Shia have numbers and power in the public sphere," he continued. "So [the regime] divides us by pursuing a sense of balance, of giving everyone our rights. Of course, they're not giving power to the *salafi* [hardliners] or the Muslim Brotherhood; it's about the preservation of their power. So this balance that they pursue is in the interest of reducing popular power—dividing power up to reduce the power of numbers."

Though definitively associated with Shia politics and stereotypes of Shia nationalism, Al-Morshed is actually married to a Sunni woman, like several other men in his immediate family.

"My wife can get angry with me for supporting [Syrian dictator] Bashar Al-Assad," he joked, "and I can get angry with her for supporting Daesh [the Islamic State]."

We shared a laugh.

"In Bahraini society, there *are* intermarriages," he pointed out. "People work together, we are neighbors. Our identity should be between individuals, not set by the state or government. Inside me, I can't believe that we are [united]. Others are clearly getting more work, benefits, housing. So inside, I cannot truly believe they are like me. You just sense that something is wrong, something is off, something is not normal. You just feel inside, as the original people, that you are somehow lost inside your own country. I have lost everything."

"The Identity Crisis"

The government's preference for global heritage and cosmopolitan culture produced a profound local question: Without a recognized national culture, can there even be a national identity? This was the implicit subject of a fascinating television debate on Al-Wasat News, Bahrain's only independent news source before it was closed by the government in 2017 for sowing division.[105] In 2003, in the wake of new government reforms and before the escalation of sectarian tensions, Al-Wasat—which literally translates to "The Middle"— invited numerous influential leaders to a televised "cultural forum." It featured Saeed Al-Nouri, vice president of the Shia-led Islamic Enlightenment Society; Hassan Modon, president of the antisectarian Al-Minbar political party; and Abdul Amir Al-Layth, an Al-Wasat News contributor, among others.

> "It must be said that the identity crisis that we are experiencing does not deny the existence of a certain level of common identity, and we are, in reality, suffering from confusion in the Bahraini and Islamic affiliations alike," Al Nouri said. "This

can be understood if we go over the indicators, as we find on the psychological level a confusion in the feelings of national brotherhood, and culturally there is the problem of the absence of a unified national culture that crystallizes our national values. There is also the absence of a joint social and political project that exemplifies mechanisms of dialogue and joint social action. And if we add to that the fact that the issue mixes efforts that work on discord and the exchange of accusations, we will find that we are facing societies within a single society, which deepens the crisis."

Taken by the idea of "the identity crisis," Modon defended Bahraini society and subtly the regime. "I believe that the issue here does not completely reach the limits of a crisis, because there are certain components that contribute to shaping and strengthening the general structure of our common national identity, and specifically I find that there is a triple component that represents our common denominators and through which we can work to establish a common national identity. These components are represented in the Islamic affiliation, the Arab affiliation, and the Gulf affiliation."

Later, Al-Layth usefully distinguished between the identity of the state and the identity of a nation. "When there is an army and a budget, there is a state with buildings, streets, and ministries. . . . But with only these things, are you able to build a homeland and one nation with a common identity? Of course not. There is a difference between the state and the nation. In the second case, you are talking about a national identity and a common culture, and creating that requires cultural components capable of achieving a common identity. . . .

"It is necessary to benefit from this oral tradition in the project of a common national identity, because through it we can find cultural elements capable of forming a homeland for all. I think that the solution comes through cultural mixing within the community, then raising certain images or flags will not create an emotional mental image."

In a careful acknowledgment of these points, Modon said, "I find that there is a problem raised in Bahrain recently related to writing the cultural history, and fortunately, His Majesty the King referred to this in one of his speeches, as there is indeed a need to rewrite the cultural history of Bahrain. . . . And I see that this is a real problem that has not been approached with courage until now, for what is written about history reflects one side of the nation's history, and therefore it reflects a certain aspect of the national identity that is closer to the official view, so to speak.

"We really do not have a comprehensive vision for writing our cultural history, and we need to rewrite this history in its entirety and with its various components. The books on cultural history that have received official marketing reflect only one view, and there are publications that reflect other visions that are not circulated at the scale of the nation as a whole. What I am proposing now is not that we work to present another narrative that is counter or parallel to the official cultural history in Bahrain, but it is necessary that we work on writing a common cultural history for this country, and take into account its various elements and affiliations, without falling into an adverse cultural reaction."

All sides here—those of reformists and apologists—implicitly recognize the artificiality of a national identity cut off from a sense of heritage. But in their prescription to "rewrite the cultural history" in a manner that reflected and fostered greater "cultural mixing," these leaders were ultimately speaking past each other. Reformists sought to craft a national story that acknowledged the presence and legacy of the indigenous Shia population and its contributions to local and global Islamic heritage—or really, any acknowledgment of the Shia at all. But instead, the regime responded to calls for the promotion of more "parallel" and "counter-" narratives by presenting Bahraini society as a cosmopolitan cacophony, one in which the Shias were but one of many communities that have anchored themselves on the island in its five-thousand-year history as a global crossroads.

Since the time of the Al-Wasat discussion, the Bahraini government has implemented a number of symbolic actions to depict the kingdom as a place of "religious tolerance" and "social pluralism." In 2008, King Hamad appointed an Iraqi-origin Jewish ambassador to the United States, Houda Nonoo, a former member of the Shura Council and the first Jewish ambassador to represent an Arab country. In 2011, he appointed a Christian woman to serve as Bahrain's ambassador to the United Kingdom, Alice Thomas Sama'an, who was also the Arab world's first woman to chair a session of Parliament when she briefly took the gavel in 2005. In 2012, the regime donated land in Awali to build the largest Catholic church in the Gulf, and then renovated Manama's old synagogue in 2014. In 2019, on a visit when he was formally honored by King Hamad, Prime Minister Narendra Modi of India launched a $4.2 million renovation of the two-hundred-year-old Lord Sri Krishna temple, the oldest in the Gulf region. During this period, the kingdom also founded the This Is Bahrain Association, which is devoted to promoting a "culture of peace" between different religions and sects, and the King Hamad Global Centre for Peaceful Coexistence; its vision of Bahrain, according to a statement from its chairman, is as "a multi-cultural society comprised of many faiths and ethnicities," a "rich mosaic of cultural diversity," and "a harmonious and prosperous society where the 'one family' spirit prevails."[106]

These gestures of goodwill have largely been directed at politically inoffensive minorities. Though Indians, most of whom are Hindu, comprise nearly a third of Bahrain's population, just about all are on temporary labor visas with no political rights. The much smaller number of Christians and Catholics are also temporary migrants, though predominantly Western and better resourced. Bahraini Jews are limited to a few families who can barely form a minyan together and fly in rabbis from abroad for special religious occasions. By raising the profile of these other communities, the kingdom ensures Bahrain's Shias do not hold a monopoly on victimhood. It contextualizes Shia (and Sunni) claims-making among a broader group of faiths that the royal court must purportedly balance.

Placing contemporary Shia-Sunni sectarian relations in a longer history of intercultural and interfaith dialogue on the island, the regime's narrative thus ignores Shias' indigeneity and their majority status among nationals, but also any inconvenient Sunni demands for favor. Like all religious, ethnic, and national groups in Bahrain, neither can really purport to represent, define, or speak to a common Bahraini identity; all groups are subsumed by their relationship with the regime. All the while, the state can uphold the concept of a centuries-old, immemorial, cosmopolitan Bahrain, which predates today's divisions and the cultures vying for recognition.[107]

Ultimately, the state does not appear to recognize heritage or customs that give meaning to would-be forms of national culture; it recognizes only its own power, to give and take away identity. Under these circumstances, national culture is reduced to the bargain that binds all parties. In exchange for their allegiance, citizens are granted state subsidies. And in exchange for their labor, noncitizens may earn far greater wages than those available to them in their countries of origin. And by sowing communal distrust, highlighting intergroup threats, and emphasizing their ability to guarantee security, the regime has found that it can reinforce domestic backing and dampen pressure for reform more cheaply than by distributing welfare benefits.[108] The "one family" spirit prevails.

In this way, Bahrain reveals how prosperity may purchase allegiance and labor, but it does not afford the rights of true citizenship; nor can it command the devotion of true patriotism. It is imaginable that were Bahrain to ever become less concerned with its social divisions or less prosperous, like a town with no more pearls to harvest, its subjects might just move down the coast.

6

Masked Conflict

Carnival and Power Relations in Trinidad and Tobago

When Trinidad was a slave-dependent plantation economy in the late eighteenth and early nineteenth centuries, there were two primary masquerades that the upper-class European planters portrayed during the annual pre-Lent Carnival. One was the *negue jardin*, literally the "garden nigger," or field slave—lowest in the island hierarchy but simultaneously an embodiment of untamed masculinity.[1] The *negue jardin* often painted himself black and wore chains; others dressed like a harlequin and recited verses from Shakespeare, Byron, and Blake. The *negues jardins* would fight with whips and sticks, a tradition that endures among today's *kalinda* martial artists. The other masquerade involved white women dressing as a *mulâtresse*, a mixed race or "coloured" woman, often referred to as "red"—the preferred sexual mate of white men, even if they were not marriageable. Devious, sensual, but inferior, the *mulâtresse* was perceived to be predatory. Still today there is a Trinidadian saying, "Nuttin' give trouble like an old car or a red woman." In these characters, the plantocracy indulged in and yearned to experience the unbridled sexuality and supposed savagery of their counterparts in bondage. Each masquerade represented a construction that publicly communicated the white planters' most repressed fears and fantasies. Denied the opportunity to engage desires unpalatable within their civilized self-understanding of whiteness, Carnival was a respite from the real world of Trinidad and Tobago but simultaneously a stage to freely express one's deepest thoughts about it. Over the centuries, the characters, fears, and fantasies have changed, but the stage remains.

Carnival Mentality

"We have a phrase called a 'Carnival mentality,'" said Kim Johnson, director of the Carnival Institute, a government-sponsored research and education organization. "It's when someone is playing himself. It comes from the idea of playing a character in a mas' [masquerade]. To suggest that a person in their

Majority Minority. Justin Gest, Oxford University Press. © Justin Gest 2022. DOI: 10.1093/oso/9780197641798.003.0006

everyday life is just playing himself suggests that the self is just a costume that someone is putting on.

"In a sense," Johnson continued, "we wear a mask every day. Teachers, priests, judges, all wear their costumes. We know what each looks like—a nerd, a Hell's Angel—and the costume tells who we are. In Trinidad, the costume is who or what we'd like to be. It's not so much envy, though there is a certain amount of contempt, but for a moment you want to behave the way that person behaves. But the white people knew they could leave it behind on Ash Wednesday, and it channeled an image of Black people being perennially irresponsible, dirty, and driven by sexual appetites. Protestantism despises the body—sex and visceral functions of being human. And all of that was placed on Black people. That conflict with the upper classes fueled the Carnival and, in a strange ironic way, it continues to benefit the Carnival. It remains a moment of excess and outrage."

Trinidad has a "Carnival mentality" all year long. On one hand, the government has embraced the annual festival as the national hallmark of a "festival society."[2] Many costumiers, tourism services, and musicians prepare for the

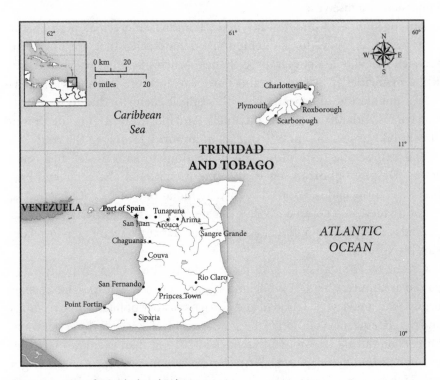

Figure 6.1 Map of Trinidad and Tobago.

next year's festivities before the streets are cleaned from the one that just took place. On the other hand, it is a country consumed by the racial "costumes" its people wear every day. In the contemporary era, whether you are Afro-Trinidadian and descended from Trinidad and Tobago's original slave population or Indo-Trinidadian and descended from the indentured servants who replaced Africans on the plantations significantly determines your views and how you are viewed by others.

Long the numerical majority, Afro-Trinidadian Creoles ruled the country for the first thirty years of sovereignty, but over time Indo-Trinidadians' prospered economically, grew in number, and challenged Afro-Trinidadians' claims of authenticity before ultimately forming an Indocentric political party and winning government power. Now comprising nearly equal, nonmajority shares of the national population, both groups view many public matters interpreted through the narrow lens of ethnic supremacy. Carnival itself is debated as one such matter, but it is also the venue for the expression of Trinidadians' fears, uncertainties, and ideals for the future of their society. Throughout its history and the demographic changes that have occurred, each year's pageant brings new answers to the old question: How do Trinidadians understand themselves?

Among the cases under study here, Trinidad emerges as perhaps the most realistic model for contemporary democracies that are unable to reconcile inevitable demographic change. Much like what will happen to white majorities in American and European futures, Trinidad's African-origin population unexpectedly lost its ethnic majority due to immigration trends and differential fertility rates. And like minorities in the United States and Europe, the Indo-Trinidadian minority leveraged the country's liberal democratic institutions and protections to gain power and equal status. Despite opportunities to redefine its national character and embrace its ethnic and religious diversity, Trinidad remains a country that is, if not divided, subject to a divisive debate over its national character that pervades every other political issue. Race constantly reemerges in recurring proxy battles.

Central to Trinidad's outward image and long the setting for politics disguised as culture, Carnival is a telling example of such a proxy. This chapter begins with a review of Trinidad and Tobago's history of interethnic relations and the concurrent evolution of the annual Carnival. Based on interviews and immersion during the annual festivities in 2019, it then examines Carnival through three different prisms. First, Carnival is a memoir for African-origin people that asserts their rightful inheritance of the land. Second, Carnival is a ritual that is ultimately repeated for its own sake—much more a national anthem than a national industry. And finally, Carnival is a contested expression of symbolic power that has the potential to cross social boundaries, but that ultimately reaffirms them.

A Caribbean Crucible

The British Empire's universal abolition of slavery in 1834 freed African slaves in Trinidad but set into motion the demographic change that would later complicate their postindependence politics over a century later. As much as it disoriented African-origin people after generations of oppression, emancipation also disoriented the microeconomies of planters whose sugar trade depended on the exploitation of forced laborers. While the Crown paid farmers compensation for the policy change, there were no laws that permitted planters to compel former slaves to work, and other laborers were in short supply.[3]

At the time, "free Blacks" and "coloured" people possessed some economic privileges after years of being burdened by civil disadvantages. Even while they were still subject to discrimination in courtrooms and barred from holding public office or joining military service, no law limited the amount of property they could hold in land, houses, or slaves—all of which could be freely bequeathed.[4] When abolition was announced, free Blacks and coloureds were already the majority of the small-scale farmers and poor householders in Port of Spain.[5] Once the remainder of Trinidad's Blacks left the plantations, the initial postabolition decades of British-Trinidadian politics were consumed by the "labor question."[6]

As elsewhere in the Caribbean Islands, Fiji, Guyana, Malaysia, Mauritius, Myanmar, and South Africa, the answer to that question was to transport laborers from India under terms of indenture. Far more slowly and later than Mauritius (Chapter 7), Trinidad would receive a steady flow of Indian indentured laborers beginning in 1845, when the former slave population could no longer demand market wages and many became unemployed.[7] Within fifteen years, 37,440 Indians had arrived for five-year terms of forced labor; by 1917, when the indenture system was terminated, 143,939 Indians had immigrated. Their free return passage after ten years in the colony, which was insisted on by both the Colonial Office and the government of India, made the Indians seem like temporary laborers, not a permanent addition to the population.[8] And the indentureship system kept most of the Indians on the estates as resident workers, severely restricting their freedom of movement and their contact with wider Trinidadian society.[9]

Largely hidden from view, the Indian population grew and began to settle. From 1869 to 1879, the British governor, Arthur Hamilton Gordon, granted Crown lands to Indians who forfeited their claim to return passage. He hoped that his action "would probably do much to induce a large portion of the Indian immigrant population, from being mere temporary sojourners, to becoming permanent colonists, a result greatly to be desired."[10] Thereafter, Indians were permitted to purchase Crown lands directly. Many did,[11] while others rented land from Indian-origin owners. By 1871, Indians made up 25 percent of Trinidad's population and 75 percent of the total sugar estate labor force; by around the turn of the century, Indians comprised 33 percent of the total population and 87 percent of plantation labor.[12] In the interim, only 21 percent of those Indians eligible for repatriation chose to return; the remainder joined a resident Indian community of "peasant proprietors," anchored by their Trinidad-born Indian children.[13]

After 1917, these "Creole Indians" in Trinidad's rural countryside developed in parallel to the Afro-Trinidadians in the cities and ports. While Indians sought to establish themselves in the island's economy, many Afro-Trinidadians began to occupy positions in the colony's bureaucracy and demand greater self-determination. Both communities grew inspired by waves of pan-African and Indian nationalism in the interwar period. Trinidad's African-origin population seized on the 1935 Italian invasion of Ethiopia—the continent's last uncolonized region—to forge a sense of anticolonial, Black consciousness. While some cultivated the symbol of Ethiopia for Black nationalist political projects, others mobilized their working-class Afro-Christian churches. Worshipers of the Orisha religion, which combines Yoruba and Catholic traditions, staged elaborate public ceremonies to invoke divine entities and entreat them to intervene on Ethiopia's behalf—all while flouting colonial laws that prohibited the exercise of *obeah* magic, drum playing, and other African cultural practices.[14]

Inspired by Mahatma Gandhi and the transnational Indian campaign for independence, Trinidad's Indian community began to leave the plantations and pursue local anticolonial activism. Literary clubs, debating societies, and the distribution of Indian cinema reconnected Indo-Trinidadians to their faraway homeland, invigorating a sense of rooted ethnic identity and a new language of resistance. These influences also imbued the Indo-Trinidadian minority with a sense of dominant Indian aesthetics, morality, religion, and political ideology.[15] The East Indian National Association and the East Indian National Congress expressed their solidarity from the diaspora, defying the image of the demoralized free Indians who gave to the Creole public the "coolie" stereotype.[16]

Over the course of this parallel renaissance, the British slowly expanded suffrage and the number of elected members in the colony's legislative council, but Trinidadians pressed for more. After a string of protests and disturbances across the Caribbean and the investigation of a royal commission, universal adult suffrage was introduced in Trinidad in 1946. After further agitation, the Crown also allowed the governor to appoint to ministerial positions elected council members, who were already responsible for practically running government departments.[17] This slow evolution from a complete autocracy to a semi-representative system to near-democracy took place under the shadow of a 1946 census report that projected Indo-Trinidadians to soon become the largest single ethnic constituency, and a majority by 1963 (see Figure 6.2).[18] When a debate about the use of birth control erupted between Trinidad's Catholics and Indo-Trinidadian supporters of Jawaharlal Nehru in the early 1950s, the Creole sociologist Lloyd Braithwaite wrote, "There can be little doubt that such a debate would have been unlikely a decade ago. Factors

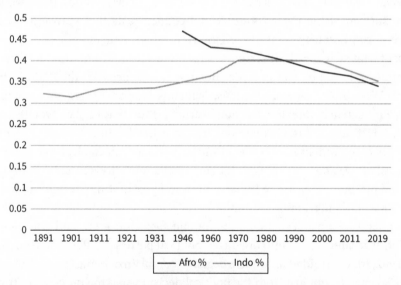

Figure 6.2 Population share of Afro- and Indo-Trinidadians between 1891 and 2019.

Note: This figure plots the relative share of African- and Indian-origin people in Trinidad, based on available census data. The remainder of the Trinidadian population is of white Creole, Chinese, or mixed ethnic background.

Sources: Jack Harewood, "The Population of Trinidad and Tobago, 1974," Paris: Committee for International Co-ordination of National Research in Demography, 1975, 95; United Nations Statistics Division, "Demographic and Social Statistics," accessed October 3, 2017, Unstats.un.org; Trinidad and Tobago Ministry of Planning and Development, Central Statistical Office, "Trinidad and Tobago 2011 Population and Housing Census Demographic Report," 2012, 94, https://www.undp.org/content/dam/trinidad_tobago/docs/DemocraticGovernance/Publications/TandT_Demographic_Report_2011.pdf; "Trinidad and Tobago Demographics Profile 2019," Index Mundi, December 7, 2019, https://www.indexmundi.com/trinidad_and_tobago/demographics_profile.html.

which make it possible were the prestige of Nehru . . . and the fact that with the emergence of the Indian group to high social status, the Hindu point of view became respectable and could therefore be contraposed to the Roman Catholic one."[19]

In the elections that followed, the ties between people's quest for ethnic consciousness and nationhood would crystallize. Eric Williams, an Oxford historian who returned to Trinidad in 1948 as an employee of the Caribbean Commission, conducted 157 meetings across the island in the lead-up to the 1956 election.[20] According to historian Raymond Ramcharitar, Williams deployed his scholarship and personality "theatrically and magisterially to dramatize the wickedness of slavery" to a Black population that was "susceptible to history as revenge plot, and Williams' performances created an oral nationalist narrative readily available to the community."[21] According to political scientist Selwyn Ryan, Williams "cast himself in the role of the providential messiah who had been preparing himself in the wilderness of the Commission so that he might with greater effectiveness 'set his people free.' "[22]

Williams and his People's National Movement (PNM) political party would win thirteen of the twenty-four elected council seats that year and would govern continuously until 1986. However, when Williams's opponents—a mix of white Creoles, Indo-Trinidadians, labor activists, and the Democratic Labour Party, led by Hindu leader Bhadase Maraj, defeated the PNM in the 1958 West Indies federal elections, Williams blamed racism. A pamphlet was circulated before the election warning Indo-Trinidadian voters that if the election was lost, "woe to our Indian nation."[23] In response, Williams said that "the Indian nation was in India. It was a respectable, reputable nation. . . . It was not the 'recalcitrant and hostile minority' of the West Indian nation masquerading as the Indian nation and prostituting the name of India 'for its selfish and reactionary end.' "[24]

Under Williams's leadership, interethnic suspicion grew, and communal identity became woven into organized political parties.[25] After independence in 1962, Indo-Trinidadian leaders began to complain of being "marginalized" and "alienated" not just from the political decision-making process but from all of Trinidadian society.[26] As their fertility rates slowed with the prosperity of the oil boom years, Indo-Trinidadians became critical of a Black monopoly on state power and an exclusive Afro-Trinidadian definition of national culture. They accused Williams of gerrymandering parliamentary districts to minimize Indo-Trinidadian representation, and there is evidence that he recruited Afro-Caribbean immigrants from nearby islands to alter the demographic balance and inflate his support.[27]

It has been argued, however, that it was the economic success of South Asians that increased Afro-Trinidadians' determination to maintain dominant political control.[28] Were they to lose political power, many Afro-Trinidadians thought that their prospects in society would grow dismal.[29] In 1970, Williams was challenged by a revolutionary group of Black Power activists who organized large protests and took hostages after Williams declared a state of emergency. In an attempt to console radicals and the disaffected poor, he expressed solidarity with the movement, removed two white ministers from his cabinet, and also moved to reduce civil liberties. The tension between Trinidad's multiethnic demography and its ethnocentric politics culminated in the experiment that was the National Alliance for Reconstruction (NAR).

Elected to power five years after Williams's death, the NAR was a multiracial coalition of defected PNM members, Indo-Trinidadian parties, and labor activists who won thirty-three of Trinidad's thirty-six parliamentary seats amid deep economic hardship in 1986. Economic stagnation after the oil boom had produced a 22 percent unemployment rate, increased substance abuse, weakened family life, and resulted in hundreds of thousands of emigrants.[30] In 1987, the *Sandesh* newspaper editorialized on its front page, "The resounding victory of the National Alliance for Reconstruction . . . is overwhelming evidence that our people have once more regained their freedom and sanity and that they no longer intend to be bound or kept divided by racial or other subversive prejudices."[31]

However, the NAR disintegrated almost as quickly as it formed. Mere months into its rule, Prime Minister A. N. R. Robinson expelled Foreign Minister Basdeo Panday, two junior ministers, and the NAR's secretary general—all of whom had political bases in Indo-Trinidadian constituencies— and the Indo-Trinidadian faction split off to form its own party, the United National Congress (UNC). Then, in 1990, a Black Muslim organization led by the Islamist Abu Bakr, Jamaat Al Muslimeen, attempted an unsuccessful coup. Though the coup had only minimal support on the fringes of Trinidadian society, its execution, subsequent looting, and the provision of amnesty for the insurgents rendered a sense of anarchy and despair. The coup's support among many Afro-Trinidadians from the slums of Port of Spain and the margins of the island suggested the government's inability to reach and protect the welfare of its people.[32] By 1991, NAR support was largely reduced to two districts in Tobago, and the party lost power to the PNM. Partisanship has been effectively racialized ever since; most of PNM's support comes from predominantly Afro-Creole constituencies, while most of the UNC's supporters are Indo-Trinidadian in origin.

Table 6.1 Key Factors in Trinidad and Tobago (Majority Minority in ~1995)

Immigration	Equality	Identity	Social Relations
Concentrated: Indentured labor migrants from India from 1845 until 1917. Since then, some immigration of Afro-Caribbeans, but significant emigration of both Indo- and Afro-Trinidadians to Canada, the United Kingdom, and the United States.	*Equal:* Universal adult suffrage introduced in 1946. After further agitation, the Crown allowed the colonial governor to appoint to ministerial positions elected council members. By the time of independence, all groups held equal status.	*Exclusive:* After the introduction of universal suffrage, interethnic suspicion grew. After independence, Indo-Trinidadians complained of being "marginalized" and "alienated" by Afro-Trinidadian assertions of control in ethnoracial terms.	*Tension:* Political parties are severely racialized. Every debate, no matter how small, has become a proxy battle in a seemingly existential war for racial and cultural supremacy.

By the following election, in 1995, Indian- and African-origin people made up constituencies of approximately equal size—40 percent each of the population—and ethnic identity determined voter choice to a degree never seen before.[33] The presence of overwhelming concentrations of either Indo- or Afro-Trinidadians preordained the outcome in most parliamentary districts, and an Indian-origin prime minister, Panday, was elected for the first time after the NAR formed a coalition with its former members. Trinidad's fragile multiethnic order—the balance between Indo-Trinidadian and European control of agriculture and commerce, and Afro-Trinidadian control over politics—had been disturbed. "Stunned, tearful and traumatised,"[34] African Creoles retreated to the space where their monopoly could endure, independent of Indo-Trinidadians' money and newfound power: national culture.

Masked Conflict

Carnival dominates contemporary and historic Trinidadian culture. Early Carnivals among Trinidad's upper-class planters masked—even from the participants—the true significance of their portrayals. One can only imagine the irony when French-Creole planters parodied their subordinates while being served by them. Similarly, the Carnival's Canboulay (derived from *cannes brulées*, or burnt sugar cane) torch procession was a parody of a dramatic event in plantation life when slaves were herded together with the cracking of whips in the event of a wildfire.[35] After emancipation, Carnival passed into the hands of freed slaves and laborers who seized the opportunity to boisterously parody the superiors who previously excluded them from the festivities. People gathered in calypso (derived from the West African *kaiso*) tents where chantwells (*chantuelles*) sang rhythmic songs that subverted authorities in a harmonious French patois (eventually, the English that British colonial officials could understand). The lower classes turned Canboulay into a memorial ceremony held annually on the night of August 1, the date of Africans' liberation.

During this period, Black laborers sought to reduce their dependence on the plantation by trying to become peasants or artisans; those who failed drifted into towns, where frequent unrest reflected an awareness of oppression.[36] Gangs fought each other because they were unable to attack the real sources of their misery or powerlessness, but they targeted the elites when Carnival provided an opportunity to articulate their resentment.[37] A *jamette* (underclass) Carnival emerged beneath upper-class fêtes. Bridget Brereton described utter bacchanalia:

> Bands of prostitutes roamed the streets of Port of Spain making "indecent gestures" and singing "lewd songs." There were traditional masques with explicit sexual themes. The most notorious was the Pissenlit (or Pisani), literally "wet the bed," usually translated as "stinker." It was played by masked men dressed as women in long transparent nightdresses; it involved much sexual horseplay and was accompanied by obscene songs in patois. The jamet bands included both men and women. The women would generally be prostitutes, active or retired, dressed in the traditional Martinique costume, always masked. At some times, and in some places, they exposed their breasts. The men were elaborately dressed, and would dance and strut through the streets, making suggestive comments to bystanders and propositioning women. Transvestitism and accompanying horseplay were very common, whether in the Pissenlit, or individually. Victorian Trinidad, in its publicly expressed expectations and norms, was certainly less tolerant and more prudish than in the days of slavery. The press made much of the alleged corruption of lower-class youth which took place before, during, and after Carnival. Perhaps it did; though in the teeming and squalid backyards of the city's slums it would have been difficult not to have got corrupted, Carnival or not.[38]

Increasingly viewed with disdain and suspicion by Trinidad's elites and government officials who feared "another Haiti,"[39] the rebellious and lascivious aspects of the festival provoked numerous measures intended to prevent disorder in the late nineteenth century.[40] In 1858, Governor Robert W. Keate' attempt to prohibit the wearing of masks was met with such popular resistance that the police were forced to withdraw. After the defeat, a group of three or four thousand Africans provocatively marched past the precinct with axes, clubs, and machetes.[41] In 1883, the government prohibited the playing of drums, tambourines, or *chac-chacs* (West Indian maraca-like shakers) without a police permit, while milder regulations were issued for European musical instruments. In response, lower-class percussionists started using bamboo stems as drumsticks.[42]

By 1881, the Canboulay—which colonial officials had moved to the Sunday preceding Carnival—was detested by police and elites. Its masked participants carried fiery torches and marched to drumming, hooting, shouting, and singing, and it was the occasion for stick fights between *kalinda* martial arts champions and rival bands.[43] Determined to address the threat, police chief Arthur Baker ordered his officers to stop the procession, resulting in an enormous riot that persisted until Governor Sir Sanford Freeling insisted they retreat to their barracks. After Freeling was recalled in 1883, Baker clashed again with Canboulay participants the following year. Despite their disgust with the *jamette* Carnival, Trinidad's press criticized Baker's actions as provocative and resented any attempt by the executive to interfere with it by force; they recognized that Carnival was the only truly "national festival," the only one the people could claim as their own.[44] Still, Canboulay, organized band conflict, and stickmen assemblies were all soon prohibited, and, within ten years, so were the grosser forms of obscenity characteristic of the *jamette* Carnival.[45]

Purged of its most debauched and bellicose components, Carnival in the early twentieth century slowly attracted the Creole middle classes previously caught between their desired distance from the former slaves and their exclusion from white elite circles. A mere twenty-six organized bands of about twenty people each were registered in Port of Spain in 1900. After the First World War, there was a sharp increase in the number of bands, and official competition centers were set up in the city where the bands presented themselves before a jury. By 1946, there were 125 registered bands, and by 1965, there were 171 bands and about 100,000 people dressed up in carnival costumes during the two-day festival in the newly independent nation.[46]

As the British Empire granted greater power to African Creoles and Indians began to leave the plantations, Carnival activities and calypsos began to turn their focus away from the upper classes and toward the curious East Indians in their midst. Intrigued by the idea of the Indian feast, including the festival of Hosay (Husayn)—an Indo-Caribbean counterpart to Carnival that was prominent in the southern parts of Trinidad—calypsos of the time frequently mentioned Indian food. Dhal, roti, curry, and *talkarie* were markers of difference and at the same time the major and easiest means toward a temporary setting aside of differences.[47] However, the feast was also a point of interethnic contact that barely concealed the differences that existed on a daily basis and polemicized Africans' cultivation of Indian women. The stereotype emerged of the jealous Indo-Trinidadian man, concerned to preserve Indians' ethnic purity, "defending with sharp cutlass the honor of his daughter, sister, or wife, or saving face after having been cuckolded by chopping up his woman and her Creole lover"—constructs just as exaggerated as the powder-faced planter waltzing but equally at home in Carnival's drama and discourse.[48]

Amid the euphoria of Trinidad's march toward independence, Carnival was more broadly embraced not just as part of the nascent nation's social fabric but also as part of its historical development. In 1957, the government created the Carnival Development Committee (renamed the National Carnival Commission in the 1980s), which to this day organizes the festival's calypso, steel pan, and masquerade band competitions, giving these traditions official recognition as part of national culture. The calypsonian, long regarded as a jester tolerated with condescending dismay by the well-heeled, became a national hero. On public squares and roundabouts, where other countries might feature tributes to revolutionary heroes or founding statesmen, the Trinidadian government erected statues of old calypsonians. With independence and Creole political dominance, however, Carnival, long an act of resistance, lacked an obvious antagonist. With the PNM in firm control and— by the late 1970s and 1980s—struggling, calypsonians and Carnival designers turned on each other. Ambient debates focused on the primacy of Africa in Trinidadian culture and the Black Power movement, as Trinidad sank into a deep recession.[49]

When Panday and the UNC took power, Carnival was in a dire state. The historian Ramcharitar observed that the tone of Carnival grew "weary and ambivalent" in the early 1990s. There were pro-coup calypsos and increasingly bitter lyrics, attendance had declined along with record sales, and the legendary designer Peter Minshall—who had transformed the festival in the 1980s and was commissioned to choreograph Olympic and World Cup opening ceremonies—declined to participate.[50] The Guardian's editorial on Ash Wednesday in 1991 asked "Is Carnival dying?" It pointed out administrative inefficiencies, the deficiency caused by Minshall's absence, and the general decline in public enthusiasm. If unchecked, the editorial warned, "the national festival is destined to continue to deteriorate to the point where creativity and the imagination would have little play in a second-rate jump-up celebration."[51] In 1995, another Guardian editorial observed "unusually small crowds at both the opening of the conventional steelband Panorama and the normally well-patronised Soca Monarch [competition]."[52] However, the backlash to Trinidad's first Indian-origin prime minister rejuvenated the festival.

"Pseudo-Racism"

Basdeo Panday was an unlikely racial justice warrior for Indo-Trinidadians. When he was ushered into government with the NAR in 1986, he had spent his entire career attempting to unite Trinidadians across racial lines in favor of class-based solidarity. The grandson of indentured laborers from Bhojpuri, Panday's first job was as a sugar cane weigher on a plantation. He would go on to obtain university degrees in law, economics, and drama in London, before returning to Trinidad after independence to work as an attorney. He joined the unionist Workers' and Farmers' Party and made an unsuccessful run for Parliament in 1966, before ultimately becoming the president general of the All Trinidad Sugar and General Workers' Trade Union in 1972. Amid political turbulence in 1975, Panday linked arms with radical union leaders George Weekes and Raffique Shah to found the United Labour Front, a new political party that challenged the PNM. Panday was first elected to Parliament in 1976, and instantly became the opposition leader. After weak results in the 1980 local elections, he merged the party with others led by Creole politicians A. N. R. Robinson and Lloyd Best. In advance of the 1986 general election, they formed the NAR. When they swept into power, they decided that Robinson would serve as prime minister because the reeling country was "not ready" for an Indian-origin leader. It was in this coalition that Panday became more defined by his ethnic background than his socialist ideals.

I interviewed Panday at his suburban home in Bryan's Gate, San Fernando. He answered the door dressed in a pink-checked, short-sleeve dress shirt and black trousers and cordially invited me into his living room. His ornate furniture contrasted with the house's modernist design, and the shelves were lined with symbolic gifts he had received over the years from dignitaries and heads of state. We removed our shoes and sat barefoot on his tasseled sofa.

"When I joined the Workers' and Farmers' Party," he told me, "we realized that the country was divided with a line down the middle: Africans on one side, Indians on the other. We tried to divide it another way, unite workers across racial lines. . . . The racial tension was extremely high and our party fell between two stools. The PNM had been in power for some twenty-eight years, and whereas some people saw that as political stability, I regarded it as political stagnation. In another attempt to bring people together, we joined together with the Tobago Democratic Action Congress, which held two seats [to form the NAR]. I thought that after the PNM had been led by an African leader for so long, the leap of having an Indian leader would be too far.

"There has always been discrimination against the Indian population in Trinidad and Tobago," he continued. "And one of our agreements was that we would end discrimination and redress the imbalance in government service. But Robinson's problem was that he was a prime minister without a political base from which to gather strength, and maybe he didn't trust us anyway. He had an unofficial cabinet and began running a government without the government—not dealing with the basic problem for which we had fought.

"One day," Panday recalled, "he brought to cabinet a list of persons to be appointed to state boards, and there were no Indians among them. We raised this, and it made him very annoyed. We asked, 'What's happening to redressing?' In another incident, we weren't consulted on a government sale, and the response was 'We didn't trust you.' We also proposed an Indian Cultural Center to teach Hindi and Indian music that would be opened by the Indian foreign minister. Ultimately, he was trying to consolidate the Afro-Trinidadian vote around him in search of a political base. There were several incidents like this that created tension. At one point, Robinson began firing our men one by one. That led to our expulsion from the party. And if speaking up on the issues that were important to us meant that we broke [the party] up, then I guess we did."

When Panday and the UNC won power in 1995, Carnival became once again the venue for resistance. The 1996 Calypso Monarch competition was won by Cro Cro's "Black Man, All Yuh Look for Dat," a sour song that rebuked Afro-Trinidadian voters for failing to vote in larger numbers. "When I sang rise African rise / and I beg Black Man please open your eyes," he exhorted. He then blamed Afro-Trinidadians who defected from the PNM to support "A man on a charge for interfering / Blackman all you still go and vote for him"— a reference to sexual assault allegations against Panday (who was acquitted). In another calypso that year titled "Mr. Panday Needs His Glasses," calypso celebrity Watchman portrayed the prime minister as an alcoholic and sexual abuser. Lady B's "Curry and Salt" alluded to fears that Black children would be miseducated under the new government.

At the same time, Panday was prodded by the predominantly Creole-controlled Trinidadian press. Shortly after his election, *The Guardian*'s front-page photo showed the new prime minister and a male member of his cabinet appearing to kiss. *The Guardian* later ran a provocative front-page headline, "Chutney Rising," a double-entendre that ostensibly referred to an increasingly popular music genre but clearly implied that Indo-Trinidadians were seizing power.[53]

As tensions quickly rose, Panday escalated matters. He ordered a boycott of the paper and denied their reporters access to government documents. He accused editor-in-chief Jones P. Madeira of being a racist and called for his resignation. He then accused communications magnate Kenneth Gordon, who owned the *Express* newspaper and multiple television networks, of being a "pseudo-racist," someone who may not be racist in their personal life but cynically employs race to provoke, manipulate, and make political appeals. "I do not believe that freedom of the press includes the untrammeled right to publish lies, half-truths and innuendo about anyone," he said at the time, "and Mr. Gordon maintains that he has an untrammeled right to do so."[54] (Gordon would later successfully sue Panday for libel.)

At the 1997 Dimanche Gras Show, which is financed by the government, Panday swore that taxpayer money would never again be used to subsidize calypsonians who use their songs to slander government or innocent individuals.[55] He also proposed censorship laws that would prohibit calypsonians from performing songs that denigrate government or incite racial polarization.[56] Since Trinidadian society was "plural and fragile," Panday said he could not allow such a symbolic national occasion as Carnival to be used to spread prejudice and misogyny.[57] Accordingly, he announced that the Calypso Monarch competition would no longer be held as part of the Dimanche Gras Show.

Panday's attacks on the calypsonians and the press were condemned as a threat to free speech—a treasured tradition in Trinidad that dates back to the calypsonians of the nineteenth century. The prime minister's intimidation recalled planter-class efforts to censor Carnival, Canboulay, and the Hosay festival, fearing the voice of the people and their imminent rebellion. To many Afro-Trinidadians who feared Indo-Trinidadians' "revenge against them for years of political and social exclusion and disenfranchisement,"[58] Carnival became a cause célèbre.

"Carnival has been both a good and bad thing," Panday told me. "The good is that it is said that it is an avenue to get rid of frustration. So when we have Carnival fêtes—Trinidadians will fête anything with drinking and dancing, maybe a hangover from slavery—but it dissipates an enormous amount of energy that could otherwise be used to make the country a better place for all.

"The bad aspect of it is that it is centered around sex, and the behavior at Carnival is not a very good example for children coming up. But then again, one has to look at many dimensions. It used to be about tremendous costumes, but—and I don't know if it's the bandleaders or the economy—they became less and less until it degenerated into a g-string. It's just a great diversion. We are teaching Carnival in schools. Why are we involving children in this behavior and dissipating the energies of our youth?

"No politician is brave enough to ban Carnival. It is a given, a fact. But how can it enhance the growth of the country? Indians will boycott it as long as calypsonians are in the pocket of the PNM. They began singing songs

chastising Indians. That turned Indians off from the tents. And that has alienated a fair proportion from the Carnival exercise."

These are the words of someone for whom Carnival is meaningless, if not
menacing. Still bitter about what he called "all these nasty calypsos," Panday lamented a country that was arguably more divided now than when he agitated
for universal workers' rights. In a 1997 poll of about a thousand Trinidadians,
more than 50 percent of the Afro-Trinidadians surveyed said that, in their
view, race relations had worsened since Panday took power, compared with
only 6 percent of Indo-Trinidadians; 50 percent of the Indo-Trinidadians
questioned said they actually had seen an improvement.[59]

When the PNM returned to power in 2002, Prime Minister Patrick
Manning would multiply funding for the National Carnival Commission
more than fivefold. With state resources, the annual festival took on fresh defiance as a battleground for "a fierce contestation of space in which little quarter
is being given on either side."[60] With its renewed raison d'être, Carnival risked
becoming a "national tradition" in which many Indo-Trinidadians felt unrep-
resented and ultimately unwelcome.

Carnival as Memoir

Carnival's cathedral is Piccadilly Greens, a dark, ramshackle stretch in the
rough southern neighborhoods of Port of Spain. At 4:00 in the morning beneath a slender crescent moon the Friday before the festival, a thousand locals
assemble on bleachers in front of Angee's Roti Shop and Alvin's Tyre Change
to commemorate Trinidad's national martyrs.

Under electric cables drooping from streetlamps, the smell of kerosene
permeates the balmy night air. A steel pan soloist drums the national anthem
before an Anglican priest blesses the "celebration of emancipation." "Thank
you, Lord, for members of the National Carnival Commission," he said.
"Amen," replied the crowd in unison.

Unlike many other Carnival events, which can begin up to four hours late,
the annual reenactment of the 1881 Canboulay Riots starts right on time.
The PNM minister of community development, culture, and the arts, Nyan
Gadsby-Dolly, opens: "Carnival is borne out of the cultural revolution of a nation . . . of a people determined to be free."

The performance begins with a counterdiscourse for contrast. Actors
portraying British colonists and the planter class wearing white masks speak
in the Queen's English and waltz to Strauss's "Blue Danube." Swiftly, the next
scene emerges with an overlay of African percussion introducing a mob of

Afro-Trinidadians. Chanting in unity, ululating, and sparring with sticks, they dance interpretatively barefoot on the asphalt. Their loose-fitting tunics and dresses are colorful—a disorderly counterpoint to the uniformed, sedate, stoic discipline of the elites.

"Everything dey got, come from we sweat!" shouts a Creole leader. "African won they freedom, but they conditions still inhuman."

"Burn the canes as an act of resistance," chants the band in chorus. "Never forget!"

A regiment of red-and-gold-draped constables arrive.

The rioters link arms and form a circle, their eyes closed in solidarity. As a shaman blows into a conch shell, machetes are brandished, exhorting the band into battle.

Afterward, the British governor, Stanford Freeling, emerges: "There was a misconception on your part that the government wanted to stop your amusement." The Queen (Victoria) has a preference for "peaceful subjects," he explains. "You may have every indulgence if you keep within the law." He then promises "no more interference" with the masquerade.

"Freedom!" cries the crowd, as the blue of dawn emerges from the horizon, behind silhouettes of corrugated metal and palm fronds. A traditional mas' procession begins to the beat of African percussion:

Black gorillas hoisting sugar cane stalks that flame blowers light afire.
Women in ballgowns stuffed to exaggerate their breasts and derrieres.
A middle-aged steel pan band called "The Jungle People."
Shirtless, muscular "juju warriors" in grass skirts and frilly grass sandals.
Zombies in shackles and demons cracking twelve-foot whips.

The masquerade is certainly a release of suppressed fantasies, fears, and resentment. To the naked eye, it is mindless, unconscious, and gratuitous. More profoundly, it is a reappropriation of antecedent tropes and caricatures of African-origin people—an inversion of social roles and a reclamation of the weapons of bondage from the nobility they mock.

"Canboulay is the essence of Carnival, the struggle for freedom," Minister Gadsby-Dolly told me afterward from her perch on a dais. "It's a deep cultural heritage, the underpinnings of the culture of the Africans and their struggle to achieve our freedom."

"Is it disappointing that more Indo-Trinidadians don't participate?" I asked. "Can they relate to this national struggle?"

"The East Indians would have had a different experience," she replied in an imperious tone. "The life of the Canboulay Riots was an African struggle . . . definitely an African struggle."

"But can it be the 'national story' when there are no Indians spectating or participating?" I pressed.

"Oh, they're some here," she said, looking around. "Their hair is covered, so you're not seeing it."

"Yes, I think a couple may have played the waltzing British."

"No, one of the leads was also Indian," she insisted, furrowing her brow to suggest seriousness. "You just can't tell under the costume. It's not a portrayal of East Indian culture, but it is inclusive."

"Do you think that Afro-Trinidadians hold these demonstrations of their culture all the more tightly because they feel like it's under threat from demographic change?"

"I would say that both pure races are losing to the mixed races. You're seeing a lot more curly-haired people, that's what I call them. And they're holding on to African culture because there was a time when our traditions were not to be shown. So you're seeing a resurgence of people wearing their natural hair and natural clothes. East Indians were permitted to keep their culture and traditions. This points to the need for African pride."

Just as I began to thank the minister for her time, she reached out with her arm. "I don't know that East Indians are not participating," she said, "but the Canboulay Riots reenactment is the portrayal, the underpinning of national culture. They weren't part of the start of the masquerade. But the evolution of the masquerade eventually included all. It's not an exclusion. It's just a fact that this was the struggle of the Africans, and we opened the way for all to participate. There has continued to be African pride throughout our history. At one point, [African predominance] was taken for granted. But once there was a challenge on the economic, political, social landscapes, people draw on their culture to remind them that they were great."

With her words, Gadsby-Dolly danced with the same agility as members of the burlesque procession: Canboulay was inclusive of Indo-Trinidadians, but ultimately something to which they could not possibly relate.

It is undeniable that Canboulay's audacious protagonists were Port of Spain's Afro-Caribbean underclass; it was Creole bands that led the *jamette* Carnival and valiantly fought their censorship. But it is also true that the same British constables used violence to suppress Hosay processions by Indians because it was a source of Indocentric self-affirmation at a time when the "coolies" were resisting plantation conditions, and because Hosay—which connected Indians to Africans—undermined the colonial desire to isolate the Indians.[61] In the Hosay massacre in San Fernando on October 30, 1884, twenty-two people (of whom eighteen had recognizable Hindu names) died and well over a hundred were wounded in the bloodiest confrontation of its kind in the history of Trinidad. Though they were never enslaved, Indo-Trinidadians do understand exploitation, oppression, and freedom—even if from a different experience.

The spirit of Canboulay is a universally human triumph, much like the civil rights march from Selma to Montgomery or the Boston Tea Party in the United States. Few Americans would ever suggest that their countrymen who did not descend from those Bostonian forbears or southern Blacks could not see themselves in these human acts of defiance. Recognizing the fleeting nature of their freedom and, more recently, the insecurity of their political power, however, Trinidad's Creoles are determined to memorialize that which is rightfully theirs and establish an indelible "national" legacy.

Indeed, it is telling that the Canboulay Riots reenactment is said to celebrate "emancipation" when the revolt took place forty-seven years after the abolition of slavery. For people of African origin, abolition did not bring true emancipation. And to many of Trinidad's leading Creole thinkers, Canboulay is a reminder that freedom and self-determination are still not fully theirs.

Enter the Dragon

One of these Creole thinkers is Earl Lovelace, Trinidad's most famous living novelist and the author of *Salt*, *The Wine of Astonishment*, and the 1979 Carnival classic *The Dragon Can't Dance*. Lovelace's disillusionment with Trinidad's elites is expressed most poignantly in the disappointment of Fisheye, the last book's rebellious "bad john" ruffian who was once enthralled by Eric Williams and the PNM's nationalism. He wanted to "become part of it, this wonderful thing that was going to fight colonialism, was going to stand up for the people, was going to create jobs and make us a nation,"[62] only to gain little from their election victories and witness the persistence of prejudice and foreign influence over Trinidad.

Lovelace lives in the bourgeois Cascade neighborhood of Port of Spain, nestled in the lush, tropical canyons northwest of the Queen's Park Savannah, the city's central park. Perched on the side of a dense bamboo-filled ravine filled with dozens of cawing birds, the house's wide wraparound patio gives the sense of a jungle treehouse immersed in greenery.

Well-to-do neighborhoods like Cascade, St. Ann's, and Belmont are surrounded by a fringe of shantytowns and slums, the residue of earlier European and Creole elites' preference to keep their staff close by. Lovelace is acutely aware of this history and insisted that we cannot understand the cultural place of today's Carnival without an appreciation of its sociopolitical origins.

"The culture has always been under threat because Africans have always been under threat since the beginning," he explained. "So it wasn't like you came on a cruise and decided to stay here. People were brought here to work, and a hierarchy, which was expressive of racism, was institutionalized. And we have been under threat. Political self-determination is only one aspect of being in control of yourself. It could be almost a screen, a blind that prevents you from engaging your sovereignty. I think that you can't just jump to postemancipation, or jump to postindependence, as if there was nothing before that created the social relationships. And they were not accidental or incidental; these were established. Even the process by which independence was affirmed—one of the questions in literature has been voice—who is seeing the world? When anyone speaks, he is coming from somewhere."

Lovelace's work has championed the formation and virtue of an authentically Trinidadian ethic, unqualified and uncorrupted by foreign influences: true self-determination. His desire to territorialize Creole identity defies its inherent cosmopolitanism—historically subject to European standard-setting, a mélange of immigrant arrivals, and a vague but yearning pan-African solidarity. Lovelace is none of the above and all of them at once. His aversion to the subjectivities of external benchmarks comes through in the nihilism of *Salt*'s Michael, a fifteen-year-old who was happy to fail his school exams:

> With a calm that announced and emphasized that his future lay elsewhere, that he was Bango's nephew and the grandson of Pappy King Durity who up to the age of eighty-one was still going from district to district to dance bongo and to sing hymns at the occasion of a death and who, according to my mother, didn't care if Good Friday fall on Christmas Eve once he had a rum to drink and cuatro to play and a woman to caress.[63]

At eighty-three years old, Lovelace is mild mannered but as irascible and combative as a teenager. He sat comfortably, if not supremely, in a round wooden rocking chair on his wide balcony in a white linen shirt, unbuttoned down to his sternum.

I asked him, "Despite sovereignty and years of self-rule, why are Afro-Trinidadians insecure?"

"I think that 'insecurity' is a strange kind of word," he said. "It suggests that you should be secure, something other than you are. Why are Africans insecure? I would ask, 'Are Africans insecure?' What is the expression of this insecurity?"

"Perhaps Carnival itself," I proposed.

"The Carnival has been one of the means by which Africans restored their gods and reclaimed their personhood," he replied. "So Carnival is not asserting a kind of security but a means of expressing yourself to your world. You also have to understand that Carnival is not just an assertion; it is a rebellion as well. We are human in a profound sense, by—well there are so many sides. One is African, and one has to understand why it has endured beyond the European Carnival, which has been largely concerned with establishing the emblems of power.

"If you look at Carnival, I don't know to what degree it is Afrocentric. That grew out of the need to reaffirm themselves and claim themselves in this place. You're talking about a society where everything African has been somehow belittled, marginalized—steel pan had a period when it was banned, religion, stick-fighting, all the things we are trying to rescue in a different kind of context. Rebellion is not only against; when you are against something, it implies you are also for something—on behalf of a vision of what it means to be human.

"Emancipation is a big, bad fake. You said you were going to emancipate people, and all you did was set them into liberty. You didn't look after them, grant reparations, deal with illnesses. However, it was at least being free from having to work for someone else, having to endure the brutality. We're talking about people who have been captured from their homeland, brought into this part of the world, and for three hundred years have been in this condition. Everything they have has been pushed down or criminalized. . . . Around 1840, the colonial authorities decided to remove the celebration of emancipation from August 31 and put it on Carnival Sunday. Instead of having two carnivals, [Europeans] consolidated it all in one place. They removed emancipation from it. How do Europeans affirm this power and keep the subjugated down? Everything they did was to keep these people in their place."

"So Carnival is the search for a subjugated identity?" I proposed. In *The Dragon Can't Dance*, Lovelace wrote that the festival was where the protagonist, Aldrick, in his dragon costume could "reaffirm his identity" since it is "only at this time of the year when the community's intransigence is permitted to manifest itself as the spectacle and outbreak of Carnival spirit in the streets."[64]

"Everybody has an identity," Lovelace told me. "People may not want to accept it, but people know where they come from. It hasn't been affirmed or shouted out for many reasons. Presenting figures like the dragon or the midnight robber, my thinking is that people are not looking to embrace 'African' necessarily. The 1970s was the period of Black Power's emergence, and once that happened, Black people knew where they came from. Even if it were a quest to return to Africa, we confront what has happened since we left. For intellectuals, it was a rediscovery of Africa. I remember how, when we dressed up in what we thought was African wear, ordinary Black people were out-raged, ridiculing us for putting on these clothes. Why would somebody ridi-cule someone for dressing in a way to connect them with that place? There is something pushing them to do so."

He looked outward, searching for words in the infinite vegetation before us.

"I find it strange," he resumed. "In the old days [before independence], there was a Carnival Queen Show on the Savannah, and all the contestants were white. And the Catholic archbishop would crown her. In 1917, the spir-itual Baptists, the 'shouters,' were banned—a Black religion that was criminal-ized. . . . This country, like many in the Caribbean, was created by Amerindian slaughter, African enslavement, and you might add Indian indenture. You can't remove this context and just see Carnival [at face value].

"If we say that Carnival mediates between the groups, then it has to achieve something. It's not so much that I'm looking for something; it's what I make of what I see. I'm looking for something that speaks for people. It has to go through all kinds of roads, dead ends, before reaching—a whole ongoing pro-cess. It's not that somebody is directing. It is just happening. It's what Carnival produces despite what people make of it. It's a way to finding oneself, but finding is a kind of endless occupation."

"And maybe that's why Carnival endures," I add.

"Right. People come with a new quest and a new expression. And even though they may be totally wrong, they are expressing a hope, a community, and there is somehow something right about it."

It begins to rain on the canopy of tin and leaves. Lovelace lights a cigarette.

"Where do the Indo-Trinidadians figure in this quest for finding oneself?" I asked.

"The dialogue was never between Africans and Indians," said Lovelace frankly. "It was between Africans and Europeans in a colonial place. The question of speaking to Indians is to come. They come from a place that they can identify and relate back and forth—unlike Africans, whose connection was cut. We have time. I wouldn't rush to judgment. In a situation where one group is asserting themselves, other groups want to as well. Indians would say that they brought their gods with them. So Indians are not looking for an identity, or anybody to invite them into a religion.

"That leads to another question—a big question. We claim to like being a multiethnic society. We know what it has meant: the domination of a ma-jority by a minority, in culture, arts, politics. . . . What does it mean when you are in charge? But I don't think Africans are in charge. In the cultural spaces of an important festival, occasion, an important season that appears to be controlled by Africans. But does that fit the people who are indeed in charge?"

"I'm a pretty discerning person," I replied, "and when it comes to Carnival, I think Afro-Trinidadians are in charge."

"Numbers don't mean anything unless you have power associated with the numbers," said Lovelace. "Only in 1946, people received adult franchise, but only six percent of the people voted. We are in charge of what? We have to see how politics have developed and on whose behalf the government acts. Africans have had political power for some time, but if you were in power, it suggests you would have empowered your people." He was really channeling Fisheye now. "But there has not been a parallel in business or politics. Africans have apparent control over culture, but there are other aspects of society where Africans do not have power and don't even talk about having power."

"How can Carnival be about dialogue if a primary constituency is not present?" I asked.

"We have a history of four hundred years on this island, and fifty-seven years of independence," said Lovelace. "There are questions caused by that past that we have to deal with first. To be human is new to this blasted place, this part of the world where we come from. Go to the Bowery and see the people half naked trying to find something to eat or smoke. And a fundamental question we have to resolve is how do we see ourselves as human. People go to theater to see things; we pay to play mas'—to play a role that helps affirm something about ourselves. We have to look in a different direction beyond concepts of power that [Europeans] have employed.

"This society developed in a way that set Africans and Indians against each other. It was in their interests to keep these groups off-balance. You have to consider the bigger good. I don't know that we have had any program or person present what multiethnicity means," he concluded.

If more Indo-Trinidadians participated and could find themselves in Carnival, the complex existential monologue that Lovelace lionizes would be ever more complicated—but perhaps in the productive way that characterized Africans' original entry into a previously exclusive European event. For decades, Carnival has been predominantly Afro-Trinidadians in conversation with Afro-Trinidadians, which has been enlightening for some people of African origin but possibly confounding for Trinidad.

Carnival as Ritual

It is significant that Lovelace repeatedly referred to Carnival as a "religion," as an exercise based on faith. In *The Dragon Can't Dance*, Carnival provides the occasion for the protagonist, Aldrick, to find meaning and purpose in his masquerade: "It was in a spirit of priesthood that Aldrick addressed his work; for the making of his dragon costume was to him always a miracle, a new test not only of his skill but his faith: for though he knew exactly what he had to do, it was only by faith that he could bring alive from these scraps of cloth and tin that dragon."[65]

The Trinidadian government, which has recently allocated as much as $47 million per year to the event, justifies doing so not out of ritualistic faith but as an investment in a national industry (see Figure 6.3). Carnival's supposed profitability has been contested endlessly in the Trinidadian press, but there is a severe shortage of reliable economic data.

With the international popularization of soca music, interest in calypso is unlikely to support itself with revenue. At the annual Calypso Monarch Final in 2019, attendants in the grandstand were docile, well dressed, and almost

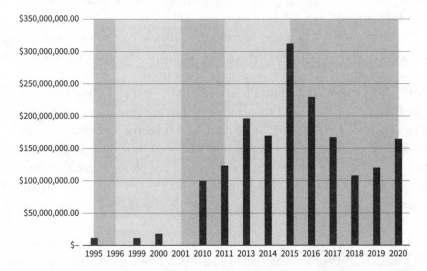

Figure 6.3 Government support for the National Carnival Commission in $TT between 1995 and 2020.

Note: This figure plots government expenditures in support of Carnival activities. Green shading denotes period when the PNM has been in government. Orange shading denotes when the UNC has been in government.

Sources: Raymond Ramcharitar, *A History of Creole Trinidad, 1956–2016* (New York: Palgrave, 2021); Raymond Ramcharitar, "The Carnival Bubble," *The Guardian*, February 8, 2017; Parliament of the Republic of Trinidad and Tobago, Divisions and Projects Financial Scrutiny Unit, "Head 62: Ministry of Community Development, Culture and the Arts," 2020, http://ttparliament.org/documents/2895. pdf; Trinidad and Tobago National Carnival Commission, "Unaudited Statement of Receipts and Payments for the Year Ended September 30, 2014," October 13, 2014, http://www.ncctt.org/new/ images/pdf/NCCs_Income_and_Expenditure_Statement_201314.pdf; Parliament of the Republic of Trinidad and Tobago, "Sixth Report of the Joint Select Committee on Ministries, Statutory Authorities and State Enterprises," 2014, ttparliament.org/reports/p10-20130308-s4-HOUS-R6.pdf.

exclusively Creole, and they filled less than half the space—not the conditions for the kind of political rebellion this art form once embodied. It had the feel of opera, the kind of historic art that survived off legend, philanthropy, and the interest of an ever-dwindling, moneyed audience.

Set against a backdrop painted with African masks and interludes of African percussion, the event was a unique mix of concert, church, and soapbox. Interestingly, government funding was a consistent theme in the lyrics. During the extemporaneous competition, one of the performers chastised the National Carnival commissioner Winston "Gypsy" Peters—a prominent calypsonian himself—for sinking the national economy and putting government funds "into his pocket." A finalist, Erphaan Alves, declared, "Culture is future," and demanded more government support for calypso and displayed an oversize government check for $500 million made payable to "Culture." In a Pollyannaish, pro-PNM calypso, Tobago Chalkie glossed over pressing social problems, poohpoohing corruption and a struggling economy, and chastised government "critics," particularly a former UNC member of Parliament, Devant Maharaj.

Maharaj, now out of office, remains an outspoken critic of Carnival, and a bigoted villain to calypsonians. Once Trinidad and Tobago's minister of transportation (2011–2013) and later the minister of agriculture (2013–2015), Maharaj entered public life as a talk radio host on a show bluntly titled *The Hindu View Point*, and then authored a newspaper column for *Trinidad Newsday* from 1998 to 2005. Since then, he has been a firebrand and a thorn in the side of PNM leaders. A few weeks before I interviewed him, Maharaj had just shared the prime minister's personal cell phone number on Twitter and urged citizens to call with complaints. At the time, he was a "person of interest" in a government investigation, while also suing the government to challenge sedition laws being used against him.

"Carnival is a myth," Maharaj told me at our meeting in a hotel lobby filled with visitors. "Try to book a ticket to go to Miami right now. There are as many Trinidadians who try to escape Carnival as stay. It's a myth that the Carnival community perpetuates on others. It is an urban [Creole] phenomenon that is forced onto rural [Indian-origin] communities. Good luck going to a beach; the born-again Christians have retreats for their flocks. The Muslims don't participate, and Carnival almost always coincides with [the Hindu holiday] Maha Shivaratri, and so the orthodox Hindus pack their temples. People will say it brings in millions, but that's anecdotal at best, and it's unclear what the cost is of closing down the country for a week."

"But is Carnival benefiting people more broadly—not financially but as a source of ritual and national identity?" I asked.

"But then, it is a national identity artificially created by the state."

"Aren't they all?"

"Well, some constructions are organic. And our state's funding, because of the oil price crisis, is short. I think there is cross-cultural participation, but not the kind of numbers that the government would like you to believe. They don't like to survey, but you'll see that one ethnic group dominates. . . . What you have playing out is Samuel Huntington's *Clash of Civilizations*, and what's fueling the Afro side is the resource of state when the PNM is in power."

"But when UNC was in power," I pointed out, "you tripled the Carnival funding." After the PNM increased the annual budget to over TT$100 million (US$15 million) in 2010, the UNC was the party that raised it to its 2015 peak.

Maharaj responded, "The UNC has the issue of, in order to validate their own national identity, they have to adopt the zeal of a new convert. They have to thump the Bible a little harder than the rest. To get by and have legitimacy as a truly national government, they have to do that. The PNM doesn't have to show their legitimacy with the Indos. It's not part of their worldview, reflective of their racial ideology. Because of how the boundaries were gerrymandered in the 1960s, they can win without Indian support.

"The UNC tried to establish not a Ministry of Culture but a Ministry of Multiculturalism. Unfortunately, it was run by [calypsonian] Gypsy Peters, and no matter how many entreaties we made, he never implemented them, and it continued to run monoculturally. You'd swear it runs as the Ministry of the Culture of Congo. It doesn't run with the diversity of the country in mind, with any semblance of equity in the distribution of funding. When you look at the media, there are about eight Indian radio stations, all privately owned. But you cannot have a single calypso private radio station running all year long. It is self-evident that the Indian community finances its own culture. Despite the disproportionate funding of Carnival, the Indian cultural expression survives without state funding virtually by itself.

"This all fits in the spectrum of Trinidadian history, when there was almost structural racism against Indians by the PNM government. For their first thirty years, they did not have a single Hindu minister. When Basdeo Panday was being sworn in as a minister in the 1980s with the NAR, they had to stop the ceremony to find a Hindu priest. I feel like Indians can't engage in a conversation on race because, as a result of slavery two hundred years ago, the Black man has a monopoly on victimhood, perpetuated by the plight of African Americans in the United States. It allows Afro-Trinidadians to be the aggressor.

"[Indians] did not advance in Trinidad because of special privileges," said Maharaj. "It's because of work, and thrift, and strength of families. My last ancestor arrived in 1910 and was assigned to a cocoa estate in Santa Cruz, and then to a sugar estate in Arouca. He later bought a lot of land from the estate. . . . I think the Indian psyche is that, if you give them a playing field, they have the arrogance and self-confidence to come ahead. They just don't have that here in terms of state largesse. The opposition will point to ethnic imbalances in lawyers, doctors, engineers, and university students, but it's not because of any state intervention. It's based on meritocracy. You're not given a pass because of the texture of your hair."

"Some Afro-Trinidadians say that Carnival is an expression of liberation," I said. "Isn't that something both Indians and Africans—in light of their shared experiences in slavery and indenture—can get around?"

"The vast majority of people don't associate it with freedom; they just want to have a good time," Maharaj insisted. "The intellectuals want to rationalize it. For the Africans, their culture began with the end of slavery. Their culture was beaten out of them. They were given European names and compelled to worship a white God. For Indians, despite the harshness of indentureship, it was by no means as painful as the oppression of slavery, and they were permitted to maintain the practices of their culture. My culture is six thousand years old. I don't have to look for it. The African is holding on to Carnival, and holding on to the political power it renders, because it's all they have."

Maha Sabha

As thousands of revelers celebrated in fêtes or prepared their costumes across the country on the night before Carnival Monday, the suburban village of Cunupia was quiet.

On Monroe Road, people gathered at the Maha Sabha orthodox Hindu temple to observe Shivaratri, a holiday dedicated to Shiva, one of the principal Hindu deities, that coincides with Carnival most years. Hundreds of pairs of shoes and sandals lined the colonnades wrapping around the rectangular building, which featured two steeples and ornate architectural moldings.

When I arrived, the temple was already completely full—about five hundred people, barefoot and dressed in the finest kurtas and saris, each vibrantly colorful, embroidered with gold thread and shimmering rhinestones. The women wore rich vermillion, fuchsia, purple, and turquoise, the men in elegant saffron, mustard, crimson, celestial blue, and white—all seated in golden chairs with red cushions.

The shrine's polished tile floors and walls of glazed wood reflected the light from a row of crystal chandeliers above a center aisle, softened by cream- and ivory-colored drapes hanging from perpendicular roof beams. Tropical palms and flowering bushes grew in pots flanking delicate water fountains in front of the temple's elevated stage. Pieces of fruit dangled from strings above—green apples, miniature bananas, bunches of black grapes, tomatoes, and okra. In the backdrop, idols of the Hindu gods Shiva, Parvati, and Hanuman looked onto a dizzying array of activity.

The congregation clapped in unison to a fifteen-piece orchestra of young musicians playing entrancing, intertwining melodies and percussion. Multiple rhythms beat from a long drum, a tambourine, a *dhantal* (a native Indo-Caribbean idiophone), and cymbals. A harmonium provided a sense of flowing continuity, while violinists, hand organists, and three female vocalists overlaid a graceful chorus. In front, congregants greeted luminaries and community elders, while children scurried along the aisle and stage. Pandit Navin, sitting cross-legged on an elevated mattress and wearing a pristine white kurta with a garland of white chrysanthemums, welcomed those in attendance. With its own music, lyrics, costumes, rituals, and spiritual leaders, another Carnival had begun.

During his sermon, the pandit acknowledged the pressures of a new era, but he expressed faith that there would be an "evolution" among Hindus.

"This is how our culture and how our traditions continue," he said, his head wobbling. "As a result, sometimes you have clashes. Their sense of thinking is different. Things that they're exposed to and what we're exposed to, totally different. . . . And so they seem to react against. The world is changing, the conditions are changing. . . . There must be a point of meeting."

But lest anyone think he was referring to relations with Afro-Trinidadians or those celebrating Carnival, the pandit made no mention of the imminent national holiday that closed all businesses for a four-day weekend. The "point of meeting" was actually to close the widening gap between older and younger Hindus, he said.

Mere miles away, the other Carnival—the centerpiece of Trinidad's culture, its national festival, Earl Lovelace's "religion"—was ignored in favor of another, competing set of rituals. There would be no "point of meeting" between these two cultures that night.

As if to drive this conclusion home, the pandit then acknowledged Sat Maharaj, the secretary-general of the Sanatan Dharmanan Maha Sabha, or Great Assembly of Eternal Knowledge, the main orthodox Hindu group in Trinidad.

The eighty-three-year-old Maharaj, who has no family relation to Devant, has provoked Creoles since he assumed the helm of the organization, which his father-in-law, Bhadase Maraj, founded, in 1977. When Basdeo Panday won

Trinidad's 1995 election, Maharaj quickly demanded that Parliament drop the Judeo-Christian "amen" from its opening prayer and abolish the Trinity Cross, named for the Holy Trinity, the highest national award. When Winston Dookeran was appointed governor of the Central Bank in 1997, Maharaj expressed delight that "a Hindu name will soon appear" on the Trinidadian dollar, even though Dookeran, while of Indian descent, is a Protestant. Maharaj once argued that the harmonium should be given equal stature with steel pans—the national musical instrument—in school musical instruction. He has also spoken out against interethnic marriage while pressing for Hindi—which many Indo-Trinidadians no longer speak—to be taught in all public secondary schools.[66] Since that time, he founded the Hindu-oriented Jaagriti radio station and an internet-based television network, which recorded his ancillary Shivaratri sermon.

Staying seated on a grand crimson and gold sofa in the front row, Maharaj was handed a cordless microphone:

"This is the best time of the year when you can witness the true diversity that exists in Trinidad and Tobago.

At this time, one section of the community, they are worshipers of Bacchus, the god of wine. In the Hindu community across the land, we are worshipers of Lord Shiva, the sustainer of the universe. What greater diversity can you find than this difference?

And we live happily together. While the ladies in the other section, who worship Bacchus, they strip almost naked and dance [in] the streets of the city, you look at our ladies here, they are the most beautifully dressed in any part of the Indian diaspora. Fully dressed, not to arouse the animal instinct in man.

You heard our pandit chanting verses from the scriptures to elevate the soul and to educate the mind. And yet you hear the same chants on the other side to arouse the animal instinct in you and they call it Carnival. We call it Shivaratri. This is the diversity that is Trinidad and Tobago.

At this point in time, we have almost one hundred fifty temples, more than calypso tents, where this worship is taking place. This is the diversity that is Trinidad and Tobago.

Tomorrow night, we'll have a twelve-hour vigil, from six in the evening until six in the morning. The other side of Trinidad and Tobago will have loud music, wining, and dining. This is the diversity that is Trinidad and Tobago.

More than that, people have the impression that that is the culture; the other side is the culture. In Trinidad and Tobago, we have a variety of cultures. And this is one of the strongest aspects in the culture and religion of Trinidad and Tobago. Some people believe that at this point, our country sees visitors coming in. If you go to Piarco Airport, you'll see hundreds of visitors coming in, but you'll see thousands of Trinidadians leaving to go, either to Canada to their family or to America. So you have a heavy traffic at Piarco Airport. That is the diversity of Trinidad and Tobago.

On Monday and Tuesday if you go to Port-of-Spain, you'll see thousands of people on the streets, worshippers of Bacchus. But if you go to our seashores, go to Mayaro, go to Tyrico, go to Maracas, and you'll see thousands of Trinidadians who don't want to worship Bacchus. They take their families to the beaches. So this is the diversity that is Trinidad and Tobago.

And I want to congratulate the Hindu community for bringing spirituality where there is devil worship."

Wanting to add something, Maharaj requested the microphone back. Expecting a more diplomatic corollary, I listened carefully for something conciliatory to dress up the brazenly divisive speech he just offered.

"On the diversity theme, if we didn't have Hindus in Trinidad to produce this kind of diversity, Trinidad and Tobago would have been another Haiti. You take that; that would have happened."

The pandit diplomatically thanked Maharaj: "So of course this is truly wonderful words of inspiration, and we indeed have to be very, very proud of our heritage, and our culture." An attendant then presented Maharaj with an elaborate gift basket to thank him for his leadership.

In an interview, I asked Maharaj why social relations must be so acrimonious.

"Because if I am representing one group, and that group is discriminated [against], I have a responsibility to speak out," he retorted combatively. "My constituency is Hindu. When the nation of Trinidad and Tobago is challenged, I stand for the nation. But inside, I fight for our space."

"But rather than transcend boundaries, the fighting reinforces them," I said.

"It is the nature of man to gravitate to those of your kind," Maharaj replied.

"Does that make it right?" I asked.

"I don't know," he said. "We are born differently, on different continents, at different times. And because of [economic] development, we are now integrated and the world has become narrow and small. The boundaries are collapsing around us."

This last statement is revealing.

Ostensibly, Maharaj's venomous address to the congregation cynically depicted Indo- and Afro-Trinidadians as living in parallel cultural universes, despite their close proximity on a small island. However, the way he portrayed their separation is as much about interethnic differences in Trinidad as it is about a deep schism within the Indo-Trinidadian community itself.

Maharaj's "boundaries" that long reinforced the construction of ethnic and religious purity are beginning to blur in Trinidad's modernity. And just as Creoles are concerned to own and control the cultural traditions they believe to be theirs, Indians are equally concerned to protect the sense of distinction that emerged with Indian and Hindu nationalism in the 1930s, when art and films cast Indians according to white European standards of respectability—the very concept of respectability that Carnival has historically contested.

Today, profound discomfort characterizes Hindu feelings about Creole intermarriage and Hindus' participation in Creole cultural habits. The differences Maharaj underscored consistently related to the role of women, audible in his references that contrasted women who "strip almost naked" with those who are "fully dressed," those that contrasted raw "animal instincts" with the purportedly asexual habits of "family," and those that contrasted religious "worship" with "wining"—a Caribbean phrase for a grinding dance duet of pelvic harmony. In so doing, Maharaj was not only signaling differences between Indians and Creoles; he was also condemning the thousands of Indians who indulge in such "national" culture.

Carnival has "emancipated" multiple generations of Indo-Trinidadian women over the decades. In the 1980s, Drupatee Ramgoonai, a popular Indian calypso singer, outraged Trinidad's Indian communities, who grumbled that she was prostituting herself by dancing on stage with Black men all around her. In the time since, a generation of Creole-Indian relationships has produced tens of thousands of mixed-race children that Trinidadians universally refer to as *douglas*—an only slightly disparaging Hindi word for "mixed." Every *dougla* is raised differently, but most identify more closely with Creoles, who self-identify as "mixed" themselves and typically embrace *douglas* more readily than Hindu communities. Many Creoles proudly tout their Amerindian, European, or Chinese genes. "That's not who we are," Maharaj implied.

After the Maha Sabha service, I asked a variety of young adults whether they planned to attend Carnival festivities or knew of anyone who managed to integrate Carnival participation into a life of devout Hinduism. Most were loath to acknowledge any such engagement inside the temple and within earshot of their families.

However, Jannessa Kalloo, a thirty-five-year-old, self-employed congregant, told me, "I have a friend who dresses the *murtis* [idols] who will play mas', but he doesn't want the pandit to know. You feel like everybody is doing it. It's the national culture, and so if you choose God, you're weird. I've lost friends because I don't participate. It's trendy, and they judge me, like I'm two steps from God. In Trinidad, they have Carnival jumpers [parties] at the schools. A lot of people try to integrate Carnival into every part of life. It's almost as if they're creating the illusion that Carnival is a religion. If Maha Shivaratri is observed for seven nights, Carnival is observed with two months of alcohol, partying, and nudity. It's so influential that it causes people to blindly follow the songs and videos."

After a brief pause, she added, "And I don't think it is a coincidence that, almost every year, Carnival falls on the same date as Shivaratri."

In fact, it is indeed a total coincidence. Both are tied to the lunar calendar, so the two holidays are linked by astronomical phenomena, not a government conspiracy to divide their society. However, it was not my place to correct her. "Can you be both a Hindu and Carnival participant?" I asked.

"If someone is trying to play mas', they haven't taken the time to understand their religion. If you understand just one scripture—not even all of them—you'd pull away from some people. I'm not judging anybody, but don't be a convenient Hindu; be a complete Hindu. Surrender yourself to God."

This mutual exclusivity of these dueling gods—present in the words of leaders like Maharaj but also the PNM minister Gadsby-Dolly—suggests that even the most innocuous foray into Creole culture corrupts the Hindu and that any acknowledgment of Indo-Trinidadians' struggle cheapens one's appreciation of the Afro-Trinidadian condition. Together, these forces undercut the development of a more universal Trinidadian identity—the kind that may loosen the shackles of colonialism and transcend the boundaries it created.

But in his angst, Maharaj also hinted at the enormous extent to which Indian and Creole rituals *are* mixing. And together, they coexist, co-influence, and co-create.

Carnival as Power

The steel pan is unquestionably Afro-Trinidadian in origin. It emerged from the streets of Port of Spain where young Creole men began beating frying pans, biscuit tin lids, and oil drums after colonial authorities banned the percussion from drums and bamboo sticks. In the late 1930s, one such youth realized that dents in the oil drums produced different tones from the same piece of metal. By 1950, equipped with pans that produced thirty-two distinct tones, ensembles were drumming everything from classical music to calypso. Pan bands attracted groups of accompanying revelers and fueled rivalries between neighborhoods in Port of Spain, often resulting in street fights that alarmed upper-class society and earned great notoriety.

But today, pan crosses social boundaries more than all the other Carnival arts. While even Trinidad's biggest bands remain amateur, they grew larger than their neighborhoods' toughest hooligans and now incorporate a broad spectrum of members and supporters—Indo-Trinidadians, women, children, foreigners. Since Prime Minister Manning declared pan to be Trinidad's national musical instrument on Emancipation Day in 1992—in no small part, an act of cultural reclamation itself—it has become part of the mandatory national music curriculum taught in public schools and Hindu academies alike. Even Hindu temples often incorporate pan into their orchestras.

Pan bands could never be too particular, anyway. The large-form groups require 120 highly trained musicians who memorize all the song notes and rely on an army of people to contribute money and sweat to assemble, decorate, and maneuver the unwieldy apparatuses. The pans are typically attached to metal scaffolding with wheels for creaky portability and, in case of rain, a roof adorned with colorful flags and frilly bunting. The bands' practice sessions are freely accessible to members of the public who visit their "yards," where drinks and food are sold from stalls. Much in the way baseball fans attend their team's spring training games, pan groupies like to "lime" in the yards and watch the assembly of each year's performance unfold over a beer.

The most devoted fans accompany the band to the Queen's Park Savannah on the day of the Panorama Final—Trinidad's largest pan competition—on Carnival's last weekend. The bands line up in a holding area surrounded by scores of tents, selling a variety of drinks, fried chicken, fried fish, corn soup, rotis, and doubles, an Indo-Trinidadian street food dish of curried chickpeas in fried flatbread. On the Savannah, they rehearse, tune the drums, and engage the thousands of people enjoying the free recitals until it's their turn to perform.

In advance of their stage time, the drummers and their hangers-on push the orchestra's heavy scaffolding across the dry grass toward the grandstand and up its ramp. Along the five hundred meters between the holding area and the ramp, the drummers and groupies avoid discarded Carib beer bottles and fried chicken cartons. Once on stage, they place wooden wedges under the wheels to hold them in place, and then scurry off in front of thousands of spectators.

What follows is an utter tour de force:120 uniformed, and therefore undifferentiated, drummers dancing and playing in perfect synchronization. The bands require immense solidarity, coordination, and discipline. The song compositions, which feature multiple strings of melody and overlapping beats, risk cacophony if the drummers are not in true harmony. For further flair, the bands are often accompanied by people waving flags, toting banners, or dancing choreographed numbers. Each elaborate performance is also accentuated by a dizzying array of strobe lights, flame plumes, confetti, and firework displays. In front, the arranger uses animated gestures to conduct the layered beats.

While members are not obligated to be local to the bands' original neighborhoods, they often are anyway. Desperadoes is a popular band from Laventille, an infamous slum on a hill overlooking Port of Spain, where pan is thought to have been invented; it is also the setting for Lovelace's *The Dragon Can't Dance*. Because of high crime in that neighborhood, however, the band can no longer practice there and recently moved to a yard on Charlotte Street downtown. The band is also featured in Derek Walcott's poem "The Spoiler's Return": "Tell Desperadoes when you reach the Hill / I decompose, but I composing still."

An Afro-Trinidadian invention, pan's broader adoption reveals Carnival culture's capacity to be truly national. Two of Trinidad's most legendary composers, also known as "arrangers," were of Indian origin, Jit Samaroo and Lennox "Bobby" Mohammed, the youngest arranger ever to win a Panorama title. The world-class sitarist Mungal Patasar also undertook a collaboration with pan drummers to found a new genre he called "pantar."

Kim Johnson, the director of the Carnival Institute who is of mixed African, European, and Chinese descent, is perhaps the world's leading steel pan promoter. In 2015, he wrote *Pan: A Music Odyssey*, a feature-length docudrama about the invention and evolution of the steel pan. He says that most of the large bands are predominantly of African origin but that everyone else is readily accepted regardless of race, class, religion, nationality, education, gender, or age.

"Afro-Trinidadians claimed pan tightly from the onset," he said. "They have always claimed it very tightly. One of the first acts the PNM government took in January 1956 was to make it a government matter with the creation of the Carnival Development Committee and the definition of national culture as carnival, calypso. and steel pan.

"When they say that Carnival is Afro-Trinidadian," Johnson continued, "they're talking about the passion and deep emotional commitment. If you were in prison for twenty years and freed, you wouldn't celebrate running down the street yelling, 'I'm free!' You would eat a hamburger or get a prostitute. The slaves wanted to do what they couldn't do before. Africans tended to celebrate when they could practice their African art forms, and those were music of groups and gangs, antiphonal drums, costuming, and dance. They also went for large hierarchical organizations. The Africans chose kings, princesses, and military titles in slavery. So in a sense, the Carnival did represent something far deeper and more spiritual to Afro-Trinidadians than to other groups, for whom it was nationalism and fancy dress.

"That conflict with the upper classes fueled the Carnival, and in a strange ironic way, it continues to benefit the Carnival. It remains a moment of excess and outrage. . . . The Trinidadian idea of reality is that the veneer of respectability is just a façade. The real reality of social relations is bacchanal—confusion, mainly of a financial or sexual nature.

"The PNM's use of Carnival is a lot less idealistic today than it was fifty years ago. Fifty years ago, Carnival was the national festival and the Carnival arts—calypso and steel pan—were the national art forms. Now, a lot of it is peripheral to the arts. The majority of young people are not interested in calypso and pan; they don't see it as representing the soul of Trinidad and Tobago anymore. It's something that [PNM politicians] use politically. Privately, they will admit that it's not what it was. I don't think they believe in its importance deeply. They see it as a tourism product rather than an expression of our soul.

"Carnival has infected other festivals in Trinidad, so that a lot of them have been carnivalized. Carnival is a public festival and one of innovation in the streets. Christmas was historically the antithesis—one of traditionalism and domesticity, with returning family. Today, the beer companies sell more beer at Christmas because the Indians participate equally. Traditional Christmas music, *parang*, now is dominated by *soca parang*, with as much smut and sexual innuendo as anything religious."

"Are you saying that Carnival lost value precisely because it tried to become more inclusive, more national?" I asked.

"It lost its value because intrinsically it has lost its value," Johnson said. "American music is rooted in the blues, but if B. B. King were to have a concert, it would mostly be white people there. Young Black people only care about hip-hop. Jazz is on the brink of starvation, even if it is at the heart of the American psyche. It's not that white people became involved; jazz became intellectual and abstract, and it could no longer be used to seduce women at a party. I can't lay that at the door of white people."

He paused for a beat.

"What happens at the popular level is not necessarily what the politicians are lobbying for. Indians may rally for traditionalism, but at the ground level, Indians are going to school and living next to Black and mixed people. Around election time, they become more Indian, but otherwise they become more Trinidadian. These things are complex and always in flux and related to internal conflicts across and within the groups. There has always been a desire to create some sort of Trinidadian national definition of itself, but that has tended to be dominated by Blacks. So Indians will say that this idea of 'national' is not national at all. And that has tended to be true. But you also have to place Trinidad in a wider Caribbean context.

"The PNM is a very conservative party, much more so than the Indian party. It's also manifest in the idea that, when a white philosopher speaks about man, he or she attempts to speak for all of humanity, but he's really just speaking for white middle-class sensibility. It's not deliberate; it's just how they think. The PNM is the same in its concepts of national culture. I don't think it's a deliberate attempt to exclude Indians; it's implicit. They are positioning Trinidad and Tobago in a wider Black civilizational culture."

"What about for the UNC?" I asked.

"For the UNC, Carnival is a political vehicle as well. One of the earliest UNC governments, they had to give more money to poor Blacks than poor Indians. It was the exigencies of Trinidadian politics. They have to show that they are 'Trinidad' and not racist, and more stridently than the PNM does. A practical example: I made my film on pan when the Indian government was in power. We got most of our funding [US$1 million] from the Indian government, and I'm certain I never would have gotten it from the PNM. [The Indians] have to prove it."

"Why doesn't the PNM have to prove that they are a party for all?" I asked.

"They are the party of our independence, nationalism, anticolonialism, and they rest on their laurels. And those are powerful laurels that they can still rest on," Johnson said. "Trinidadians are very given to hyperbole and will throw the 'racist' label at each other, but there has never been a lynching or any of that. . . . You have to put the racial politics into context. Race is gamesmanship, and a kind of naïveté. 'Racist' equates people with racists in Johannesburg or Atlanta. You have to take it with a grain of salt."

"And people do?" I asked.

"No. They live a bifurcated life. [They are susceptible] around election time, but the rest of their lives, they are more accepting [of] their school friends and lovers. That doesn't mean it's hunky-dory. There are still vestiges of colonialism; it has continued with modern means. But it's thoughtless. It's a neurosis; not a psychosis.

"I think the exclusively Afro-Trinidadian view is wrong, but that is the political and population's view of Carnival's role. It does involve the contribution of all ethnic groups. . . . I think it is Carnival's ability to incorporate different groups that has made it so protean and adaptable to other environments. Even though it is not as large as Rio's, somehow it has been able to spawn more other Carnivals all over the world—precisely because it is not exclusively

African. . . . The steel pan, for example, uses the chromatic scale developed in Europe. . . . The true approach sees how Carnival has grown by embracing, but that's not a politically accepted point of view."

Chutney Soca

With chutney soca, Carnival has grown, but not necessarily by embracing.

In 1987, Drupatee Ramgoonai's debut album, *Chutney Soca*, blended Indian musical instruments with soca beats and bawdy Carnival eroticism, and Indo-Trinidadian culture was never the same. Through the 1970s, "chutney" had been a popular Indo-Caribbean music genre emerging from Bhojpuri-derived songs by women accompanied by *dholak* (a small two-headed barrel drum), *chac-chac*, *dhantal*, harmonium, synthesizers, and drum machine.[67] Ramgoonai's innovation blended Indian-oriented orchestration and melodic contours with a soca-like groove to gain enormous popularity.

Before this, Indians' Carnival activities took place very much inside an "indigenous" Creole framework; they participated but were alienated from the Carnival itself. Indeed, Prime Minister Williams once referred to Indians as mere "transients." The move of chutney soca into the calypso space climaxed during the 1995–1996 Carnival season—karmically, the 150th anniversary of Indians' arrival in Trinidad. In December 1995, Creole calypsonian Scrunter won the soca-parang competition with a chutney-style tune, "Chutkaipang." The following month, private impresarios staged a massive Chutney Soca Monarch Competition, which drew over fifteen thousand people, prizes as large as those of the Calypso Monarch awards, and established chutney soca as a fixture of the Carnival season.[68] The 1996 Carnival socas included several chutney socas by Creoles, but none bigger than Indo-Trinidadian Sonny Mann's "Lotay La," which broke records for cassette sales. While "Lotay La" was popular with non-Indians, election-inspired ethnic tension was not far beneath the surface when he was pelted with cans and bottles by a predominantly Black audience at the Soca Monarch Final.[69] Still, chutney soca symbolized the cultural arrival of Indians at the same time as their political arrival.

Chutney soca was the canary in Trinidad's cultural coal mine. Many in the Indian-origin community were not pleased about the way these new art forms gave their young people entrée into the Trinidadian mainstream. For all their complaints about their marginalization on Trinidad's cultural fringe, their sudden integration raised even bigger questions. Observers noted the way that women "outshine" the men in their enjoyment of the dance, a sort of "hypnotic frenzy":

When the music stops, it is almost as if the trance-like state is ended. The audience participants part company unceremoniously, sometimes not even uttering a word to their respective "partners," and move back to their group or their seats. In this popular village-type theatrical event the vulgar becomes natural and the obscene, joyous. It is anti-authoritarian, anti-pretence and anti-traditional for it has come out from behind the purdah (curtain) unto the proscenium stage with all this raw sexuality, banality, and bacchanalia. Can you recognize the similarity of this chutney music to calypso and soca in carnival? They are literally the same.[70]

This flouting of the social inhibitions previously restricting Indian dance, and its recontextualization as a form of public culture among women and men, was dramatically new and led to backlash by Indo-Trinidadians and Creoles alike.[71] Especially in the context of Panday's election, Indo-Trinidadians' entry into mainstream Carnival arts mobilized many Creoles to reclaim these arts more tightly. Chutney soca, and the interethnic exchange it symbolized, was not for everybody.

Jahaji Bhai

Each year, Carnival starts with a rite of passage on Monday: J'ouvert, short for *jou ouvè*, but pronounced "JOO-vay," the Creole French word for "daybreak." And like any rite of passage, it equalizes all.

Participants preregister with one of dozens of groups or bands and meet at about 3:30 in the morning for a slow saunter through Port of Spain. Derived from a coterie of artists and writers, my band, Friends for the Road, broadened its ranks to include a number of ex-pats, diplomats, and middle-class professionals who were of mixed races, gay and heterosexual, young and old, male and female—a cross-section of the world, even if not a cross-section of Trinidad.

The band arranged an accompanying convoy of flatbed trucks, subcontracted from logistics companies, each laden with the essential materials: dozens of six-foot speakers, subwoofers, and a full bar stocked with white rum, dark rum, cognac, and mixers. A "Rhythm Section" occupied the front flatbed and beat African percussion, while a deejay spun the latest Carnival soca at levels that shook the trees around the Queen's Park Savannah. It is a roaming caravan—a feast, not as much movable as it is just moving—along a designated route. Rather than walking the route from Wildflower Park in St. Clair and around the Savannah, participants danced the entire way.

Multiple people wheeled around bathtubs and cannisters of mud, which participants slap onto each other's faces. They then dusted each other with the colorful paint powder characteristic of Hindu Holi celebrations. In between, they photograph, kiss, wine, urinate, and solicit frequent top-offs from the rolling bar truck. While many of the revelers arrive with friends, it is impossible to stay among them and not disperse among the mobilized chaos of dancing, drinking, and pounding bass. By sunrise, it is nearly impossible to tell people apart underneath caking layers of mud and pink, red, blue, and yellow paint.

One cannot fully understand Carnival without joining a band for J'ouvert and marching down the streets surrounding the Savannah. Soca's pounding beat and universally catchy choruses drive drunk, exhausted people together and onward. There is nothing subtle or layered. Stripped of any respectability and any of the markers that signal race, class, or origins, the universal feeling was "We are all somehow one, and the city is ours."

This is the healing sentiment captured in one of the most famous calypsos ever recorded, and in impeccable irony, it placed second after Cro Cro's divisive scolding in the 1996 Calypso Monarch Final. The song is "Jahaji Bhai, Brotherhood of the Boat" by Brother Marvin, a *dougla* musician. A humanitarian appeal, its lyrics leverage the experiences of his mixed-race lineage to identify the common struggle that Indians and Creoles share and urge "love for one another" in a unified Trinidadian identity:

Jahaji Bhai, Brotherhood of the Boat (1995), by Brother Marvin

I am the seed of meh father
He is the seed of meh grandfather
Who is the seed of Bahut Ajah [great-grandfather]
He came from Calcutta
Ah stick and ah bag on he shoulder
He turban and he kapra
So I am part seed of India.

The indentureship and the slavery
Bind together two races in unity
Achcha dosti [good friend]
There was no more Mother Africa
No more Mother India, just Mother Trini

Janmabhoomi [my home]
My Bahut Ajah planted sugarcane
Down in the Caroni plain
So Ramlogan, Basdeo, Prakash and I
Is Jahaji Bhai
Brotherhood of the boat, Jahaji Bhai
Brotherhood of the boat, Jahaji Bhai

I would be ah disgrace to Allah
If I choose race, creed or colour
Bahut Ajah had to make that journey
For I to have Zindagee [life]
So it is ah great privilege
To have such unique heritage
Fifty percent Africa, fifty percent India

I have "do chuttee" [two holidays]
Emancipation and Arrival Day
Aant bhala so bhala
Since Fatel Rozack made the journey
150 years gone already
Bahut achcha . . . [very good]
Whether you're Hindu, Muslim or Christian
Let's walk this land hand in hand
We could only prosper if we try
As Jahaji Bhai
Brotherhood of the boat, Jahaji Bhai
Brotherhood of the boat, Jahaji Bhai . . .

Chal tahalna ek matt [let's stroll together]
Agal bagal [side by side]. . . .

For those who playing ignorant
Talking bout true African descendant
If yuh want to know de truth
Take ah trip back to yuh roots
And somewhere on that journey
Yuh go see ah man in ah dhoti
Saying he prayers in front of ah jhandi

Then and only then you'll understand
What is ah cosmopolitan nation
Haat melawo [let's join hands]
There's no room for prejudice at all
United we stand, divided we'll fall
Bete baat ko garro [child, pay heed to what I'm saying]
So to all races here in Trinbago
Aapko kalyan ho dhaniaho [may you be blessed, may you prosper]
Let us live as one under the sky
As Jahaji Bhai
Brotherhood of the boat, Jahaji Bhai
Brotherhood of the boat, Jahaji Bhai

Indo and Afro Trinibagonian,
We should learn to be one
Our Ancestors came by boat,
is the salt water in yuh throat

Great grand pa and grand mama
One was ah slave and one was indentured
But the religion or color
Didn't interfere with their love for one another [nahe nahe]
I am the proof of racial unity
And that is the way everybody should be [Achcha sante]
Everybody should have the tone in their prayer
Let show each other we care
As we all know

Jahaji Bhai
Brotherhood of the boat, Jahaji Bhai
Brotherhood of the boat, Jahaji Bhai

Instantly, "Jahaji Bhai" became an anthem and common refrain in Trinidad. And Brother Marvin, an embodiment of Trinidad's cultural geography, was immune to accusations about the reappropriation of Indian or Creole culture by the respective orthodoxies.

Carnival ought to have the same kind of immunity. Rich with human symbolism and subject to divergent, irreconcilable interpretations, Trinidad's annual festival remains the same cauldron of cultural alchemy it was in the eighteenth century. Its masquerade invites position-taking by all sides balancing their desire for the familiar (ethnonationalism) and the forbidden (the other). In inviting excess and outrage, it also continues to invite deep introspection. The assembly of all its masks is a representation of who Trinidad is and, more accurately, who it wants to be.

However, like any institution and any country, its form is conditional on its composition. And so long as many Indo-Trinidadians perceive Carnival to be unwelcoming or dismiss it as a foreign ritual of empty hedonism, and as long as Creoles are concerned to righteously proclaim their inheritance and guard its gates of entry, Carnival cannot claim to truly represent the essence of Trinidad any more than when it was just a group of powdered planters waltzing in a ballroom. If Trinidad is ever to transcend the social boundaries that divide it, Carnival must be its communion.

The Stage

It is telling that Carnival was ultimately invigorated by the ascendance of a predominantly Indian-origin government in 1995—the political manifestation of Trinidad and Tobago's majority minority milestone. As I discuss in chapter 2, national identity is easiest to assert when it is defined against some threatening Other. However, this reinvigoration also reveals something about culture: it is enlivened by contestation. For too long, Carnival was in a stagnant, internal conversation among Afro-Trinidadians and its participants were preaching to the proverbial choir. The legacy of British colonialism and the European plantocracy had long faded; the conventional targets of the calypsonians had left the islands. It is also at this moment of contestation that greater Indo-Trinidadian influences began participating in the music and national pageantry.

Though this contestation is an expression of the social relations that historically split Trinidad and Tobago's Indian- and African-origin communities, it is also characteristic of a healthy public arena where these constituencies are equally represented. This stands in brutal contrast to Bahrain and Singapore, where such contestation is, respectively, ignored or not permitted. There is no such arena. There is no such stage. Trinidad's cultural leaders are constantly playing to a crowd to lay their claim to an evolving nation. In Bahrain, the only crowd that matters is the royal court and, in Singapore, crowds are prohibited from gathering. Unsurprisingly, and by design, their nations have not evolved much.

Democracies make such contestation possible, but they are also prone to the centrifugal forces that have paralyzed social progress in Trinidad and Tobago and are beginning to make diversifying countries like the United States un-governable. First, entrepreneurial political candidates and officials begin to leverage latent racial tension to build constituencies and win elections. Racial tension produces more racial tension, as more political choices are explained or defined in terms of identity differences. Parties then become racialized, which drives the creation of racialized electoral boundaries, which makes the parties more exclusively subject to a single racial constituency and spills over into civil society and broader associational life. Eventually, it seems all decisions are viewed through the lens of identity differences, and even the most trivial debates are proxy battles in a war for cultural supremacy.

If democracies make such contestation possible, though, they also make evolution possible. Beneath the boundary-patrolling rhetoric of politicians like Devant Maharaj and Nyan Gadsby-Dolly, Trinidadians are transgressing the lines of Creole and Indo-Trinidadian identity in small but meaningful ways. Creoles frequent roti and double shops, Indo-Trinidadians are emerging soca stars, pan and cricket are for everyone, intermarriage continues to grow. If such trends continue, there will come a time when there will be less of a market for politicians who leverage racial differences for electoral gain, when exclusive constructions of Trinidadian identity will ring hollow. Indeed, in the words of Gadsby-Dolly herself, "both pure races are losing to the mixed races." Their loss will be Trinidad's gain.

7

Where We Belong

Maroon Villages and National Memory in Mauritius

Le Morne Brabant is a breathtakingly stark mountain peninsula on Mauritius's southwestern extreme. Nearly two thousand feet high, its sheer cliffs are multicolored—red, orange, tan, and blond in the sun's changing light. Toward the summit, green springs from the many albizia trees. Beginning in the seventeenth century, maroons—fugitive slaves who escaped the island's sugar plantations—occupied six rock shelters on the summit, inaccessible except by the most advanced climbers and largely hidden from the coastline below. According to popular legend, a group of maroons inside this inviolable refuge in 1835 spied a battalion of soldiers approaching their position. As the story goes, unbeknownst to the fugitives, the soldiers had come to inform them of their emancipation and exculpation. With dramatic irony, the maroons feared recapture and leaped from the precipice to their deaths rather than relinquish their freedom. This story is held dearly not only by the African Creole people of the adjacent village of Le Morne but also by all those who see themselves as the descendants of Mauritius's slaves.[1] It crystallizes the defiance of the African Creoles' identity, placing them in opposition not only to colonial oppressors but also, more subtly, to Indian indentured servants who distinctly accepted their coercion by the British in return for small parcels of land. It renders the African Creole identity a fundamental purity of principle that contrasts with the morally compromised instrumentalism of others and roots them in the wilderness that once provided them with shelter. This is the kind of evocative story that forms a nation. But for African Creoles in Mauritius, theirs is a nation that was never realized—a community that remains undefined.

A Freedom Never Felt

Africans accounted for at least three-quarters of Mauritius's population until the 1820s, but there is precious little information about most aspects of their

Majority Minority. Justin Gest, Oxford University Press. © Justin Gest 2022. DOI: 10.1093/oso/9780197641798.003.0007

lives. Africans first arrived on Mauritius in 1641 as Malagasy slaves imported by Dutch colonists who had settled land on the hitherto uninhabited island east of Madagascar. The first permanent human inhabitants were the slaves who had escaped the Dutch and were left behind when colonists abandoned Mauritius in 1710. The Dutch lacked the manpower to police the slaves, many of whom established maroon settlements in Mauritius's woodlands, where they were able to live unmolested. These maroons then inherited the island until French colonizers arrived five years later and renamed the island Île de France. French planters cleared vast expanses of the verdant rain forests and palm savannahs to bring almost the entire island under sugar cultivation by the end of the eighteenth century.[2] After 1722, maroons operated either in isolation or in small bands that were forced to find refuge in areas that are even now almost entirely inaccessible—on the remotest mountaintops, in secluded rock shelters, and in underground lava tunnels—or pass as freemen in the burgeoning port town of Port Louis.[3]

During ninety years of colonization, the French imported tens of thousands of slaves from different regions around the Indian Ocean's rim. They came

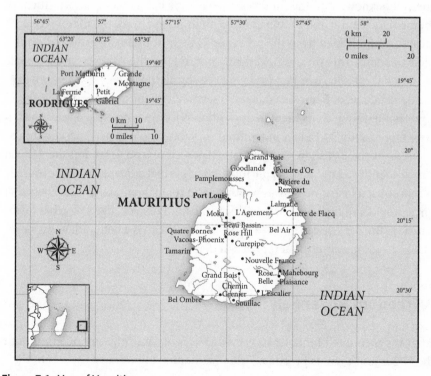

Figure 7.1 Map of Mauritius.

from Mozambique, Ghana, Madagascar, the Comoros, the Seychelles, Réunion, India, China, Java, Malaysia, and eventually West Africa. By the end of the eighteenth century, there were more than sixty thousand slaves in Mauritius, tending to the fields and providing domestic, manufacturing, construction, and maritime labor. The National Assembly's 1793 decree abolishing slavery throughout the French Empire was ignored in Mauritius, and the slave trade continued unabated; another thirty-five thousand slaves landed in the Mascarenes region before British occupation brought an end to the legal slave trade in 1810.[4] To placate the restive French planters now operating under the British flag, the first British governor recommended that Mauritius be exempted from the 1807 ban, a request that the secretary of state for the colonies promptly denied. Within months of his decision, the island became notorious as the center of an illicit trade that brought over thirty thousand more slaves by the mid-1820s.[5] By 1830, Mauritius had the third-biggest slave population in the British Empire, exceeded only by Jamaica and Barbados and nearly double that of the Cape Colony.[6]

When the British government emancipated slaves in 1834, Mauritius was the first colony to recruit indentured laborers from India. The seventy-five indentured laborers who arrived that year proved to be the vanguard of more than 451,000 men, women, and children who reached the island before the program came formally to an end in 1910; more than 294,000 of these immigrants remained permanently in Mauritius, where their presence rapidly transformed the colony's social and economic landscape.[7] In 1846, just twelve years after the end of slavery, Indians comprised more than 35 percent of Mauritius's total population, and by 1861, they made up 62 percent of the colony's residents—a percentage that has remained relatively constant to the present day.[8] Within a generation of their liberation from bondage, Mauritius's African Creoles were outnumbered before they ever had an opportunity to claim nationhood—let alone self-determination—on the only land they had ever known.

This simultaneous sense of indigeneity and marginality also consumes the populations of many countries today where diverse immigrants are projected to soon outnumber historic ethnic majorities. But unlike natives elsewhere who have lost their numerical advantage in a territory they still inhabit, Mauritius's African Creoles long for a land that was barely ever their own, a majority that never held power—a freedom they have never felt. As a result, their circumstances are worth understanding because they exhibit the power of nostalgia even in the absence of historical reference points. What does this yearning tell us about the nature of nationalism in a multiethnic setting?

This chapter begins by examining the segregated history of social relations in Mauritius: first, of African Creoles and their descendants; second, of Indian immigrants and their descendants; third, in the postindependence era when these two groups began to interact in an open public sphere of the so-called Rainbow Nation. In the aftermath of what has been termed the "Creole malaise," I explore the way Creole identity is understood and constructed in the modern-day sites of two maroon villages, Le Morne and Chamarel—rare symbols of Creole self-determination in an Indian-dominated country. Much like the maroons who preceded them and briefly inhaled the sweet scent of sovereignty, today's Creole population is still trying to understand who they are and carve out a corner of their island where they belong.

Grand Marronage

The defiance of Mauritius's earliest slaves who evaded Dutch colonists grew into a legacy among future generations in what became known as the Maroon Republic. Some would run away from their plantations for a short period of days or weeks and then return—a strategy of resistance referred to as *petit marronage*. Less prevalent but far more powerfully, others would permanently remove themselves from the fields in an individual's surreptitious act or a plantation-wide breakout, called *grand marronage*. Even after the French government cleared the jungle that shrouded the earliest maroon settlements and created maroon-hunting units that systematically sought out their havens, 11 to 13 percent of Mauritius's slaves would still escape in any given year.[9]

Almost immediately after taking control of Île de France, French governors were confronted with the problems of *marronage*. In 1722, only a year after the French arrived, runaway slaves occupied a military post in the district of Savanne after expelling the soldiers; in 1732, they took possession of the military post in Flacq, forcing the colonists to abandon the whole district.[10] In 1724, Governor Denis De Nyon complained about the maroons and asked that a number of Africans from Bourbon Island be sent to help fight them. By 1735, Governor Bertrand-François Mahé de La Bourdonnais armed and trained his own loyal "slave catchers" and set up an organization of twenty-four men with distinctive uniforms and a well-defined command structure to become Black maroon hunters.[11] Military posts were established to protect French settlers, and throughout the eighteenth century rewards were given to anyone who captured a maroon, dead or alive. The "Maroon Detachment" was required to present the right wrist of the maroon and a written statement from their supervisor certifying the capture. Heads were also cut off and exhibited in a public place. Hands were buried either at the cemetery of Port Louis or in the slave cemetery.[12]

While maroonage was detrimental to the plantation economy, officials were equally concerned about the threat maroon communities posed to the viability of colonial governance. Colonialism not only exploited Africans for their labor; it also sought to disconnect them from their native traditions, religions, and norms. Colonizers Christianized their slaves, who intermingled their residual cultures with European norms to produce a Creole ethic. Maroons evaded the field labor, but also this cultural tyranny. In Jamaica, the establishment and successful maintenance of fugitive slave communities in the Cockpit country eventually left colonial authorities with no other option but to recognize the maroons as a separate community within the local body politic and to negotiate formal treaties in 1739 clarifying their status and position in Jamaican society.[13]

Mauritian maroon communities, however, never achieved such status. Archival and archaeological accounts suggest that their existence was basic and unstable. District registers and police records show that desertions lasted anywhere from twenty-four hours to decades,[14] but nearly all were eventually caught as part of a persistent, cyclical struggle of escape, rebellion, recapture, and again escape. While free, maroons lived in communities that staged fierce and elaborate raids that pillaged and set fire to plantations, sometimes murdering their authorities with weapons made from small pieces of metal they collected.[15] One band reportedly sent an innocuous-looking woman named Antigone to scout out sites by day, pretending to look for information while assessing the suitability of the site for an eventual attack at night.[16] These raids were not merely vengeful; they provided the means of survival. Archaeological digs from Trois Cavernes in Plaine St. Piérre suggest that maroons "eked out an impoverished existence for a limited period of time."[17] In the system of circuitous caves, scientists found an abundance of animal bones and charcoal but few other artifacts like ceramics and metal tools. This suggests a band of people exploiting domesticated animals, trapping, and hunting whatever was available at a given time—heavily dependent on the location of the nearest plantation.[18] In the face of such desperation, the persistence of maroonage led many observers of eighteenth-century Mauritian life to attribute it to Africans'—rather than humans'—continuing "love of liberty."[19]

Alas, French planters' love of forced labor was as strong as Africans' love of liberty. The magnitude of the clandestine slave trade led English abolitionists to charge that local officials had actively thwarted attempts to suppress it, charges that culminated in the appointment of the Commission of Eastern Inquiry to investigate.[20] Already exempted from the French prohibition and then under pressure from the new British government and local abolitionists, planters began to consider alternative labor sources in the early nineteenth century.

When slavery finally ended on February 1, 1835—later than elsewhere in the British Empire—planters established a new "apprentice" system under which the ex-slave "praedials" were required to work without pay at the rate of seven and a half hours a day for a total of forty-five hours a week, Sundays and holidays excepted, in exchange for food rations or land for cultivation.[21] Strict, unfavorable ordinances governed apprentices' labor, and nearly 8 percent of the apprentice population was apprehended for desertion in each of its first years of enactment. In anticipation, Governor Sir William Nicolay sent a dispatch to London on the eve of abolition that included a copy of an ordinance that amended, rather than abolished, the laws relating to runaway slaves.[22] Once the apprenticeship system was terminated in 1839, Nicolay reported that "a great number of the large sugar estates had been almost wholly abandoned by the former ex-slaves," attributable to their "predilection for establishing themselves in particular parts" of Mauritius, "owing to their comparative local advantages over others."[23]

Any such advantages may have related to the growing presence of *gens de couleur*, free people of Black or mixed racial heritage who even today occupy an intermediate socioeconomic position between the European and African Creole communities. Between 1806 and 1825, Mauritius's free population of color doubled in size to more than fourteen thousand, or 17 percent of the island's total population. By 1830, 18,109 *gens de couleur* accounted for two-thirds of the island's nonslave inhabitants and a fifth of its total population.[24] Granted the right to vote in 1790 but residentially segregated in urban regions,[25] *gens de couleur* remained marginal in Mauritian society until the 1830s. They tended to earn their living in the service sector as bootmakers, hatmakers, seamstresses, servants, and wigmakers, and owned small one-room *cazes* and precious little land, if any at all.[26] In 1806, after almost forty years of active involvement in the public and private real estate markets, free colored holdings amounted to only 7.1 percent of all inventoried land, and almost 30 percent of Port Louis's free colored households owned no taxable property.[27]

As their resources grew, however modestly, the *gens de couleur* emerged as passionate abolitionists.[28] They pressured the Colonial Office to repeatedly strike down vagrancy ordinances designed to force ex-slaves to sign labor contracts.[29] They also frustrated planters' attempts to drive their former apprentices back onto the sugar estates by offering new freedmen viable alternatives to farm work.[30] Through independence, the *gens de couleur* dominated Catholic and many nonreligious civil society associations that represented the *population generale*, advocating for multiethnic, class-based causes related to poverty alleviation. By the 1840s, Mauritius was an island with a sizable, free African majority with very few resources, very little power, and very little time before they would lose their numerical advantage.

The Great Experiment

Concerned with their ability to coerce labor as early as 1816, the colonial government decided to experiment with the use of Indian convict labor, and Mauritius's planters began dispatching recruiters to China, Singapore, Ethiopia, and Madagascar. Between 1839 and 1857, some 4,601 workers from Madagascar, 2,739 from China, 433 from Aden, 320 from the African coast, and 206 from Comoro Islands arrived in Mauritius.[31] The planters' gaze returned inevitably, however, to the "seemingly inexhaustible manpower" of India.[32] By 1839, some 25,000 Indian laborers were engaged on Mauritian plantations, 77,996 by 1851, and 192,634 in 1861 in what was called "the Great Experiment."[33] Housing their new field laborers in lines of thatched huts in the sugar estate camps under the oversight of *sirdars* (foremen), French planters had replaced their slaves and initially managed them no differently.

British and Indian public outcry about the planters' exploitative treatment of Indian immigrants forced the government of India to suspend emigration to Mauritius late in 1838. It resumed in late 1842, however, after repeated complaints from the colony's governor and the local sugar industry that the continued suspension of the "coolie trade" would spell economic ruin.[34] With the resumption of Indian arrivals, the British Protector of Immigrants agency was established and tasked with processing indenture contractors and arbitrating cases of alleged exploitation. Between 1860 and 1885, 110,940 complaints were lodged over the breach of labor laws or indenture contracts, which planters always preferred to finalize verbally to minimize paper evidence. Most complaints concerned the late payment of wages, while others related to poor housing and rations, a lack of proper medical care, and harsh penalties for missing work and leaving estates without permission.

In response to their exploitation and oppression, many Indians deserted their plantation duties, much like the Africans who preceded them. Between 1860 and 1886, around 209,000 complaints were lodged against Indian immigrants by sugar estates, three-quarters of which alleged illegal absence from work or desertion.[35] In 1871, 9,471 indentured laborers signed a petition for greater oversight of labor rights, authored by Adoplhe de Plevitz, the humanist estate manager of Nouvelle Decouverte Sugar Estate, who advocated for labor rights. This helped mobilize an 1872 Royal Commission that investigated Mauritius's treatment of Indian immigrants and found that the "traditions of slavery" still persisted and that the local police force continued to engage in periodic "maroon hunts." Directed against the tens of thousands of indentured Indian laborers in the colony, these operations were conducted under the authority of desertion and vagrancy ordinances modeled upon the old fugitive slave laws.[36] Lest Indians and Creoles bond over their experiences of subjugation, the plantations instituted a "pass system" that restricted laborers' mobility and inhibited Indian-African dialogue, let alone mutual understanding.

For many Indians, commerce and landownership were the paths toward economic mobility in a land they came to dominate numerically even if not yet politically. As increasing numbers of immigrants completed their indenture, many entered nonagricultural industries. According to the 1851 census, Indian-origin people made up one of every seven persons employed in trade, manufacturing, and commerce such as domestic service, peddling, and gardening, occupations hitherto dominated by ex-apprentices.[37] In 1851, Indians accounted for less than 3 percent of all professional people and less than 5 percent of all independent proprietors. Just thirty years later, Indians comprised 25 percent of Mauritius's professional classes and 27 percent of the colony's independent proprietors.[38] During this period, the intensity of trade with India led the Indian rupee to become the only legal tender in Mauritius.[39]

This expansion of economic activity enabled many Indians to then invest in land when it became available. Between 1883 and 1887, a drop in sugar prices spurred larger planters to sell portions of their more marginal estate land to gain some financial relief while retaining Indians on the plantations. The process, known as *grand morcellement*, continued until 1920, by which time about 40 to 45 percent of Mauritius's cultivated area belonged to small landowners and planters, mostly Hindu and Muslim Indians.[40] During the First World War, the net value of Indian investment in real estate soared 280 percent and doubled yet again during the first half of the 1920s.[41]

Much as the gauntlet of slavery and its indiscriminate treatment of Africans ignored the ethnic boundaries within *négritude*, Indians' experience also unified a heterogeneous population. The immigrants belonged to hundreds of different Indian castes, religions, and ethnic communities that steadily consolidated into kinship networks or social groups.[42] And the initial absence of any religious infrastructure in the sugar colonies made even those who previously practiced Hinduism or Islam only "marginally religious."[43] Eventually, Hindu sects of orthodox Sanatanis and Arya Samaj—a Mauritian religious movement that would peak in the 1960s—emerged but featured no major distinctions in practice and pervasive intermarriage.[44] Unlike Africans, who were subject to colonialism's "civilizing" cultural agenda, Indians were able to maintain not only their traditions but also a direct connection with a home-land. Any remaining lines of distinction among them were blurred by the rise of Indian nationalism across the sugar colonies in the early twentieth century.

When Gandhi visited Mauritius in 1901, he observed the plight of the inden-tured laborers and sought to send an Indian emissary thereafter. Six years later, Manilal Doctor, a barrister trained in England, arrived with the purpose of improving the general conditions of Mauritius's indentured laborers and to instill a sense of pride among the population.[45] He swiftly employed legal means to pursue the termination of the indenture system and protect Hindu religious practices. On March 15, 1909, Doctor began publishing a fort-nightly newspaper, *The Hindusthani*, with the motto "Liberty of Individuals, Fraternity of Man, Equality of Races." In the first issue, he set the tone for his secular nationalist political agenda: "Our paper does not favour any particular race, sect or people. . . . We therefore call upon Hindus, Mussulmans, Parses, and Christians to join hands, and strive with unanimous effort for liberty, equality, and progress."[46] Progress would come, but not for all.

Le malaise créole

While social movements led by Indian nationalists and *gens de couleur* worked in parallel for greater self-determination and social justice, Mauritius's Creoles remained subject to significant political and economic disadvantages. Their plight was unchanged by the creation of a new Constitution in 1948. Fearing

Table 7.1 Key Factors in Mauritius (Majority Minority in ~1861)

Immigration	Equality	Identity	Social Relations
Concentrated: Indentured labor migrants from India from 1835 until 1917. Since then, some emigration of middle-class Creoles during the mid-nineteenth-century "Hindu Peril."	*Equal:* Though there were different entitlements for Creole ex-slaves and Indian-origin ex-indentured laborers, they were equal before the law. Any adult who could write their name could vote in 1948, and universal adult suffrage was introduced in 1959. All voted in the independence referendum.	*Exclusive:* After the introduction of universal suffrage, interethnic suspicion grew. The independence vote divided civic identity and associational life by ethnicity and religion. Indian-origin officials rely on patronage from the police to mail carriers, with token Creole representation.	*Tension:* Political parties are divided by ethnicity and religion, in some cases overtly. *Le malaise créole*, observed in the 1990s, described hopelessness, frustration, and racial resentment among Creoles subject to racialized disadvantage and unresolved problems derived from slavery.

domination by the growing number and wealth of Indians and the possibility of postindependence annexation by India—a "Hindu Peril"—many *gens de couleur* left the island for Australia, Britain, and Canada. This "Coloured Exodus" narrowed Creole ranks to lower-class "Black African" people who identified as *ti-Kreol* and reduced their overall share of Mauritius's fragile demography.[47] Perhaps more significant, their departure dealt a considerable blow to the ranks of Creole leadership. Those who remained identified less with Francophone and Catholic culture and more with a working-class socioeconomic experience that yearned for a sense of rooted heritage.[48]

When the prospect of independence was considered by Westminster in 1959, these underlying ethnic or religious tensions hardened into political divisions that separated Hindus, Muslims, and members of the *population generale*.[49] Accordingly, Hindus largely backed decolonization and organized around the pro-independence Labour Party and its Hindu leader, Seewoosagur Ramgoolam, who would later be called "Father of the Nation." The Muslim community organized around Comité d'Action Muselman, led by Abdool Razack Mohamed. The white Franco-Mauritian descendants of Mauritius's planter class allied with their fellow Catholics, the Creoles, and the anti-independence Parti Mauricien Social Démocrate, run by Jules Koenig and, after 1967, by Gaetan Duval, a charismatic but polemical Creole leader figure who called himself "the King of Creoles." Violence called the "Race Wars" erupted in the months before the independence decision. Mauritius's ethnic boundaries now defined its political boundaries, and this would remain true after independence was announced in 1968 and Ramgoolam became Mauritius's first prime minister.

In the 1970s and 1980s, Mauritius underwent a period of modernization that spurred rapid economic changes and stratified its ethnoreligious groups. While most Indo-Mauritians shared the ranks of the lower classes with Creoles during the colonial period, Creole exclusion in society, politics, and the marketplace became more pronounced after independence as a predominantly Asian middle class began to develop and Hindus increasingly dominated government and the civil service.[50] The institutionalization of Asian languages and the palpable exclusion of Kreol in language policy became synonymous with Hindu hegemony.[51] Kreol—which about 90 percent of Mauritians speak—was barred from use in Parliament and not permitted in a variety of workplaces, effectively disqualifying thousands of Creole people who did not speak French or English. Even today, the majority of Mauritians have not mastered English.

During a February 1993 ceremony commemorating the abolition of slavery in Mauritius, one of the few Creole Catholic priests there, Father Roger

Cerveaux, articulated a general feeling of discontent with a country in which Creoles had become the face of the poor and the marginalized.[52] Describing widespread feelings of hopelessness, frustration, and resentment in the Creole community over their extreme poverty and lack of relative economic progress, *le malaise créole* became a popular discourse for understanding Mauritian social tension as a collection of pathologies and problems derived from slavery.[53] More implicitly, the statements of Father Cerveaux recognized the limits of the Catholic Church's civic focus on social services. A legacy of its complicity with slavery's civilizing mission, the church did not provide an ethnicity-specific platform for Creole empowerment in a way that fit into the emerging logics of multiculturalism.

Other Creole leaders long believed that their plight was in part attributable to Creoles' inability to politically mobilize around a consolidated ethnic identity that the state would be forced to recognize and support. In 1969, Sylvio and Ellie Michel founded the Organisation Fraternelle, one of the first civil society organizations dedicated to the interests of "Afro-Creoles." A registered political party by the 1970s with some clerical support, the organization pursued an Afro-Creole identity centered on the legacy of slavery. It erected Mauritius's first monument dedicated to the memory of slave ancestors in Port Louis's Jardin de la Compagnie in 1976 and set the tone for a number of future movements influenced by the period's Black consciousness, Rastafarianism, and pan-African *négritude*.[54]

This distinguishes the Creolization of Afro-Mauritians from the Creolization of Afro-Trinidadians. In the Afro-dominant Caribbean, Creolization was first a discourse of hybridity and evolved into a triumphant consolidation of pre- and then postindependence power. But in Mauritius, rather than seek out and embrace their untraceable cultural hybridity, Creole activists focused on a consolidated pan-African diasporic identity that demanded accommodation by Mauritian multiculturalism.[55] Subject to an inversion of power with the majority Indian-origin population, Mauritian Creoles struggled to develop a collective consciousness free of the complicated dependencies and entanglements of French Catholicism and a set of distinctly Afro-Creole cultural goods that communicate their indigeneity without contradictions from the state. *Le malaise créole* was a drifting, anomic sentiment yearning to assert a cultural legacy on the island.

This assertion was eventually made by Joseph Reginald "Kaya" Topize, a young Rastafarian activist and musician widely known as the father of "seggae," a blending of the musical and philosophical elements of Mauritian *séga* and Jamaican reggae that embodied the simultaneous narratives of Creole nativity and pan-African solidarity.[56] Alongside the Kreol language, rhythmic *séga* was one of the few cultural artifacts that Creoles could rally around and embrace as authentically "African."[57] On February 21, 1999, Kaya was arrested for smoking marijuana at a rally to promote its legalization and died in police custody shortly thereafter. Riots ensued, the most severe political violence since the 1968 Race Wars. Protestors blocked main roads, looted, ransacked police stations, and burned hundreds of vehicles, shutting down commerce, government offices, schools, the port, and public transport in Port Louis for multiple days.[58] An autopsy would find trauma lesions on the musician's body and attributed his death to an internal hemorrhage. Creoles across the island assumed foul play by the predominantly Indian police and hailed Kaya as a martyr for Creole freedom.

Kaya's death inspired not only a new generation of music but also identity politics. Later in 1999, the Muvman Morisyen Kreol Afrikain opened Mauritius's first newspaper written from the perspective of the Afro-Creole. *Lavoix Kreol* was a forum for public discourse in a developing Creole public sphere—distinct from the Catholic public sphere—that became popular within working- and middle-class Creole households.[59] It became a counterbalance to the opinions expressed in the long-standing Hindu-run *Mauritius Times*, the Muslim-run *Star*, and the mainstream *Mauricien* and *L'Express* newspapers. Ten years later, the government instituted a Truth and Justice Commission mandated to investigate the legacies of slavery and indentured labor over a period of 370 years. In November 2011, its 535-page report detailed the way that Mauritius's descendants of slaves were disproportionately subject to inadequate housing, illiteracy, and manual labor positions, while being underrepresented in the agricultural economy, small-business sector, and politics.[60]

It was also during this period that Indians and Creoles raced to apply for the island's first UNESCO World Heritage Site, and thus define its global cultural emblem. While Creoles pushed the candidacy of the Le Morne Cultural Landscape—the monumental mountain peninsula that long protected maroons—Indo-Mauritians and the government favored and ultimately submitted a dossier for the Aapravasi Ghat, the harborside depot in Port Louis that processed the arrival of hundreds of thousands of indentured servants from 1849 onward. Literally meaning "Immigrant Shore," it was a sprawling campus where many Mauritians' ancestors began their life on the island, 98 percent of whom were from India. Aapravasi Ghat's 2006 selection and the debate around it only solidified the cultural boundaries that divide Mauritius and did nothing to transcend them. After a feverous push for the government to later submit the Le Morne dossier to UNESCO, the ancient maroon refuge was inscribed on the World Heritage list in 2008, formalizing its centrality to Creole self-understanding.

Le Morne

Le Morne is the capital of the Maroon Republic, the mountain its unconquerable national landmark. Historians believe its summit began to be occupied only after the French colonized Mauritius in 1715 and began clearing away the tropical jungles and slopes that previously sheltered maroons. The earliest association of maroons with Le Morne did not occur until 1736, although its extraordinary topography is mentioned in Dutch accounts more than a century earlier.[61] Its apex features panoramic views of the Indian Ocean and any boats that may approach Mauritius's west from the African mainland. To reach these hideaways, it is thought that maroons built a wooden bridge on the southern slope that they subsequently withdrew. The archaeologists whose work contributed to Le Morne's UNESCO recognition had no choice but to hire a helicopter in 2002. Too small to allow any form of habitation, the rock shelters were the last resort of a community of maroons who likely resided in a seaside village called Trou Chenilles, where many freed slaves congregated after their emancipation.

Allan Ramalingum's ancestors once resided in Trou Chenilles, before it was destroyed by a cyclone in 1945. The Creole population then rebuilt their community on the southern coast of the peninsula, and Allan is its handsome, forty-one-year-old, mixed-race Creole mayor.

"We talk a lot about the past," he said about his fellow Creoles. "But we have lost a lot, and we have nothing on paper. Truthfully, we have no idea if we own the land under our homes. We have no legal documentation. We just know that we have been here for a very long time."

In fact, French-origin families and the government formally own the land around Le Morne, and Allan's grandparents were evicted from their longtime home a few kilometers away from where he currently resides. Every day he drives past their old house, now overgrown with bush and blackened by fire. His sense of precarity is not innate; it is from experience.

"You are in your own country, but you are not controlling anything," he says. He points to Le Morne Mountain's peerless silhouette in the delicate morning light. "This is our monument. It is all that we have. It's what our ancestors left for us as a sacred memory. And it is visible, undeniable."

Le Morne village is made up of one main street that runs parallel to the coastal highway and a variety of small cross streets lined with one- and two-story houses. Each house is unique and built by its occupant with whatever materials seem to have been available: in the best case, concrete and cinder blocks, but often sheet metal.

Bougainvillea flowers drape over the fences and spill into the street. Electrical lines and clothes lines dangle from above, while stray dogs roam below, skipping over concrete gutters that collect the morning rain and bits of discarded rubbish. The mountain rests in the distance, never really out of view behind the village's papaya trees and coconut palms. Seggae music pulses from a nearby porch for all to hear.

"For us Creoles," Allan said, "to be Mauritian is very important. It is us who fought for Mauritianism, for everyone to get equal opportunity. It is religion that threatens to divide us."

Allan's great-grandfather was an immigrant from Madras in southern India, hence his Tamil surname. When his grandfather was young, the French baptized him and instantly transformed a Hindu Indian into a Creole—a demonstration of how religious differences supersede co-ethnicity in Mauritius. Most of the island's Hindus likewise do not identify with Muslim Indians, and they assign any nonwhite Christian to Creole status. Allan's grandfather and father would marry others of African and mixed ethnic ancestry, all Catholics.

"When the Indians came, they got the majority because the Indians would never refuse to accommodate [the wishes] of the French or British," he said. "But Creoles would talk back. They have suffered and they want to be free. The Indians were not tortured like us. But the maroons, you have to understand, they were very strong. They were rebels. It's in our DNA."

We walked along a side street toward his parents' home.

"*Tout bien, tout bien.* The Indians think everything is *tout bien,*" he said, referring to the public image conveyed by the Mauritian government of a pragmatic, harmonious Rainbow Nation. "It is us for whom it is not *tout bien.* That we get along, it's something we say. It's something we have to say. But it's not real. Real life is here."

He points to a pile of cinder blocks in the shadow of a guanabana tree. Indians, he said, want to suppress any evidence of ethnic conflict because the instability threatens their elevated position in Mauritian society. So they will insist that there are no tensions, and that the island is the beacon of multiculturalism and coexistence symbolized by its multicolored flag.

"We have had a racial war. But why should we expose tourists to our problems? They are our economy. Otherwise, the war will reach the gates of the St. Regis Hotel."

Allan works as a nature guide and is heavily dependent on hotels for business. Nearly a quarter of Mauritius's economy comes from tourism today.[62] His grandfather was a shaman, who specialized in plant-based remedies and taught him his trade.

His father, Joe, is a retired social worker and a former mayor of Le Morne's village. We met on his front porch.

"It's simply not a system of merit," Joe told me. "Indians have greater resources, and access to public-sector jobs, even in cases when a Creole has better certificates of qualification. Because of this discrimination, there is no meritocracy here. Where there are Creoles in places of power, it is for political reasons. The hotels offer us more opportunities because their owners are usually French and Catholic—Christian, like us. The French remain on top. But the French still use Creoles in the same way they used us when we were colonized. They are still colonizing. They are annoyed when people do not speak French, and they have taken all our land. We followed them, from sugar cane plantations, to manufacturing, and now to resorts.

"Look at this village. We are all stuck in small houses, with acres of empty fields next door. They don't just move us out of our house. They literally moved our entire village and then fenced off our old land."

Mario, Joe's brother, who works as a hotel cashier, joined the conversation. "Everyone in the village knows each other," he said. "They marry between each other's families. But they question parents who push their children to go far in school. One of the reasons is that they don't believe they'll be rewarded for it. . . . When you have a Hindu name, it gives you a better chance of getting a job. People help their own. My daughter managed to get a government job, but it's because of our [Indian last] name.

"So we earn our living by fishing and working in hotels," Mario added, "not in the front office, but in the kitchen and housekeeping. People are discouraged from pursuing the top jobs. The Creoles act like they don't want to leave their misery. They're happy with their five hundred rupees (about US$14) for the day."

Today, fishermen may live on less. The Mauritian government recently signed an agreement that grants Japanese companies access to fish in Mauritian coastal waters, which feature reef cod, tuna, sea bream, squid, shrimp, crab, and lobster. Le Morne's fishermen, who once finished a day's work at 9:00 a.m. in rowboats, now require motorboats to access free, unpolluted water away from hotels' cordoned-off seascapes. As I walked toward the beach, I saw several fishermen returning with their catch well after noon. One of them was a thirty-two-year-old gentleman named Robbie.

Lounging topless on a beach mattress that he laid against the trunk of a tree overlooking Le Morne's azure lagoon, Robbie was chatting with a number of friends when we met. In between drags from a joint and sips of a bottle of *lambique*, a moonshine rum, he reflected about the Creole predicament.

"If I were the prime minister, I would shut down every hotel on Le Morne and fill their rooms with local people from the village here," he said. "People don't realize, we would be champions in everything, if we just had the materials."

Pointing his bottle toward the Le Morne peninsula, he continued, "But if we want to surf over there, white Mauritians will start a fight with us and kick us off the land. We are locked in here. We can't move. And yet, it's ours. When I was a kid, my grandfather taught me how to swim, how to surf on that beach. We should be able to enjoy what we have here."

In 1998, when Robbie was twelve years old, the people of Le Morne village protested and successfully prevented Les Pavillons Hotel from appropriating a major part of the peninsula's public beach, an already small segment of the peninsula's otherwise walled-off resort space. In 1999, a number of Creole organizations also opposed the development of cable car facilities on the mountain. Since then, the government has continued to approve applications for the construction of new hotels and golf courses.

"The Indian perspective is clear: 'You can't go further than me,'" Robbie said. "You stay here. There is a barrier. People say they'll change things, but they get bought off by the government to keep them quiet. If I spoke English well, I would speak with the prime minister myself. But I speak Creole and they would not understand. However, when I sing, I speak in every language."

His friends raised their bottles to that.

Across the road, facing the water, is the home of Madame Zanane. A respected woman of high status in Le Morne, she is a sixty-four-year-old shaman healer—a sort of witch doctor and village elder. She claims to be able to remedy otherwise lethal stings from stonefish and jellyfish, backaches, and sore throats. Her home is set back from the street, which contains both the serenity of lapping coastal waters and the loud rush of passing buses. The front yard was a dirt driveway with several parked motorbikes and a family of puppies leaping around. She stood on her patio awaiting us.

Clearly a woman concerned with appearances, she greeted us in a red and white halter top, white leggings, and a pearl necklace with matching pearl bracelet. Large silver hoops hung from her ears. She was quite slender and spoke in a deep voice. Her natural white hair was styled in a nicely groomed afro.

"Creole people are born looking like Rastafarians," she said, referring to their natural hair and dreadlocks. "You have to tell Africans what their roots are. Long ago, when you had a *séga* night, the people would dance in modest clothing."

As an exhibit, she showed me an old photo of herself, posing glamorously in front of Le Morne Mountain in a rich, cream tunic with a matching headdress. As I admired the image, she lit a cigarette.

"Our roots are our culture," she said, "our music, a patrimony that our ancestors made sacred. How to prepare African food? We prefer to cook fish, octopus, mussels, and yams on the *raseau* grill. Long ago, we only ate meat on special occasions and holidays like Christmas."

She placed the photo next to her and tapped the cigarette into a conch shell that she used as an ashtray.

"The position of Creoles in Mauritian society is not good. There are a lot of Africans who have lost their identity, and they are being recruited to be Muslims and Hindus, who sometimes even offer them money. We now have Creole priests assembling people together to define our identity as Mauritians. But you know, Catholicism was imposed, too.

"In my dreams, I always wanted to do something for the children here," she reflected. "So I hold *séga* nights to show the importance of our roots. *Séga* and the *ravanne* drum bring us to a pre-Catholic past."

She begins to rhythmically tap an empty green metal petrol tank lying nearby.

"Creoles came first, but India is taking over and there is no equal opportunity. The African community must be together, and here in Le Morne, we really are together. Even the Hindus here feel like they are Creole. They live the same way.

"As recently as around 1960, I saw people who were direct, pure descendants of the maroons—Zulu, Jambo, the ones with the very short hair. They were living nearby, and a French Mauritian family threatened a number of them. Shortly thereafter, the British sent lorries to pick up the Africans and deport them to Mozambique or Madagascar."

Madame Zanane told this story on live Mauritian television a couple years ago, and then received phone calls from the police warning her about speaking ill of the French family. Although no one has been able to verify it, she continues to share the story at will.

"Today, Creoles can go anywhere they want. We have the liberty that the maroons could not have."

She caught herself.

"Well, we know there are places Creoles cannot go. We have freedom, but we are not completely free."

Madame Zanane's, Robbie's, and the Ramalingums' views reflect Creoles' sense of profound frustration. They see themselves as the keepers of

Mauritius's heritage. A people of principle, they defied colonizers but continue to pay for their resistance. The closest thing to indigenous people Mauritius has, they are looked down upon as primitive for being so close to the land and sea. And they are resigned to their disadvantaged status in a society controlled by people they continue to view as foreigners occupying their land.

A concept of their nation remains elusive, but they believe that it has remained so because of the barriers inhibiting their cultural practices and self-determination. If they could just speak in their own language, control their own land, make their own decisions, they frequently remark. And yet they have found ways to assert their heritage and cross social boundaries through music, nature, and ongoing intermarriage. Heritage, to Madame Zanane, is available and it must be taught.

This is the irony at the center of the Creole plight. A blend of all of Mauritius's different ethnoreligious communities and their respective heritages, they are claimed by none. And so they draw enormous strength from the defiant legacy of maroons. Outsiders of mixed origin, they have resisted oppression since their forced arrival. The people of Le Morne quite literally live in their shadow on land that remained unconquered by colonialism—an ever-present reminder of their indomitability, even in the worst of times.

"We're always running," Allan Ramalingum told me. "Running away from the police. Running after being shooed off the beach, and out of the lagoon. We're still running."

Chamarel

If Le Morne is the soul of the Mauritian Creole life, the village of Chamarel is its heart. Access from Le Morne is via a circuitous motorway that clings to the cliffside as it winds up the Black River Mountains and narrows to a single lane at one point. Panoramic vistas of the turquoise western coastline display Mauritius's natural beauty and the mountains' isolation.

Chamarel is shrouded in a kind of mystery. Long a shelter to maroons, its buildings are embedded in a dense, misty jungle—banana plants, plumeria, traveler palms, papaya trees, ebony, and towering bamboo—that thrives in the cooler humid air one thousand feet above sea level. The foliage is inhabited by thousands of colorful songbirds, pheasants, boar, and tortoises. The human inhabitants, however, are surrounded by a string of encircling walls that designate the boundaries of adjacent coffee plantations, banana groves, sugar cane farms, and privately owned savannahs.

"Chamarel is a village inside a fence," locals often say. The wooden fence is incomplete for extended areas. At one point, all that remains is a lonely gate covered in vines with no walls attached on either side. Over the years, its mostly Creole residents uprooted many of the fence's logs and repurposed them to build homes and open up the otherwise empty prairieland and rain forest. The flora continues to hide the persistence of prohibited African culture.

A few hundred meters into the trees off Route Royale is the Nyahbingi Tabernacle, Chamarel's principal Rastafarian temple and one of Mauritius's most important Rastafarian religious spaces for the past twenty years. It is marked by a single sign posted to a log alongside the motorway, in front of a narrow dirt path through the jungle. The way is marked by short posts painted in the characteristic Rastafarian green, yellow, and red stripes, which lead to a clearing. There lie a number of log benches and wooden alters. Every Sunday, a congregation of a few hundred people assembles for ceremonies and groundings. Deeply tranquil, the space is nevertheless contested, like so many other Creole landmarks. The coffee producer Case Noyale, Ltd., which owns vast amounts of land near Chamarel, claims that the temple is occupying their ground and must be removed.

One of the Nyahbingi congregation's elders is Monsieur André. A very tall, skinny gentleman, he greeted me in the street barefoot, wearing a loose-fitting khaki collared shirt with breast pockets and a pair of baggy shorts that drooped below his knees. His black hair was in one large lock that wrapped around his head like a turban, with about a dozen small dreadlocks dangling above his narrow neck; from a distance, it appeared a jellyfish had perched atop his head. Spectacles hung from a black lanyard over a distinguished, shaggy white goatee.

He casually invited me into his home. Around the side of a souvenir shop he owns, he opened a sliding gate to reveal a tidy garden with coconut palms, orchids, and a blooming yellow bell flower tree, a brugmansia. In a sandlot, stray cats roamed along with a small family of turtles. He lives in a spacious home behind his store, Roots of Chamarel, which sells a variety of African cultural items and souvenirs.

His living room had a pristinely clean white floor with several sofas. A keyboard, electric guitar, and large windpipe leaned against the wall. He sank into a large easy chair. When he spoke, he stiffened his posture and spoke passionately—extending his long, angular arms into the space around him, and emphasizing the beginning of phrases like a preacher on a pulpit.

"The Rastas raise up the Creoles," he said. "We meet in the temple for prayer, but also to organize ourselves. The original Creole community was implicitly

Rastafarian. There was no Catholicism. Rastas came from the maroons. They escaped to find"—he paused to correct himself—"to return to their way of life in Le Morne, Chamarel, and the Black River region."

Rastafari developed in Jamaica in the 1930s wave of pan-African diasporic consciousness and revivalist Christianity. Based on an interpretation of the Bible, Rastafarians worship Jah—God, who manifested as Jesus Christ but also in Haile Selassie, the emperor of Ethiopia from 1930 to 1974. It likens the oppression of the African diaspora by Western societies to the oppression of Jews in Babylon, with the African continent its Zion and promised land.

"When the French were here, they brought medicine to persuade people to convert to Catholicism and destroy what they believed to be the devil's culture. So they turned one population into two and introduced many cultural elements. We began to live the way they lived, and this has displaced us from our ancestors and our God. . . . Catholicism distances Creoles from their roots. Catholics will not bring people to their heritage; it allows the French to bring people to *their* way of life. Rastafarianism introduces them to their past.

"Now we want to know who is our God," he added, "what to wear, how to pray, what to eat. But it's difficult to return. With each generation, the Creole population is more estranged from our past. So we need to create our African life here, now."

"What is stopping you?" I asked.

"The government is Indian, and if it's not Ramgoolam, it's Jugnath," he said, referring to the two dynastic families that have long dominated Mauritian politics. "Two families. If they could remove Creoles from this island, they would. But they can't; we were here first. So they run meetings in languages that Creoles typically do not speak [English]; they have a minister or two that are Creole [for the sake of appearance], but it doesn't help. They're the minister of sport, or the minister of equality. They are jobs created for a [token] Creole.

"The Indian religion is not indigenous," Monsieur André continued. "Mauritius has become India. They have taken our country and made it in their image. But we were here before them. We were the ones who developed, who built this land; the ones who did the hard jobs that made this country. The roads, houses, the ones who cultivated the sugar cane. The stone buildings in Port Louis, each rock was laid by African hands. This country is ours.

"The Indians have visa-free entry into India," he listed on his fingers. "The Muslims can go to Mecca for hajj. Nobody is coming from Africa to tell us the African way of life. We haven't had an opportunity to see how Africans came here. We have suffered a lot, and we have been cut from our roots. The Africans don't have a passage to our roots. The religion is this passage. This is what scares people about us [Rastafarians]. It gives us a way of life that nobody else can control."

"This is reminiscent of the maroons," I said.

"Maroonage initially divided the Creoles. The Catholics persuaded many Creoles that it was a bad choice. But the maroons wanted to follow their culture, to find who they are. They were not André or Christopher or Pierre. They were Chikulu, Chilulu, Kaliku. Those were our names. I was born a Catholic to Catholic parents, but I wanted to search for my roots. I am still searching."

"Do you think the death of Kaya was a turning point for Creoles?" I asked, referring to the late Rastafarian seggae musician.

"Nothing has changed since Kaya," he replied swiftly as if he had considered the question before. "It has only become worse. Last year, there was an incident in which the police beat up a Rasta community in Port Louis for smoking ganja [marijuana]—which is a fundamental part of our religion. Our prayer starts with it."

Of course, contestation over marijuana is what led to Kaya's original arrest, and it remains a source of political debate two decades later. Rastafarians, for whom marijuana is an integral part of practice, claim that its criminalization violates their cultural and religious rights. And even though arrests and prosecutions disproportionately target Creoles, the Mauritian government has not wavered. In fact, the government has enacted more severe drug laws and cites such violations on convicts' public "character" profiles, hurting their future job prospects.

Chamarel is defiant. Numerous kilometers deep into the surrounding Black River Mountains' jungle lies a clandestine marijuana farm, accessible only via an unmarked trail. Unlike the island's plantations for the past three hundred years, the farm is run as a cooperative. There are no bosses, no *sirdars*, no hierarchies. Those who are more experienced help administer the farm and train newcomers. "If we are caught by the police, we will all go to jail," they say.

One former farmworker estimated that about 60 percent of Chamarel's male population has worked on the farm at some point in their lives. The workers evenly split the profits from sales to a variety of wholesale-to-retail dealer-distributors. Typical earnings are about 80,000 Mauritian rupees (about US$2,400) for a three-month harvest, which is split between four people who tend the crops on an occasional basis to earn extra money. "People need to survive," he said.

In this model, the farm embodies a sort of alternative, Creole philosophy of economics, an implicit rejection of and resistance to the imperial business model that shackled their ancestors and exploited laborers for centuries. But it operates under the cover of a leafy tropical canopy. And lately, the crimes its workers commit come with stiffer penalties. "It is Africans who tend to grow and sell ganja," said the farmworker. "And so it is in the government's interest to stop them—to keep them from making money, to keep them in their place."

Taken together, the people of Chamarel and Le Morne are actively reimagining and reconstructing what it means to be an African in Mauritius today and historically. In so doing, they are creating a parallel Creole existence: Rastafarianism as an alternative to Catholicism, cooperatives as an alternative to capitalism, ecological preservation as an alternative to property development, all of which takes place through gaps in barriers that otherwise control their access to land and sea. It is little wonder that Creoles feel out of bounds.

Where We Belong

Music has long been the cultural means of transgressing colonial order. The fisherman Robbie referred to the way his singing crosses ossified social boundaries. The witch doctor Madame Zanane uses *séga* as a portal to the forbidden past. Monsieur André and his Rastafarian congregants evoke the memory of the musician Kaya and his freedom to communicate until his subversion became tangible. Much like Kreol, *séga* and the *ravanne* drum are uniquely African and were developed independent of, indeed despite colonial power. Mauritian journalist Jean-Clement Cangy once explained that *séga* percussion was "born in pain, in the sufferings of slavery, the humiliations and privations . . . but also in revolt against horror, crime against humanity, in maroonage."[63] Today, Creole music offers a critique about a modern society that precludes their class mobility and most positions of governance.

On my way out of Chamarel, I visited the members of a popular seggae band, aptly named The Maroon Brothers. Roy and Chiku were seated on a patio outside the home they share with their father, Toto Lebrasse, one of Mauritius's early pioneers of seggae. Situated on a *kikuyu* grass hill above a small creek and garden, the parquet wooden patio was surrounded by ferns and overlooked Chamarel's neighboring Piton Street.

There, the two brothers lounged with a friend, inhaling deeply from a plastic Coca-Cola bottle they had converted into a reliable water bong. Roy is a lean, handsome man, while the younger Chiku is taller and more muscular.

"We are expressing the maroon legacy through music," Roy told me. "Through it, we keep the brotherhood of our ancestors. We tell the history that we learned from our parents, and translate it to the nation."

It was clear that when Roy said "nation," he meant all of Mauritius.

"We want to create a sense of equality, to create one universal world. But we have been divided by religion and politics. When we came to this land, we were together, but we have since been separated. In slavery, the French separated the strong from the weak."

"Are you also trying to reconnect Mauritius to Africa?" I asked.

"This isn't Africa anymore" was Roy's answer. "It's India. The culture of Africa has been dominated, so we cannot live the way we want. There are some Indians who want to live in harmony with Creoles, but others do not. Indians listen to our music; the music is universal, but politics divide. Music is a way to bring people together, and to communicate points of view that would not normally be welcome in casual conversation.

"Indians are programmed to tell you that everything is fine between us. But the police are all Indian. And the prohibition [of marijuana] is a way to suppress us. Meanwhile, ganja preceded the arrival of Indians. Some people even say it was the Indians who brought it to Mauritius." (Indeed, the word "ganja" is actually Indian in origin.)

"The ganja makes us think a lot," Roy continued. "About the future. It opens our mind to think differently. By banning marijuana, they also block the freedom of our minds. This was African land, but it could have stayed natural and we would have been richer, spiritually. We would live differently, free from the society defined by others.

"For Rastas, Kaya was a prophet. He spoke for poor people. And when they killed him, they blocked our means of communication, they blocked our message. There are lost songs, things that will never be diffused by radio."

In the background, the voice of Kaya's musical heir, The Prophecy—one of Mauritius's most popular seggae musicians—drifted through the air. It was the title song from his 2018 album, *Where We Belong*:

> Put Rasta in jail cause we consume natural products
> Prohibit of spirituality; Tell us what really more
> Mauritian politics comes dirty
> Pointing figures we always guilty
> One day the truth will be reveal about them conspiracies
>
> Jah will need a helping hand
> Cause our culture is near extinction
> Then try to eliminate cause that we wanna face them weakness
> Behind the door
> Jah see the light
> Jah see the light

Where we belong (Where we belong)
Where we belong
African identity
Where we belong (Where we belong)
Where we belong

Cause I inner getting braids
Cause I inner getting braidlock man
I let my hair keep growing on my head it's my choice man
I wanna to stay my culture It's mind

Jah will need a helping hand
Cause our culture is near extinction
Then try to eliminate cause that we wanna face them weakness
Behind the door
Jah see the light
Jah see the light

Where we belong (Where we belong)
Where we belong
African identity

Where we belong (Where we belong)
Where we belong
Mauritian identity

Originally recorded in English, it seems directed beyond Creole people to the government. And it is not clear whether the artist is rhetorically questioning "Where we belong?" or asserting that Mauritius *is* "Where we belong." In the chorus, he alternates between "Mauritian identity" and "African identity," as if he is weighing their attributes, combining them, or perhaps even choosing between them.

For Creoles in Mauritius, of course, there can be no choice. Their African identity *is* their Mauritian identity. It is the wider Mauritian identity that cannot be African, under current demographic and social constraints.

Whether musical or prosaic, Creoles' political demands are not calls for equal status or minority rights—the kind of claims one might otherwise expect from an outnumbered community of people who have never really experienced self-determination. They are claims for sovereignty—the kind one might expect from a people with an indigenous claim to the land under them.

Out of Bounds

The Creole response to Mauritius's legacy of demographic change reveals how nostalgic nationalism does not require a history of power, like the histories that motivate contemporary nationalism in the United States and Europe today. Nationalism can also be a righteous sense of entitlement, a moralistic argument independent of practical circumstances. It is a matter of where one belongs.

Unlike Indian-origin Mauritians, who were able to maintain a direct link to the subcontinent, Creoles were cut off from their ancestral African origins. They cannot belong anywhere but the island of Mauritius. And so they leverage their limited cultural resources as the Maroon Republic to assert their liberty and ownership of it. While some of their assertions engage the Creole imagination to consider a vision of their history outside the boundaries of plantation life, this is the nature of nationalism more broadly. It assembles cultural artifacts to create an identity and moral claim to sovereignty.

While Creoles are an unlikely parallel to nostalgic, far-right populations in the United States, Britain, and elsewhere in Europe, they all speak of a country they deserve to inherit. While these white, disproportionately working-class communities in the West are interested in preserving their status in the face of multicultural liberalism, Creoles seek a status their ancestors enjoyed only as fugitives from a system designed to oppress them. Each is sensitive to conspiracy theories—an implicit expression of helplessness—and each somehow feels out of bounds in countries they once defined.

As in other multiethnic and multireligious societies, it didn't have to be this way in Mauritius. Mauritians of African, Catholic origins and those of Indian Hindu or Muslim origins were subjugated by the same extractive system of plantation labor. However, by the time they were both free to engage one another and bond over their shared history of servitude and exploitation, the structures of colonialism and the politics of independence had placed them on divergent trajectories—dividing civic identity and associational life by ethnicity and religion. These divisions ultimately reproduced the inequities of colonialism in a democratic setting, deepening Creoles' marginality.

In the divisive identity politics and culture wars that pervade the Western societies that today approach majority minority milestones, similar path dependencies are created. Every action that excludes or vilifies one social group is another that must be undone to unite a diversifying people. White Americans' and Europeans' history of power makes many less willing to relinquish or even share control of their respective countries. Mauritius's Creoles, however, are generally resigned to their status as a minority; they can seek only moral victories.

8

Internal Affairs

Why New York's Irish Still Run the Police Department

The old New York Police Department (NYPD) joke goes like this: *They let Italians into the police department so all the Irish could have St. Patrick's Day off.* Rain or shine for 257 years, on March 17 thirty-six blocks of Fifth Avenue shut down to make way for a six-hour procession of what is now 135 marching bands, seventy bagpipe and fife-and-drum groups, and thousands of police officers striding alongside city councilmen, members of Congress, the New York City mayor, and the New York State governor.[1] Today, the parade is conventionally understood as an innocuous celebration of Irish American culture. Two million diverse spectators line the sidewalks wearing shamrock-shaped sunglasses and dangling plastic pots of gold, but make no mistake about it: it is a demonstration of raw power. From its inception in 1762, when a group of homesick Irishmen serving overseas in the British colonial army dressed in Kelly green—then prohibited by the British colonial government in Ireland—defiantly marched in New York to fête their homeland on the day of its patron saint, the parade has always been a gathering place for a diaspora, its church, and its servicemen. As the Irish grew in number and emerged as New York City's most reviled ethnic minority—distrusted because of their Catholic faith and detested for their poverty—the parade became an expression of organizational clout and a mandatory event for political officials. When Mayor Bill de Blasio waved a miniature Irish flag and walked lockstep with Police Commissioner Jimmy O'Neill in the shadow of St. Patrick's Cathedral in 2019, he followed a long line of non-Irish predecessors dating back to A. Oakey Hall, who walked the route in a garish, all-green, long-tailed suit in 1870. Today, Irish Americans are a predominantly middle-class constituency and arguably the insiders of New York politics in a city of two hundred other nationalities, and yet the parade goes on long after their integration into mainstream society, long after the presidency of John F. Kennedy—the legacy of a scorned minority desperate to protect itself.

Majority Minority. Justin Gest, Oxford University Press. © Justin Gest 2022. DOI: 10.1093/oso/9780197641798.003.0008

Legacies of Marginality

New York City's Irish communities could be understood as a best-case scenario in majority minority societies. Most arrived destitute from the Potato Famine of the 1840s and 1850s, but after just a generation of residence Irish immigrants defied prejudice to build civic institutions and demand accommodations by their government. Today, the vast majority have moved out of the tenements in the Lower East Side and the ghettoes of the outer boroughs into New York's leafy suburbs, with a significant number in the professional classes. Now universally accepted as part of the United States' white racial majority, their present circumstances bear zero resemblance to the marginality and penury of their ancestors.

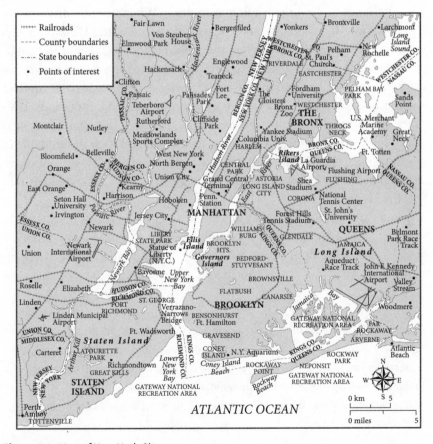

Figure 8.1 Map of New York City.

While several historical observers have portrayed the Irish Americans in New York City as frantically seeking entry to a world of white privilege, the Irish community saw themselves engaged in a bitter cultural conflict rooted in sharp differences based on race, national origin, religion, and even physical appearance.[2] As a result, when they obtained power by leveraging large coalitions of voters or inserting their countrymen into seats of government and influence, the Irish moved not to break down the barriers between their community and their Anglo-Dutch detractors but to carve out domains of their own control—independent clout to counter that of the resident majority. "The struggle for political and cultural power—indeed, the larger conflict over the meaning of Americanism," writes historian Terry Golway, "was at its heart a battle between the political machine's mongrels and the descendants of the *Mayflower*."[3]

There should be little doubt that much of this antagonism was born of the Irish experience under British colonial control. "When men are driven away by unjust laws—by starvation and the fear of death," writes Golway, "when they are forced to snatch their wives and children and take them three thousand miles across the sea to save them from the jaws of famine, when they see plenty and luxury all around them—their memories of home become motives of hatred, and will feed the fires which time cannot quench."[4] Indeed, the Irish propensity to build their own power rather than join the establishment is equally a reflection of the absolutism of the British and their descendants in New England. "The Irish in America live in 1846," noted T. P. O'Connor, an Irish member of the House of Commons, in 1918,[5] but the same could be said of his British counterparts.

The antagonism should equally be viewed as a human political response to the experience of immigration—certainly skepticism, but also the desire for self-determination among people who left their homeland to define their own destiny. Irish American novelist and historian Peter Quinn has written:

> The Irish in America—at least the Irish I grew up with—were still in the defensive crouch they'd arrived in during the Famine, still sensitive to the distrust and dislike of a *real* America, to the suspicions about our loyalty and supposed proclivity to raucous behavior. We were forever reminding ourselves—and the rest of America—of how many Irish fought with Washington, how many died at Antietam, and how many won the Congressional Medal of Honor, a litany of self-justification that implicitly accepted it wasn't enough that we've been here for over a century.[6]

For these Irish men and women, pursuing work with the police and the broader civil service was an act of self-justification and a grasp at security. To this day, Irish culture and NYPD culture are deeply intertwined, the subject of an ethnic stereotype and but also great folklore. If an officer dies in the line of duty tomorrow—no matter his or her ethnic heritage—the casket will be covered in a kelly green police flag and followed by bagpipes. The past four commissioners were Kelly, Bratton, O'Neill, and, most recently, Dermot Shea. The head of the officers' union, Patrick Lynch, is abrasive, vitriolic, and prone to talking out the side of his mouth. For many, the drink of choice off the beat remains Jameson's Irish Whiskey, and gallows humor is ubiquitous. As recently as 1972, police patrolled the city in kelly green models of the Plymouth Fury squad car. There are hundreds of multigenerational Irish American NYPD families, some of whom pass on their badge numbers to their children as if the police department were a medieval guild.

Over time, though, the NYPD has undertaken a massive and deliberate effort to diversify its ranks to better represent the changing ethnic composition of New York City. Puerto Ricans, Bangladeshis, and Chinese officers now also pursue the stability and symbolic acceptance that police jobs offer. During the same period, many Irish Americans have taken police jobs with suburban Suffolk County or the Port Authority, known to be easier work that pays better. Those who grew up in surrounding Long Island, New Jersey, or Westchester County are also tempted by other occupations, despite NYPD regulations that allow people who do not reside in the five city boroughs to still serve—a carve-out that many attribute to Irish influence. But ultimately, despite its evolution, the NYPD remains a living legacy of Irish power and politics in the nineteenth century.

But what does it say that it remains so? Why do the Irish seek such protection in light of their position as New York's ultimate insider ethnic constituency? Why do the Irish still become police? While this question is far more specific than those that motivated my research in the other case societies, New York is at a much more advanced stage in its majority minority evolution. Its demographic turning point may have taken place years after Mauritius's, but whereas the relationship between Mauritius's Indians and Creoles is effectively unchanged since the early twentieth century—offering us a sort of time capsule—the status of New York's Irish population has changed dramatically. The bond between the Irish and the NYPD is one of the few remaining vestiges of early Irish American life that allow us to tap into the enduring logics of their social positioning and behavior.

In this chapter, I explore these questions through a variety of interviews with Irish-origin police leaders and observers. It is worth acknowledging that this is a self-selecting sample of people. The Irish are an immigrant-origin community at an advanced stage of assimilation, and these are individuals who continue to hold aloft the ethnic torch. They are part of what sociologists Roger Waldinger and Claudia Der-Martirosian have called an "immigrant niche," which makes them more connected to their ethnic or religious identity than other Irish Americans who left New York City and chose careers outside the police department.[7] However, they are also invaluable portals to New York's Irish American past, who carry forward the culture, norms, and traditions that produced this "niche" in the first place.

Three reasons emerge to explain not only their enduring connection to the police department but, more fundamentally, their self-understanding as a minority. First, across my interviews with Irish-origin police leaders, there remains a strong culture of risk aversion that is a response to enduring insecurity about their social status. Second, and in response, the Irish American community continues to grasp for power, protection, and the sense of family that the NYPD has provided for generations. Third, as the Catholic Church has lost credibility and occupied a less prominent space in the New York public sphere, the police department reinforces these Irish Americans' desire for moral scaffolding to help structure their lives.

That some Irish Americans can still see themselves as insecure underdogs reveals how some of the most integrated immigrant-origin Americans still don't feel totally at home and yet still can't identify fully with the plight of other ethnic minorities. The reasons why say something about the history of Irish integration and marginality in one of the world's most successful multiethnic democracies. If the Irish are a best-case scenario, then their experience suggests the limits of what a majority minority society can ultimately become. Legacies of marginality do not disappear easily, and compensatory actions to accumulate power persist well after they appear to be necessary. New York City exhibits the variety of possible majority minority scenarios when multiple minority constituencies compete for power and recognition rather than a single counterpart to the majority group. In New York, interethnic politics between the Irish and Anglos could not be zero sum forever.

Starved for Power

"The Irish are people who didn't come with inherent skills or entrepreneurship," author Peter Quinn told me. "Their power was political, not economic. They came from one of the weakest economies in Europe to the most industrialized nation in the world. They were the most rural people in Western Europe at the time of the Famine. And within days, they're in the fastest- industrializing city in the world. They stayed in the city because there was power in numbers. They're not people of Wall Street or the Ivy League. Their power was in their [organization]. Their only crime was not having enough to eat."

After they gained independence from the British in 1776, Americans took on a new, exalted status in the eyes of Ireland's Catholics.[8] However, American perceptions of Irish Catholics were not so different from those of British colonials. Since the Reformation, many Protestants generally looked down on Catholics as corrupt Christians whose religious life was guided by superficial formalities and superstitions rather than genuine individual faith.[9] Due to the peculiar nature of Christianity in Gaelic Ireland, which incorporated elements of pre-Christian traditions and customs, British Protestants despised the Irish as "pagans" and "barbarians."[10] Despite this skepticism, many Irish migrated to New York and New England to work in the growing number of factories, to build the Erie Canal and the Croton Aqueduct, or to work as carters, longshoremen, seamstresses, and domestic help.[11] Beyond the job opportunities, the Irish also supported a Jeffersonian pursuit of freedom of speech, freedom of the press, easy naturalization, voting eligibility, and religious liberty—all of which were heavily contested in Ireland at the time.[12]

Even in New York, which had been more tolerant of ethnic diversity than the rest of America since Dutch colonial rule, the Irish were greeted with disdain.[13] There was a pervasive view that Irish poverty was a product of innate character flaws rather than the product of circumstances beyond their control. Nativists argued that Irish immigrants were predisposed to "vices of their condition, wretchedness, beggary, drunkenness, deceit, lying, violence, treachery, malice, superstition, and naturally hostile to Protestant values of temperance, education, and cleanliness."[14]

According to the historian Golway, public officials, journalists, and clergy in New York and London constructed a transatlantic narrative of Irish degeneracy, a narrative arguing that Irish poverty, intemperance, and corruption made them unworthy of charity and unable to rule themselves:[15] "They might have sailed three thousand miles from their homeland, but the enemy hadn't changed; the enemy still was the moralizing reformer, the civic elitist, the high-church Protestant who believed that Catholics had to shed their superstitions and their cultural identity before they could be politically and socially redeemed."[16]

Initially, these pre-Famine migrants did not have the critical mass to sustain political agitation in the United States, nor were they mobilized by a sense of persecution.[17] Too weak to protect themselves with their own civic institutions but generally distrusted, Irish Americans initially portrayed themselves as "political exiles from English tyranny."[18] This both encouraged a sense of solidarity with American republicans and also avoided the application of state-level immigration policies in jurisdictions like New York and Massachusetts, whose early poor laws had a provision that prohibited the landing of "persons likely to become a public charge" without bonds.[19]

Irish immigrants, however, were accustomed to political mobilization thanks to the organized Catholic struggle against the British in Ireland. A culture based around saloons and parishes reinforced their will to create fraternal clubs, unions, and political machines.[20] On October 29, 1841, just before he was appointed the first archbishop of the Archdiocese of New York, John Hughes announced the formation of a separate Catholic political party, dubbed the "Carroll Hall ticket" for the venue in which Hughes made his announcement.[21] After insisting that it was "not [his] province to mingle in politics," he proceeded to list to his supporters the names of candidates who had his personal approval.[22]

When all ten Democratic State Assembly candidates endorsed by Hughes won and late Carroll Hall entries split the Democratic electorate in three other districts and led to Democratic losses to Whigs, the message became clear: Irish Catholics held the balance of power in New York City. In a sign of this power but also the Democratic Party's initial distance from the Irish in 1844, the Protestant mayor, Robert H. Morris, consulted Hughes rather than his party's own intelligence-gathering operation about Catholic opinion. Acknowledging a string of Catholic church burnings in Philadelphia, Morris asked the archbishop whether he was concerned about similar incidents in New York. "Are you afraid that some of your churches will be burned?" he inquired. Responded Hughes, "I am afraid that some of *yours* will be burned."[23] Even before the Famine migration, Irish Americans had begun to recognize their power and sought to entrench themselves.

Beginning in 1845, however, the initial wave of Irish immigrants was eclipsed by one of the greatest influxes of immigrants the world had ever seen. A deadly fungus introduced from the Western Hemisphere, *Phytophthora infestans,* spread across Irish farms and sent millions fleeing hunger and misery. At the time, the British official in charge of relief efforts, Sir Charles Trevelyan, complained that the "great evil with which we have to contend [is] not the physical evil of the famine, but the moral evil of the selfish, perverse and turbulent character of the [Irish] people."[24] Two and half million Irish arrived in the United States in a single decade—a million of whom settled in New York, where the gentry condemned "their drinking and carousing and their foreign religion, with its lax attitude toward the Sabbath."[25] While 48 percent of Irish immigrants were estimated to be skilled workers in 1826, only 12 percent of the Famine migrants had a trade, and only 2 percent had been merchants or professionals.[26]

In response, a public charge rule was passed as part of an 1847 act by the Whig-dominated New York state legislature. Framing the arrival of the Irish in apocalyptic terms, the Know Nothings proposed a twenty-one-year naturalization period for immigrants, a ban on Catholics in government, and the deportation of foreign-born criminals and paupers.[27] Even New York's Irish-born men of "rank and property" greeted the unprecedented influx of unskilled immigrants with some trepidation; they worried that the recent arrivals might sully their reputation and reinforce stereotypes.[28] They also believed that less affluent Irish immigrants were coming to America wholly ignorant of the hard work involved in succeeding in the United States.[29]

The new arrivals responded by huddling together for mutual protection in neighborhoods—segregated not just by nationality but by counties at times—that nearly replicated the social atmosphere of pre-Famine rural Ireland's coasts and glens.[30] Inside these enclaves, they could perpetuate traditional social patterns, including boisterous wakes and "Paddy funerals," in comparative isolation from New York's censorious middle class.[31] To the despair of New York's politicians and labor leaders, these working-class immigrants usually reacted to injustice by assembling in militant, ethnic associations reminiscent of the secret societies that undermined Protestant landlords back in Ireland.[32]

And despite their best efforts, nativists in New York could not counter the power of the Irish numbers. Manhattan's population was 371,000 in 1845; it grew to 630,000 in just ten years as the hunger took hold in Ireland.[33] By the time the Famine wave receded in the mid-1850s, more than 25 percent of New Yorkers was a native of Ireland, and 52 percent of the city's residents were foreign-born.[34] When the 1848 Treaty of Guadalupe Hidalgo ended the Mexican-American War and yielded nearly 500,000 square miles of land between Texas and modern-day California, many non-Irish people departed the industrializing East Coast,[35] while the Irish stayed behind and took manufacturing jobs in New York City, swelling their share of the population and propelling some into a more stable middle class. By 1850, the Irish comprised about a quarter of the population of not only New York but also Boston, Philadelphia, and Baltimore.

The famine migration fundamentally altered New York's civic and political life. Democratic leaders at their Tammany Hall headquarters recognized this demographic shift and ended their invocations of nativism. The Irish were already inclined to support them, thanks partly to historic alliances between Irish (Protestant) exiles with the followers of Jefferson and Jackson, partly in opposition to the strong anti-Catholic strains running through the Whigs, Know Nothings, and Republicans, and partly owing to patronage and their desire for a sense of belonging.[36] During campaigns in antebellum New York's Irish neighborhoods, the discussion of substantive issues was superseded by candidates' skill at wielding quid pro quos[37] and violence, often by rivalrous volunteer fire departments.[38] According to Tammany stalwart Richard O'Gorman, New York City's politics was "a filthy pool of shabbiness, falsehood and corruption."[39]

In this environment, power was wielded by and through the police department. In the early nineteenth century, crime prevention was the work of a small full-time force of employed constables and marshals and a ragtag night watch of moonlighting part-timers appointed by ward aldermen and endowed with no more legal authority than any other citizen.[40] Party loyalty was the qualification that counted most for these jobs, and the aldermen sometimes used their office to reward the unfortunate or infirm.[41] As New York grew into a global commercial capital, though, the state legislature responded to increases in crime by creating a unified, day-and-night police force of eight hundred men appointed in New York City by the mayor.[42] It was almost impossible to get such a full-time position unless aspirants had demonstrated allegiance to the party in power in previous campaign efforts. In return for one of these coveted jobs (a $12 weekly salary in the mid-1850s), officers were expected not only to continue laboring for the party at election time but also to contribute about 2 percent of their salary to party coffers and use their influence to assist party members who might run afoul of the law.[43] Remarkably, forces would be fired and hired after each municipal election. Control of the police was estimated to be worth 10,000 votes in a mayoral election at a time when fewer than 100,000 votes were cast.[44]

While most Irish Americans in New York were employed as manual laborers and domestic servants, the famine generation sought public employment over riskier ventures in the boom-and-bust private sector, and their fluency in English gave them an advantage over other European immigrants. Until 1870, the Democratic Party generally excluded the Irish from elective office. When they were nominated for minor posts, Protestant Democratic voters often scratched them from their ballots; if they still managed to win, Irish-stock politicians were often more focused on looting city coffers than cultivating more Irish representation.[45] Consequently, rather than elective office, the party "machine" was far more likely to deliver employment opportunities in the civil service or the newly professionalized police and fire departments.[46]

Few did so more strategically and shamelessly than Fernando Wood, twice elected mayor between 1855 and 1862. Secretly a member of the nativist Know Nothings and notoriously corrupt, Wood outwardly sympathized with the plight of the Famine migrants and enraged the city's moralizing aristocracy when he staffed the municipal police force with Irish immigrants to curry their favor. After he first entered city hall in 1855, 17 percent of the officers appointed to the police department were Irish-born.[47] Reporting on an 1856 election, the *New York Times* lamented, "As for the Irish, they have gone in a drove—as they always do—for the regular Democratic ticket. They will probably never do anything else, as long as they remain Irish, and it takes at least two generations to convert them into Americans."[48] Newly arrived immigrants were said to report to the courts with Tammany Hall–stamped notes that read, "Please naturalize the bearer."[49] In 1857, Wood's corrupt control of law enforcement motivated the Republican majority in Albany to disband the municipal police force and replace it with a state-controlled Metropolitan Police Department. Wood and his officers, however, refused to acknowledge the order and exchanged gunshots in a bloody—ultimately unsuccessful—battle against the state forces on the steps of city hall.

Even with the new police force, patronage politics would persist, and the Irish population gradually emerged from poverty and marginality. The ranks of the fire department, public school faculties, and labor unions were stacked with the Irish, and after Wood was reelected mayor in 1860, 309 Irish immigrants were serving in the police department.[50] The patronage did not immediately affect the share of Irish New Yorkers working in low-paying, unskilled jobs—around 50 percent between 1860 and 1900[51]—likely because the number of Irish grew as fast as the job openings. However, over that same forty-year period, the share of Irish Americans in the professions and white-collar clerical work grew significantly.[52] In 1880, New Yorkers elected an Irish Catholic immigrant mayor for the first time, and by 1900 Irish Americans were a disproportionate share of skilled laborers.[53] This was more a story of relative desirability than social enlightenment, however, as the Irish were deemed more tolerable than new waves of Italian, Jewish, and other European immigrants that followed them.

The Irish took little solace in their new mobility, and rather than join New York's social and civic institutions, they created their own. They founded a network of Catholic orphanages, asylums, dispensaries, hospitals, and shelters for unwed mothers that were constructed in defiance of the worthiness-based criteria applied by established charities imbued with evangelical Anglo-Protestant values.[54] Across the United States between 1870 and 1921, the Irish-dominated Catholic Church constructed thousands of cathedrals, churches, rectories, convents, parochial schools, colleges, and seminaries and the official Catholic University of America in Washington, DC, in 1889.[55] Between 1880 and 1920, the number of parochial schools in the United States increased from 2,246 to 5,382, and their combined enrollment rose from 400,000 to 1.7 million, a growth rate faster that of the nation's Catholic population.[56] The Irish developed their own ideas of civic morality that challenged the Protestant framework of disinterest, temperance, and laissez-faire economics,[57] and applied them to their institutions. Through it all, the NYPD remained one of them.

In their history of New York policing, James Lardner and Thomas Reppetto write that, more than other municipal agencies, the police are governed by "unwritten and, in some cases, even unarticulated rules."[58] While this makes the jobs challenging, it also gave the Irish great, subjective, arbitrary power and the opportunity to shape department norms. As the years have passed, modern leaders have established policies and an official chain of command to promote greater police accountability. The struggle to achieve this accountability reveals how difficult it is for civilian leaders to suppress what Lardner and Reppetto call the police department's "inner life," "the traditions, the fears, the lore, and all the lessons, official and unofficial, spoken and silent, that cops pass along from generation to generation."[59] Even as the Irish now enjoy a smaller share of the NYPD's ranks, their hold on its inner life is unquestioned. Based on interviews with police officers and the people who observe them, the remainder of this chapter explores why.

Forever Insecure

Risk aversion continues to drive a significant number of Irish Americans to value and pursue jobs with the NYPD and other civil service agencies a century and a half after the horrors of the Famine. The Irish have historically been more engaged in New York City politics than other constituencies, so it is natural that they would be better positioned than other constituencies to take advantage of patronage. They were also more eager to seek such jobs. "For the Irish peasant transplanted in New York, fear of joblessness replaced fear of eviction," Golway writes. "The solution was the very institution that had facilitated eviction in Ireland but that offered protection in New York: the government."[60]

Golway, an Irish American himself, is a senior editor at *Politico*, a Washington-based news publication, and has covered New York City and state politics for forty years. An accomplished historian and former member of the *New York Times* editorial board, he has authored more than a dozen books, among them a rich history of Tammany Hall. I met him in a brasserie in Hell's Kitchen, once a rough Irish American neighborhood just west of

Times Square between Chelsea and the Upper West Side, today a hub for Thai restaurants, gay bars, and luxury high-rises.

Golway's father frequently encouraged him to take the civil service entrance exam.

"I'll never forget," Golway recalled. "He said, 'Yo

u'll never get laid off, you'll retire in twenty years, and you'll have a pension.' He never mentioned the part about getting shot in an alley or having a burning building collapse on you!

"That hunger for security and the suspicion of capitalism is at the root of the Irish's enduring affinity for civil service," he continued. "You'll have a stable income, in a larger community, and you'll be part of a culture that is imbued with your own. You'll be okay, and that's okay.

"The fear of being a victim of capitalism's excesses and faults, I still have it myself," Golway confided. "You gotta protect yourself against the whims of capitalism. And I find myself telling my twenty-two-year-old children the same. 'Be careful. Don't take unnecessary risks. Start your own business? Are you crazy?'

"The Irish are not an entrepreneurial culture, and the history of Ireland suggests that. Nobody I knew, any of my Irish friends, started their own business. It wouldn't have occurred to them. And that may be a reflection of

Table 8.1 Key Factors in New York (Majority Minority in ~1880)

Immigration	Equality	Identity	Social Relations
Continuous: A fair number of Irish immigrants had already migrated to New York City by the 1820s, but enormous numbers arrived due to the Potato Famine in the 1840s and 1850s. New waves of Germans, Greeks, Italians, and Jews followed later in the century.	*Equal:* Although informally reviled and distrusted for being Catholics, the Irish were recognized as white and therefore exempted from institutional discrimination reserved for African Americans. Unlike other white ethnic groups, the Irish spoke English, which better prepared them to compete for political power. They organized voting blocs, and soon their own political and social institutions.	*Inclusive:* Despite Whig Party xenophobia and the rise of the nativist Know Nothings, Irish voting power ensured that New York's identity politics generally recognized them as legitimate members of the city and country. This recognition deepened as the Irish took up more civil service patronage jobs, and with the arrival of other diverse immigrant groups.	*Redefinition:* Once an Anglo-Dutch stronghold, New York was redefined by Irish social institutions like churches, hospitals, universities, and clubs that ensured separate but equal status, and political institutions like Tammany Hall that ensured their clout. Irish integration set a template for future American religious and ethnic minorities after immigration control was federalized.

colonialism. The entrepreneurial class in Ireland is Protestant. That wasn't a value that the Catholics brought across the water.

"The Irish were good at politics. It wasn't just the numbers, which helped. But despite colonialism and before the Famine, the Irish did participate because they had the right to vote. In the 1820s, the Reformation was still alive and well as colonialism, and while most Irish men could vote, laws dating back to Henry VIII forbade them from holding office."

"Shouldn't the authority that came with police jobs have satisfied any Irish insecurities long ago?" I asked.

"It's weird to think of police officers as anti-authority, but they do see the politicians and the brass as people they are at war with," he replied. "There is a spirit of the secret societies from rural Ireland that is alive and well in the [police] union—the notion that the bosses are suspect. The anti-authority baked into the union is part of the secret society mentality that manifested in the [Irish Republican Army]—the notion of a brotherhood that is forever challenging the hierarchy. The union operates basically like a secret society, and it's very subtle. Their negotiating style, the chip on the shoulder, the ways in which they are so easily offended. They can be begrudgers. And when you look down the list of Irish stereotypes, being easily offended is one of them." He starts to laugh. "The way the police acted when [Mayor Bill] de Blasio came on the job—turning their backs on him [at a 2017 funeral for a slain officer]—that was a very Irish thing to do. It certainly was dramatic. More than anything else, it was a sense of grievance that seemed over the top. And I associate that with parts of Irish America. I was mortified by that display. Just the other day, a friend who was a detective went on about how [Mayor Michael] Bloomberg didn't give them respect. But [Mayor Rudolph] Giuliani didn't give them a good contract. Well what do ya want!?

1. "The Irish feel like the elites look down on them, just as they did in the 1850s," Golway continued. "Academics, journalists, but particularly businesspeople look down on them as Irish, as cops, as Catholics. They are ready to feel the effects of snobbery. And that sense that they're being criticized by their social betters, that is quintessentially Irish." He paused with a look of exasperation, smiling. "But otherwise, they're utterly assimilated."

Golway is close with Quinn, the author of numerous fiction and nonfiction works about the New York Irish. Though I did not meet them together, each asked me to share friendly barbs with the other. Quinn grew up in an Irish American household in the Bronx, the city's northern borough and the subject of many of his works.

"When I was growing up, the Jewish population in the Bronx was about a million," Quinn told me. "The amount of creatives, writers, artists, and scientists was incredible. We [Irish] weren't concentrated on those kinds of dreams; we were just looking for a job. I went to Catholic grammar school, Catholic high school, and the goal was for everyone to pass the civil service exam; that was the underlying thing. Everyone should have the skills to get a civil service job. A large part of the Jews had lived in cities before and had entrepreneurial skills. The Irish were serfs essentially.

"The Irish in a sense—people forget this—they created their own society in America," said Quinn. "You had a Catholic school system, Catholic hospitals, Catholic jobs, and 'Catholic' in those days just meant 'Irish.' And by doing so, they created their own destiny. After the Famine, the Irish went into a defensive crouch. It wasn't about how the Irish become white, but how the Irish stayed Irish.

"Their identity felt threatened. There was the Protestant crusade in Ireland, resistance to their admission to America, and Catholicism was the bête noire of that era, more threatening than Islam is perceived today. What keeps groups together is not self-love, but fear of the enemy. They felt like they would disappear if they scattered. They just reformed into groups like Tammany, the police, the church, and the unions. This is about the reorganization of an immigrant group. The first thing you do with power is keep it out of the hands of your enemies."

"Do you think the Irish feel any less white or American?" I asked.

"The Irish were white to begin with, but people don't organize their own churches, schools, and unions if they were being accepted into whiteness. The Irish weren't accepted as Americans. Into the 1920s, the KKK was not so concerned with Blacks, who were powerless. They reacted to immigration in the border states. Even when Kennedy runs, there was the suggestion of [Catholic] disloyalty, lasting into the 1960s. My parents graduated from college, and there were clubs in [the waterside town of] Shelter Island that they could not join. It's not all that long ago that the hate and discrimination went away. When you left, you became susceptible. It's about safety. The Jews aren't clannish; they're not. They know the enemy is still out there. No one is going to Catholic churches and shooting people up."

Many Irish Americans have kept their guard up anyway.

Walter Harkins is a fourth-generation NYPD officer in a five-generation NYPD family. His great-grandfather, Patrick J. Harkins, served from 1884 until 1919 and rose to the rank of inspector. His grandfather, Walter E. B. Harkins, served from 1922 to 1964 and retired as chief of Staten Island. His father, Walter E. Harkins, served from 1959 to 1998 and was a first-grade detective on the Manhattan Homicide Squad. For his part, Harkins joined the force in 1993 and is a detective, detailed to the FBI's Child Exploitation and Human Trafficking Task Force when we met.

He grew up in East Flatbush, Brooklyn, and, like so many other Irish Americans in the 1970s and 1980s, his family moved to the Long Island suburbs. Both of his sons are pursuing careers with the NYPD; one of them had recently taken the entry exam, much to the chagrin of his mother. "My ex-wife hates the PD and hated my job," Harkins told me with some pride.

We met over drip coffee near the FBI substation downtown. I asked him if he wore his father's badge number.

"My old man said, 'No, you get your own shield. That's not the Harkins way. You make your own name.' My old man could tell you some stories, I tell ya."

"Across all these generations of your family, everybody had a secure middle-class life," I said. "You're no longer discriminated against and excluded. Why do you think Irish Americans like you still become police?"

"I remember when my grandmother in Flatbush told me that she made food for people because [my grandfather] had a job during the Great Depression," Harkins said. "And I remember hearing a lot of stories from my grandfather about how much respect the police got. He told me about his wool coat with real brass buttons, and they had a wooden rack that you could slide onto the coat to polish the buttons without damaging the wool. When it was the real police department, the city used to have Police Day, and it was a holiday. I don't know when it ended. He told me some good stories."

Harkins's nostalgia is not merely about the glory of his father's and grandfather's stories; it's about their security. His references to brass buttons and public holidays reveal his desire for recognition, a reassurance of status. His reference to the Great Depression was one of many I heard in interviews, and it suggests a sense of never feeling very far from ruin.

"It was not just stability; it's respect," said Ed Conlon, a retired Irish American NYPD detective. "Even if you go five generations as a free citizen, there are one hundred generations of being legally second class and dirt poor. We are people who come from peasantry. It's not as if we were talking about the Potato Famine every week, but the Irish have a tendency toward morbidity. As soon as people stop talking about their exclusion, the moment passes.

"In the eighties, when crime was an ordinary everyday reality, the city was thought to be a dangerous place. Getting mugged was normal when I graduated from high school in 1979. There was a lot of junk psychology about [Irish Catholics and] authoritarian personalities, and it's there, but I don't think it's prevailing. But it's a mythologized job. And the myth still holds currency."

Nearly two centuries removed from the Famine, many Irish New Yorkers are still not quite settled.

Part of the Family

Conlon is part of another multigenerational NYPD family from Yonkers. He is now the department's deputy commissioner for strategic communications. He was a beat cop, turned detective, turned bestselling book author. After penning the "Cop Diary" column under the pseudonym Marcus Laffey in the *New Yorker* magazine for a number of years, he published a gritty 2004 memoir, *Blue Blood*, which detailed his trajectory from a rookie cop patrolling Bronx housing projects. The book, which generated a million-dollar advance from Penguin publishers, offered a raw depiction of modern law enforcement but also violated police norms that frowned upon publicizing police work. Not so subtly, he was put onto the midnight shift by the NYPD, and, after a stint as a police intelligence liaison, he handed in his gun and badge in 2011 to concentrate on fiction writing for seven years before returning to the department.

The culture against making police affairs public is closely connected to Irish distrust of Anglo-British authority. In Ireland, the worst thing to be accused of was being an informant—a "rat," a "snitch." Conlon didn't explicitly violate anyone's trust, but he breached the "blue wall of silence." As in the secret societies, the mentality among police officers is *We're in this together—I've got your back, and you've got mine.* It is instinctively defensive. And to comply, cops have overlooked misconduct, even by colleagues and superiors they loathe. "No matter what you say," young officers are often told, "say nothing."

Conlon's job today is to consider the public image of the NYPD—to portray police work and tell police stories in the best possible light. We met at Stout, an Irish gastropub, a ten-minute walk from NYPD headquarters at Police Plaza.

He entered wearing a black leather jacket, frayed around the collar, concealing his gun. With coiffed hair and deep-set eyes that closely examine his surroundings, he resembles popular television depictions of police officers. When he is photographed, he instinctively poses with his arms crossed or in his pockets. However, he is not a conformist. A Harvard graduate, he articulates an external perspective about police work, which lent itself to his strong writing. He seems to have always had one foot in and one outside the police department's circle.

"My father was a cop, briefly, almost nominally," he told me. "He grew up in the Depression, and civil service jobs were the way out, the thing to shoot for in his time and place. His younger brother Eddie became a cop, his sister became a nurse, and his youngest brother went to the fire department. These were jobs that would keep you for life with a pension. My father was in the marines and went to law school at night. He had bigger ambitions, and he ended up going to the FBI because it was a higher-prestige position.

"My father was ambivalent about what he did," Conlon continued. "He had a law degree and an MBA, and there was some self-doubt. Instead of being a glorified cop taking mandatory retirement at age fifty-five, he could have been a judge or big-time lawyer. But he always knew people and could fix things. A bartender got locked up for drunk driving, he made a call. When something went wrong, he could put you in touch with somebody who could fix it. He could get you a job. He was like a one-man Tammany Hall." He paused. "In a good way!" We laughed.

"Nobody expected any of us to go on to be a cop," Conlon said reflectively. "I always wanted to be a writer but didn't know how I'd make a living. But people grow up on the stories. If your father works at a bank or an insurance company, you'll hear his stories about deals and secretaries. But I heard stories about robberies, chases, and other crazy things.

"One story was when he was young, working on the waterfront, and he knew a trick thieves had. They'd take off their cap in a deferential gesture to police, but they would hide a razor blade in the brim and cut the cop's face to make a getaway. So when a guy reached for his hat, dad drew his gun. In another story, he was making an arrest without his gun—which would never happen if he were a beat cop, but maybe in the FBI—and he had to walk this guy to his car. And he did the incredibly cheesy movie gag of sticking his finger into his trench coat to fake a weapon as he walked the guy down the street. There was this double message of deep cynicism—damned if you do and damned if you don't—and great enthusiasm, of having real fun. The fun is a great part of it. It was fascinating to me."

He took a drag from an electronic cigarette.

"We talked broadly about [my becoming a cop]. I started a criminal justice job in Brooklyn after college, and he encouraged me to maybe be a prosecutor. I had a ponytail at the time, and [FBI Director] J. Edgar Hoover had been dead a few years, so I wasn't sure if I'd fit inside [FBI] culture. I went to the police academy to see if I liked it. It's the police department, it's not the Foreign Legion; you can leave if you don't like it. I remember reading once that doctors' children make for better-adjusted doctors. They have a more practical appreciation of what they can and can't do. And the same is true for cops' kids."

Alice McGuillion, a police officer's niece herself, held a position similar to Conlon's. Between 1980 and 1989, she was deputy commissioner for public information, tasked with controlling the flow of information to the news media and public. As a rare woman in the NYPD's upper management, she said she kept her Irish maiden name and touted her Washington Heights roots to reassure men on the force that she was a "part of the family."

"It's a complicated place," said McGuillion, now a public relations executive. "I think there's a flip side to the blue wall of silence. When I worked with [New York Police Commissioner Bob] McGuire, he had very strong anticorruption practices. He felt like that protected the family—that if you allowed broad corruption practices to go on, you were damaging the whole. And I agreed with that one hundred percent. I never thought that burying it made sense, just as it doesn't make sense in families either. Breaking that silence, by exposing corruption, made the PD stronger. I saw crazy behavior by even chiefs who didn't want to face up to certain things. And in many cases, it cost them their careers. Just because they didn't want to be forthcoming. There was a sense that we don't need to air our dirty laundry, and that has its consequences."

With multigenerational legacies throughout the NYPD, the Irish were among the last ethnic groups to found a fraternal order—a nonaffiliated, nonprofit organization that operates on the fringes of the department. They didn't need to create a sense of family; in so many cases, they literally were a family. To this day, ethnicity and religion inside the department remain quite clannish. There is a Holy Name Society for Catholics from the Bronx, Manhattan, and Staten Island, and a separate Holy Name Society for Catholics from Brooklyn and Queens. The Jews have Shomrim. There is a Bangladeshi Police Association of America and a Pakistani American Law Enforcement Society. There is the Steuben Society for Germans and Pulaski for Poles. There are thirty-six ethnic and religious orders in all.

When the Emerald Society was created by Irish American officers in 1952, it was just at the time when they felt like their dominance was on the brink.[61] Uncomfortable with perceptions that the Irish still rule the police department and resentful of stereotypes about hard-drinking cronyism and associations with white privilege, it can be a touchy and cagey group. (Their representatives did not respond to my formal outreach.) But like the other orders, the Emerald Society organizes banquets for a benevolent cause or charity referred to as "rackets" or "10-13s," named for the NYPD code meaning "officer needs help." Along with retirement parties, these are the venues for police bonding, where the sense of kinship is rekindled. Far more visibly, they convene the NYPD's Pipes & Drums Band, a marching bagpipe- and-drum orchestra. More than one hundred volunteers strong, they play at rackets and funerals and follow the New York City mayor and police commissioner in the St. Patrick's Day Parade every year.

One of the officers most closely associated with the Emerald Society and the NYPD's sense of "family" was Steven McDonald. He was a marine medic who returned to New York City and worked as a hospital administrator, but he dreamed of being a cop. Admitted to the force in 1984, he was transferred to Central Park's anticrime unit in 1986. On July 12 that year, he was following a pattern of gunpoint bicycle robberies in plain clothes when he identified a group of men in the area. A foot chase ensued. McDonald caught up with them after thirty yards, identified himself as a cop, but—realizing they were mere teenagers—never pulled his gun. When he bent over and inquired about a suspicious weapon-shaped bulge in one of the youth's trouser legs, another stood over him and shot McDonald three times in the head, throat, and spine, paralyzing him from the neck down for three decades before he died of complications in 2017.

At the time of the shooting, McDonald's wife, Patty Ann, was three months pregnant with a son, Conor, whose life was instantly oriented around the police department from birth. Thirty-one years later, Conor is now a sergeant in the office of the chief of the department. Previously, he was an officer in the Midtown South precinct and a detective in the Queens Warrant Squad. I met them both for coffee two blocks south of Central Park, just before they attended an NYPD Christmas party.

"My dad was extremely proud of our Irish Catholic heritage," said Conor, who was named for the Irish folk hero Conor Larkin from *Trinity*, the 1976 novel by Leon Uris. "He grew up walking up Fifth Avenue for St. Patty's Day, he joined the Emerald Society, and the most important part of that was the NYPD. The men and women who came into our lives when he was injured, they took care of me.

"We Irish come from big families," Conor continued, "and the PD is one big family. When you get into the academy, into your first house [precinct], it becomes a second family—a dysfunctional family sometimes, just like any family, but with a lot of love.

"I work with people who are different religions, ethnicities, and sexualities my whole career. One of my earliest partners was a West African Muslim guy fresh off the boat in Queens, but he was one of my favorites because I knew he always had my back. He was always going to protect me. If we can feel that sense of duty with a partner, if he can have that feeling and guys answer the call, we're together. I'd pick up the next shift because I just loved being there.

"A lot of guys with an Irish background, we're just raised with that sense of duty from our fathers and mothers. A lot of my closest friends are Irish cops, college graduates, and we were all raised in that same way. . . . It's like you were magnetically drawn to it. But it was also me coming to the reckoning that this is what I was called to do. My heritage, my dad, and with what's going on in society, it was a higher calling.

"His pain was so excruciating," Conor continued. "Sometimes he would lay in bed and just scream. But anytime he would get a call to come speak at a graduation, an event, at a roll call, he'd call the nurses to get him going, get into the [wheel]chair, and get him out there as soon as possible. It's tough to explain how hard it was for him physically to do anything. But he had a sense of duty."

Patty Ann leaned toward me. "Steven's roots," she said, "both his uncles, his father, his brother, great-aunt, his grandfather, were all police. Seeing that tradition, it was almost ingrained to help people. If Steven was to have gotten out of that chair after being shot, he would have gone back to patrolling the streets. Steven once gave some neighborhood kids our home phone number. Am I gonna change that? He was a better husband and father than some able-bodied men. And I'm glad that we were married at the time."

Her eyes glazed, as tears welled up.

"My mother loved that Steven was so close to his Irish roots," Patty Ann said. "He got an Irish passport, and every year, he would march in the parade. And after he was shot, he would march every year thereafter to benchmark his recovery. We would get him home and he would be freezing. So we'd get him into bed, my mom would make corned beef and cabbage, and he'd watch [the 1952 film] *The Quiet Man*. Through all the ups and downs, the one consistency was the Irish."

The McDonalds made news when they publicly forgave Steven's assailant, Shavod Jones, who was fifteen years old at the time of the attack. When Conor was a teenager himself, he volunteered at a youth homeless shelter and mentored an African American boy who reminded him of Jones, who died in a motorcycle accident three days after being released from his nine-year prison sentence.

"I had a vivid dream of Shavod," Conor recalled. "In it, he said, 'That kid is me.' And that was my affirmation. Understanding a young boy, I understood how that anger could happen. I felt like I could work with Shavod. It opened my eyes. My parents had protected me so much after what happened to my father. I felt like I could work with kids like that. No one pushed me to do this."

"I can say I didn't," Patty Ann said.

"There was no defiance or apprehension. My mom could hear it in my voice."

"I wanted him to be a lawyer," said Patty Ann. "He was my only child. Being a cop was not a profession I would have chosen for him, with what happened with Steven. But Conor was in the top ten of his class at the academy, and I asked myself, 'How come he couldn't do this in high school and college?' He was so determined and dedicated there, it was something he really wanted. He studied and passed the sergeant's and lieutenant's exams. When it's in here"— she gestured toward her heart.

"Some people want to do their twenty [years] and out [to retirement]," she said, "and then there are others who could be making a lot more money elsewhere. But you have to love the person enough. And when you love someone, and you see that this is something they want to do, it's inside of them, you have to support them. But you know what the risks are. There are some women and mothers who don't want it, but you know what they say: 'If you love something, let it go.'"

Even since Steven's death, the McDonald family continues his tradition of community service. Patty Ann now serves as the mayor of a small Long Island town and works with other police officers' wives and widows through the NYPD's Survivors of the Shield program.

"Our faith sustained me and always has," she said. "We had mass in his room at Bellevue [Hospital] every day when he couldn't swallow anything. And with everyone who came into his room, we held hands and said the prayers. Even Mayor de Blasio. The Catholic faith sustained him all those years."

Clutching his father's rosary, Conor said, "Scientifically, something kept him alive for twenty years, but there was something else there, too. I've struggled with my religion, but I still have strong faith because of the church. You have a lot of stuff you go through as a cop, but when the world is falling to pieces, I always feel centered when I go to church and I pray. That Catholic faith continues to be passed down to us because we were persecuted for it for so long."

Lords of the City

After the famine, a "devotional revolution" took place among many Irish American immigrants. Their church was the one thing that was familiar in a new land, and the only organization that was truly transnational. Undoubtedly, the Irish were also embracing their faith in response to its vilification; they were disdained for their Catholicism. It is what made them different from Anglo-Dutch Protestants, many of whom were phenotypically indistinguishable. And when Bishop John Hughes emerged as the Irish community's primary political interlocutor as the Famine migrants washed ashore, civic and religious identities merged. The bond between the Catholic Church and the NYPD persisted deep into the twentieth century.

"If the Cardinal ever wanted anything, a police escort or something, there are no questions asked; you just did it," former NYPD commissioner Bob McGuire told me in an interview.

"There has always been a close relationship with the archdiocese. And there was an expectation—whether it related to topless clubs, pornography, or gambling—that the police commissioner was going to do the right thing by the archdiocese, and that pulled apart as the laws defied Fiftieth Street," he said, referring to the cardinal's diocese and St. Patrick's Cathedral.

McGuire had been a commissioner under Mayor Ed Koch from 1977 to 1983. Before that, he worked as a prosecutor and defense attorney. He was appointed after the Knapp Commission on police corruption delivered a sobering call for reform of the NYPD. McGuire grew up in Throgs Neck in the Bronx, which he described as "a little bastion of lower-middle-class respectability," populated by cops, firefighters, and public custodians. Raised by religious parents, he had a younger brother who initially went into the Jesuit priesthood, an older brother who joined the military, and a sister who became a nun. His father was an NYPD captain, his mother went to mass and communion every day, and they insisted on morality, good grades, and athletic excellence from their children. I met McGuire, eighty-two years old, at his Madison Avenue law office in Midtown East. He wore a dark navy suit with a six-inch lapel and a tie with navy blue and gray stripes.

"In a way, it reminds you of the influence of the Catholic Church in the United States, which was largely Irish dominated," he said. "There was a puritanical aspect to it, unlike the laissez-faire Italian Catholic Church, which acknowledged people's humanity; people are going to have girlfriends, they're fallible. With the emergence of Irish Catholic schools with their nuns and priests, it would not be unusual to have Irish American teenagers coming out of those high schools wanting to [be a police officer]—doing God's work of keeping compliance with the rules. You got security, your pension, you keep your nose clean, have a decent salary and healthcare. So those were all the components, but there was an overlay of a job that was more than a job. You had a badge and a gun; you kept the law. There was something greater than yourself in the vocation.

"Then you got into the department and reality hits you. There was a lot of corruption, a fair amount of brutality, and you realized that you had a lot of power. And not just for the Irish. They acted out either by becoming corrupt or racist or physically abusive. And sometimes the same cop would do all three. And I think that was a significant minority of the PD, and not an insignificant number of Irish Americans."

"Why?" I asked.

"There was an awful lot of racism in our society, and young men go into an urban police department wanting to do good. But then they confront reality and the use of violence, guns, organized crime, narcotics, a lot of money changing hands. And the young idealistic cop who sees this corruption going into the higher echelons of the PD, I'm not sure how you resist those temptations. And if your elders are whacking around African Americans on the street—Everybody wants to be accepted. Some people could withstand all these influences, but it's not easy.

"My father made a deliberate choice," McGuire said. "When he was promoted to sergeant, he was assigned to a plainclothes unit in the vice squad, which looked at prostitution and gambling. And twenty years ago in the vice squad, it was hard for anyone to be clean. So he swapped jobs with someone in the harbor precinct so that he could avoid that stuff and stay off the street.

"I think you could make an argument that, for the Irish, every day was a fight. To move along in society, to get jobs. These were not philosophers coming from Ireland. These were lower-middle-class people just trying to find a way out. The PD, maybe tinged with patronage, was the way. It allowed them to control the culture of the department. It gets complicated to figure out why—how a group of people who themselves were vilified at the bottom of the cultural ladder turn on other minorities when they got into power. You know, 'Irish need not apply,' dogs turned on Irish people. Maybe because they wanted to be integrated into society. There was a pecking order sixty years ago. Blacks and Hispanics at the bottom, Italians above them, and then the Irish above them. And then you have the emergence of an Irish culture in the NYPD that went on for many years. Jonny Wynn, Bill McQuaid, Cotter, Donnelly, O'Brien," he listed examples, "the beat went on.

"There were connections between the immigration, the church, the way we were taught a morality of repressed sexuality," he said. "Drinking was okay, whacking someone around was okay, but it's hard to understand how they justified the corruption. They distinguished between clean money and dirty money—'grass-eaters' and 'meat-eaters,' we used to say. If there were gamblers—not organized crime or drug dealers—they would put cops on the pad [payroll]. This was not a big moral issue, and it spilled over.

"I went to Catholic schools all the way," McGuire continued, "and then I applied to five law schools in 1958—you know, Seton Hall, Fordham, Notre Dame, and I went to St. John's. I never thought of applying to a non-Catholic school. Many high schools wouldn't send your transcript to non-Catholic universities. When you were a kid, you could go into the priesthood, but if you liked girls, [police] was the next best thing. An upright job, a guardian of the law, making sure it was enforced. You got respect."

The office phone rang. McGuire obliges.

"Hey, pal, how ya doin'? . . . You get my message? . . . I know. It never stops."

After a quick exchange, McGuire hangs up.

"You know, today, most of my friends are Jewish, and I think the Irish and Jews have a lot in common. That ironic, fatalistic sense of humor, the importance of family. [The Jews] are the funniest people in the world because they are the most cynical people in the world.

"At the press conference after my appointment as commissioner, the [WNBC television] reporter Gabe Pressman asked Ed Koch, 'Isn't McGuire's appointment just another example of the continuing Irish domination of the NYPD?' Without missing a beat, Koch puts his hand on my shoulder and said, 'Bob! You told me you were Jewish!' And I said, 'No, I said I *look* Jewish!'"

I doubled over, laughing.

"That same sense of humor shapes this sense in the Irish of doing good. Your religion tells you that's what you're on earth for, and then you confront your fate."

He paused, pensive.

"If you talk to enough Irish people, you might conclude it comes back to the Catholic Church. Human nature is so complicated. When you look back on the Catholic Church—and all denominations really—the fundamental predicate and message is one of love and forgiveness. Love thy neighbor and lead a moral life, the antithesis of brutalizing people and corruption of money. How could young men go into the priesthood, dedicate their lives to the service of God and humanity, and become serial abusers? It's almost impossible to get your arms around this. And it's not insignificant numbers. It's sobering about the frailty of human beings, which only opened up after people entered the priesthood. You wonder if there's another cohort of Irish American men who go into the police department, and a lot of them were totally honest, church-going, peaceful men, and they also went to the dark side. Is it just human nature playing itself out? There are some parallels."

Jim McShane has an answer. He started his career as a police officer in the Bronx, then became a firefighter in Washington Heights, but he returned to the NYPD and retired as a deputy chief for narcotics. Now sixty-seven, he is Columbia University's vice president for public safety. McShane's father was born in Cross Maglen, County Armagh, a hotbed for the Irish Republican Army. He was a staunch anti-English Irish Catholic, and McShane has outwardly wondered if he came to the United States as a fugitive. His mother was an Anglophile from County Clare who worked as a nurse during the Blitz in London. The two met in New York in 1948. With his proximity to Ireland, McShane marvels at the New York Irish as an insider who knows too much.

"Every Irish family has a cop and a priest," he said, as if it were a matter of fact. We are sitting in his office in the basement of Columbia's iconic Low Memorial Library. His walls are covered in NYPD and New York Yankees baseball memorabilia. "I guess these are positions of honor. And you can get that honor and job security relatively easily, without a certain level of education. But cynicism creeps in. Every kid in the academy wants to do good. But after a few years, you're so beaten down by the system. Watching criminals walk, watching people make shit up—bad guys and cops—you just get cynical. To know you might not come home at night, it's hard to keep that motivation. You start running red lights; free coffees turn into free hamburgers and free massages. At midnight in your squad car, you're the lords of the city, and it's all based on faith that you're going to do the right thing."

Lords of the city, priests and police possess awesome power over others. They occupy a space defined by the duality of good and evil and are endowed with religious and legal authority. Communities place faith in their judgment and leave them unmonitored to protect the peace, to execute God's will. They are unaccountable in their most pedestrian interactions, and they are protected by inscrutable, silent, medieval institutions. And today, both are subject to losses of faith. The Catholic Church is subject to pervasive accusations of pedophilia and sexual abuse, and the police have been subject to high-profile accusations of abuses of power and racist brutality. This is not to suggest Irish proclivities but rather a common Irish experience in New York institutions they defined.

"There are two kinds of cops," McShane said. "There's your scared old, Irish Catholic mentality. A lot of the Irish would come poor and hungry, and once they got a little bit, they morphed. They would become hard-nosed, toughest on their own, forgetting where they came from. They got a house with three kids and they became racist and [anti-immigrant]. What are you afraid of? You think you have a rough life. You got a fuckin' house in Rockland [County], you got three cars, your kids are educated, and there are people on the streets of New York City who eat worse than peasants in India—when, fifty years ago, these people were our parents. My parents were immigrants, and I'm glad they got in. How can you be anti-immigrant when this country was built on them? Sometimes, cops are their own worst enemies.

"A lot of it had to do with the [decline of the] Catholic Church. The Irish were all Catholic and the church values were controlling. But with the pedophilia scandals and the hypocrisy, the church's influence waned. The church is not the pillar, and cops had to look elsewhere for moral direction. And it's not clear where. A lot of people call themselves Catholic, but they don't go to mass. And now people think they are holier than thou, but they're not. You don't always catch the bad guy, but you always catch the victim and you have to help restore their sense of trust and person. You need to have a humanity about you. You need to have a pure heart and a willingness to do the job. But you know, there are criminals out there, with or without the church.

"The other kind is the 'wild geese,' as [former New York police commissioner Bill] Bratton would say. They're adventurers, they had higher social values, and they didn't forget where they came from. They took pride, and were willing to go the extra step and risk their lives. The Irish used to wander the world. They're everywhere, and those are the good, positive forces out there, as opposed to the people who forget where they came from."

Bratton was alluding to Irish mercenaries who left Ireland to serve in continental European armies in the sixteenth, seventeenth, and eighteenth centuries. Until the British outlawed it in 1745, the Catholic Irish gentry were permitted to discreetly recruit soldiers for service in the militaries of Catholic countries like Spain, Italy, and particularly France. Colonial authorities worried that grounding so many unemployed youths would be more disruptive than letting them fight for their imperial adversaries. Intentionally or not, Bratton invoked a Catholic morality to orient the consciousness of his force— on one hand, suggesting that police follow a higher calling; on the other hand, implying the risks of their idleness.

"I don't know where people get their morality from these days," McShane said. He pointed to a poster photograph of former NYPD commissioner Ray Kelly, on the bottom of which is printed "It's a matter of pride."

"If you're doing the job right, you're proud of who you are. If people attack you, you get your back up against the wall. The cathedral is not a particularly spiritual place, and most of us don't read the Bible. We can't quote from scripture. . . . But that sense of belonging, that's what you get from the PD, and it never leaves you."

Logics of Multiculturalism

When one of his primary antagonists wrote an 1841 commentary in *Freeman's Journal* asserting that the United States was a Protestant country, Bishop Hughes authored a stinging reply: "That a great majority of the inhabitants of this country are not Catholic, I admit. But that it is a Protestant country, or a Catholic country, or a Jewish country, or a Christian country in a sense that would give any sect or combination of sects the right to oppress any other sect, I utterly deny."[62]

Hughes saw all minority religions, not just Catholicism, as vulnerable to an oppressive dominant culture, and he advised his followers to align with other minority groups rather than assimilate the dominant culture's values.[63] "If the

Jew is oppressed," he said, "then stand by the Jew. . . . There is no such thing as a predominant religion, and the small minority is entitled to the same protection as the greatest majority."[64]

In Belfast, there were two sides—British-backed Irish Protestants and Irish Catholics—and so they fought for zero-sum supremacy. Once third, fourth, and fifth ethnic groups were introduced to New York politics, Hughes and his Irish American followers recognized that they had no choice but to consolidate, to negotiate, to leverage, to organize. Ultimately, the Protestant leaders of Tammany Hall didn't care about ethnicity or religion; they cared about votes. By crafting a multiethnic definition of New York City's identity, their politicians recognized the Irish integration as American citizens despite their insistence on separate institutions. On the streets of the Lower East Side, modern American ethnic politics—and multiculturalism—were born.

The irony is that, once in control of the NYPD, the Irish sought cultural dominance and assimilation in the most nineteenth-century Protestant tradition. The department became their sphere of influence to counterbalance their marginality elsewhere and to wield their power outside of an ethnicity-specific context. This became less and less possible as New York City diversified, however; the Irish entered other professions, and pressure grew for the NYPD to reflect the communities it serves and protects. But rather than seeing themselves in the eyes of rookies from different ethnic backgrounds, the Irish expected their own style of policing from people of different normative traditions. Despite centuries of integration and social acceptance, they wanted to keep the department their own.

"The demographics changed fast," said Deputy Commissioner Ed Conlon. "When I left the detectives squad, it was Coakley, Crowley, Conlon, and now it's a lot of Latino guys who are all short and bald. Good guys and good detectives, but it was a rapid change.

"The stereotypical difference between the LAPD and the NYPD is that LA has pressed uniforms, ramrod posture, and military style. That's not how you'd describe New York cops. They're more likely to be talkers and problem-solvers. That style is taught. Blacks, Hispanics, they all become Irish cops. That's our prototype. Throughout the seventies, when the PD was more Irish than not, the way you deal with people is how you're socialized. So Jamaicans and Ukrainians did it the way Patrolman Murphy did it. The hallmarks are humility and some cynicism, a distaste for grandiosity and self-importance on duty. Off duty, the storytelling, barroom tradition. They all go to cop bars and tell cop stories."

The diversification effort was led by the NYPD's two most famous recent commissioners, Ray Kelly (1992–1994 and 2002–2014) and Bill Bratton

(1994–1996 and 2014–2016). Despite his Irish heritage, Kelly is an out-lier. A longtime NYPD cop born on the Upper West Side, he had no close relatives in policing, and his Irish background was not core to his identity. His father was a milkman and his mother worked in the dressing room at Macy's. A marine lieutenant and Vietnam War veteran, he ascended the ranks quickly, partly because his time as an active military officer counted toward promotions.

"There are a fair amount of father-son situations [in the NYPD]," he told me in an interview. "You need the DNA to do it, and fathers do hand it down to sons. But the city is majority minority, forty percent born outside the country. We wanted a department that reflected the population, and I was the impetus behind that diversification and outreach. But it makes the job easier. When there are problems in certain communities, it was nice to have someone from the community to help. It was also the right thing to do. When I left, we had officers born in a hundred six countries. And I preached not lowering the standards. It's not a panacea. Because of the nature of the job, police do things that make people unhappy because of the use of force or arrests. But in those situations, you want someone who has credibility in that community."

"I know you don't wear your Irish Catholic heritage on your sleeve," I said, "but did your background affect your ability to facilitate this reorientation?"

"Yeah," he acknowledged. "Here's someone, me, born on the West Side, having worked on twenty-five assignments, it gives me some credibility. I didn't ride in on a pile of pumpkins. [My background] was helpful in making it happen. I've actually had people tell me that."

"What do you make of reactions to the department's diversification?"

"I think there is a natural propensity to pull the ladder up," Kelly said. "You don't want someone to replicate or diminish what you have. Yeah, there are tensions even within the ethnic groups inside the police department. And it's a funny thing, and the PD is so big that you have so many fraternal orders, and those traditional groups—the Italians and Irish—have lost some power, and the internet has helped connect people. I don't see it as Irish; it's more of a human condition.

"But what's interesting," he added, "I was commissioner for a long time, and I went to promotion ceremonies once a month promoting as many as four hundred people, and they would all want pictures with the commissioner, often as a couple. And the diversity in officers and their spouses I was exposed to was amazing. [Intermarriage] is just not a head-turner like it once was, and you become acculturated to diversity and accept it more and more. It just stops being a big deal. You don't have the bias that you did when I was way down in the ranks. The department has changed; its people have changed."

Bill Bratton was born and raised in the Dorchester neighborhood of Boston, long an Irish Catholic area. While his father was Irish, his mother was French Canadian, and he had few police influences in his youth. He was inspired by police-related television shows from the 1950s and 1960s like *Dragnet*, *Naked City*, *Adam-12*, *Barney Miller*, and *Car 54, Where Are You?* He has also led police departments in Boston, Chicago, and Los Angeles.

"The idea of the image of the PD being so Irish-centric is based in statistical reality in that the majority of its members were Irish," he said. "But even as that began to change, the Irish imagery still dominated. Some of that has to do with the green symbols on the department flag, the green lights outside the station houses. And for a period of time, the cars were kelly green. Some of that had to do with the commissioners and leadership. Some of it comes from the fraternal organizations, the Pipes and Drums [Band], and the Emerald Society is one of the more active and so prominent, along with the heavy domination of the Catholic Church in New York by the Irish. Most of the cardinals have been Irish, despite heavy minority representation. Their histories are inextricable. No matter whether you're burying a Black or female officer, the Pipes and Drums and the color guard are present. But let's face it. The Irish have a strong sense of self-confidence. They're not shy about making their presence known. It's ironic that a group that had been at the bottom of the pile for so long, they have been aggressive in their climb for the top."

"In your experience in leadership across so many cities, is all this unique to New York City?" I asked.

"You have two totally different departments between Los Angeles and New York. The LAPD has almost no Irish influence whatsoever, even though my number two was Jimmy McDonald, who was as Irish as Paddy's pig. When they did a St. Paddy's Parade they had to go up the same street block multiple times because there wasn't anyone there. We were outsiders who migrated. The average neck sizes are fifteen inches in LA, eighteen inches in New York, and twenty-one inches in Chicago."

We laughed together.

"LA is now a Hispanic department. New York, that influence is still a generation away. There has been a conscious effort for the departments to reflect the population they serve. The Irish, Italians. Jews never amounted to a significant number because it was not culturally something that they went to. Because of the perception of police as an oppressor, it was not a prestige job for Black people. For Latinos, it is seen as something of status—much as it was for the Irish.

"The LAPD is much more focused on appearance and procedure," said Bratton. "In LA, I wouldn't touch the traditions of the uniforms or car markings. It's iconic. There is a pride in the organization that has nothing to do with the ethnic makeup. Appearance was so much of their ability to control. They looked sharp and were in control. They were focused on officer safety. To give you a sense of LA, everyone in the NYPD wants to get out of the bag [uniform] as soon as possible. In LA, officers take much greater pride in being in the uniform."

"How connected to these differences is the normative influence of the Catholic Church in New York City?"

"[In New York,] the Catholic Church heavily dominated; it's joined at the hip, really. Less so now, because of the sex scandals. So [many in] the leadership of the church in both cities were Irish. Cardinal [Richard] Cushing, [Cardinal Bernard] Law, et cetera. In Los Angeles, the department was never closely aligned with the Catholic Church, and the Catholic influence came from the Latinos. The white leadership, if you will, was much more midwestern Protestant. And the rigidity of the LAPD far exceeded anything I experienced in Boston, Chicago, or New York. Policing has been historically interpreted as a tool of oppression for those in political control and influence. So the department is historically a reflection of who is in power in the city."

Long after they were subject to pervasive prejudice and social marginality, many Irish Americans still yearn for the recognition conveyed by multiculturalist politics—the creation of group-specific institutions, the celebration of minority cultures, and government recognition and protection of group-specific norms. But so much of Irish culture is now American culture. The logic of multiculturalism was always time-sensitive; multiculturalist politics prescribed accommodation of ethnoreligious differences in the short term, but only in the interest of long-term integration, when such accommodations are no longer required. Do Irish New Yorkers feel like they remain too marginal and weak to let go of the institutions that protected them for so long? Or do they want it both ways: acceptance into the majority identity and protective institutions to secure their supremacy? Can minorities ever gain true acceptance in a society that once subordinated them? Is it ever possible to reconstitute a national identity in an inclusive manner?

The answers hold implications for majority minority societies more broadly.

Pipes & Drums

As the NYPD and New York City diversify, the Emerald Society's Pipes & Drums Band has become the most overtly Irish element of the department. In public appearances, the kilted band members are very much the public face of the NYPD, but as a fraternal order, they are not compelled by politics to veil their Irish affinities or reflect a broader demography. Put another way, the Pipes & Drums allow the Irish to communicate their cultural domination of the NYPD at a time when their actual domination is no longer palatable or feasible. To be clear, the NYPD has an officially recognized Police Band, but it is the Pipes & Drums who follow retiring officers out of the precincts on their last day of work, who follow the caskets of fallen officers in public funerals, who have been invited to play for popes and presidents and on live primetime television.

The Pipes & Drums Band is therefore the closest thing to a multiculturalist accommodation for this once-ostracized minority. It tenders Irish Americans a rare license to be proudly Irish—and, more subtly, white and Catholic—in a country that has come to embrace them as part of the ethnic majority. On the band's official web page, it describes its members as "comprised of the Irish born; the sons and grandsons and great grandsons of Irish warriors who came to this country and found a better life. Only active and retired police officers are afforded the privilege." In American society, such overt exclusivity is typically claimed only by organizations that assemble or represent the interests of people of color and other disadvantaged social groups. But the Pipes & Drums can get away with it because, despite their overt Irishness, they aren't actually so exclusive.

"The Pipes are no longer an Irish thing; they're a police thing," said Rob Gault, the commanding officer of the NYPD's Times Square Unit and a long-time piper. "We're an Irish pipe band, and we march with an Irish flag and an American flag, but we march at events that have nothing to do with Ireland. And it's not like we show up in places; we're invited to these things everywhere. And now there are pipe bands in cities without any legacy of Irish police. St. Patrick's Day is one of the biggest parties of the year, but there is no shortage of non-Irish people there celebrating Irish heritage. I don't think you see that with other ethnic celebrations."

Gault has a military-style flattop haircut, bushy blond eyebrows, and a double chin. We met in his precinct office before he was scheduled to monitor a Washington Square protest by the Black Lives Matter movement, a racial justice group agitated by police brutality against African American suspects.

"Do you think Irish Americans can relate to today's minority groups' struggle to ascend and integrate?" I asked.

"I think our struggles are different from other groups'. There's not a race issue. [The Irish] struggle was more of a Catholic struggle and discrimination, but I think Irish people are proud of where they are now relative to where their grandparents were in such a short period of time. In New York, I don't think your working-class, second- or third-generation Irish American fails to see the struggles of other groups. Our struggle was only a couple generations ago. My parents grew up in the inner city, in an Irish ghetto. My mother had eight brothers and a sister, and they were by any measure dirt poor. They didn't really have anything. I am the child of that, and I don't have to look far to understand today's struggles. And that is unique with the Irish. It didn't take them a long time to raise their status. Maybe because of the Democratic Party, maybe because of civil service, but maybe because of the culture of sacrifice, charity, and faith. It's just not that distant in New York."

"What if it's more because the Irish were more quickly accepted as white Americans?" I suggested.

"I remember playing for [slain NYPD officer] Omar Edwards. It was very much a Black funeral. And we did the slow march to the church. It makes you very proud to be Irish, though, you know. The event wouldn't be the same if we weren't there. [Slain NYPD officer] Miosotis Familia, on the Grand Concourse in the South Bronx. That was a straight-up assassination just because she was wearing a police uniform. And her kids, that was a powerful one. When a hero dies in the PD, that's part of the send-off: there's gonna be an Irish flag there."

I reconnected with Gault at the 2019 St. Patrick's Day Parade, when the Pipes & Drums tuned up in the West 43rd Street staging area. They wear soldier-like uniforms with a matching kilt. The drummers wear a black balmoral, while the pipers wear a busby, an ostrich feather bonnet. Their uniforms are elaborated with a horsehair sporran and white spats over black shoes, and each member wears a gun belt with his weapon loaded in the holster. It reminded me that, for a time, the English outlawed the bagpipe because it was deemed to be a war instrument.

The clean, yearning legato of bagpipes suddenly filled the air. Pipe sergeants adjusted their chanters to conform to the pipe major, Andrew McEvoy. The sergeants then visited each of the other pipers—many of whom were of higher ranks inside the NYPD—to calibrate their instruments as well. The bagpipe consists of two tenor pipes, a bass pipe, and a chanter, which provides the melody—all emerging out of a sheepskin bag. The bag is squeezed to keep the tune playing when the piper needs to take a breath.

In between short rehearsals, the pipers and drummers mingled like it was a high school reunion. Though the band meets regularly and plays in scores of events each year, not every member participates each time, but they all assemble for the St. Patrick's Day Parade. While some diligently adjusted their pipes and stretched their lungs, others were preoccupied with the forceful back-slapping and shoulder-grabbing of the moment.

As the officers assembled, city janitor Yomi Baptiste, a Haitian American street sweeper, walked by. That morning he embellished his green coverall jumpsuit with a metallic green and gold garland, and he laughed as he brandished a handful of golden leprechaun coins. He paused to tidy up the curbside in front of the General Society of Mechanics and Engineers headquarters, as Congressman Peter King, a fourteen-term Republican from Long Island, stepped out and walked toward his assignment in the parade route on Fifth Avenue. He passed through hundreds of uniformed police officers, all gathering to march to 79th Street. The officers huddled around a food truck sponsored by the police union that provided breakfast items, including baguettes dyed with kelly green food coloring. They wore their full dress uniform with badges, ceremonial cords, and their usual nameplates: Castellano, Chou, Matthews, Murphy, Schwab, and Suero.

One piper, Lt. David Nisthaus, had skin a shade darker than the rest. He was born in La Paz, Bolivia, and migrated to New York City with his family when he was five years old. He joined the NYPD in 1990 and heard the Pipes & Drums play at his graduation from the police academy. His beat partner in Spanish Harlem dared him to join.

"So I called up the Emerald Society, and I asked if I could learn," he said. "They told me where to go, and before we hung up the phone, I said, 'I want you to know, I'm not Irish. I'm Bolivian.' And there was a looooong pause. And then the guy said, 'All right, just come on down.'"

He roared with laughter.

"I definitely kept it low. The chiefs would look at me funny at times. I got so tired of explaining the whole story, I just started telling people I was adopted! People always say, 'You don't look Irish.' So I always ask them, 'You like Chinese food?' And they say, 'Yeah.' So I say, 'That's funny. You don't look Chinese.' That shuts 'em up."

Patrick O'Connor, a retired bomb squad detective and longtime piper, approached us. His father died in the line of duty in 1971, and his funeral was the first ever attended by the Pipes & Drums, beginning the tradition.

Pointing at Nisthaus, I stirred the pot. "You know he's not Irish?"

"Well, we have to have one Bolivian in the band, you know," O'Connor replied.

Nisthaus guffawed.

"When the Irish first came over," Nisthaus continued, "they spoke English and it was a good-paying job, a good way to move up. So it paved the way for a lot of success. And that's true for me too. Look at me, I risk my life so my son can go to Xavier High School. When he says a Hail Mary at dinner, I think to myself, 'That's worth fifty thousand dollars a year.'"

Julio Torres is the only other Latino in the band. His father was Puerto Rican, but he was raised by his Irish American mother.

"My mom pronounces my name 'JOO-lio,' and so I do too. But as long as you show a deep commitment to the instrument and an appreciation of Irish culture, these guys don't care."

A few feet away, Brian Meagher Jr., a third-generation piper, prepared to march next to his father, the last original member of the Pipes & Drums still marching.

The experience was all a bit surreal to retired NYPD lieutenant Patrick Heraghty. Though born in the United States, he was raised in County Offaly in Ireland.

"To this day," he proclaimed in a moderated brogue, "they still say that everybody is Irish on St. Patrick's Day. What other nationality says that, but us? Why don't the Dominicans or the Puerto Ricans say that?"

"Why do you think that is?" I asked.

"Because this is the warmest, most welcoming nationality in a very diverse city."

"It is very warm," I agreed, "but do you think it was also a way to better integrate themselves in New York?"

"Every race has gone through that persecution," Heraghty said. "The Mexicans are going through it now. The Puerto Ricans, the Italians, everyone has to go through it."

In 1841, Bishop Hughes called upon his Irish American flock to protect other minority groups from systematic disadvantage. He believed no ethnic or religious people or group of peoples had the right to oppress or dominate others in the United States. Now accepted into the white American majority, like other white American ethnicities, however, Irish Americans struggle to identify with new immigrants and people of color.

Ultimately, the wonder of Irish Americans and the NYPD is not the story of how the department attracted the Irish; it is how those subject to strong Irish ethnic identities have continued to be attracted to policing. Ultimately, many Irish Americans have realized that the NYPD is now just as meaningful to the futures of recent immigrants as it once was for their ancestors in the late nineteenth century. But after generations teetering on the edges of status and stability, not all Irish Americans are ready to let it go.

I walked toward the Fifth Avenue parade route and encountered the current NYPD commissioner, Jimmy O'Neill, who would soon resign and be replaced by Dermot Shea. I asked him what St. Patrick's Day meant for—not the Irish but the NYPD.

"It gives us a chance, a day when New Yorkers show their appreciation for the NYPD," he said.

He paused a beat, realizing he needed to correct himself.

"Although that's also true for Puerto Rican Day and Dominican Day, too," he added.

Old habits die hard.

Minority Mentality

To say that New York was "redefined" by the influx of Irish immigrants in the mid-nineteenth century exaggerates the extent to which New Yorkers embraced their incorporation. The social and political organization of the Irish Catholic community left the government little choice. The earliest large minority to immigrate to the United States after the end of the slave trade, the Irish created a template for the integration of future ethnic and religious minorities in America: solidarity networks, separate institutions, political blocs.

The enduring legacies of Irish Americans in the nineteenth century exhibit the lingering consequences of a minority's marginality. The Irish-origin police officials I interviewed reported a general sense of insecurity among their ranks, distrust of outsiders, and a propensity to take compensatory actions to accumulate power that persists well after it appears to be necessary. That any such sentiments linger almost two centuries later suggests America's inability to fully convince some Catholics of the country's evolution and their incorporation into the mainstream. It's not just that the "minority mentality" is hard to shake, something also observed among Singapore's Chinese; it's that the evolution of a national identity is an enormous challenge.

The Irish American experience in New York perhaps lowers the expectations of how open any state can be. New York is as much a story of *recomposition* as of redefinition. New York City, in particular, didn't choose to recognize the Irish; the city became too Irish to ignore. And with the growth of Germans, Greeks, Italians, and Jews, post-1890 New York became unrecognizable to the pre-1840 eye. But even in a country designed to evolve with its demography and without selective immigration laws at the time, New York's Anglo-Dutch, Protestant majority was still largely unwilling to evolve with their population. Is it reasonable to expect later generations of an even more entrenched white American majority to act any differently? Only if the past goes unrecalled.

As I'll explore in chapter 12, the mass arrival of the Irish and other European immigrants in the late nineteenth century set the stage for what would be the

United States' first majority minority milestone, when English Protestants, the original US majority, comprised less than 50 percent of the American population. What should have been a momentous milestone in the nation's history was ignored because the mainstream majority broadened its membership to include these ascendant white ethnic groups. With the incorporation of Irish Americans into twenty-first-century concepts of "whiteness," the lessons to be drawn from their ancestors' marginality risk being scrubbed, like Fifth Avenue after the St. Patrick's Day Parade is over.

9

Culture Change

How Hawai'i Found Harmony in Its Demise

Hawaiian legends link the birth of King Kamehameha I, the archipelago's unifying monarch, to tropical storms and the appearance of a bright star, Kokoiki, shooting across the evening sky over the Big Island of Hawai'i. It was said these were omens that foreshadowed the arrival of a great warrior chief to mystics around 1736. Kamehameha's mother knew she was carrying the heralded child and fled before rival chiefs, who were wary of these beacons at a time of civil war, could threaten him. It is believed that she escaped the island by boat to give birth to her son, initially named Paiea, in the safety of the sea. Ordered to be put to death, the child was hidden and immediately handed off to relatives to be reared in the inaccessible Waipio Valley, a lush region of canyons carved into towering green cliffs that open to the island's north shore. There, isolated from the tumult, he was renamed Kamehameha, "The One Set Apart."

Kamehameha's later brutal unification of the Hawaiian Islands in 1810 ended a long period of inter- and intra-island warfare and coincided with the arrival of Westerners who might otherwise have exploited their divisions. His victories were also unquestionably dependent on Westerners, who supplied his forces with guns, ammunition, and the formula for gunpowder.[1] In many ways, Hawai'i's history followed that of its greatest king. Born at sea, set apart from the nearest mainland by three thousand miles of ocean, Hawai'i was a world unto itself. At the time of Kamehameha's rise, it was an isolated but thriving civilization with its own language, religion, and governing structure that delivered order and prosperity. As with Kamehameha's dynasty, Westerners both made the unified Hawaiian Kingdom but also brought irreversible complications that would ultimately lead to its demise. This tension never left the self-understanding of the Hawaiian people.

Restoring a Nation

Cultural norms are for much of the world what the oceans around Hawai'i are for tropical fish; they structure the society around us but are invisible and

Majority Minority. Justin Gest, Oxford University Press. © Justin Gest 2022. DOI: 10.1093/oso/9780197641798.003.0009

atmospheric in nature. It is only with their disappearance that we fully appreciate their power. After the arrival of Americans early in the nineteenth century and their subsequent conquest of the islands, Native Hawaiians were like fish out of water—their kingdom toppled, their identity suppressed, their cultural norms undermined. And by the time Hawaiians organized to resurrect their suppressed national identity during the 1960s "Hawaiian Renaissance," the nation's composition had changed. For many years, Native Hawaiians had intermarried and intermingled their traditions, their culture, and their genealogies with people from China, Japan, Portugal, Puerto Rico, the Philippines, and the United States.

In attempting to reclaim their lost national identity and cultural norms of the past, Hawaiians suddenly faced the complicated question that confronts all societies facing demographic change: Who are we? Drawing hard lines across a population ignores the ways that social boundaries have blurred over generations of global mobility, intermarriage, and statecraft; those boundaries also resist the global diffusion of ideas and identities that have weakened territorial links between blood, soil, and self. What happens when the "We" and the "Other" are indistinguishable?

In Hawai'i, global mobility both nearly eliminated Native culture and characterizes who Hawaiians are today. What makes Hawai'i so valuable as a case study in demographic change and national identity is that, in defining their nation, Native Hawaiians have had no choice but to formulate a vision that internalizes this diversity and accepts its contradictions. This obviates debates about "authenticity" and "heritage" that have plagued discussions in the United States and European states, all of which have been subject to previous waves of migration—whether by Ottomans or Arabs, Visigoths or Vikings—that left indelible but unrecognized marks on their supposedly pure national character. Even with the advantage of having already accepted their multiplicity, Hawaiian movements to reconstruct their nation have still had to decide: On what basis should they exclude? To what extent can they include while still sustaining a sense of national distinction?

After reviewing the history of Hawaiian social relations, this chapter explores four different ways Hawaiians have sought to renegotiate their sense of identity and power in the aftermath of demographic transformation: (1) the reestablishment of genealogical bloodlines and the status they once bestowed, (2) legal quests to reassert Hawaiian national sovereignty in the face of American hegemony, (3) the resurrection of the Hawaiian language and its use as a conduit to the past, and (4) the reclamation of ancestral lands and the revival of sustainable farming cooperatives. Each movement

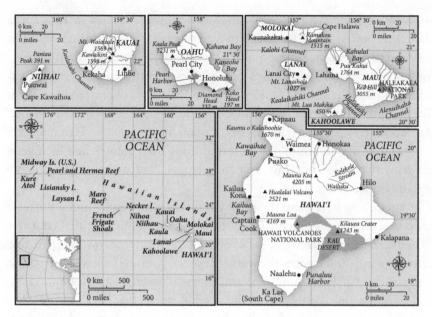

Figure 9.1 Map of Hawai'i.

reflects a different human inclination in the process of nation-building. The first two ways—the identification of bloodlines and litigation—are inherently political in nature; they seek to reassign power to the nation. The second two ways—the revitalization of language and cooperative land cultivation—are inherently cultural in nature; they seek to change what the nation means. After interviewing the people at the helms of these efforts, I ultimately find these divergent approaches—like the Hawaiian identity itself—to be more connected than they appear.

The Road to the Renaissance

By the time of his death in 1819, Kamehameha I had united Hawai'i's islands into a stable kingdom with an orderly succession. Each island was assigned a governor that maintained the authoritarian *kapu* system of religious law and a feudal line of hierarchy down to the smallest *lahui* community. Despite the inauspicious death of the English explorer Capt. James Cook, who was killed in a 1779 battle, partnerships with Westerners enriched Kamehameha I and the Hawaiian Kingdom. Under his reign, the government monopolized the sandalwood trade and imposed port duties on visiting ships while prohibiting human sacrifice and enacting new laws that protected the security of civilians. Hawai'i was a feudal, God-fearing society fed by subsistence farming and fishing, with strong leaders who navigated delicate relationships with imperialist powers thirsty for conquest. Kamehameha's savvy, however, could not stop Western diseases from killing two-thirds of his population by 1823. It is this demographic shift that forever changed the complexion and future of the archipelago.

The mortality rate did not alter the kingdom's population on its own; Native Hawaiians still comprised 97 percent of the national population as late as 1840. Rather, it was the combination of disease and the industrialization of the sugar economy. Native Hawaiians were less inclined to work on plantations in the first place, and among those who were, they could not satisfy the Western planters' voracious appetite for labor. Accordingly, the planters pressured the government to contract workers from foreign countries. Alternating between Chinese, Japanese, Filipinos, and Portuguese to ensure no single foreign-origin minority grew to significant size, plantation recruitment whittled Native Hawaiians down to 36 percent of the population by 1898 (see Figure 9.2). Among plantation workers, Hawaiians and part-Hawaiians made up an 82.8 percent share (3,184 workers) in 1872 and a mere 25.1 percent share (2,575 workers) just ten years later.[2]

During this demographic transformation, the kingdom sought to protect the status of the decimated Native Hawaiian population and the material interests of the European American planter class, which installed proxies in high-level government posts. Foreign laborers' incomes were taxed, but most were not able to vote; the Hawaiian Constitution of 1887 limited suffrage to male residents of "Hawaiian, American, or European descent."[3] The predominantly Asian laborers were also unable to own land, and many intermarried with Native Hawaiians in part to access their spouses' entitlements. In 1883, the Hawaiian government had already restricted Chinese entry to six hundred immigrants in any consecutive three-month period, and three years later they prohibited the entry of all unskilled Chinese. This all coincided with a global wave of laws oriented to exclude so-called Asiatics from immigrant admission and naturalization. When the planters seized control of the Hawaiian government and established an American republic in 1893, they wrote a new Constitution that required voters to

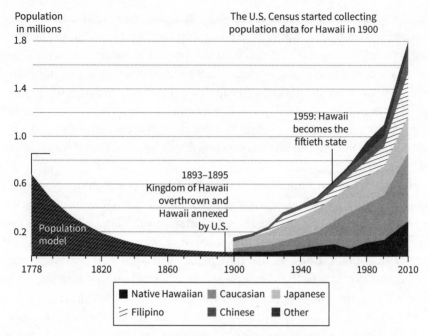

Figure 9.2 Racial population distribution of Hawai'i between 1778 and 2010.

Sources: Katie Armstrong, *National Geographic*. Data: Office of Hawaiian Affairs' Native Hawaiian Data Book; David Swanson, "The Number of Native Hawaiians and Part-Hawaiians in Hawaii, 1778 to 1900: Demographic Estimates by Age," US Census Bureau; Imani Altemus-Williams and Marie Eriel Hobro, "Hawai'i Is Not the Multicultural Paradise Some Say It Is," National Geographic, May 17, 2021, https://www.nationalgeographic.com/culture/article/hawaii-not-multicultural-paradise-some-say-it-is. Supplementary statistics available in Ronald Takaki, *Pau Hana*: Plantation Life and Labor in Hawaii, 1835–1920 (Honolulu: University of Hawai'i Press, 1984), 28.

be citizens of Hawai'i and able to read and write in either the English or Hawaiian language.[4] Asian plantation workers effectively lived at the discretion of the sugar companies.

Presaging Hawai'i's future during this period, the kingdom and Native Hawaiians displayed countervailing inclinations about political ethnocentrism and cultural openness. From the earliest contact between Hawaiians and people of European or American origin, Hawaiian women *ali'i* (nobility) married white ship captains, businessmen, and entrepreneurs, whose children grew to form a class of mixed *hapa* elites.[5] Nativists outside these circles, however, pressured King Kalākaua to preserve a "Hawai'i for Hawaiians"— to rein in the sugar industry, limit immigration of Asians, and spend resources on improvement for Native Hawaiians.[6] Unwilling to compromise the booming plantations, Kalākaua responded symbolically by reviving public *hula* performances, building the 'Iolani Palace, and commissioning an iconic statue of Kamehameha I. He sought to reassure Native Hawaiians about the recruitment of foreign labor by spending national resources on finding a "kindred race."[7] He also sponsored Native Hawaiians to attend many of the world's leading universities and established initiatives to document Hawaiian genealogy, science, and arts.

The preoccupation with preserving racial differences extended to plantation life. As plantations evolved from crowded barracks and unsanitary camps into villages with family-oriented cottages, racial differentiation dictated the location of housing and segregated social halls, baby nurseries, recreational sports teams, public school classrooms, and plantation wage structures.[8] Relegated to working in the fields, the Chinese, Japanese, and Filipinos were divided into separate "gangs," paid different wages to incite resentment,[9] and often assigned different tasks according to stereotypical attributes determined by the Hawaiian Sugar Planters Association.[10] These classifications lumped subnational groups with different languages, religions, and cultural traditions into national composites—all holistically distinguished from a *haole* counterpoint of reference.[11]

On the margins of plantation life, Native Hawaiians' natural and social ecosystems were not exempted from the disruptions caused by industrialized farming. The Native Hawaiian *ahupua'a* system of land division typically comprised a watershed that channeled rainfall through cloud forests down to orchards, taro patches, and eventually to seaside fisheries. The *ahupua'a* resources were primarily produced and consumed within the extended family networks of *ohana* and shared with the ruling chiefs.[12] As planters accumulated land, they diverted water sources away from Native Hawaiian families and subsistence farmers, unsettling these interdependencies. While some Native Hawaiian families retained ownership of their ancestral lands amid the Hawaiian government's distribution of titles, most eventually became the planters' tenants and provided crops in lieu of payment. These disruptions, however, also brought Native Hawaiians into closer contact with Asian immigrants. Like the Hawaiians, the Chinese and Okinawans farmed taro, and it was common for them to share their skills and labor with each other.[13] Commercial exchanges between subsistence farmers and fishers produced early interracial marriages that led to further ways Hawaiians introduced foreign practices and traditions into native culture.

After the United States overthrew the monarchy in 1893 and annexed Hawai'i in 1898, the drive toward assimilationism led to the abolition of countless Hawaiian cultural practices but also to the broadening of informal conceptions of Hawaiian identity. American control coincided with an enormous influx of Japanese and Filipino workers between 1890 and 1920, whittling Native Hawaiians down to a 16 percent minority across the archipelago. In

1899, about twenty-six thousand Japanese plantation workers arrived, and by 1900, almost 40 percent of Hawai'i's population was Japanese.[14] When a strike paralyzed O'ahu plantations in the summer of 1909, Tagalogs, Ilocanos, Visayans, and Pangasinans were recruited from the Philippines to replace the strikers. Filipinos would grow to comprise 10 percent of the Hawaiian population by 1920 and 20 percent by 1930.[15] These trends largely stopped, however, when Congress passed the Immigration Act of 1924 and prohibited the entry of Asians[16] into American territory, against the passionate objections of Hawaiian planters.

Their labor supply cut off, planters turned to the assimilation of Asian plantation children to develop a future workforce. Without completely jettisoning race-based policies, plantation camps became more family-friendly and geared toward the cultural reorientation of their inhabitants to a consolidated set of American and Christian values. This began with the dissolution of Japanese schools. For the decades before American rule, Japanese families sent their children to be educated in Japan or Japanese schools in Hawai'i, which were initially supported by plantation managers with free land and donations.[17] Under the assimilationist push after the turn of the century, these schools were thought to be antithetical to the integration of the Japanese into an English-speaking, American workforce. Planters therefore began to open public schools and recreation centers for children; for adults, they invested in English classes, social halls, baseball teams, and cinemas.[18] By 1927, enough Hawai'i-born youths entered the plantation labor force to effectively crowd out the need for migrant labor. The acute period of demographic change was over.

Mixing in classrooms and playing fields, the multiethnic laborers and children developed common ground and a sense of local identity. The daughter of a Portuguese laborer told historian

Ronald Takaki how her mother would make gifts of her bread and "little buns for the children in the camp. The Japanese families gave us sushis [*sic*] and the Hawaiians would give us fish."[19] Pidgin English, which was not commonly employed by the white *haole*, soon superseded the native tongues of immigrant-origin children and fostered a sense of understanding with Native Hawaiians. Takaki describes this process in rich detail:

> As the immigrants transplanted many of their old customs and traditions and foods to the new land, built new churches and temples near their cottages and gardens, gathered in clubhouses and on baseball fields, became acquainted with fellow laborers from other countries, and spoke pidgin English to each other, they developed a unique working-class culture and community in the camps. As they gazed at

morning rainbows brilliantly arching over the Koʻolaus and other mountain ranges, took walks into misty valleys like ʻIao and Waimea, and fished and picked ʻopihi at secret beaches, they also began to feel an attachment to the islands. Perhaps they belonged here, they thought. And as they watched their children grow up and play in the camps—children born far away from Kwangtung, Kumamoto, the Azores, Pusan, Luzon, and other places familiar only to the first generation—they began to think of themselves as people of Hawaiʻi.[20]

Soon, intermarriages—which were often encouraged by Native Hawaiian families[21]—and the children they produced made Native Hawaiians indistinguishable from foreigners. Native Hawaiians had surnames from China, Japan, Korea, Portugal, England, and Spain via the Philippines. Naturally, these *hapa* Native Hawaiians also inherited the physical attributes of people from China, Japan, Korea, Portugal, and the Philippines. According to government censuses, there were about 50,000 "pure-blooded" Hawaiians and 2,500 part-Hawaiians in 1870—a twenty-to-one ratio. Within two generations, the ratio was approximately one to one; in slightly more than another generation, the ratio was one to ten, and by the beginning of the twenty-first century, it was believed to be about one to one thousand.[22] Because assimilationist policies historically differentiated between white people and effectively everyone else, all people of color were implicated, and a new solidarity developed. After organizing a successful strike bolstered by the participation of Filipinos, Chinese, and Portuguese in 1920, the Japanese Federation of Labor decided to become an interracial union and change its name to the Hawaiian Laborers' Association[23]—a name that reflected the way that the union, including its working-class members, adopted a regional rather than ethnic identity.

American involvement in the First and Second World Wars enlisted Hawaiians, pureblooded and mixed, to shed blood for the new flag. American bonds were deepened by the casualties suffered at the hands of the Japanese at Pearl Harbor. These sacrifices are thought to have distanced many Hawaiians from their allegiances to and their memory of the kingdom and demonstrated their devotion to the United States. After multiple petitions were ignored by the mainland, statehood was finally granted in 1959. By that point, 90 percent of all Hawaiians already held US citizenship, and the referendum was supported by 93 percent of those who voted. About six thousand voted against it, and thousands more abstained. But rather than leading to the fuller assimilation of Native Hawaiians into American society, as ethnic studies scholar Davianna McGregor has written, "statehood sparked a reassertion of Native Hawaiian rights and revitalization of Native Hawaiian language, culture, and spirituality."[24]

Ironically taking place just after Hawaiʻi's formal Americanization, this Hawaiian Renaissance sought to recover the artifacts of Native Hawaiian culture long suppressed by their mainland countrymen. The movement inspired many pursuits—from the revival of *hula* rituals to a return to wayfinding, using celestial navigation on double-hulled voyaging canoes— each of which simultaneously honored these traditions and exhibited their ancient civilization's sophistication in the face of 1960s modernity. Small groups of Hawaiians and non-Hawaiians began to form farming cooperatives to grow taro to reestablish the foundation of an antecedent Hawaiian livelihood.[25] The unearthing of Native Hawaiians' endangered traditions coincided with their popularization and commercialization worldwide, ensuring their survival but also their corporate commodification and corruption. As a result, the same transethnic alliances that strengthened earlier union activity now mobilized Hawaiians against their economic, political, and cultural marginality as part of the antihegemonic spirit sweeping through postcolonial spaces in the 1960s. That which was once shameful was now a source of communal power.

One of the greatest local beneficiaries of Hawaiian statehood was the Bishop Trust—the estate of the Hawaiian noble Bernice Pauahi

Table 9.1 Key Factors in Hawaiʻi (Majority Minority in ~1890)

Immigration	Equality	Identity	Social Relations
Concentrated: After decimation of Native Hawaiian population by Western diseases, waves of Chinese, Japanese, Filipinos, and Portuguese immigrants were recruited for plantation labor. This whittled down Native Hawaiians from 97 percent to 36 percent of the population within fifty years by 1898.	*Unequal:* The kingdom sought to protect the status of the Native Hawaiian population by taxing foreign laborers' incomes, prohibiting them from voting, and making them ineligible to own land. The preoccupation with preserving racial differences extended to plantation life, where racial differentiation dictated employment, wages, and the segregation of social and residential life.	*Inclusive:* Despite initial nativism, there was extensive intermarriage between Natives and foreigners. Because harsh American assimilationist regimes differentiated between white people and effectively everyone else, all people of color were implicated, and new solidarities developed. Native Hawaiians became indistinguishable from a growing *hapa* population of foreign origin.	*Redefinition:* The Native Hawaiian self-understanding evolved with its mixing gene pool. This was aided by the assimilationist mission's new, cross-ethnic public schools and the formation of cross-ethnic labor unions oriented in solidarity against the plantocracy. Either way, Native Hawaiian identity became more civic than ethnic in nature.

Bishop—which, at the time of her 1884 death, controlled nearly 10 percent of all Hawaiian land. Pauahi's will directed the trust to establish a pair of "Kamehameha Schools" (named for her great-grandfather) for Native Hawaiian boys and girls in O'ahu. After statehood, the Trust resolved to elevate the standards of these schools to a global elite level and open extension programs for children who were unlikely to be admitted, to complement public education and promote Hawaiian culture. By the mid-1960s, Kamehameha's extension division served six thousand children in thirty-eight communities on six islands and included "workshops in Hawaiian culture; large-scale production and dissemination of Hawaiian studies materials for use in public schools; weekend enrichment activities; summer classes and cultural activities; agricultural and environmental initiatives; canoe-making projects; night classes for adults; and pre- and postnatal classes for young, first-pregnancy mothers."[26]

Over the years, Kamehameha Schools upgraded to a six-hundred-acre Kapālama campus in 1955 and opened satellites in Maui in 1996 and the Big Island in 2001, around the time it was reported that several non-Hawaiian students had been admitted. No historical records about these non-Hawaiian students were maintained, however, and so little was known about their experiences and numbers. These exceptions aside, the Trust was sued numerous times on the grounds that the Hawaiians-first admissions policies violated American civil rights laws. Despite several multimillion-dollar payouts, each time the possibility was raised that non-Hawaiians might be admitted, Hawaiians organized to resist.[27] In a world where culture was increasingly commodified, Kamehameha Schools were viewed as one of the last institutions of Native Hawaiian culture to be preserved for Native Hawaiians. In seeking to protect that culture, however, the ever more diverse population confronted a complicated question: Who is Hawaiian?

Each of the four movements I will now explore attempts to answer this question and fulfill the promise of the kingdom's motto, which was crafted when the monarchy was restored after the first Western attempt to conquer the islands in 1833: "Ua Mau ke ea I ka'āina I ka'pono," which is loosely translated to "The *ea*—the breath of life, the spirit—of the land is perpetuated in righteousness." The phrase was adopted as the state motto in 1959, but in 1993—the hundredth anniversary of the American coup—the Association of Hawaiian Civic Clubs unsuccessfully attempted to alter the motto to the imperative "*E* Mau ke ea I ka'āina I ka'pono," "*Let* the *ea* of the land be perpetuated in righteousness." In different ways, Hawaiians continue this effort to perpetuate the *ea*.

Hula and Heritage

For centuries, Hawaiians perpetuated the *ea* through genealogical providence, *moʻokuʻauhau*. One of its components related to deriving human understanding, *ike*, from lived experience. "You might drive up to the top of Mauna Kea, but that does not constitute that you've been there," one Native Hawaiian told me. "You've been there if you took a dip in the Waiʻau pond at the top. You have to have a deeper connection to claim a connection at all." But what does such a standard mean for defining what qualifies someone as a Hawaiian?

Civil rights lawsuits such as those against the Bishop Trust thrust this question of "Hawaiianness" into the public sphere. In the case of *Rice v. Cayetano* (2000), the US Supreme Court reversed the Ninth Circuit Court of Appeals and declared unconstitutional a law that excluded non-Hawaiians (as defined by those with less than 50 percent blood quantum) from voting in trustee elections for the state's Office of Hawaiian Affairs. While the state attorney general argued that Congress has the power to enter into special trust relationships with indigenous peoples—including but not confined to American Indian tribes—the majority opinion ruled that the state had enacted race-based voting qualifications and therefore violated the Fifteenth Amendment.[28] By designating Hawaiians as a race rather than an indigenous people subject to special protections, the case undercut Native Hawaiians' capacity to preserve Hawaiian-specific institutions, as well as Hawaiians' genealogical claims to special recognition in their colonized, ancestral space. In light of the Court's decision, what does being "Hawaiian" mean?

Hui Hui Kanahele-Mossman has a firm answer. She comes from a family of women educators who kept Native Hawaiian culture and language alive during the period of American suppression and now directs the Edith Kanakaʻole Foundation, named for her maternal grandmother, one of those Hawaiian cultural guardians. Channeling Native Hawaiian logics of biomimicry, the organizational hierarchy mimics the structure and management of ancestral fishponds, *loko iʻa*. Calling itself a "cultural-based non-profit organization," the foundation was established in 1990 to "maintain and perpetuate" the teachings, beliefs, practices, philosophies, and traditions secretly preserved during the assimilationist period—particularly *hula* rituals.

We met in her single-story, open-plan office next to a preschool on the outskirts of Hilo on the Big Island. While support staff conducted business from desks across the room, Kanahele-Mossman worked from a large round table that could seat six; the chair she offered me was positioned at a distance.

"People don't understand that there were just a handful of rebellious people in the late 1800s who believed *hula* needed to be passed on. And you can trace the hundreds of dancers today to that small handful of people," whom Kanahele-Mossman refers to as the "carriers," as one might with an inherited genetic predisposition.

"My grandmother instilled in us that 'whoever wants to learn, teach.' She was an educator throughout the state and then the world. She spoke fluent Hawaiian and never gave it up, and she loved her community—not only the people, but everything else. She loved that the beach was right here, and where to collect *opihi* [ocean creatures] and where the whales came in the wintertime.

"My grandfather, her husband, was from an area at the very south of the island, Ka'ū. He was born into a cowboy tradition, and they kept their survival practices. They knew the land like the back of their hand and where the trails were. Over miles of dry area, they knew where to find fresh water. They knew how to raise animals and how to make food from what's around them. They made whiskey from *ti* leaves.

"My mother was one of six children, and although she was very spoiled, she was very determined to hang on to her culture and language. So all of her brothers and sisters are one hundred percent Hawaiian, from blood quantum. She touts that fact, and she says that is all she knows and no other way. And that's how we were raised.

"The generation above me is concerned by the thinning of our blood quantum, and they worry that soon there will be none of us left. And whatever ancestral knowledge will die along with it. And so that is a challenge. However, we're still here, even though some of us have a pinky's worth of Hawaiian blood. We still know where that comes from, who that ancestor was, and where she lived hundreds of years ago. That has created a very dynamic celebration of who we are and how we preserve this local culture. . . . Even that pinky full of Hawaiian is chained to the healthfulness of the island. And I think you'll find that in anybody who has Hawaiian blood, especially today, they celebrate the fact that they are so integrated."

"Is the rest of your family also one hundred percent Hawaiian?" I asked.

"My father was not one hundred percent Hawaiian, and neither is my husband. I know my language, I know my practice, I know this island, and so I didn't feel the need to find someone one hundred percent Hawaiian. But I think there was a need for me to personally find someone with Hawaiian blood, and personally I think there is a need for all Native Hawaiians to seek that out."

"That's a really controversial thing to say," I pointed out. "If there were newspaper reporters here, that would make headlines."

"I think it is controversial. I personally know a whole bunch of Hawaiians who married *haole*, and they would consider it controversial. But I believe in that fact because, you know, because I am a practitioner of the language and I have personally found true identity and unbreakable connection to this island through that bloodline. It goes to say that, even though they may not have found that connection yet, they have it in them. We are an island, a people in the middle of the Pacific who can trace its race to the *ti* leaves and coral. And no matter where they go in the world, they have that birthright, that *aha*, to the natural phenomenon here."

"But if the oral history is so strong, why does bloodline even matter?" I pressed.

"The oral history is totally dependent on the genealogy. One of the creation [*hula*] chants is fundamentally a genealogy, which starts to even mention family names. There are seventeen chapters in that genealogy, and not until chapter eight does man come into reference. So even with a touch of Hawaiian blood, you can trace your name. If you don't, you can practice language, *hula*, or carving but, at some point, that connection between you and the land stops."

"Aren't you rocking the boat of harmony here?" I asked.

"The boat has been rocked. But we're ocean people; we know how to steady boats."

We shared a fleeting moment of levity.

"I'm not saying it hasn't been brought up," she continued. "The ideal has been around for generations since foreigners started coming to the islands. There was a point in time when whatever was Hawaiian was not permitted or popular. However, besides being white, other things like Chinese language or Filipino culture weren't accepted either. So all of those cultures have seen oppression. And because we were the host culture here, a lot of the others spoke Hawaiian, and their acceptance of the host culture—their assimilation—was part of the reason why everyone got along to a certain extent. I'm not saying that we've all been happy, skipping into the rainbows holding hands. Those of us public school students have seen discrimination firsthand between peers and from authority figures. But it hasn't gotten to a certain point where it becomes violent or a barrier to moving forward together in taking care of this island [because they have adopted this island as passionately as the native]."

"There are a lot of Native Hawaiians—those who have, besides their name, no other clue about who they are and where they come from," she continued.

"And immediately, they are my biggest concern, because that's a lost opportunity. And some of them really want to learn. The thinning of the bloodline and all these other ancestors, they are an identity to be celebrated, but they are a missed opportunity."

"But some people, who don't have Hawaiian blood but want to contribute to the island, feel very insecure," I said. "In my discussions with them, they will place caveats on their role in the movement you're promoting by saying things like, 'But you should know that I'm not Hawaiian by blood,' as if it may disqualify them from participating. Who knows how many other potential allies are alienated?"

"To me, it's unnecessary to feel [insecure] about their *haole* status," she replied. "I can't tell you how many non-Hawaiians have stood by me in a fishpond or *hula* class and repeat that they're not Native Hawaiian. But they feel like there's a need to say that. I don't get the feeling that they are communicating not being welcome. For a number of people, I think it's out of respect. They know that they're not part of the culture, but grateful for participating and for the provision of the artifact. I think it's more a form of gratitude."

The most polemicized artifact is, without a doubt, *hula*. Because hula is a ritual, it dies without practice. Even its plant-derived garments and ornaments are perishable. Recordings and framed photos are insufficient for authentic reproduction. It is an oral tradition that relies on each new generation to carry it forward. It is for this reason that its decades-long prohibition under the US government and subsequent commercialization was so grave and its preservation so treasured today.

In the minds of Kanahele-Mossman and her fellow *kumu hula*, no Supreme Court case can overrule the exclusivity that Native Hawaiians have on the inheritance and passage of *hula* rituals. In its intangibility, *hula*—and therefore true, authentic Native Hawaiian culture—remains out of the hegemon's reach. And so, with the reduction and assimilation of the Native Hawaiian population, the future of *hula* is also at stake.

Pua Case is a *kumu hula* in Waimea, a town perched about three thousand feet up the northwestern face of the Mauna Kea volcano—the world's highest mountain if measured from seabed to summit. She is of mixed ethnic lineage, tracing ancestors back to Puerto Rican and Portuguese plantation workers, whalers from Normandy via Nantucket, and a Hawaiian princess. She is devoted to her guardianship of the *hula*, but also to the sanctity of Mauna Kea—which already hosts some of the world's largest astronomical telescopes and where scientists plan to build an additional thirty-meter lens on land that was protected by a Historical Preservation Act for its significance to Hawaiian culture.

I met Case in a Chinese buffet restaurant in Waimea Town strip mall anchored by a KTA Supermarket and McDonald's. She wore dark glasses and was emotionally exhausted from a draining week of protests at the thirteen-thousand-foot peak. She spoke in a soft but firm voice—a voice of caution after painful betrayal.

"*Hula* is a ceremony to me, a ritual," she said. "It's sacred. I don't teach it far beyond Hawai'i ever. I teach it to interact with the spirit world, to remember who I am beyond Christianity and colonization. In its purest sense, it still allowed for the practices that came before the [assimilationist] laws and the attempts to keep us from remembering and doing that which the Westerner could not understand—so that they could break us and control us. And that's not to say that a practitioner won't struggle still when told that their rituals are breaking a Christian taboo. We have gone through that, and those who learn *hula* on the mainland or Japan don't have to; they can do it for the love of *hula*. When you are in the depths of *hula*, you are not performing; you are living through the art form and the life ways.

"The difference between *hula* and all of the other practices is that *hula* retained a complete set of practices, prayers, protocols, chants, and dances that guided the manner of going through the process. Much of the other lifeways were actually a manner of living. *Limu* [seaweed] gathering might have had two prayers, whereas *hula* has one hundred. That is the difference between ritual and art forms and daily ways of survival. More than survival, it was like eating or drinking water or planting; they're for survival, but far more. There are gods attached to the weaver; there was nothing superficial about the way of life of the indigenous.

"But that doesn't mean that they are all to be looked at equally," Case warned. "*Hula*—as an art, life form, and manner of recording history—is different from fishing. One feeds your body, the other your spirit. We are presenting right here between you and I a glimpse of a lifeway and cultural way of being that you must live to understand. We are sitting at a table for an hour, and that is different from following me for a year."

"Why is *hula* so critical to the preservation of Hawaiian culture?" I asked.

"*Hula* is a central focus of us retaining our cultural identity."

"But why is that?" I asked, trying to reach the core.

"*Hula* is all we got. It's not a weapon. But it's the only thing we have that they do not. I'm not talking about the dance—prayer, practice, a way of standing and holding oneself. I'm talking about kneeling at the crater and calling out the name of Pele, and sobbing because you are still able to do so. There is hope, rejoicing, light-heartedness, reverence, unity, balance. Why would we die to keep it? The heartbeat of our culture are the drums of the *hula*. That is what we have. When we are standing in those [*hula*] lines, that is what we stand with.

Because in the *hula*, the spirit lives, and our ancestors come forth because we call them. And so in that case, it is pivotal in everything we do."

She paused and took a deep breath, peering through a window into the adjacent parking lot. A pickup truck passed by.

"Mauna Kea is a new opportunity to realize that we are from a proud, brave people. Something is not right. Rent is too high. There is too much [commercial] development. There is less access to water. And then we remember that we come from a brave strong people. We have no choice but to rise. Mauna Kea is a unifier, no matter what anyone says. It has brought us together in a way that no one else ever could. What we risk is being in a place that does not recognize us anymore."

People inside Hawaiian social movements refer to people like Pua Case and Hui Hui Kanahele-Mossman as the "tip of the spear." This suggests a sense of solidarity with their desire to preserve Hawaiian traditions but also their polarizing approach to facilitating social change. Just as spears' edges cut both ways, the exclusivity of the *kumu hula* I interviewed deepens Native Hawaiians' bond to their heritage but undercuts efforts to broaden that alliance to others in a diverse, American society today.

Hannah Springer believes in the capacity of Hawaiian cultural identity to adapt without corrupting its essence. The descendant of Hawaiian *ali'i* nobles and wealthy American planters, she thinks of herself and other modern Hawaiians as a "confluence of Yankee ingenuity and Hawaiian sensibility." With this "hybrid vigor" of science and sensitivity, she has advised many organizations and companies about how to manage Hawai'i's natural resources. "They get painted with broad brushes as traitors and bon vivants," she said about people attempting to thread the cultural needle, "but I think there was a genuine and deep, sincere curiosity about the world, and a desire to continue the evolution of Hawai'i."

I met Springer at her midcentury ranch house, which overlooks a panorama of the Kona coast from about a thousand feet above sea level. The wide single-floor home had hardwood floors, and its walls were lined with bookshelves, family heirlooms, and acrylic portraits of Hawaiian landscapes. Sliding doors opened to the breathtaking vista above a grassy lawn that sloped downward to the eucalyptus trees on the side of the Big Island's Māmalahoa Highway. As we sank into well-worn upholstered chairs facing the ocean and sky, I referred to the *kumu hula* I had previously met.

"Does hybridity get in the way of the achievement of righteous *pono* culture?"

"When you speak to someone with a pure Hawaiian parent and who lives as a paragon of culture like Hui Hui, most of us don't live that life," Springer said.

"I admire that life. I have studied with her mother, aunt, grandmother, and father, and they are tremendously important in my life."

She looked out to the luminous view and thought of her husband, who was slaughtering cattle elsewhere on the ranch. "We live here now, and my husband is *haole*, and I'm very self-conscious of that. One of my grandfathers was also *haole*, and both of my parents are direct descendants of the *Mayflower* party. It just becomes such a complex conversation. A unique thing about [the Kanaka'ole] family is that they have retained their occupation and access to the poetry and protocol through the practice of *hula*. But adapt or die!" she chuckled. "I don't disagree with Hui Hui, but she's not pure either."

Springer continued, "A part of the conversation about being *hapa* is that if you're *hapa* Asian—Chinese, Japanese, or Filipino—you can pass for greater Hawaiian than if you're half-white. And those peoples are not necessarily any more sympathetic to the cause of Hawai'i than *haole*. Their kids just pass more easily."

I asked her, "In light of the rigidities of identity in other countries, I suppose it is remarkable that there is even an openness to 'passing' as Hawaiian in the first place, no?"

"I think there is something about the geographic location of Hawai'i—its isolation, the benign climate, the productivity of the land—that allowed for the development of a sensibility that was not afraid of the Other," Springer answered. "Unlike people in the high latitudes, we aren't struggling to enjoy our day. And I think when you live in those circumstances, your social and spiritual evolution is different than when you struggle to get warm or stay cool. . . . And even with the first example of the British snatching of the *ea* [the Hawaiian spirit, or breath of life], it went so well that we could believe that the second occurrence fifty years later would lead to its ultimate restoration. [Queen] Lili'uokalani's plea for the United States to restore the *ea* in light of the facts being presented to the government demonstrates her belief in the power of those facts and the power of the law. And that is a disappointment that we're still smarting from.

"But even Hui Hui's sister, Kekuhi, is teaching *hala'uhi'a*, the *kanaka* [Hawaiian] sensibility, and I have heard her say that 'If you are breathing in the air of Hawai'i, you're Hawai'i. If you are drinking the water of Hawai'i, you're Hawai'i. If you are eating food grown in the soil of Hawai'i, then you're Hawai'i. And if your bones are in that same soil, you're Hawai'i.'

"There are things about Hawai'i that are only for my children and me, but if a measure of success upon a landscape is the intelligence with which you live on that land, my *haole* husband is as *kanaka* as the rest of them."

She smiled, and then adjusted her seat.

"Having said that, given the demographic pressures today, I feel Hui Hui's urgency.... The math supports her urgency. But I and our children have been tremendously fortunate in that our non-Hawaiian spouses have been willing and able to enter into the lifestyle of living within our environmental means."

It is this personal, intimate experience with mainlanders that inspires Springer's confidence that not only must Hawaiians broaden the reach of their cultural movement for it to be successful but that newcomers have the capacity to match the *kanaka* sense of guardianship as surrogates. She concluded with an allegory.

"An ancestor went to the summit of Mauna Kea. He followed the protocols that gave order to the relationships between man and deity. He later retreated from the mountain before deity settled on the summit. No matter where we think we are in the social and political hierarchy, there is always something higher than us. There are many examples of *ali'i* who got a little big for their *malo* and were disciplined for their breach of the order—whether it's the family, political, or environmental order. And our growth area is in restoring the environmental, natural order."

As opposed to the genealogical family or political order, clearly. A pragmatist, Springer believes the natural order—the integrity of the land, the *'aina*, that which feeds—remains in Hawaiians' control.

"And that is something that can be taught," Springer said, reassuring herself. "I pray so."

Struggles for Sovereignty

A fundamental assumption in Springer's optimism is that she believes Hawaiians—natives and otherwise—can serve as custodians of the land without the restoration of property rights. A vocal set of activists disagrees. Since the Hawaiian Kingdom extended landownership to Western planters and missionaries, Hawaiians have seen the incremental exploitation of their water, soil, and seas. Accordingly, an integral part of the movement to revitalize Native Hawaiian culture has been the belief that the US annexation of the kingdom and the appropriation of its land was the original sin, redeemable only with the return of Hawaiian sovereignty directly by the United States or at the direction of supranational institutions.

In 1976, a group of activists occupied Kaho'olawe, an uninhabited Hawaiian island that the US Navy used as a bombing range, in an effort to make a claim for self-governance and resist the American destruction of Hawaiian land. Approximately forty such sovereignty organizations have evolved since then to reclaim the control of lands lost to the US government.[29] However, the concept of sovereignty is amorphous and could mean a completely independent Hawai'i under the exclusive or predominating control of Hawaiians, limited sovereignty on a specified land base administered by a representative council but subject to federal regulations, legally incorporated land-based units within existing communities linked by a common elective council, or a "nation-within-a-nation" on the model of Native American Indian nations.[30] Even though Native Hawaiians are divided over whether sovereignty should even be pursued in the first place, multiple voices claim to represent the will of the approximately half-million people with some indigenous ancestry.

Prominent among them is the Nation of Hawai'i. Still mobilized by the Kaho'olawe protests in 1978, a subset of activists took over the lighthouse at Makapu'u Point, the southeastern-most point of O'ahu and a symbolic landmark as the historic landfall for all sea traffic from the US West Coast to Honolulu. The lighthouse was originally built due to a petition and support from American shipping interests in 1888 in the lead-up to Hawai'i's annexation. Led by Dennis "Bumpy" Kanahele, organization members filed an heirship deed before forcibly overtaking the lighthouse. After a month of occupation, they were arrested and removed from the site. Kanahele served a year of jail time and was on parole until 1991.[31]

In 1993, Kanahele and a group of about 150 activists occupied state-owned Makapu'u Beach, a mile west of the lighthouse, claiming the land as sacred refuge because it contained a *heiau*, a Native Hawaiian temple, and in light of his rights to the land as a direct descendant of the Kamehameha bloodline.[32] When state police moved in to evict them, Kanahele began a fifteen-month negotiation that culminated in an extraordinary agreement allowing members to relocate to "traditional housing" on forty-five acres and a watershed just inland in Waimanalo.[33] State employees cut a road into the rain forest and brought in water lines, electricity, and portable toilets to the site.[34] Members built homes, organized a local government, cultivated crops such as beans and taro, and carefully scrutinized visitors before entry was permitted. With a fifty-five-year lease, the Nation of Hawai'i was born and Kanahele was its head of state.

Swiftly, the members moved to exempt themselves from American authority and assemble a base of popular support. In November 1993, they were invigorated by President Bill Clinton's signing of the "Apology Resolution," a joint congressional resolution that "acknowledges that the overthrow of the Kingdom of Hawai'i occurred with the active participation of agents and citizens of the United States and further acknowledges that the Native Hawaiian people never directly relinquished to the United States their claims to their inherent sovereignty as a people over their national lands, either through the Kingdom of Hawai'i or through a plebiscite or referendum."[35] Citing this resolution, Nation members spoke in public forums with local residents about sovereignty and authored the Proclamation of the Restoration of the Independence of the Sovereign Nation-State of Hawai'i and the Hawaiian Constitution. They manufactured and issued Nation of Hawai'i driver's licenses and insurance cards, with instructions to display them to police officers if detained. Participants handed out pamphlets at various areas in and around Waikiki, nonviolently telling the *haole* tourists to "go home."[36]

Today, the nation and its *pu'uhonua* (refuge) survives on subsistence farming and the sale of products deriving from a marijuana greenhouse. It runs a weekly medicinal marijuana clinic and recently introduced AlohaCoin, the "world's first and only crypto currency with a national identity and land base, the national monetary system of the Nation of Hawai'i." Police do not enter the refuge, though they maintain communication with the nation's leadership. Though now a peaceful movement and colony, its black iron entry gate is a relic of the nation's adversarial history. It is adorned with the nation's black and yellow flag on the front and upside-down Hawaiian state flags on the back. The adjacent guardhouse has signs draped across it, demanding "Free Hawai'i" and "Restore Hawaiian Sovereignty," and a "Free Mauna Kea" bumper sticker. When I arrived, the dark backdrop of the windward Ko'olau Mountain Range was a dark, forbidding shade of green dramatized by hovering clouds.

At fifty-five years old, Bumpy Kanahele still cuts an imposing figure. Broad-chested with thick legs and fleshy, paw-like hands, he exudes the casual confidence of a folk hero when he furrows his brow and speaks about himself in the third person. A shock of gray now mixes into his straight black hair that falls to the sides of his head. He greeted me in a sort of all-terrain golf cart that had a yellow "SOVEREIGN" license plate. We drove slowly uphill through the nation he founded—a modest village of several dozen prefabricated homes with small orchards, cars parked on lawns, and dogs wandering under metal canopies and palm trees. About seventy people live there full time.

"I've built everything that we've done on the 1993 Apology Resolution; that was the magic potion," he said as we entered his office in a trailer on the top of a promontory. "And today, it's starting to really reach people differently across generations. . . . How can you build a society off of a wrong—something so devastating to a population of nationals? The Apology Resolution made the foundation so strong because finally America admitted to the overthrow. It doesn't just go away now that you've said you're sorry. They can't walk away; restitution kicks in. It was federal recognition of a form of government, and I took the path of independence because it afforded us that right. . . . Throughout the whole thing, I got picked up by the feds in August 1995, accused of harboring a fugitive, threatening federal agents—just political things to get Bumpy Kanahele off the streets and slow this thing down."

"During the period that you were struggling to pursue sovereignty so aggressively," I said, "there were others fighting against Western and American domination using Native Hawaiian culture. Why was the cultural movement more tolerated than the political?"

"The Hawaiian language, the [*hula*] dance, was becoming stronger at the same time [as sovereignty movements]—which created thousands of new Hawaiians," he explained. "And that spirit did more—it had the biggest impact—on things. The revitalization had many parts. Koʻoholawe in the 1970s brought understanding to people outside the movement. In the 1980s, we got heavy into land occupation. . . . But without the communications media, people didn't have access to the information about the cultural practices being shut down—until the language was taught in the schools and the *hula* came back out. Then the ocean stuff, the *hokulea* [voyaging canoe]. What got them there was the funding. The *aliʻi* trusts like Kamehameha, Hawaiian Homes—they're not necessarily anyone's friends—I found it difficult to get any help from these guys. But they supported the cultural movement. . . . People didn't know that the action we were taking on the streets was revitalizing the interest in the culture and the arts, and the language is what revived the spirit of *aloha* in such a way that everybody started to see how the nation came about. If the arts and crafts connected with us, they risked getting cut off. But we stuck by these things for twenty-five years."

"Are you saying that the cultural movement sapped political energy?" I asked.

"The culture is more fun; kids are involved," he said, as a green gecko began to crawl across the wall behind him. "Promoting that takes people away from building a country, the political side. Because of the law, we realized we didn't need anybody's permission to create a nation."

"So what's the vision?"

"If America released Hawaiʻi, [it would set a precedent]. People come here looking for that spirit. Everybody comes here looking for that, the secret is *aloha*. But we cannot fight back, we cannot pursue violent things, because that's the way *aloha* works. No more boundaries. Transportation, energy distribution, and communications each dissolve boundaries. . . . So we're not talking about sovereignty anymore; we're talking about connectivity. That has cut off a lot of the geographic laws that were previously associated with boundaries. That's the dream."

He leans across the table in front of me.

"To get there, small people need to be empowered to reach out and not be [stuck inside] the boundaries that kept us in our place. Today, people can become citizens without residency. They have e-residents like Estonia. We are doing the same thing." Quoting a speech by the former president of the University of Hawai'i, Harlan Cleveland, Kanahele said, "We are one of the most intriguing experiments in the building of a multicultural society."

Indeed, this pluralism is what separates the Nation of Hawai'i's approach from that of Kanalehe-Mossman, the *kumu hula*, and the exclusivity she places on Hawaiian identity and the transfer of its essential traditions. Beyond his occasional invocation of his personal Kamehameha lineage, Kanahele isn't concerned with blood quantum. His refuge of Hawaiian sovereignty and "connectivity" neither mandates nor implies any hereditary prerequisites. One of his administrative deputies was a white American *haole*, and multiple residents lack Native Hawaiian roots. He is looking for allied citizens, not kin.

This is also true for Ke'anu Sai, a retired US Army captain and lawyer who has spent the past three decades contending that Hawai'i remains in a state of war from 1893—that the United States unlawfully acquired the Hawaiian Kingdom's territory and that American regulatory power is therefore illegitimate. Since 1995, he has attempted to activate the Hawaiian monarchy's regency to assume the function of a government exiled from an occupied state and declared his ideas to Hawaiians, irrespective of their ethnic background. In 1998, under Sai's influence, Big Island resident Lance Larsen discarded his driver's license and plates and drove his truck around Hilo with a placard of Section 6 of the 1859 Hawaiian Civil Code displayed. Larsen refused to pay a variety of fines because he said doing so would recognize American authority in Hawai'i and constitute an act of treason against the Hawaiian Kingdom. Sai escalated the case to the Permanent Court of Arbitration in The Hague—*Larsen v. The Kingdom of Hawai'i*—which implicitly recognized the kingdom's enduring existence in agreeing to hear the case. In August 2018, Hawai'i County Councilwoman Jen Ruggles refused to cast votes on behalf of her constituents because of her concerns that her votes may "constitute war crimes" against the Hawaiian Kingdom. Her colleagues ejected her from the council chamber, and she did not run for reelection.

Though Sai dismisses Kanahele as "simple" and his Waimanalo refuge as "artificial," they agree that Hawaiian identity is not only about bloodlines. "The issue here is nationality, not Hawaiian ethnicity," Sai said. "You can be *haole* and be Hawaiian. 'Hawaiian' is short for 'Hawaiian subject' and, in 1893, people could acquire Hawaiian citizenship by natural birth, parentage, and naturalization. So we have to be mindful of that. But people are operating on the ethnic lens: they basically manufactured a crisis of being colonized and its inherent racism. All of that was post-1893. That irresponsibly plays the race card back to Captain Cook, and suggests that our people were not agents but rather subjugated by foreigners. That reifies a false narrative. We are the by-product of our denationalization everywhere. They don't realize what power we have in our hands as a state."

No matter how peaceful or legalistic the sovereignty movement has been recently, however, it is inherently adversarial and asks modern Hawaiians to effectively choose between an indigenous heritage most can barely conceive of and the familiarity and convenience of their American incorporation. "Being torn is part of being spoiled in [American] society today, with all the com-forts," Kanahele said. "We are Hawaiians by birth, Americans by force."

The refuge residents continue to accumulate dozens of unpaid traffic and parking violations that they refuse to acknowledge because they were assessed by American officers. State police are still not permitted to enter the refuge. "The cops ain't our enemy," Kanahele said, "but I'm not going to just let your ass in here. . . . Once we get to the resources, that's going to help us make it easier to communicate, because right now we're just focused on survival. The real *akamai*, the smart ones, they're thinking about how to get a base to engage."

A Universal Language

For many activists, schools have been that base of engagement. The Hawai'i state public education system is the only state system in the United States in which indigenous students comprise the largest proportion, more than a quarter, of the total enrollment.[37] As a result, and in the tradition of the ante-cedent Japanese schools, there remains a demand for semi-autonomous ed-ucational spaces governed by local communities in the interest of ensuring that Hawaiian language and culture are taught. Article 10 of the Hawai'i State Constitution even states, "The State shall promote the study of Hawaiian cul-ture, history and language and provide for a Hawaiian education program consisting of language, culture and history." The proportion of native charter schools as a share of all public schools in Hawai'i also exceeds that of all state public education systems in the United States,[38] and most of these schools focus on teaching the Hawaiian language, 'Ōlelo Hawai'i, often in full immer-sion environments.

In 1980, a mere two thousand Hawaiian native speakers remained in the world, and only twenty-five of them were under ten years of age. Fearing the language's extinction, Native Hawaiians noted the examples of linguistic education set by Maori schools in New Zealand and Mohawks in Canada, and they pursued approval of Hawaiian as an acknowledged state language to be taught in schools.

In 1987, when the first immersion program started at the Pūnana Leo Schools, there were only four people who were teaching Hawaiian in classrooms in just two schools, one in Oʻahu and one on the Big Island. For them, the Hawaiian language was a portal to their past, access to heritage, because Hawaiian values are embodied within the language, rendering a way to communicate and define Hawaiians' politicized relationship with the natural earth.

One of those four teachers was Lehua Veincent. Of mixed Chinese, Portuguese, and Hawaiian descent, Veincent was raised by a Catholic family and sent to the same private Catholic school that his father and grandfather attended. His mother was beaten for speaking Hawaiian early in life and, although she swiftly assimilated and attended standard English schools across town rather than the local Hawaiian school, she still practiced traditional Hawaiian fishing and farming. From this upbringing, Veincent saw how language could stitch marginalized peoples together and persist despite assimilationist pressures. Today, he is the *poʻo kumu* (principal) of the Hawaiʻi campus high school for Kamehameha Schools, once an instrument of assimilation and later a lightning rod for Native Hawaiian nationalism.

We met inside his office on the Kamehameha Schools' sprawling modern campus in Keaʻau, eight miles south of Hilo. Set on 312 acres of hilltop forest-land, the $225 million campus looks like a small university with state-of-the-art athletics, arts, and classroom facilities, all on nicely landscaped grounds. Veincent's office was a jumble that reflected the many demands placed on a school principal. His walls were lined with books, wood carvings, and framed photos. In the foreground sat a stack of plastic file boxes, a large stuffed animal, his bicycle, and a hat stand with his academic regalia and a mylar balloon. He sat with his legs crossed in front of a large photograph of Bernice Pauahi Bishop, the schools' founding benefactor.

"What share of your students identify as Native Hawaiian?" I asked him.

"All of them," Veincent responded without hesitation. "In one way or another, they do. That's something that's ingrained in them from a young age. But I always make mention that we are mixes. I wouldn't know my Chinese and Portuguese side if I didn't know my Hawaiian self first. . . . Many of these students may not have the ethnic background. So they may also not have the cultural practices. What the immersions and charters did was create opportunities to educate themselves in a system that was Hawaiian. So the values became taught equally across them. That's how people knew they were more similar than they were different. We never said that we were doing this to save our race; we did it to build a strong foundation as people to take care of our land, ocean, songs, communities. And that crossed everybody. Just because Hawaiians are preferenced [for admissions], our own awareness of our Hawaiianness creates greater awareness of our other cultural backgrounds. We have come a long way since 1987. We were always taught about blood quantum in my family. We were very concerned about genealogy. I was also a product of Hawaiian Homelands [residences], which required us to have a certain blood quantum. But it depends on whether families transfer this awareness. Families need to have those conversations constantly."

"How would you define the Hawaiian identity?" I asked. "Personally. In the way you wish for your school to convey it?"

"The standardization of who we are as Hawaiians needs to stop, because we are built by our different senses of place and the various foundations, the five *ike mauli*. We understand that we live in a dualistic society at this point. *Kumulipo*, our creationist genealogy chant, explains who we are as a land and people. It speaks about how you can't have one without the other. A *pakukui* fish in the ocean and the *kukui* tree on the land—they are counterparts. The *kauila* eel is balanced by the tree of that name on the land. You cannot have wellness without illness. Everything exists in duality. That is transferable to education—the premise of Hawaiian charter and immersion schools. To have an intellectual foundation, you must balance it with a cultural foundation. And so we can still be very focused on college—Harvard, Stanford, the military—but we have also strengthened the students and their families' concern with their cultural foundation of who you are and where you come from."

Wary of what a nationalist might think about shipping Hawai'i's best and brightest to the mainland, I asked, "Is this focus on Western understandings of achievement betraying authentic precolonial roots?"

"I think we have to adjust and adapt ourselves," Veincent said. "Whether you existed before Captain Cook's arrival or now, part of being Hawaiian is to adapt. Nothing stays stagnant. I'm more than sure that some of our prophets were insightful about change. Ke'a Ulumuku was a prophet who told his chiefs of the coming of foreigners. He foresaw the breaking down of the Hawaiian temples and the death of Hawaiians from sickness. And whatever they shared with their *ali'i* [nobles], they had to prepare for. So we still know that we need to prepare as well because we know that the future has. We put our students on college visits so that they can come back and plan better. They will not be blind to the political and economic challenges that exist locally or globally."

"But why not resist greater American hegemony?" I asked. "Why not orient education in a more antagonistic way?"

"It's about allowing choices for our children. How can we approach our learnings from a Hawaiian focus in order for them to choose their own pathways? We provide them with an understanding of our own Hawaiianness to build resiliency that allows them to make positive and reshaping choices."

He paused and took a deep breath.

"Look, there is a lot of insecurity. How can we operate a Hawaiian school with people of such diverse ethnic makeup? But this is the role of the schools, to consolidate disparate peoples into a common *oiwi* consciousness and understanding that you congregate here with the obligation to return back to your land. That is the truest application, what they do when they go back home."

As Kamehameha Schools have evolved to attract and promote the most ambitious and high-potential Hawaiian youths and their parents, Veincent said, he and his colleagues must work harder to achieve these goals. Students and parents are looking for an advantage in the capitalist race for resources, imposing Western understandings of relationships toward an end. In response, Kamehameha administrators offer what they call the "*oiwi* edge," the advantage of indigenous Hawaiian sensibilities—which suggests that their relationship to their *lahui* community is the end itself. When parents work hard to "get out of the taro farms" and want to see their children excel on American terms, it is the Hawaiian language that communicates the compatibility between Native Hawaiian thought and these modern ambitions.

"Any time you invoke Hawaiian language, you are uniquely thinking in Hawaiian terms," says Cheryl Ka'uhane Lupenui, the director of the nonprofit Kohala Center, which has worked to infuse Native Hawaiian values into the state's schools. Lupenui previously served a four-year term on Hawai'i's Board of Education and was the CEO of the Young Women's Christian Association of O'ahu for a decade. We met in a conference room at her Waimea Town office.

"You're not trying to translate an English construct," she explained. "It's a deep-rooted, ancestrally grounded understanding, and so don't try to use a one-word interpretation. We strive for a state of *pono*, a deep-rooted Hawaiian construct—something you can't understand without coming from Hawai'i."

Her last statement was reminiscent of the *kumu hula* and the exclusivity she placed on the Hawaiian identity, but then Lupenui made a critical pivot.

"We need to engage with as many people who want to engage respectfully with the island as possible. It is an inclusive expectation. And there is a need for us to understand levels of readiness. So we don't exclude anybody from the party. So I'm a hybrid, with my Italian, German, French, English, and Hawaiian roots, and my husband is Spanish, Portuguese, Scottish, and Hawaiian. And I feel like those of us who have come from that place of hybridity, we bring a unique perspective and have a role to play. I can navigate multiple worlds; it's a strength. There was a time when I felt more comfortable in front of a board of white CEOs than with Native Hawaiians. Hawai'i is dealing with multiple cultures, and we can't devalue one or another. I don't want to homogenize our culture. Love is love. I don't believe in marrying for gene pool. We will [eventually] lose those who can claim one hundred percent Native Hawaiian background, and that is a huge loss. But I also feel like Hawaiian culture is a lived and practiced experience and that is open to everybody.

"I think that there is a difference in that I can trace my ancestors to these islands and that gives me a *kuleana*, a responsibility through lineage and genealogy. That being said, as the Japanese and Chinese have come postcontact, that gives them *kuleana*, too. And Hawaiians have such a vocabulary to define their relationship to these islands. *Kama 'āina* [being a person of the land] is not reserved for Native Hawaiians."

The Hawaiian language has an elaborate set of expressions that specify different relationships between people and the land of the Hawaiian archipelago. Many of these expressions modify the word *hoa*, a grammatical construct typically associated with parents and inherited relationships:

> *Hoa hanao* denotes a biological relationship from birth.
> *Hoa loha* refers to a beloved friend.
> *Hoa 'āina* refers to a tenant or caretaker of the land.
> *Hoa noho* refers to residing or sitting.
> *Malahini* is somebody who is not familiar with a place, but that is not just a tourist.
> *Kupa 'āina* refers to someone who has been on the land for a long time.
> Only *kanaka ma'oli* refers to someone who is ancestrally connected to Hawai'i.

In interpreting all relationships to be somehow unchosen, *hoa* discourse presumes that they are all somehow inherent and organic rather than volitional. More subtly, the Hawaiian language—and through it, Hawaiian culture—incorporates everybody into the natural balance of society.

"Culturally, there is a recognition that we can live in dualities and multiplicities without being in conflict," Lapenui continued. "Hawaiians can embrace the missionaries' god while continuing with their polytheistic religion too. There was an acceptance that they were not necessarily in conflict. They lived in the 'and and and' space. And there was such an acceptance of intermarriage . . . so we don't think that we will lose our culture if we accept another culture."

The power of the Native Hawaiian language derives from the pluralistic mindset it enables its students to articulate. But is this a strategy to renegotiate the Hawaiian identity more broadly? The 2010 census reported that only twenty-four thousand households identified Hawaiian as their dominant language, and about ten thousand people are estimated to be fluent speakers—six times the number in 1980 but less than 1 percent of the state's current population.[39] And although more than twenty-five hundred students annually enroll in the eleven Hawaiian preschools and twenty-one immersion and charter schools, and another eight thousand study the Hawaiian language in other higher education settings each year, this remains a fraction of Hawai'i's youths.[40]

However, Lapenui believes that language is merely one portal to the pluralism of Hawaiian thinking: "The cultural practices and 'āina, land-based work are also . . . an entry point for those who want to learn. . . . Our journey now is how to normalize that thinking every day in multiple spaces that are not Hawaiian, and how to shift spaces to be more Hawaiian. And in this adaptation, we need to have multiple ways of doing something and [advocating] that 'āina [a relationship to the land that feeds] is not exclusive to Hawaiian culture. In Italy, if you are running a vineyard for a hundred years, that is 'āina, too."

Sons of the Soil

There is a Native Hawaiian legend that says when spirits pass on to the afterlife, they must be accompanied to come over the Waianae Mountain Range and its crest at Ka'ala on the leeward west coast of O'ahu. The spirits that were not accompanied remain in that region and are thought to be disgruntled and mean-spirited. Such is the reputation for the people of Waianae today. The working-class, agrarian town about thirty miles northwest of Honolulu is notoriously the "roughest" neighborhood in Hawai'i, and one of its poorest. But in the middle of the hot, arid valley where one of the earliest Hawaiian homesteads was established, a farm is using Native Hawaiian agricultural practices to endow a new generation with Hawaiian norms and values.

MA'O Farms is a social enterprise—a nonprofit that generates revenue. Covering forty-one acres, it is the largest organic farm on O'ahu in size and in revenue. The farm grows fifty different indigenous and introduced crops—beets and bananas, pak choi and eggplants, rainbow chard and several varieties of radishes—rotating them all year round to control pests and let the soil recover. Its grounds feature an open-air communal kitchen, a dining area, and a canopied production line where the day's harvested crops are sorted, washed, and packaged for shipment to a variety of statewide retailers like Whole Foods and Foodland. Its daily operations are run by community college students from the Waianae community—all of whom must be seventeen to twenty-four years old with high school diplomas and aspirations to complete a bachelor's degree. The farm will hire anyone who applies and signs them to a two-year contract that requires sixteen to twenty hours per week of harvesting, packaging, and delivering the produce in exchange for full university tuition and a monthly stipend. In their first year, the employees learn every aspect of farm operations and are taught life skills related to self-reliance and resiliency. In the second year, they are asked to lead a team of first-year workers and model the desired work ethic.

"We like to be eloquent middle fingers to what that narrative of Waianae is," said Kamuela Enos, the farm's director of social enterprise for the past decade. "We've built ourselves into a defiant identity. This is a space to show what agriculture should look like for Hawai'i. It's not about being part of a global supply chain, which is giving us Type 2 Diabetes at 7-Eleven. Our ancestors were the first organic farmers. An important part of organic farming is soil regeneration, so we see soil as an endowment that future generations have access to. The soil is the principle, and the crops are the interest, and we would never cash our principle and call ourselves 'rich.' So we've tried to indigenize to repurpose the colonial structures and systems that were thrust upon us and turn them into vehicles for our ancestral responsibilities: to always bequeath abundance and intact social and ecological systems—products of a nonextractive economy."

Underneath a trucker's hat and a shaggy salt-and-pepper beard, Enos speaks swiftly but with razor-sharp acumen. A lecturer in the University of Hawai'i–Manoa's Department of Urban and Regional Planning and once a thirty-six-year-old commissioner on President Barack Obama's White House Initiative on Asians and Pacific Islanders, he is as confident and defiant as the messages he conveys. I spoke with Enos alongside MA'O Farms cofounder Kikui Maunakea-Forth. Like Enos, she is an agrarian intellectual in a trucker's hat, with overt ambition, a warm disposition, and an axe to grind.

"Everything is about land tenure," she said. "The problem with the old movement is that they didn't insist on owning their land. That's what makes us so different. We're going to do whatever it takes to get land and make sure it is dedicated into perpetuity to feeding ourselves."

"You can't just say no to development," Enos added. "You have to create authentic economic development. But how is that brought into a contemporary space? This isn't just growing food; it is organizing communities through the act of growing food—the severing of the relationship between people, land, and practice. There's no way to reestablish anything until you reestablish that symbiosis."

It became clear that MA'O Farms has very little to do with agriculture; it is about power.

"We're no longer angry Hawaiians," Enos said. "We're degree providers. We understand where power sits, and we plop our asses right there. Our ancestors understood how to live sustainably on our islands. And that's what the world is asking itself how to do—realizing that we have one finite shared biosystem. . . . Our ancestors asked the same questions: How fit are the people? How abundant is the landscape? How is the water quality? We want our young people to be entrepreneurial, but we also want them to be here and grounded in the land. That is how we unlearn poverty. Our ancestors were never poor."

In confronting modern Waianae's poverty and disenfranchisement, MA'O also confronts Waianae's diversity. The student workers come from a variety of ethnic backgrounds, some with Native Hawaiian bloodlines and others without. Enos and Maunakea-Forth do not discriminate in whom they adopt, and they understand Hawai'i's demographic change as part of a colonial system that used blameless foreign laborers to achieve disruptive economic restructuring.

"What changed with demography was land tenure," Maunakea-Forth said. "Hawaiians moved away. They didn't have land anymore, and that made them lose their community, their identity, and their self-determination. The lines were formed around you. That's what the paper [deeds] said, but that's not what your genealogy said. Demographic change doesn't diminish or dilute your being *maoli*. . . . Our way is to be inclusive, *ma'alama*. We have processes through which you can be part of my family, *hana'i*—taking in somebody. And when you go from one million to forty thousand people, there are a lot of orphans. By chance, we are still here. Whether it was natural or man-made, we are still here to be among our plants and our animals. There is nothing I can say to exclude anyone from helping what we love."

"We remind people that being indigenous relates to continuity on the landscape as much as it is genetic," Enos said. "What it meant to be *maoli* was a fluency in your landscape and how your community lived there. The water, the land, and the people. And that's the highest and best way to maximize your profit. You can be non-Hawaiian, and if you create abundance, you're fuckin' *maoli*.

"Hawaiians should have a real broad diversity of opinions," Enos continued. "And to make us feel the need to be homogenous in our voice is wrong. I'm of the mindset that I'm only Hawaiian as much as Hawaiians serve humanity. I don't see being Hawaiian as entailing a retreat from the [modern] world. We honor the brilliance of our *kahuna*, but it's incumbent upon us to keep our intellectual property. The bringing in of other cultures gave us richness in diversity and gave us good problems to solve; it's not necessarily a bad thing. To have ethical, moral quandaries is really good; it foments powerful dialogue about race and class. You don't see the kind of segregated housing here that you see elsewhere. We have so many ethnicities, how are you gonna split us up?

"That's a nuanced conversation that Western society is wrestling with," he added. "At the heart of it is the struggle for authenticity. Who can speak? Who is entitled to a practice? And we hope to show that, no matter where you start, authenticity is earned. And you can earn a place next to our *kapuna* when you invest here. To be *maoli*, a sign of your development and growth is how things are grown around you—not your material accumulations.

"It's identity. Look at the social media feeds. People are being divided. The conversation about who America is and who gets to be American are erupting and creating fault lines. My dad used to say, 'Shut up and work.' If you focus on being productive in your relationships with others and the landscape, you're acting like a Hawaiian.

"We can no longer be siloed into species. That's the awakening. We can't step away from the big system and check out, we have to heal it. . . . If you rise to power and people don't rise with you, you're a dead chief. The land and water must rise with you."

In 1976, Enos's father, Eric, led a number of fellow activists to occupy two hundred acres of empty land deep in the Waianae Valley, back up against the green velvet foothills. They initially received permission from the state to camp and hike, but as they cut their way into the wild, they encountered hundreds of ancient *kalo* (taro) terraces. The discovery inspired them to restore the native agriculture that once characterized the site, and they began secretly diverting water from the main stream running from nearby Kanewai. They were cited and pursued by enforcement officers from the state's Department of Land and Natural Resources, until an anthropologist found a historic map showing that the two hundred acres of terraces were used for taro cultivation as early as 1906—justifying its restoration under law.

The Hawaiian language has over three hundred names for taro, a sacred staple of the Hawaiian diet and one of the world's earliest cultivated plants. It is a root vegetable of 250 varieties grown in deep, moist, or swampy soils, primarily for its edible starchy bulb. After harvesting the bulb, its root top (*huli*) and lush, frilly triangular leaves (*luau*) may be replanted for future cultivation. A metaphor for this regeneration, the native legend of Haloa says that the first *kalo* sprouted over the grave of the stillborn first child of the gods Wakea and Ho'ohokulani, after the soil was flooded by the tears of his grieving mother. Like the *huli*, Ho'ohokulani later gave birth to another son, whom she also named Haloa. Consistent with the theme of the duality between man and nature in Native Hawaiian thought, the first Haloa is thought to be the first *kalo*, and his younger brother became the first Hawaiian. In Hawaiian language, the *kalo* root is called *oha*, the root of the word for family, *ohana*.

Ka'ala Farm itself therefore embodies the regenerative crop it grows. Today, it remains a working farm but is primarily run for educational purposes. About five thousand children pass through every year, beginning with fourth-graders when they first encounter the Hawaiian history curriculum in school. Its terraces burst with lush vegetation and are perfumed by the creamy, coconut fragrance of flowering *kamani* trees. The sounds of birds and water trickling through ponds and paddies are everywhere.

When I arrived after driving a mile of dirt road into the rugged countryside, I was greeted by the farm's seventy-one-year-old manager, Butch Detroye. An unlikely ambassador, Butch is a skinny, leathery *haole* draft-dodger from the Vietnam War era. He arrived in O'ahu as a twenty-five-year-old in 1973, without a job, home, or family member on the island. After an initial struggle to fit in, Detroye met his Native Hawaiian wife on Kea'au Beach, where they lived for two years; from her, he says, he learned true *aloha*.

"My wife eventually introduced me to all of my friends," Detroye said, while we walked alongside the farm's *kalo* terraces. "Everything was good with the *wahine*, but it took time for the guys to check me out. All of her friends were different ethnicities, so you had the Chinese, the Portuguese, the Japanese, the Samoan, the Hawaiians . . . but they were all brothers and sisters. I knew I was an outsider, and I tried to stay away from a lot of the *haole* on the beach. I was more humble and I was a good listener. It helped a lot, because I was listening to their stories instead of putting out my own."

After working at an orchid nursery, Detroye joined Ka'ala Farm in 1995. From practicing traditional Hawaiian farming techniques, he says he found his place as a Hawaiian.

"I can be *Ha-Wai-I*," he enunciated slowly. "*Ha* is Hawaiian for the breath of life. *Wai* is the water; *I* is the creator. So I can be *Ha-Wai-I*, even if I'm not Hawaiian."

He sat quietly on a bench near where he and Enos had built a traditional Hawaiian memorial for his wife.

"I always wondered why was I placed here," he confessed. "And then a psychic on Maui said that I had been here in another lifetime, as a caretaker, a *kahu*, of the land. And there I found my *piko*, my center, and my *kuleana*, my natural responsibility."

We sat for a minute in silence, absorbing the enormity of the beautiful mountains, forest, and water before us. Birds suddenly cooed above us.

"What are those?" I asked.

"Doves," Detroye said. "Like the invasive plants, they found their way here and did okay."

"Well, you're kind of a dove yourself," I said.

"I guess I am."

Identity Politics

Even the most jingoistic American observer will recognize that Hawai'i is ultimately the product of settler colonialism—the occupied land of Native Hawaiian people, whose kingdom agreed to sacrifice their demographic advantage to thousands of foreign laborers but never agreed to sacrifice their sovereignty. Despite social tensions and disagreements about how people of Native Hawaiian descent should negotiate their relationship with American *haole* and their tortured relationship with American identity, Hawai'i is today a source of harmony in the context of other majority minority settings. Thanks to extensive intermarriage and the pluralism of Native Hawaiian thought, people with indigenous blood have redefined the Native Hawaiian self-understanding in a way that creates space for evolution and avenues to earn membership, unlike any other place in the world.

New research led by developmental psychologist Kristin Pauker finds that children raised in Hawai'i take less notice of racial differences and rely less on racial prejudice when assessing other people, which predicts less outgroup stereotyping even when controlling for gender, age, race, and social context.[41] When Pauker and her colleagues studied the racial attitudes of white *haole* students who moved from the continental United States to Hawai'i, they found a significant reduction in the students' propensity to generalize about race over their first year of university residence.[42] This reduction was correlated with increases in the racial diversity of the white students' acquaintances and an increase in the white students' egalitarian attitudes and cognitive flexibility. As the students spent more time in Hawai'i, Pauker and her colleagues measured further reductions in their levels of racism and further increases in cognitive flexibility. While this may say a lot about the social environment in Hawai'i, it also suggests that Hawaiian cultural norms are transferable to other Americans, if not other populations elsewhere in the world.

The loudest voices of Native Hawaiians' charge to foster allies in the restoration of their land, culture, and identity have historically been the most politicized: the occupiers of Makapu'u Point, protestors at the summit of Mauna Kea, the court-room litigators suing for sovereignty. But have they been the most effective?

National identities are lived and experienced, and it is Hawai'i's ingenious cultural leaders in the farms, fishponds, and schools who appear to most per-suasively engage the islands' people and unite them into a broader, pluralistic Hawaiian identity as a counterbalance to American hegemony. Their perspec-tive is that, in light of so many people's estrangement from their attenuating Native Hawaiian roots, Hawaiian membership today must be renovated—but earned, not bestowed. Accordingly, in a historical moment of populism and nationalism in the face of globalization, they are opening Hawaiian culture to all who are willing to speak Hawai'i's language, till Hawai'i's soil, clean Hawai'i's air, and protect Hawai'i's water.

To mediate this duality, I met with two elders of the Hawaiian Renaissance—one who has been a fierce legal advocate for the independence of Hawai'i from American jurisdiction and one who has dedicated her life to the unification of the Hawaiian population. Poka Laenui, seventy, is an attorney who has served as a delegate to the Hawai'i State Constitutional Convention, as a trustee of the state's Office of Hawaiian Affairs, and as the lead political advocate for the World Council of Indigenous Peoples at the United Nations and International Labor Organization. Puanani Burgess, seventy-one, is a poet, storyteller, Zen Buddhist priest, and a conflict mediator who has led and advised many public organizations concerned with community-, family-, and values-based eco-nomic development. Laenui and Burgess happen to be married.

I met them at Flamingo's, a local, counter-service diner in Waianae in a nondescript roadside building that just as easily could have been in the back of a small warehouse. The interior had monochromatic walls and bright red and yellow particleboard booths that looked like they were bought second-hand from Burger King in the 1970s. The pair go to the restaurant so often that, when we arrived, the cashier already knew what they wanted for lunch.

"Why has there been such an estrangement from Native Hawaiian history?" I asked. "Why has it been such a struggle to revitalize Native Hawaiian iden-tity and facilitate unity?"

After Laenui, who is known as "Uncle Poka" to many, offered a lengthy his-tory of Christian American missionaries and their strategic proselytization of the Native Hawaiian chiefs, Burgess told a short story.

"Nobody talked about the overthrow in college," she began. "These are family stories. I have a Japanese friend who teaches Hawaiian history in a high school, and whenever she came to the period of the *mahele*—when land became property—she noticed that the kids would turn off. The children said they didn't want to know that their ancestors were so stupid, so lazy, as to give away their land. So one day, before class began, she wrote on the bulletin board, 'STUDENTS: REGISTER TO OWN YOUR CHAIRS IN TWO WEEKS OR LOSE THEM.' Two weeks later, the kids arrived to find no chairs in the classrooms. The students complained, 'You didn't tell us this was real.' So to understand what happened to your ancestors, understand that they were told something in a language and value system that was not theirs. The ancestors were not stupid; people did not understand the scale of the change that was coming. Nothing like that had ever happened before, and the *ali'i*, who might have understood that process, didn't tell them."

My response: "I feel like this embodies the difference between the approaches the two of you have taken throughout your careers. Uncle Poka is very direct and literal and refers to the political conflict, while Aunty Pua tells a story to illuminate the way the past is experienced socially."

Laenui shook his head. "When Westerners look at indigenous societies, they fail to see the deeper culture within them. There was a humanitarian approach and a deep culture that had already persisted—an underlying set of rules that allowed society to amalgamate. The conflicts and wars tend to define societies, but there were so many others that were loving, peaceful, and kind—sometimes even within the context of wars."

He paused for a moment.

I knew that ultimately he was about bringing people together into coexistence. He once wrote that the greatest enemy of Native Hawaiian people is not the US government, the State of Hawai'i, or the Office of Hawaiian Affairs. Rather, it is Native Hawaiians' failure to unify.[43]

"I used to teach tai chi," he said. "Nothing is absolute. When you come from a culture of stark comparisons, you cannot understand complex realities. American society is caught between definitions of male and female, native and foreign; it's a recognition that the extremes are the extremes. The nature is that we are mixed in different ways. And because of that, we can allow and accept intermarriage and religious differences living together. People ask me, 'What are you?' And I say that I'm eclectic."

"Aren't you Native Hawaiian?" I asked.

"My mother is pure Chinese and my father was half-Hawaiian, half-white," he answered. "I am whatever works."

In fact, Laenui's birth name and legal name is Hayden Burgess. Without government filings, he unilaterally changed it to his preferred Hawaiian name, which translates to "Explosive Force and Great Wisdom."[44]

"The white fish and the black fish in the yin and yang," he continued. "The white fish has a black eye, and the black fish has a white eye. So each is in its opposite. If you look at Pua as a softer cultural approach, you don't understand her. And if you look at me as confrontational, you don't understand me. In Hawai'i, the political and the cultural are indivisible."

"[The civil rights movement] had a political strategy that played out in cultural ways," Burgess interjected. "And I thought, this is a powerful way to move. It looks like you're doing one thing, but you're really doing something else, in their *piko*, in their gut. Culture is a road there. It seeps into your pores. And when you do it in a way that recognizes the humanity of the other person, it allows you to slip in the cracks."

Burgess referred to the conclusion of a poem she wrote in 1994, after a visit to the 'Iolani Palace. Recounting her solitary visit to the room that once confined Queen Lili'uokalani for an eight-month period after a failed attempt by Hawaiian royalists to restore her to the throne in 1895, Burgess wrote:

> She stood with me at her window;
> Looking out on the world, that she would never rule again;
> Looking out on the world that she would only remember
>   in the scent of flowers;
> Looking out on a world that once despised her,
>
> And in my left ear, she whispered:
> E, Pua. Remember:
>
> This is not America.
> And we are not Americans.
>
> Hawai'i Pono'ī.

"That's the black eye on the white fish," Laenui admired.

Burgess looked at me, ever peacefully.

"That," she paused for emphasis, "is confrontation."

Hoa 'Āina

Critics will debate what conclusions we can confidently draw from Hawai'i. Ultimately, the kingdom's extraordinary social evolution took place only after it had been toppled. Would Native Hawaiians have been capable of such an enlightened approach if they had not been subjected to draconian US assimilation regimes that grouped them indiscriminately with nonwhite people of foreign origins? Did the American conquest of the archipelago alter Native Hawaiians' perceptions about the inviolability of their nation, opening their minds to change? Did the diminished numbers of Native Hawaiians leave them little choice but broaden the boundaries of national identity?

A skeptic may believe that these circumstances disqualify Hawai'i as a model for today's majority minority societies, where the majority group maintains a great deal of power and does not face such a dire demographic future. However, when the Hawaiian monarchy was still in place and moved to privilege the status of Native Hawaiians amid their dwindling numbers, the boundaries of national distinction were already blurring. Indeed, Hawaiians' openness to and even encouragement of intermarriage—with American *haole* among the *ali'i* and with Asian laborers among working-class Native Hawaiians—is unique among the cases observed in this book. Even though intermarriage is now prevalent in most cases, no other ethnic majority so readily embraced newcomers as suitable for marriage in the midst of demographic anxieties.[45] In Singapore, Lee Kuan Yew described intermarriage in transgressive terms; Bahraini women who marry foreign men risk losing their citizenship; *douglas* in Trinidad were relatively rare until recent decades; Indian Mauritians still frown upon marriages with Catholic Creoles; and in New York, Protestant-Catholic marriages did not become commonplace until well over a century after the influx of Irish in the 1840s.

Therefore, even if Hawai'i provides fewer clues for how governments may successfully manage a majority minority transition, Hawai'i is a paragon for how an ethnoreligious nation comes to adopt a civic identity. In the words of Cheryl Ka'uhane Lupenui, the Kohala Center director, Hawaiian culture is "a lived and practiced experience" contingent upon a person's connection to the land and heritage as much as their blood quantum. "Culturally," she said, "there is a recognition that we can live in dualities and multiplicities without being in conflict. . . . So we don't think that we will lose our culture if we accept another culture." And in its many idiomatic expressions for different relationships between people and the land, the Hawaiian language validates foreigners' membership in a way most other nations struggle to articulate. Today's majority minority societies must ask themselves: What is our word for *hoa 'āina*—honored guardians of a land where we are not necessarily indigenous?

While nativists in today's societies approaching a majority minority milestone might view Hawaiians' adaptation as a compromise of their national interests, Hawaiians viewed their culture's adaptation as vital to their national interests. Just as plants and animal life must evolve to survive, Hawaiians' adaptability is for the sake of their nation's preservation. The designation of caretakers and the dilution of the bloodline may attenuate genealogical links to Native Hawaiian heritage, but ultimately it ensures that its associated norms, language, and traditions live on forever. Had Native Hawaiians resisted demographic change in the way today's nativists advocate, their culture would have disappeared with their gene pool.

In statehood, it has been Hawaiian culture that has protected the sovereign interests of the Hawaiian nation in ways that political activists cannot. The United States has swatted away lawsuits with ease. Campaigns to return the monarchy or some semblance of sovereignty are fringe and generally unpopular; Hawai'i has changed too much. But US democracy could not stop the oral traditions that passed on *hula* rituals, the Hawaiian language, and traditional techniques of farming, fishing and wayfinding. In maintaining these lived experiences, Hawaiians have ensured that, while states come and go, their nation endures.

PART III

REDEFINING THE PEOPLE

10

From Backlash to Coexistence

How Institutional Choices Determine Social Boundaries

From Backlash

We have already seen that in many of the countries studied the realization of immigrants' enfranchisement and formal equality signaled to natives a change in the status of the migrant population—that they would be permanent citizens, recognized as fellow nationals, and, in some cases, granted exceptional, even advantageous, treatment. Equal recognition is therefore a pivotal step in the course of majority minority social relations. Where governments resisted the recognition of equal status for migrants, systems of stratification emerged that preserved such value. But the case studies also show how inclusive identities can supersede initial social and political inequality (e.g., Hawaiʻi and, to some extent, Singapore) and how exclusive identity politics produce seemingly irreversible tension between constituencies subject to equal treatment under democratic laws (e.g., Mauritius and Trinidad and Tobago).

Across all six majority minority societies, responses to the demographic changes are therefore contingent on the scope of national identity construction. National identities can be broadened to include newcomers of different ethnicities or religions and produce a reconstituted majority, as in New York. As Hawaiʻi shows, the alteration of national identity constructions is not implausible; feelings of groupness and linked fates change over time and are conditional on context. In a study of twenty European countries, however, political scientist John Sides found that anti-immigrant sentiments are most associated with a desire for cultural unity, a fear of cultural pluralism.[1] Sides later drew similar conclusions from a study of American voters who shifted their support from President Obama to President Trump in 2016.[2] He found that they were motivated by a desire to preserve the Christian faith, deport undocumented immigrants, and reduce immigration, and that they scored high on metrics of racial resentment. Identity construction is therefore pivotal to successful coexistence in majority minority societies but also among the hardest public attitudes to change.[3]

Majority Minority. Justin Gest, Oxford University Press. © Justin Gest 2022. DOI: 10.1093/oso/9780197641798.003.0010

It is perhaps not surprising, then, that across the six case studies, I find backlash to transformational demographic change to be effectively unavoidable. Of course, the human instinct to focus on co-ethnic preservation is one degree of separation from the ethnic nationalism that underlies many political disputes.[4] When individuals believe that their environment is changing, the in-group becomes the priority.[5] But even though demographic change has remained a persistent attribute of human civilization for centuries because of conflict, conquest, and resource scarcity, it has become extremely politicized as white majorities in some of the world's largest democracies have feared their numerical decline.[6]

In all six of the majority minority cases, demographic change led to calls for greater power-sharing by once-subjugated social groups. The subsequent backlash should be observed in the context of political liberalization and democratization since the late nineteenth century. Particularly in the postwar period, a number of trends have contributed to a gradual shift from minority rule to majority rule in countries worldwide.[7] Whether thanks to decolonization, democratization, or rights-based movements, hegemonic minorities have found it increasingly difficult to sustain rule in multiethnic societies.[8] While these changes are conventionally thought to be a good thing, political liberalization carries the potential for conflict because competition for political spoils suddenly and increasingly follows a different logic: that of majoritarian democracy.[9]

Amid the usual alteration of borders, migration, and nation-building projects since the turn of the twentieth century, the evolution of more liberal norms and democratic institutions has meant that political power is increasingly subject to, if not solely derived from, the composition of national populations. Expanded freedom of expression allows for more combative language about ethnic identities. Greater freedom of assembly facilitates mobilization and uprisings along ethnic lines. Moreover, democracy's coupling of population and resource distribution raises the stakes of relative group size in a manner distinct from minority-led regimes that derive their power from violence, ideology, and/or patronage systems that operate more independently from population dynamics.[10] Understanding this politicization can help illuminate the connection between backlash to demographic change and pathways to coexistence.

The previous six chapters complement my comparative historical analysis, which resumes here, by researching each case more specifically and exploring the consequences of historical actions in contemporary times. The results leave little doubt about how pivotal majority minority milestones were to foundational elements of each nation—the nature of everyday identity politics, the construction of a national narrative, the self-understanding of a country. Each country's journey began with the industrialization of the British Empire

(Stage 1), the importation of labor (Stage 2), the segregation of foreigners and the segmentation of labor markets (Stage 3), and then, critically, whether foreigners were granted equal status and formal voting power (Stage 4). How did states resist demographic change? What are the crucial actions that inflame division thereafter? And what are the actions that pivot entire societies from inevitable backlash toward more harmonious coexistence?

Stage 5: Nativism and the Reconstruction of Identity

Equal status and/or incorporation of immigrants into their new societies eventually inspired nativist revivals that sought to reconstruct the national identity in the face of its dissolution. The arrival of immigrants prompts a search for national consciousness—a sense of "we" to confront the seemingly unified, distinct sense of "they." To substantiate demands for immigrants' integration, natives feel an obligation to clarify the identity and culture to which immigrants must integrate. The results are often cacophonous, contradictory, and constructed understandings of heritage that scramble for a narrative, usually not found. While in some contexts, native majorities strove to exclude the newcomers, in others, reconstituted identities were built to incorporate the newcomers without losing long-established national foundations.[11]

This story has been repeated over and over with each successive wave of immigration into the United States. The arrival of Irish Catholics in New York aroused stereotypes of Irish destitution and complacency and stoked paranoia about a papist takeover by people with foreign allegiances. This contrasted with an aspiring American self-image rooted in a creed of independent, industrious Protestantism. Nativist activists such as William C. Brownlee and Samuel F. B. Morse published anti-Catholic propaganda to "warn our Protestant friends of the insidious Jesuitical working of that abomination, showing its demoralizing, debasing character."[12] The city became a haven for Irish and immigrant life, defying the xenophobia extant elsewhere in the United States and even elsewhere in New York State. This came to a head in May 1857, when the Irish-dominated New York City Municipal Police fought the state legislature–backed Metropolitan Police, who were attempting to arrest Mayor Fernando Wood on corruption charges, in front of city hall. In the face of new influxes of Jewish and Chinese people later in the nineteenth century, however, the diminished Anglo-American majority came to adopt the Irish into the fraternity of "whiteness" in order to preserve its numerical advantage.[13]

It is precisely this sort of American disorder that the governments of Bahrain and Singapore sought to avoid by ensuring that the national character is never in question. While the Bahrainis have historically limited who may naturalize into the indigenous identity, the Chinese in Singapore have sought to naturalize themselves as the rightful inhabitants of their otherwise Malay region. Despite Chinese rule and demographic dominance, the Singaporean government has recast the city-state's history in museums and textbooks as the triumph of a "multiracial" society founded on "balance." Wary of the island's fragile demographics, Bahrainis initially recruited laborers from other Arab countries during the 1970s oil boom to preserve the island's Arab national character. Even though these migrants were ineligible for naturalization, the kingdom feared a revolt in the name of the era's pan-Arabism. South Asians, on the other hand, were deemed to be a more servile replacement; they lacked other Arabs' sense of entitlement but were largely of Sunni Muslim background. Shortly after Bahraini citizens discovered that a growing number of new Sunni Arab immigrants were naturalized and suddenly so entitled, public protests took place in 2009 and 2011.[14]

In the face of demographic change in Trinidad, conflict over the national character played out in public institutions and local newspapers, the domain of the incumbent African-origin Creoles. The country's principal twentieth-century periodical, *The Guardian*, was the primary battleground for raging debates over identity and equality. These debates intensified and spilled into social relations after Basdeo Panday—Trinidad's first Indian-origin prime minister—and the United National Congress (UNC) formed a coalition government in 1995. There were accusations of racism and stereotyping, from references to the UNC victory (as "Chutney Rising") to disparities in access to education; there were questions of national symbolism, from the nomination of the steel drum as the national instrument to divisive lyrics in calypso music; and there were Creole attempts to delegitimize an outright UNC majority in 2000. This took place amid an Africanization of Creole culture, in which some emphasized their transnational connections in the face of local diversification. During this period, Trinidad American professor Selwyn Cudjoe formed the National Association for the Empowerment of African People, which became an umbrella for existing pockets of Afrocentrists and Afrocentric ideologies that had persisted from the Black Power revolution of the 1970s. The organization embraced traditional African dress, initiated resistance strategies like a "buy Black" campaign, and argued for reparations in light of historical slavery and colonial oppression. Each such effort constructed a Trinidadian national character that was foremost African in origin.[15]

Many Native Hawaiians formed civic organizations to protest the end of isolationism and the various concessions made by the kingdom to foreign governments from the 1840s until its annexation in 1898. By then, there were few venues to express their dissent and fewer Native Hawaiians remaining. The US government imposed a harsh assimilation regime that, likening Native Hawaiian culture to savagery, prohibited the use of its language and banned *hula* rituals in an attempt to civilize its people. On the brink of extinction, these cultural components survived in private homes, where they were practiced as surreptitious acts of protest. During the anticolonial 1960s, Hawaiian culture experienced a revival that would produce the reinvigoration of Hawaiian nationalism. After decades of hiding their unpalatable Hawaiian backgrounds, people of mixed Hawaiian descent embraced their heritage and engaged in projects that reclaimed ancestral lands, returned fishponds and farmland to their original state, founded Hawaiian-language schools, danced *hula*, and used traditional canoes and wayfinding navigation to demonstrate the sophistication of early Hawaiian civilization. Because the Hawaiian population was by this point largely of mixed, multiracial descent, the nativism was an unusually (but necessarily) inclusive movement with a largely inclusive identity.[16]

Three Ways States Assert Control

To quell this nationalist backlash, states have limited options. As I write in chapter 2, the phenomena that produce demographic change—fertility, mortality, emigration, and intermarriage—are largely outside the state's power. But this doesn't stop the state from trying.[17] Across the six cases, states employ a variety of techniques to slow down or mitigate the impact of demographic change. I classify these instruments by the outcomes they seek to achieve: who comes; who counts; and to a much more limited effect, who connects. "Who comes" refers to the attributes of immigrants admitted and the state's monopoly on border control. "Who counts" focuses on the distribution of electoral power among people already present and the state's attempts to alter it. Finally, "who connects" refers to the extent to which different population subgroups meaningfully interact with one another.

Who Comes?

Assuming there is no change in a country's territorial boundaries, there are only two ways that national populations grow: (1) by immigration and

(2) when births outnumber deaths—what demographers call "natural increase." Because they struggle to control natural increases in population, states can sustain one subgroup's numerical advantage only through immigration controls. This may entail recruiting or favoring admission applicants who share the dominant subgroup's ethnic or religious background, or restricting the admission of foreigners who do not share the dominant subgroup's background.

Such tactics were prevalent across the cases. To this day, Singapore's immigration admissions system overtly discriminates according to racial criteria in order to maintain its current population distribution. In Bahrain, as elsewhere in the Arab Gulf region, the government employs the *kafala* labor sponsorship system to ensure that its large number of immigrants do not have access to citizenship and are subject to regular review and visa renewals. Also, to an extent unlike that of any other Gulf country, the government embarked on a program to recruit and naturalize a significant number of Sunni Arabs, the *mutajaniseen*, most of whom serve in the police or security services. Trinidad's PNM party historically recruited Afro-Caribbeans from neighboring countries to tilt the demographic scales. In New York, the Whig Party and Know Nothings sought to remove Irish deemed to be "public charges." And in Hawai'i, the kingdom deliberately recruited laborers from what it called "kindred races" to placate nativists concerned about the dwindling share of Native Hawaiians in the nineteenth century.

Who Counts?

Confronted with the statistical reality that the manipulation of immigration admissions is unlikely to freeze demographic change, many governments simultaneously pursued policies that suppressed the political power of certain population subgroups. In short, if the government cannot halt demographic change, it can mitigate certain subgroups' representation. These actions target people's eligibility and ability to vote, the marginal effect of their vote, and the distribution of political power.

Again, such tactics were prevalent across the cases. In Singapore, the equal residential distribution of people of different races commensurate with their national population shares is ostensibly a means of integrating its population; however, it also ensures a 72 percent Chinese majority in every tower block and every electoral district, limiting racial mobilization and organized action. In Bahrain, the *mutajaniseen* not only tip the demographic scales; they also vote and are deeply allegiant to the royal court. Trinidad and Mauritius are subject to partisan—and therefore racial and religious—gerrymandering. In New York, the Irish population grew too fast for any such maneuvers to undo their solidaristic politics. And in Hawai'i, the kingdom declared foreign laborers ineligible to vote or own land.

Who Connects?

Government actions to mitigate the power of growing minority populations is facilitated by those populations' geographic isolation. When large subgroups are segregated, their power is more vulnerable to tactics like gerrymandering and redlining—the systematic denial of government services. It is worth acknowledging that a minority subgroup's geographic diffusion can also weaken them because they will constitute dominant population shares in fewer legislative districts. However, segregation is far more common and far more problematic because it also prevents different subgroups from interacting. When ethnically different neighbors or countrymen do not have regular and meaningful exposure to one another, empathy and understanding become less likely.

The legacy of segregation—an enduring strategy of control by plantation colonialism worldwide—is present across all cases and endures today. Though Singaporeans are residentially integrated, people of different ethnolinguistic backgrounds attend different schools, receive social services from racially specific agencies, and continue to speak in Mandarin, Malay, or Tamil at home, despite being generations removed from their countries of origin. In Bahrain, neighborhood segregation persists, and even nationals of different Islamic sects sustain different dialects, reinforced by a lack of interaction. Town and country were long associated with African-origin Creoles and people of Indian-origin planters, respectively, in Trinidad and Mauritius. In New York, the Irish American community built a network of Catholic institutions like schools, universities, hospitals, and charities to compensate for their exclusion elsewhere. And on Hawai'i's plantations, racial differentiation dictated employment, wages, and the segregation of social and residential life.

In chapter 1, I referred to the defensive way that individual people tend to react to demographic change in the contemporary era. In these social and psychological studies, however, respondents were alerted to demographic change suddenly rather than gradually through interpersonal exposure—the way demographic change is actually experienced. Another set of researchers has examined the effect of living in an ethnically diverse environment and the interethnic contact that inevitably takes place, through schools, marriage, or otherwise in today's Western settings where white majorities are diminishing. Of course, it is reasonable to expect self-selection: more tolerant white people are more likely to move to or remain in diverse communities; intolerant white people are more likely to leave diverse communities; and nonwhite people are likely to move to communities known to be more tolerant. Because this might make tolerant communities even more diverse, identifying the true effect of demographic change is challenging, but the results suggest that experiencing demographic change is wholly different from reading or hearing about it. On one hand, researchers have found that the pace of demographic change is fundamental to the backlash because people are less reactionary when the minority's baseline population is already large or grows incrementally.[18] Rapid demographic change, one would suppose, is not that different from suddenly being notified that your society is changing substantially; people may think the worst or respond defensively. A meta-analysis of 171 studies since 1995 finds that increasing demographic change is associated with a greater sense of cultural threat among the native-born.[19]

On the other hand, this same meta-analysis also finds that diversity is associated with reduced threat in smaller communities of five thousand to ten thousand people.[20] Indeed, new research on Americans' electoral responses to demographic change inside small voting precincts fails to even find such backlash.[21] Another study finds support for the generally pro-immigration Democratic Party in places where elevated levels of highly skilled foreigners have settled.[22] More powerfully, in a meta-analysis of twenty-seven studies that randomly assigned young people with different backgrounds to more meaningfully interact with each other and then studied outcomes at least one day later, researchers have found that intergroup contact typically reduces prejudice.[23]

Researchers are still unsure about what conditions are more likely to produce greater empathy and less prejudice, but it is fair to conclude that intergroup competition and defensiveness is mitigated when the dominant group experiences interaction with the minority by whom they might otherwise feel threatened. Psychologists have found that socialization in diverse and multiracial environments reduces young people's propensity to stereotype and increases egalitarian attitudes.[24]

Such socialization is threatening for regimes seeking to leverage fear and discomfort for short-term political gain precisely because diverse environments appear to inoculate voters from such appeals. In North America and Europe today, many people are exposed to population diversity in expressions of national culture because culture is the accessible realm of the more cosmopolitan intelligentsia, artists, writers, scientists, athletes, and urban professionals. Nationalist politics directly confront popular ideas that promote fluid, intersectional identities. Without being able to physically prevent intergroup contact, many nativists counter the fluidity in cultural spaces by increasing the salience of racial and religious identity boundaries between subgroups and casting their politics as zero-sum.

Stage 6: Political Backlash

Political backlash is merely the translation of nativist anxiety into discriminatory regimes, proxy debates, and other grasps for social control. For control is at the core of all nativism under circumstances of swift demographic change. Nativists seek to control the demographic distribution, the means of violence, the national culture, and, if nothing else, the historical narrative. While backlash plays out in competitive politics in democracies, in nondemocratic spaces there is instead competition between groups for favor and symbolic representation.

Karen Alter and Michael Zürn define backlash politics as comprising three necessary elements: (1) a retrograde objective, aiming to revert to a prior social condition; (2) extraordinary claims, demands, and tactics that challenge established norms and consider the status quo as deficient; and (3) a threshold of influencing public discourse so that the movement's objectives and/or tactics becomes normalized features of politics.[25] The authors find that important companions of backlash politics include (a) emotive elements, often suffused with the haze of nostalgia; (b) taboo-breaking and new political strategies; and (c) challenges to procedures and institutions associated with the previously dominant norms. In my research, I find that demographic change produces each of the necessary elements for backlash politics theorized by Alter and Zürn across the six cases.

First, backlash to demographic change is inherently retrograde. Often expressed through nostalgia and perhaps forms of disengagement or rebellion, the principal agenda of the threatened subgroup is to return to an earlier era when their members held superior numbers and power.[26] Nostalgia exudes a sense of predictability but also allows the storyteller to reframe the significance of past events and attributes. It hits the brakes on unwieldy social change. This backlash takes place concurrently with the rise of nativism and, across the six cases, principally relates to immigration.

Immigration policy is a primary policy domain for backlash because immigration was, in all cases, the core driver of the demographic change in the first place.

Governments recruit those immigrants deemed to be of desirable origin to reinforce their dominance and oppose the naturalization of others. In Trinidad, the PNM facilitated the unauthorized entry of African-origin people from other Caribbean islands. In Singapore, the government has been accused of altering its standards to facilitate the admission of people of Chinese origins. Just as Bahraini Shias have protested the naturalization of South Asian Sunnis in the twenty-first century, Native Hawaiians resisted the naturalization of Europeans and Americans when the kingdom first opened to foreign commercial interests in the mid-nineteenth century. Often, governments selectively deported individuals in the interest of making a public demonstration against certain groups. While this tactic was less common in New York, where the Irish were quickly entrenched in municipal agencies, it was very common in the nearby Commonwealth of Massachusetts.[27]

Second, because backlash to demographic change perceives the earlier population distribution to be preferable, it often entails extraordinary efforts to disrupt the norms and institutions of the status quo. Where immigration cannot turn back the demographic clock in election-based systems, nativists turn to the electoral institutions that determine how and where power is distributed. Naturalization may determine who has the right to vote and be counted. However, governments can also amend voting rights, revise the census rules, and alter constituency districts (gerrymander) to mitigate the political impact of demographic change. Each of these techniques was employed in the Trinidadian public sphere in which all decisions were perceived to be zero-sum. In Singapore, policies of residential balance also served to ensure that there were no significant concentrations of Malay- or Indian-origin people to organize dissent or support the opposition party. In Mauritius, a 2011 Truth and Justice Commission detailed the way that Creoles were disproportionately subject to inadequate housing, illiteracy, and manual labor positions while being underrepresented in certain business sectors and politics. These actions become particularly contentious in contexts where partisan differences have become racialized—where parties formally or informally represent and pursue certain ethnic constituencies' interests.

Third, because identity politics are core to backlash against demographic change, the accompanying discourse is essentialist and often existential. Demographic change has downstream effects on cultural, economic, and political power, giving the impression of a universal threat. Absent the ability to actually reverse-engineer the population, backlash leaders pursue symbolic victories, in which rhetorical narratives bind together the endangered constituency and political actions may change one life but comfort millions by rendering a false sense of control. When nativists cannot control the demographic distribution, the means of violence, or the national culture, they at least seek to control the historical narrative—questions of heritage and identity that they can monopolize. The Mauritian government ensured that the Aapravasi Ghat, the harborside depot in Port Louis that processed the arrival of hundreds of thousands of Indian indentured servants, was the island's first UNESCO World Heritage Site instead of Le Morne peninsula, which long sheltered African maroons. In Hawai'i, after an 1881 world tour to promote bilateral relations in the face of domestic nativism and foreigners' colonial ambitions, King Kalākaua launched a number of programs to promote the prestige of the Hawaiian national identity. He revived the public *hula* performances, built the 'Iolani Palace, commissioned an iconic statue of King Kamehameha, and held a formal coronation ceremony.[28] He also sponsored Hawaiian natives to attend many of the world's leading universities and established initiatives to document Hawaiian genealogy, science, and the arts. A century later, Native Hawaiians have personally pursued similar symbolic acts of nationalist resistance behind a more civic—rather than ethnic—identity. In Trinidad, Creole-led governments tightly embraced the Trinidad Carnival. Though a universal festival, Carnival is culturally African, with its embrace of Afro-Caribbean music, costume, and calypso. Successive governments consistently increased funding for the annual event and turned two-day celebrations of Afro-Caribbean culture into a global expression of the Trinidadian national character.

One truth emerges across all these examples: by the time societies engage in backlash politics, it is often too late to alter the state's demographic future. Indeed, backlash takes place only when it is already recognized that the native or incumbent constituency's majority status is under threat. The backlash that nevertheless ensues is not merely futile; it often poisons social relations for decades to come and pointlessly polemicizes debates over immigration. Alter and Zürn write that there are three possible ways these politics end: (1) through a loss of internal energy, (2) by achieving the retrograde change, or (3) by being transformed into a cleavage that gets absorbed into ordinary politics. The existential nature of backlash to demographic change ensures that its energy persists and it is physically impossible to achieve the retrograde change nativists seek. Consequently, the question is: What are the variable ways that demographic cleavages are absorbed into ordinary identity politics?

Identity Binaries

What separates majority minority societies with sustained or suppressed backlash against the ascendance of certain subgroups from those that better reconcile their differences? The answer relates to the construction of national identities. Stemming from this comparative analysis are five key identity binaries that push us toward a politics of either inclusion or exclusion (see Table 10.1). These binaries help explain the ways that New York and Hawai'i eventually evaded divisive social tension, for example, while Bahrain, Mauritius, and Trinidad seem forever defined by such tension. Interestingly, Singapore has constructed an ostensibly inclusive identity that distracts from a social structure rigidly defined by race. Beyond the conceptual map laid out in Table 10.1, I provide examples of the inclusive politics that came to develop in multiethnic Hawai'i, which features the most hopeful outcome of the six cases I examine and ultimately pivoted toward coexistence since statehood in 1959 in each of the five binaries I identify.

Table 10.1 Identity Binaries

Pivot to Coexistence	BINARY	Pivot to Inflammation
The production of universalist, transcendent ideologies—and the creation of an inclusive national identity: a. Intermarriage b. Religion to unite c. Socialism d. Labor solidarity e. Authoritarian ideology	*Ideology*	The production of ideologies of inferiority and favoritism—and the creation of an exclusive national identity: a. Residential segregation b. Religion to divide c. Stratification d. Supremacy e. Eugenics
Inclusive socialization: a. National language policy b. Universal conscription c. School integration d. Textbooks	*Socialization*	Exclusive socialization: a. National language policy b. Selective conscription c. School segregation d. Textbooks
Promotion of inclusive national cultural attributes: a. Music b. Cuisine c. Sport d. Tradition and custom	*Culture*	Promotion of exclusive national cultural attributes: a. Politics of memory/truth b. Invigoration of historical disputes c. Tradition and custom
Inclusive commercial experience: a. Market interdependencies b. Reduction of inequality c. Distribution of state resources	*Commerce*	Exclusive commercial experience: a. Labor market segmentation b. Racialized poverty c. Politics of reparation and affirmative action
Focus on sources of external threat to produce inclusion: a. War b. Encroachment c. Pan-ethnic political movements	*Threat*	Focus on sources of internal threat to produce exclusion: a. Census politics: gerrymandering and representation b. Racialized partisanship

The first binary relates to the use of inclusive or exclusive state ideologies that unite or divide a multiethnic population. After the arrival of Americans early in the nineteenth century and their subsequent conquest, Native Hawaiians were dominated and disoriented—their kingdom toppled, their identity suppressed, their norms undermined. By the time Hawaiians organized to resurrect their principal normative components during the 1960s Renaissance, the nation's composition had changed. Native Hawaiians had intermarried and intermingled their traditions, their culture, and their genealogies with people from China, Japan, Portugal, Puerto Rico, the Philippines, and the United States. Global diffusion therefore both nearly eliminated Native Hawaiian culture and helped shape today's Hawaiian national identity. In defining their nation, Native Hawaiians have had no choice but to formulate a vision and ideology that internalizes this diversity and accepts its contradictions. This has obviated debates about "authenticity" and "heritage" that have plagued identity politics elsewhere. Contrast this vision with that of Bahrain, where the state guards the image of and access to its kingdom—a state derived from an indigenous nation, which hosts guest workers at its discretion.[29]

The second binary relates to the socialization of children into inclusive or exclusive state programs with normative instruction. Hawaiian developmental psychologists have found that children raised on the islands take less notice of racial differences and rely less on racial prejudice when assessing other people, which predicts less outgroup stereotyping even when controlling for gender, age, race, and social context.[30] When researchers studied the racial attitudes of white students who moved from the continental United States to Hawai'i, they found a significant reduction in their propensity to generalize about race during their first year of university residence.[31] This reduction was correlated with increases in the racial diversity of the white students' acquaintances and an increase in their egalitarian attitudes and cognitive flexibility. While this may say a lot about socialization in Hawai'i, it also suggests that Hawaiians' cultural norms are transferable to other Americans, if not other populations elsewhere in the world. Again, Bahrain provides a contrast: the government does not attempt to socialize migrants. They are admitted under two-year renewable contracts—biennial reminders of their contingency—and migrants' children are admitted on the basis of parents' demonstrated ability to financially support them. Meanwhile, by keeping migrants in segregated neighborhoods and quarantined dormitories, the government ensures no socialization will take place anyway.

The third binary relates to the promotion of cultural attributes that either transcend or reinforce social boundaries. Hawai'i's recent cultural revival has been powerful because it has welcomed all who are interested in reinvigorating the archipelago's ancestral traditions. This is a strategy for inclusion as well as a necessity in light of the extent of intermarriage in Native Hawaiian society. The revival has related to the restoration of ancestral agricultural and fishing practices, the establishment of Hawaiian-language schools, and the teaching of *hula* rituals. Its popularization and commercialization have also made it appear more innocuous to those who cannot trace their heritage to the indigenous kingdom. While the Trinidadian government's tight embrace of the annual Carnival has been similarly popularized and commercialized, its political effect, in contrast, has been to alienate many Indian-origin Trinidadians from the country's purported heritage.[32]

The fourth binary relates to a system of commerce that either reproduces social disparities or segregation in the economic sector or overlooks them for the sake of mutual benefit. The initial segmentation of the labor market was as stark in Hawai'i as in the other cases I've outlined. Native Hawaiians were less inclined to work on plantations, but when their access to land and water was disrupted by planters, most eventually became the planters' tenants and provided crops in lieu of payment. These disruptions brought Native Hawaiians into closer contact with immigrant-origin Asians. Like the Hawaiians, the Chinese and Okinawans also farmed taro, and commercial exchanges between subsistence farmers and fishers produced early interracial marriages that led to further ways Hawaiians introduced foreign practices and traditions into their native culture. In contrast, the segmentation of the labor market early in the histories of Mauritius, Trinidad, and Bahrain have endured. In all three societies, the private and public sectors have been historically separated along ethnic and national lines. This severely constrains the opportunities for different constituencies to interact in encounters of mutual dependency.

Finally, the fifth binary relates to whether the state's identified threats are external, and thereby unifying, or internal, and thereby divisive. The orientation of Hawai'i's cultural revival has been unequivocally against the hegemonic history and persistent power of interests from the mainland United States. Beyond creating an awkward relationship with national countrymen, military, and the tourists driving its top industry, this shared sense of threat has also brought multiethnic, working-class Hawaiian people closer together. Similarly, in the case of New York, the Irish benefited from the arrival of other immigrants whose religious and ethnic differences distracted Anglo Protestants from their own and ultimately made the Irish appear relatively familiar.[33] Despite the unignorable presence of British colonizers in Bahrain,

Mauritius, and Trinidad, their original majorities have principally focused their attention on internal threats to the respective constituencies' ethnic supremacy and rightful claims to power.

This set of binaries is easily applied to any society grappling with identity politics. And much like the six cases examined here, no society will pivot only to coexistence, just as no society will pivot only to inflamed social tensions. Hawai'i, which I have held up here as a near-paragon of postcolonial coexistence, has a history of social division. At any given point in time, a mix of countervailing rhetoric and actions will exist. Indeed, in most societies—particularly those with large populations and land areas—there will be examples of inclusive and exclusive actions on each side of the same binaries in different regions or among different subgroups. In the United States, each of the observed expressions in Table 10.1 has been observable at one time or another, in one place or another. The question is where the national balance lies.

The Power of Institutions

It is thought that smaller societies are better positioned to peacefully manage ethnically, racially, or religiously diverse populations because they are more socially interconnected and more collectively vulnerable to external threats.[34] While certainly none of the six cases we consider here experienced civil war, the historical evidence demonstrates that neither were they without social tension and anxiety about demographic change. They clearly feature divergent outcomes, however: Singapore and Bahrain suppressed social tensions to facilitate peaceful coexistence and sustain Chinese and Sunni Arab control, respectively. Democracies in Trinidad and Mauritius succumbed to tempting incentives to exploit latent social tensions and harvest them for electoral advantage. Meanwhile, New York and Hawai'i ultimately redefined the image of their societies to amalgamate a "white" ruling class in New York and regroup a mixed-race underclass in Hawai'i.

With such variation in outcomes, despair and conflict are not structurally inevitable. Countries can orient themselves toward coexistence or conflict; majority minority relations are—at their core—governed. Focusing on such government actions, I find that divergent outcomes are contingent on whether the state equally enfranchises the newcomer population and whether its subsequent redefinition of the national identity is inclusive or exclusive. While inclusive redefinitions override historic inequities (New York and Hawai'i), governments that pursue exclusive identities are confronted by latent or suppressed social tension in states with structurally unequal constituencies (Singapore and Bahrain) and overt contestation in states with equally enfranchised constituencies (Trinidad and Mauritius). See Table 10.2 for an overview.

More simply, the state has two sequential choices: First, political leaders must decide whether they will:

A. Emphasize ethnic divisions and seek to establish the predominance of one constituency (whether it is a majority or minority)

or

B. Minimize the salience of such social boundaries and try to construct an inclusive polity that provides equal opportunities for leadership and influence (New York and Hawai'i).

Should political leaders elect to emphasize divisions in the interest of one group's supremacy, a second choice is whether they will:

C. Formalize the marginalization of subordinate groups by enacting discriminatory laws that, while affording the subordinated groups an economic role, reduce or remove the prospects for political power (Singapore and Bahrain)

or

D. Sustain the veneer of equal opportunity and equal power while relying on informal discrimination to reduce the prospects for the empowerment of the subordinated constituency (Trinidad and Mauritius).

A further secondary alternative, unseen in these cases, is where:

E. Political leaders seek to wholly subordinate the opposing constituency even with coercion, if required.

Importantly, the evidence exhibits how states are not bound by their prior course when the majority and minority compositions change. That is, even states with prior structural inequality can indeed become inclusive (e.g., Hawai'i), while states that had enjoyed formal structural equality can turn confrontational if the majority elects to impose discriminatory policies to protect their political dominance when their demographic advantage wanes (e.g., Trinidad and Tobago). This does not mean that formal legal

Table 10.2 Descriptive Overview of Stages for Each of the Cases

	Industries	Labor	Segregation	In/Equality	Identity	Relations
Bahrain	Pearls Oil	Continuous: Sunni Arab, South Asian Sunni	Kafala system; Segmented public and private sector	Selective naturalization	Exclusive nationality attainable via royal edict	Tiered corporatist society; suppression
Singapore	Tin Gambier Commerce	Continuous: Chinese, Tamil, Indian	Enclave-based settlement; *kapitan* system	Bifurcated, racialized visa system	Adherence to ethnoracial quotas	Housing, education, immigration by race
Hawai'i	Sugar Whaling	Concentrated: Chinese, Japanese, Filipino	Plantation labor camps; restricted landownership	Subordination of "colored" populations; unions	Intermarriage, diffused Hawaiian heritage	Inclusive, antihegemonic spirit
New York	Manufacturing Commerce	Continuous: Irish, Italian, Jewish, German	Residential segregation; bloc mobilization	Early franchise and political power	Incorporation of the Irish and Italians to whiteness	Ethnicity-contingent "nation of immigrants"
Mauritius	Sugar Coffee	Concentrated: Indian	Land grants after indenture; mobility restrictions	Cross-ethnic voting rights	Pan-Africanism; Indian nationalism	Racialized partisanship and poverty
Trinidad	Sugar Cotton	Concentrated: Indian	Land grants after indenture; urban/ rural divide	Cross-ethnic voting rights; labor socialism	Pan-Africanism; Indian nationalism	Racialized partisanship and poverty

foundations of equality are irrelevant. Indeed, where they are in place, they produce a sense of entitlement to equal opportunity that makes populations more conscious of discrimination and more likely to voice their concerns and make demands of the government. They may also require the state to rely on informal—often cultural—means to sustain ethnic predominance. Legal foundations for inclusion do not, however, necessarily predict whether or not the state will be or will remain inclusive. And they do not prohibit the eventual development of a sense of entitlement and a desire for status among historically subordinated populations.

The power of political institutions is important today, when divergent outcomes are beginning to emerge in different subnational units inside the same state. Differing responses to demographic change characterize different regions inside Australia, Britain, Canada, Germany, Switzerland, and the United States. Such regions—some of which are semi-autonomous—are subject to the same institutions but feature local governors who have responded to demographic changes in divergent ways. Many regions with large populations of immigrant-origin, ethnic minorities—like California in the United States and British Columbia in Canada—have become more inclusive and adaptive to demographic changes. Others, particularly in regions that are predominantly white—such as Alabama in the United States and Alberta in Canada—have sought to preserve their dominance, often employing identity binaries similar to those outlined in Table 10.1. The evidence I have presented about the power of institutions to orient societies toward conflict or coexistence, however, produces a subsequent question: How do institutions communicate exclusion and inclusion?

The Power of Rhetoric

For all of this focus on the power of institutions to pivot social relations, the case studies show how inclusion or exclusion is often communicated by the rhetoric of those governing these institutions. Rhetoric is what defines state ideologies and characterizes threats to the nation. Rhetoric sets an example of language in the socialization of children, and the telling of a national story. Rhetoric is inherently a part of cultural practice, particularly in the way leaders invoke, symbolically interpret, and curate the artifacts of national heritage. And leaders' rhetoric can also define the way we understand commercial relationships and whether we humanize or commoditize fellow nationals in the marketplace. Across the cases, we heard terms like "racial balance" in Singapore, "globalized heritage" in Bahrain, "pseudo-racism" in Trinidad, *le malaise creole* in Mauritius, "public charge" in New York, and a variety of ways to define people's relationship to the land, *āina*, in the Hawaiian language. Rhetoric is quite simply the public face of institutions; it is the language of recognition.

Problematically, across all the cases I consider, political leaders demonstrated a propensity to appeal to colonial ideologies and hierarchies to justify their status rather than defy these legacies and construct new social systems. The various nations populating the different states examined here are frequently defined by colonial or ethnoreligious constructions, even in modern times. Long after the British left America, perceptions about the problematic character of Irish Catholics endured. Pan-Africanism and Indian nationalism remain powerful in Trinidad and Mauritius to this day. Bahrain and Singapore continue to fulfill British visions for them to serve as useful crossroads for regional commerce in the neoliberal global economy. These various societies asserted their territoriality as postcolonial states but maintained a sticky colonial mindset about race, ethnicity, and religion. This suggests that in the contemporary era, historical tropes and imaginaries are unlikely to suddenly disappear.

The pursuit of harmony, therefore, lies in the state's institutional and rhetorical re-creation of the boundaries of such social hierarchies to make them unconditional on birthright or to redefine the lines of national distinction. Many of these case societies have managed to preserve the dominance or self-determination of one ethnic group over another. But the question remains: At what cost? Bahrain is characterized by a draconian system of segregation. Singapore artificially touts multiracialism while preserving Chinese hegemony. People of Indian and African origin in Trinidad have pursued separate agendas to an unsatisfying draw. On the other hand, Native Hawaiians lost control of their kingdom but gained a social stability grounded in anti-imperialistic reverence for their ancestral past and sublime hybridity. Taking two steps forward in majority minority societies, it seems, requires the state to first take one step back.

These findings suggest that the process of allaying the backlash in parts of the United States and Europe today can begin by engaging institutional elites to embrace immigration and demographic change as conducive to national survival, rather than as an existential threat. But important questions remain: What messages best communicate belonging and inclusion? Are such messages subject to the identity of the messenger? In the six case studies, there are precious few examples of influential political leaders and public officials who dared to defy the logics of ethnoreligious nationalism to rethink their nation's identity for the sake of its endurance. Here, where history ends, today's contentious political environment offers a laboratory.

11

Nation-Building

Messages and Messengers That Cultivate Coexistence

Follow the Leader

If a state seeks successful coexistence as it approaches a majority minority milestone, the evidence thus far suggests a strategy: redefine the nation by broadening the inclusivity of national institutions and the sense of shared identity. As chapter 10 concludes, these institutions may relate to (1) state ideology, (2) children's socialization, (3) cultural activities, (4) systems of commerce, and (5) the orientation of national security threats. But more inclusive institutions can take a generation or two to build or reform. Particularly in democracies, such institutions often move *slower* than demographic change.

Meanwhile, divisive political rhetoric moves *faster* than demographic change. Long before demographic transformations actually take place, politicians exploit people's fears and anxieties. Vitriolically, they jump to conclusions about small social changes that sow uncertainty. As we see across the case studies, politicians leverage divisions for short-term electoral gain but then never work to reunify their countries once they assume office. Precisely because national institutions move too slowly to mitigate rhetoric-induced panic, therefore, leaders who are concerned with coexistence must also work to construct unifying narratives about the nation and its identity.

The political issue that attracts these conflicting narratives is frequently immigration—the principal driver of demographic change. Before the onset of the 2020 global coronavirus pandemic, immigration was among the most salient political issues across a number of different countries.[1] This saliency was problematic for two reasons. First, the people who rank immigration as an issue of top priority tend to be those who wish to drastically restrict it.[2] Second, immigration attitudes are also simply more challenging to move than most attitudes toward other public policy and social phenomena.

Political and psychological research has shown that deeply embedded attitudes like prejudice rooted in intergroup animosity are very stable and therefore less influenced by elite rhetoric.[3] More generally, attitudes that are rooted in group-centric concerns, which are well-rehearsed, strongly held,

Majority Minority. Justin Gest, Oxford University Press. © Justin Gest 2022. DOI: 10.1093/oso/9780197641798.003.0011

and emotionally charged, have been found to be more resistant to change than most other political attitudes.[4] While much of this research has focused on anti-Black prejudice in the United States, it has been assumed that immigration attitudes, which are also rooted in group-based antagonism, are similarly stable and resistant to elite rhetoric.[5]

The evidence from the six earlier cases, however, suggests otherwise. In each of those cases, leaders have leveraged their political capital within specific ethnic and religious subgroups to deepen social divisions, but they also occasionally invoked these same credentials to call for unity. Despite his thinly veiled concern with Chinese hegemony in Singapore in the 1980s, Prime Minister Lee Kuan Yew previously went to great lengths to communicate a "race-blind" meritocracy that placed Singapore's Malay and Indian minorities on equal footing with the Chinese majority. That meritocracy is today validated with the endorsements of Tamil-origin senior minister Tharman Shanmugaratnam. After losing a Senate election in New York to a Tammany Hall–backed candidate, Franklin Delano Roosevelt set aside his moralizing, Protestant progressivism to align with the urban, Catholic, Tammany Hall "machine" to become governor of New York in 1928.[6] This set the stage not only for Roosevelt's 1932 presidential run but also for the integration of the Irish into national Democratic Party politics for a long time thereafter.

Looking at the contemporary United States and Europe, there have been few other times in recent political history when the cues coming from political leaders are so clear on issues of race and identity.[7] Immigration attitudes are increasingly linked with vote choice[8] and have spilled over into other policy attitudes and predispositions.[9] There is already extensive scientific evidence about the power of elite political influence, but it could also be the case that increasingly clear partisan cues from elites are now shaping mass opinion sufficiently to nudge even the most hardened viewpoints. And according to emerging psychological research, exposure to messages from elites who share in-group identities with citizens can change those citizens' attitudes on divisive issues, particularly if the message is surprising but believable.[10]

In this chapter, I report the results of two novel experiments that test the power of elite opinion makers. First, I apply my conclusions from Hawai'i, where Native Hawaiians ultimately embraced immigrants more completely than did the native-born majority in any of the other case venues because they came to see newcomers as partners in the endurance of their own indigenous culture. Accordingly, I test the effect of messaging that frames immigrants as integral to the nation's survival on attitudes toward immigration across nineteen European countries. To account for the power of far-right elite counterarguments that are also concerned with a sort of cultural threat, I test the durability of any changes in opinion when people are exposed to nativist rhetoric.

Second, I apply my conclusions about the power of elite messengers and test the extent to which white, Republican Party supporters in the United States update their attitudes toward immigrants when they are exposed to impersonated audio messages from in-group—white Republican—elites who provide welcoming messages about immigration. Using this "shallowfake," the question is whether Republicans become more liberal on immigration when a party leader indicates that he is also moderating on the issue. The results validate the power of elite messaging that incorporates immigrants into the nation-building project.

Words That Work

References to "messaging" are ubiquitous in modern-day Washington, London, Brussels, and most other political capitals. Nearly all policy professionals are now acutely aware of the psychology of issue framing, once the domain of communications professionals. In his book *Words That Work*, and over the course of a career of polling and communications consulting, Frank Luntz popularized the impact of portraying estate taxes on large inheritances as a "death tax," of generating more support for environmentalism by referring to "climate change" rather than "global warming," "energy efficiency" rather than "conservation."[11] These successes suggest to policy professionals that behind any public opposition lies majority support for one's perspective if it could just be unlocked by the right language and framing.

Between the 1960s and 1990s, American and European immigration advocates could afford to be less concerned with communications strategy. Western European countries generally facilitated labor migration since the end of the Second World War, and the United States featured an open family-sponsored, even if poorly regulated, system that was supported by ethnic minorities and businesses that benefited from population growth. Because any costs of this system were diffuse, the opposition was not especially intense.[12]

In the United States, this changed swiftly when the Republican Party began to politicize the issue of undocumented immigration, first in California in the 1990s and then nationally after the September 11, 2001, terrorist attacks, when some politicians associated immigration with national security threats. Conservative opposition grew against everything from new labor migration visas to regularizing the status of the undocumented childhood arrivals. Intense calls emerged for far-right programs of mass deportation and refugee prohibitions. During the same period in Europe, far-right parties stirred Islamophobia against growing Muslim minorities and refugees and even began to turn against visa-free movement within the European Union.

Over the course of the past two decades, pro-immigration advocates have cycled through three principal messaging themes to reframe and humanize the topic. A typical frame views immigrants through the lens of the economic contributions they bring. In this view, immigrants fill large, unmet labor needs, both in unskilled roles that native-born Americans are unwilling to accept and in highly skilled professional roles where there are severe shortages. Public information campaigns tout the country's reliance on immigrants to care for children, harvest fruits and vegetables, prepare meals, keep people healthy, and build homes and offices. Others show the disproportionate number of immigrant entrepreneurs, innovators, patent holders, and—during the global pandemic—essential personnel on the front lines of a public health crisis. Critics have lamented the ways these narratives commoditize immigrants and frame the decision to admit them as a commercial transaction. They have argued that the movement must seek more than functional or practical reasons for welcoming newcomers.

A second, concurrent frame depicts immigrants as a humanitarian obligation. This view emphasizes the vulnerability of many immigrants, a number of whom are forced migrants who leave their countries of origin in fear for their lives. Even those who are not forced migrants sacrifice material comfort, status, and other advantages in their countries of origin to pursue opportunities abroad. They arrive with few allies, a variable grasp of English, and little familiarity with their new home. In this understanding, welcoming immigrants connects to a higher moral purpose to which we are subject as people with greater resources and stability. Critics have argued that such portrayals broad-brush too many immigrants as weak and net "takers," stimulating public concerns with resource scarcity.

In the United States, a third common frame views today's immigrants as a national legacy. It taps into practically all Americans' ability to trace their family lineage to a newcomer, born in another country but who emigrated to this country in search of new opportunities or freedom. Through this frame, immigration is cast as an inherent component of American national identity, a heritage that unites citizens across generations, ethnic groups, and religious background, independent of legal status. Public information campaigns invoke Emma Lazarus's poem inscribed on the pedestal of the Statue of Liberty and the founding of the country as a refuge for religious minorities. In this spirit, some advocates have begun referring euphemistically to immigrants as "new Americans." Alas, critics argue that many Americans are now too far removed from their immigrant ancestors to make that connection and that this frame underestimates racial and religious prejudice against recent waves of immigrants who disproportionately come from Latin America, Asia, and Africa. Researchers have found that Americans also differentiate between the moral deservingness of their ancestors and the undocumented by virtue of their legal status.[13]

As signals of their failure to persuade or even assuage opponents, these messaging campaigns ran throughout the two decades leading up to the 2016 presidential election of Donald Trump, the 2016 Brexit referendum, and the coinciding success of nativist parties in Western Europe. After this wave of nativism, a series of confidential postmortems were commissioned by a number of philanthropic foundations that had poured tens of millions of dollars into the pro-immigration movement in Europe and America. Written by independent experts, these documents—several of which were eventually leaked or published—revealed the extent of popular skepticism about immigration and the struggles of related messaging campaigns.[14]

A 2017 report commissioned by the Four Freedoms Fund, an American foundation that supports better integration of immigrants into society, found that support for immigration in the United States was "a mile wide" but only "an inch deep."[15] Though researchers regularly find that over 60 percent of Americans recognize the benefits of immigration and support the regularization of undocumented populations, the report emphasized that large numbers also express concern about border security, Muslims, and refugees. While further research showed growth in general support for immigration later in the Trump administration, there remains a large "intensity gap" between those who casually support immigration and the fervent restrictionists who oppose it.[16]

In 2018, London- and New York–based Unbound Philanthropies—a liberal funder of the immigration movement in the United States and United Kingdom—commissioned a brutal, "sobering" report on the state of American support for immigration.[17] "There is no existing pro-immigrant, pro-immigration base in this country," it stated in its first section. "We do not have a large base of everyday people who are die-hard, organized, activated supporters on immigration issues." In seeking to understand why, the report's authors learned that, despite the immigration movement's emphasis on messaging, "[p]eople don't know who we are or what we want" and "don't have confidence in our ability to handle the issue, or think we're honest about its pros and cons." They attribute the failure to a general lack of "passion for immigrants and immigration among liberals" and the general perception of immigrants as a "risk factor, not as a group of people to fight for." A remedy, they wrote, will require more time, effort, creativity, and rigor.

A historical perspective may also help. The six case studies in this book exhibit the way that immigration is not interpreted so literally by societies in the midst of a demographic transformation. Rather, where the national identity is viewed as static and ethnically or religiously specific to the state, the arrival and settlement of foreigners is understood as the agent of zero-sum social change—an existential threat to the country itself. Under such circumstances, the desire for a sense of control and status in one's own country outstrips the value of any immigrant's labor or entrepreneurship. Under such circumstances, natives cannot see past their own vulnerability to recognize the vulnerability of immigrants. Under such circumstances, the legacy, heritage, and identity of the country is not honored but thought to be endangered by each new arrival.

Pro-immigration groups have struggled to make immigrants seem more innocuous. And if time is of the essence, short-run solutions cannot reinvent public perceptions of the national heritage. Few strategies have sought to leverage the perceived fragility of the nation as a justification for welcoming newcomers. It may be challenging to inspire a "passion" for immigrants, but a passion for the nation already exists.

National Survival

As I outlined in chapter 2, the fire of nationalism is stoked by immigration and demographic change because the arrival of newcomers raises broad, existential questions about how a nation should be defined and what its future ought to be. The native-born always understand their national identity with more complexity and nuance than they understand the identity of newcomers.[18] Consequently, immigrants' culture and attributes always appear far more cohesive and unified than one's own. This truth was inadvertently expressed by *Financial Times* columnist Christopher Caldwell in his alarmist 2009 book about the threat Muslims pose to European democracies, *Reflections on the Revolution in Europe*. In it, he referred to European societies as "hospitable," "insecure," and "malleable." In contrast, he depicted Islam as "anchored," "confident," and "adversarial." However, Islam is a religion with dozens of sects, thousands of traditions, and a cacophony of beliefs that has left it irreconcilably splintered. Imagine how "anchored," "confident," and "adversarial" twenty-seven European states appeared when they aligned into a supranational alliance called the European Union.

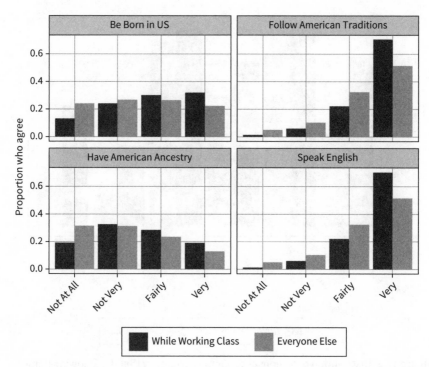

Figure 11.1 The distribution of responses to "To be truly American, how important is it to . . . ?" among white working-class people and everyone else.

Source: "2016 Time Series Study," American National Election Studies, accessed March 15, 2021, https://electionstudies.org/data-center/2016-time-series-study/.

The threat of immigration to national heritage is perceived to be far greater among those who derive more of their self-worth from that heritage. According to my analysis of American and British survey data presented in Figures 11.1 and 11.2, white working-class people—a constituency that disproportionately supports nativist parties and candidates—place greater value in heritage-based attributes than all others when defining American and British identities. More than the general American population, white people without a university degree believe that to be truly American, people need to have American ancestry, American traditions, an American birth, and fluency in English. More than the general British population, white working-class respondents believe that to be truly British, people needed to have British ancestry, a British birth, and, in some cases, a Christian faith.

It is reasonable to deduce that similar sentiments pervaded public opinion among Afro-Trinidadians in 1995, Protestant New Yorkers in 1855, and Native Hawaiians in the late nineteenth century. Conscious of this popular craving for a reinforcement of heritage just after Hawai'i's

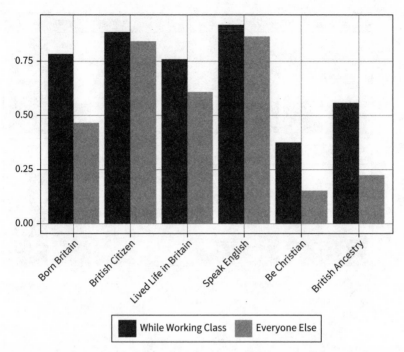

Figure 11.2 Distribution of responses to "Some people say that the following things are important for being truly British. Others say they are not important. How important do you think each of the following is?" among white working-class people and everyone else.

Source: United Kingdom Department for Transport, "British Social Attitudes Survey: 2013," July 3, 2014, https://www.gov.uk/government/statistics/british-social-attitudes-survey-2013.

indigenous population was shrinking, King Kalākaua took numerous actions to reinforce the strength of Hawaiian heritage. The appetite for this acknowledgment of indigeneity and lost sovereignty endures today in the politics surrounding Native Hawaiians' exclusive access to Kamehameha Schools, eligibility to vote in trustee elections for the state's Office of Hawaiian Affairs, and the Hawaiian Home Lands public housing program, which is limited to Native Hawaiian adults with "not less than one-half part of the blood of the races inhabiting the Hawaiian Islands previous to 1778."[19]

The concern for native bloodlines in Hawai'i, however, dissipated with the recognition of allied foreigners as integral to the survival of native heritage and way of life. Could similar recognition extend to foreigners in the rapidly aging countries of Europe? If European nationals believe their population and way of life is threatened, could this belief be wielded to justify greater tolerance of foreigners who extend or rejuvenate threatened components of French, Italian, or German heritage?

In August 2020, political scientists Tyler Reny, Jeremy Ferwerda, and I fielded a survey to nationally representative samples across nineteen European countries. In total, we polled 20,896 people in Austria, Bulgaria, Czechia, Denmark, Estonia, France, Germany, Hungary, Italy, Latvia, Lithuania, the Netherlands, Poland, Romania, Slovakia, Slovenia, Spain, Sweden, and the United Kingdom. We randomly assigned participants to a control group (6,937 people) and asked the remainder to read a news article. The article's language and Eurostat-provided data are accurate and adapted for each participant's current country of residence. Here is the British version:

Birth Rates Declining in the UK;
Experts Argue More Immigration Needed From Outside Europe

According to demographers, birth rates in the United Kingdom are significantly below the level needed to maintain the native British population. If conditions remain unchanged, the average citizen in the United Kingdom will be 46 years old by 2040. This trend is expected to place pressure on the economy as the share of retirees expands and rural areas become less populated.

Even though over 3 million immigrants have already entered the UK over the last five years, government advisers have argued that to maintain current population levels, the United Kingdom will need to accept significantly more immigrants from countries outside of Europe with higher birth rates, such as Muslim-majority and African countries.

The first paragraph primes participants with information about the fragility of native British demography, cuing readers to connect with the kind of feelings that characterized Native Hawaiians observing the deterioration of their population share between 1860 and 1960. However, these are also the kind of data employed by far-right elements to fearmonger about what has been termed "Grand Replacement," a conspiracy theory contending that elites are progressively replacing white European populations with Muslim and African peoples thanks to immigration and low native birth rates. To clarify the detrimental effect of population loss, the paragraph emphasizes the economic consequences of the current imbalance.

On this premise, the second paragraph affirms the interest of the government to maintain current population levels and reports experts' recommendation to admit more immigrants. A significant amount of European migration originates from inside the European Union. In numerous countries, more than half of all immigrants enter via the EU's free mobility arrangement. To make this a particularly hard test of demographic justifications for liberalizing immigration policy, we note that immigrants may come from

Muslim-majority and African countries, which more xenophobic Europeans find less familiar and more threatening than fellow Europeans.

After viewing the news article—adapted for each of the nineteen countries—all respondents were asked whether immigration to their respective country should be kept at its present level, increased, or decreased. As I emphasize at the beginning of this chapter, because the question of immigration levels is connected to emotionally charged group-centric concerns, they are among the most difficult political views to alter.[20] In Europe, the question of immigration is often even more sensitive than in the United States because EU countries do not have the same continuous legacy of welcoming newcomers. Moreover, unlike the American identity, European concepts of the nation are more directly rooted in an indigenous people, less apt to "evolve" with the composition of their population. And in some cases, their populations and territory are quite small and more sensitive to the influx of foreigners.

Still, invoking the need to "maintain the native [national] population" was sufficient to significantly nudge average attitudes toward increasing immigration on a 5-point scale—by .10 points across the nineteen European countries surveyed and by .14 points among the Western European countries that have historically experienced higher levels of immigration.[21] In the Czech Republic, Denmark, Spain, and the United Kingdom, the two paragraphs produced better than a .20-point shift in attitudes toward increasing immigration. When we limit the results exclusively to those respondents who passed an attention check that ensures they are carefully reading the survey questions, the effects are amplified. The need to "maintain the native [national] population" moved average attitudes toward increasing immigration by over .13 points across all nineteen countries on a 5-point scale, and by just under .20 points across the Western European countries—.31 points in Spain and .30 points in Denmark, whose population of under 6 million people has enacted some of Europe's most anti-immigrant legislation in the years following the 2015 influx of migrants and asylum seekers.

Of course, our prime about demographic population loss is insulated from nationalist rhetoric that would otherwise contend that immigrants do not extend the nation's survival but are precisely the elements that threaten its endurance. To test how resilient our original priming is against such rhetoric, we exposed another subgroup (6,976 people) of the survey sample to a corollary paragraph immediately after the first two. Invoking the specific words of far-right Hungarian prime minister Viktor Orbán, the corollary—again adapted for each country, but here reproduced for the United Kingdom—reads:

Some worry that this trend could eventually cause the UK's culture and way of life to disappear as native Britons become a minority. One politician recently said: "In all of Europe there are fewer and fewer children, and the elites' answer is more migration. But population replacement is a reality that cannot be denied. Elites are introducing foreign elements into our society and diluting it so that our nationality will disappear."

This is where Western and Eastern Europe diverge. Western European respondents were resilient to the nativist rejoinder, and the average effect of the full three-paragraph intervention was to nudge attitudes .14 points toward increasing immigration on a 5-point scale. However, in Eastern European countries, the effect drops to .03 points and loses its statistical significance, demonstrating the appeal of nativism to Eastern European respondents. The average effect across the nineteen countries drops only slightly to about an .08-point shift toward increasing immigration, and remains statistically significant. While the shift in Spain and the United Kingdom is unaffected by the nativist rejoinder, the effect shrinks substantially in the Czech Republic and Denmark, where far-right political movements have been more successful. Filtering on the attention check amplifies this divergence. Western Europeans who pass the check are more persuaded, while no effect is detected among Eastern Europeans who pass the check.

The durability of the Western European results suggests the power of this unlikely reorientation of "national survival" rhetoric. The intervention is most effective among women, respondents between thirty-five and forty-nine years old, respondents who place themselves on the ideological left or ideological center, respondents with low or moderate levels of formal education, and respondents with low and middle incomes. The "national survival" intervention was also significantly more effective at shifting the attitudes of people who expressed less concern about the coronavirus pandemic, which was receding but ongoing in Europe at the time of the survey's fielding. This suggests that the pandemic could have exerted downward pressure on the magnitude of our treatment effects, which would have been larger outside of a pandemic context.

Overall, the results of this experiment exhibit the promise of messages that focus not on the virtue of immigrants who are worth saving but rather the virtue of a *nation* worth saving. This reorientation will challenge pro-immigration groups, who are predisposed to the welfare and humanity of the population they serve. This predisposition, however, is unnatural for the national population they must convince to change public policy on immigration. In short, immigration advocates should consider "meeting people where they are."

Look Who's Talking

For most liberal advocates of immigration and integration, broadening the way one communicates about immigration is far preferable to broadening one's political alliances to include more conservative leaders. Including conservatives may rankle current allies and entail uncomfortable compromises, when it is far "cleaner" and less morally complicated to simply persuade conservative voters without engaging their leaders.

The problem with that strategy is that social scientific research suggests that language choice and message framing have a limited effect on exclusionary attitudes. One of the most comprehensive tests of framing and public opinion found surprisingly weak or nonexistent effects of different messaging frames on public opinion toward immigrants and immigration.[22] The researchers considered the effect of wording differences, such as "illegal" versus "undocumented" immigrants, but also differences in approaches, such as those that humanize immigrants and those that present statistical data. If these frames do not move opinion in a laboratory environment, it is even less likely that they will persuade citizens when met with competing messaging frames in a competitive media environment—notwithstanding the earlier results from Europe.[23]

Psychological research on persuasion suggests why approaches that focus exclusively on message content might not work. Individuals, particularly the nationalists or skeptics that immigration advocates need to reach, will be predisposed to resist persuasion from messaging campaigns. This research suggests that individuals are inclined to dismiss evidence and reasoning that does not match their preexisting views or beliefs.[24] Further studies show that yielding to persuasion can threaten a person's self-image,[25] threaten self-esteem derived from ideological or partisan identities,[26] and increase feelings of vulnerability.[27] This makes targeting those with conservative positions on immigration a particular challenge. As I have emphasized before, it is also reasonable to expect persuasion to be *even more difficult* to alter attitudes toward immigration. A successful and scalable persuasion approach, then, must first reduce resistance to persuasion before delivering a persuasive message.

Recent evidence suggests that Americans are more prone to persuasion from in-group elites even when it comes to durable attitudes related to race, ethnicity, and immigration.[28] Most promising, in 2017 political scientists Brian Harrison and Melissa Michelson found that surprising or counter-stereotypical cues from trusted in-group elites facilitate attitude change.[29] While Democrats increasingly line up behind liberalizing immigration policy reform and follow clear cues from Democratic elites, Republicans similarly receive increasingly clear and unified conservative messaging against immigration, a drastic change from even fifteen years ago. This caused me and my colleague, Tyler Reny, to wonder: What would happen if Republicans received pro-immigration messages from Republican in-group elites who are willing to break with the party consensus? Do these elites need to be well-known figures to facilitate persuasion?

In August 2020, we fielded an online survey to a sample of 9,393 Americans benchmarked and weighted to national demographics. After participants answered a number of questions about their demographics, political leanings, and contact with and impressions of a variety of population subgroups; we randomly assigned them into a control group and five different treatment groups. The first treatment group was exposed to a thirty-second video featuring a photograph of popular Fox News commentator Sean Hannity.

We selected Hannity because, in 2019 pilot research on a variety of Republican luminaries, he was among the most liked, most trusted, and most influential on Republican respondents—slightly more than even Vice President Mike Pence and significantly more than the Reverend Franklin Graham, quarterback Peyton Manning, and JP Morgan Chase CEO and billionaire Jamie Dimon.

Hannity has since been one of the most vocal opponents of immigration and one of the most loyal advocates for Trump's nationalist policies. At that moment in American politics, by virtue of his proximity to President Trump, he was as much of an institutional leader as any public official.

Respondents exposed to an intervention featuring Hannity were first asked to read a short introduction before accessing the video:

> Yesterday, Fox News commentator Sean Hannity spoke at a meeting of Republican Party officials and volunteers. Click the video on the next page to listen to a clip of these remarks.

When the video begins, a professional voice actor impersonates Hannity:

I'm a conservative Republican. I have been my whole life, and I'm worried about the way our country governs immigration.

> For years, I have fought against open borders and amnesty for illegals, but I have come to realize that Congress' gridlock on immigration has amounted to de facto amnesty anyway. Something has to be done. So, let's make some compromises. Everybody wants a secure border, but immigration governance doesn't stop at the Rio Grande. We need to treat immigrants fairly once they're here and give them an equal shot at the American Dream.

The second paragraph of this message was derived from speeches that the late U.S. senator and Republican presidential nominee John McCain made on immigration. Though a decorated ideological conservative who was once his party's standard-bearer, McCain held centrist views on immigration policy and persuaded many Republican voters and legislators to take more liberal positions in his attempts to pass comprehensive immigration reform.

The rhetoric is clear but hardly extraordinary. In fact, Hannity espoused similar views around the previous time the U.S. Congress considered a comprehensive immigration reform bill. In 2012, he reportedly told radio listeners, "It's simple to me to fix it. I think you control the border first. You create a pathway for those people that are here—you don't say you've got to go home. And that is a position that I've evolved on. Because, you know what, it's got to be resolved. The majority of people here, if some people have criminal records you can send them home, but if people are here, law-abiding, participating for years, their kids are born here, you know, first secure the border, pathway to citizenship, done." He added, "You can't let the problem continue—it's got to stop."[30]

Research suggests that the first paragraph of the impersonated statement is crucial. Its principal goal is to establish a sense of shared identity with the listener, what is called an "identity prime." It is reasonable to expect that the Republicans we intended to persuade identify with and relate to these statements. They are also likely to be longtime conservatives concerned about immigration policy. Once the speaker's credibility is established, we hypothesize that listeners will be much more open-minded about whatever message follows.

Meet John Wagner

In our 2019 research on the selection of Republican luminaries, we were surprised to find that a man no one had ever heard of was nearly as appealing as Sean Hannity and more persuasive than any other Republican we considered: John Wagner.

In the four other treatment groups, we misled our participants to believe that Wagner, a fictitious white male, is the co-chair of the Republican National Committee or the co-chair of the Democratic National Committee. (At the time of the survey, the Republican chair was actually Ronna Romney McDaniel, and the Democratic chair was Tom Perez.) In our research on Republicans, Wagner's common name, white, fifty-something male profile, and Republican credentials were enough for him to be nearly as likable and trustworthy as some of the real Republican leaders.[31]

While we were most interested in leveraging Wagner's profile as a Republican, we portrayed him as a Democrat to an equal number of respondents in order to check the difference party identification makes when all other qualities and messaging are held constant. (See the appendix for a list of the treatment groups.)

All four treatment groups were asked to read a short introduction before accessing the video with Wagner:

> Yesterday, John Wagner, co-chairman of the [Republican/Democratic] National Committee ([RNC/DNC]), spoke at a meeting of [Republican/ Democratic] Party officials and volunteers. Click the video on the next page to listen to a clip of these remarks.

The video that followed featured a photograph of the fictitious Wagner and a voice-over. Both groups with the Republican Wagner heard the John McCain–inspired paragraph that was also delivered by the Hannity impersonator, but only one group received the identity prime (the first paragraph). Likewise, only one of the two groups with the Democratic Wagner received the identity prime. This allowed us to isolate the effect of the identity prime on public opinion about immigration.

After viewing the video, all respondents were asked a series of questions intended to measure immigration policy attitudes and attitudes toward immigrants. The former was a set of five policy items measuring support for expansive immigration policy, including support for deportation, legalization programs, job-training programs for immigrants, granting immigrants broader access to public benefits, and establishing a Hispanic heritage month. We combined these items into a 0-to-1 scale of immigration policy attitudes.

The questions about immigrants asked whether they are doing enough to assimilate, whether they strengthen the country, whether they are a burden on the economy, and whether they increase the risk of terrorist attacks in the United States. These items were combined into another 0-to-1 scale of immigrant attitudes. Finally, respondents were asked a question about their feelings toward the speaker portrayed in the video.

Looking first at policy attitudes, we found that most of the treatments appear to move the full sample in a liberal direction, though it is clear that the Republican Wagner treatments, which are counter-stereotypical, exert a larger effect than the Democratic Wagner treatments. Breaking down the results by participants' political affiliations yields results consistent with what we expected. Democrats are largely immune to these messenger effects. Independents, who are less likely to be prone to partisan group-specific messengers, appear to move in a liberal direction in response to both Democratic and Republican Wagner messages. Finally, Republicans, our core group of interest, do not move in response to Democratic Wagner treatments but shift their attitudes in a liberal direction after exposure to Republican Wagner treatments.

The respondents who received the Republican Wagner message without the co-identity reinforcement prime were 1.7 percentage points more liberal on the policy attitude scale than the control. The effect is significantly larger, as we expected, when Wagner reinforces his shared identity, moving respondents an average of 3.8 percentage points more in a liberal direction relative to the control and 2.1 percentage points more in a liberal direction relative to the message without the co-identity reinforcement prime. This is a significantly larger effect than the one generated by the Hannity treatment, which—even with the co-identity prime—also moves Republican policy attitudes, but only by 2.2 points in a liberal direction.

This finding confirms that Republican immigration policy attitudes can be swayed with simple messages when the messengers are trusted members of the in-group. Emphasizing their shared values and identity through a co-identity reinforcement prime reduces resistance to persuasion much more than a party label alone.[32] The technique is most likely to move respondents' attitudes about a pathway to citizenship, job-training programs, welfare benefits, and establishing a Hispanic heritage month, all policies aimed at accommodating immigrants. It did not, however, change attitudes about deportation. Remarkably, the effects of the Wagner co-identity treatment hold independently of how strongly respondents previously identified as Republicans[33] and independently of respondents' preexisting attitudes toward immigrants.[34] There is little variation across the board, suggesting this is a powerful treatment.

None of the treatments had such an effect on attitudes toward immigrants themselves. Americans, and Republicans in particular, may follow elite cues to become more tolerant with respect to how the government treats immigrants in the United States, but the movement we see is clearly not a function of attitudes about who immigrants are or how they contribute to the United States. When analyzing the four immigrant attitudes items separately, the only movement we see comes from Republican respondents exposed to the identity prime from the Republican Wagner who become more likely to believe that immigrants strengthen America. These divergent responses are likely due to the fact that our treatment message is predominantly focused on moving attitudes about policy rather than about who immigrants are. It is possible that a message focused on immigrants themselves may have nudged Republican attitudes more effectively if accompanied by a trusted Republican messenger.

The most significant effect size—nearly 4 percentage points—is not enormous. However, this was produced by just a thirty-second intervention that targeted American public attitudes shown to be among the most challenging to move. So it is reasonable to imagine an even greater effect if there were a concerted effort to recruit multiple, trusted, credible messengers who leveraged their partisan or ethnoreligious bona fides to combat nativism and ethnocentrism in diversifying societies. This experiment should thus be understood not as a panacea but rather as a meaningful proof of concept for a broader strategy to mitigate backlash to immigration and demographic change.

The effectiveness of the fictitious Wagner as a messenger reduces the pressure on immigration advocacy groups to recruit celebrities or other influential Republicans to communicate their ideas. In fact, the fictitious Wagner was more persuasive than the widely known Hannity, who was respected and trusted by most Republicans. This lowers the bar for pro-immigration groups; for example, they don't need to approach Hannity or Pence. Even little-known Republican leaders can help persuade voters to liberalize their views about immigration and reduce anxiety about demographic change. Wagner's impact should embolden such groups to find ways to broaden their coalitions in any way possible.

It is likely that influential Republican public officials who may otherwise be sympathetic to the need for immigration may be concerned about criticism from their supporters. However, our research finds this concern to be unfounded. Indeed, we found no backlash against in-group elites.[35] If anything, Wagner's image in the eyes of respondents was only enhanced after sharing his more moderate views. This suggests that elites have broad latitude to shape attitudes even on contentious issues without turning public opinion against themselves.[36]

Meeting People Where They Are

The survey experiments described in this chapter take a similar approach. They meet native-born citizens, who may be wary of immigration or demographic change, where they are. The message my coauthors and I test employs demographic anxiety as a justification for immigration, while the messengers we test are likely to be credible to those we try to nudge. Much like solving a bamboo finger trap—a cylinder that tightens when victims instinctively try to pull their fingers out—the way to escape the hold of nationalism is to move with its momentum to loosen its grip.

This represents a departure from the conventional approaches of immigration advocates in the United States and Europe today. During the period in which nativism has grown to prominence, the focus has been on enhancing the image of immigrants without concerning themselves with the values of the people they wish to convince. In many cases, those values relate to the sanctity and preservation of the nation. As a result, advocates have struggled to foster relationships with potentially sympathetic constituencies like unions, religious congregations, or law enforcement agencies. These are groups that found many Trump administration actions against immigrants distasteful if not outright objectionable. Many recognize the virtues of immigrants and immigration, but they also value an orderly and fair system of rules.

During this same period, we witnessed the emergence of the #AbolishICE movement, which argued for the abolition of the U.S. Immigration and Customs Enforcement agency—a position that many Americans equated to lawlessness. The effect was to discredit pro-immigration advocates and distance moderate and conservative Americans from more active support of immigration. The Irish in nineteenth-century New York disputed public charge rules as grounds for deportation but never disputed the need for law enforcement. Quite the opposite, in fact: they joined law enforcement and defined it.

As immigrants and their allies consider how they may better define or redefine their country and its institutions, racial differences between native-born Americans and new immigrants are a persistent challenge. Earlier generations of immigrants simply had more inherently in common with the nation they wished to join. The inescapable context of Irish exclusion in New York City is that they always occupied a level of status above African Americans and were followed by waves of other, even less desirable immigrants of Italian, Jewish, and Eastern European backgrounds. The integration of the Irish (and eventually these other European ethnic groups) demand a deeper exploration of American conceptions of whiteness, which may presage today's American experience with demographic change.

12

Borderline White

The Past and Future of Race in American Politics

Los Tejanos

Of all the different storylines that emerged from an extraordinary 2020 Election Day in the United States, few were as counterintuitive as the results from Texas's Rio Grande Valley. Democrats had long been targeting Texas's Electoral College delegates because they believed the pace of demographic change played in their favor. Much like elsewhere in the American Southwest, an aging, white, working-class population was giving way to more transient, liberal, urban professionals and immigrant-origin minorities—the principal components of the Democrats' coalition. Early in the evening, presidential candidate Joe Biden was winning by a significant margin in the sprawling suburbs encircling large, liberal cities like Houston, Dallas, San Antonio, and Austin. But just when observers thought Texas might tilt blue, the results from the state's southernmost precincts returned with unexpected margins favoring President Donald Trump.

After Hillary Clinton won by 33 points in 2016, Zapata County flipped red in 2020.[1] Webb County doubled its Republican turnout from 2016.[2] In Starr County, Republicans recorded the single biggest swing to the right in the entire country—a 55 percent shift from 2016.[3] The Trump campaign saw similar numbers from white working-class regions in the Upper Midwest and Rust Belt in 2016, but Zapata, Webb, and Starr counties were, respectively, 94, 95, and 96 percent Latino.[4] (See Figure 12.1.) In fact, Trump performed 10 points better across Texas's eighteen Latino-majority counties in 2020 than he did in 2016 and won five of them.[5]

In the crosshairs of Trump's retrogressive assault on demographic change, these voters were the Mexican Americans whose allegiance, virtues, and values he had questioned. And they lived up against the border he wished to militarize, the border to which he attributed so many of America's ills. How, many wondered, did Trump's rhetoric not sufficiently prime the Mexican and Latino identity of people in the Rio Grande Valley to mobilize greater Democratic support?

Majority Minority. Justin Gest, Oxford University Press. © Justin Gest 2022. DOI: 10.1093/oso/9780197641798.003.0012

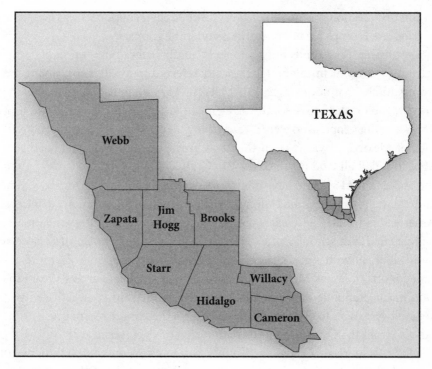

Figure 12.1 County map of South Texas.

As many Democratic Latino advocates emphasized in the weeks after the election, voting patterns in South Texas were the exception that proved the rule. Biden won Texas's Latino vote by double digits, and he won more of the nationwide Latino vote than Clinton did in 2016.[6] Enormous Latino margins propelled Democratic victories in Arizona, Colorado, Nevada, and New Mexico, and their growing numbers contributed to Democratic victories in Georgia, Pennsylvania, and Virginia, and close races in North Carolina and Ohio.

Latinos are a remarkably heterogeneous constituency. The label is used as a catchall for people of Hispanic origins, but it includes dozens of nationalities, diverse racial and religious backgrounds, and a range of socioeconomic and educational backgrounds that intersect with political preferences in ways that may produce Republican preferences. In postmortems about the Rio Grande Valley, local party officials lamented neglect by the state and national Democratic Party[7] and highlighted the economic concerns of people who work in the oil and gas sector.[8]

But the question was not how voters justified their support; it was how they overlooked Trump's assault on Latinos and immigrants.

The answer was simple: most people in South Texas do not think of themselves as Latino or immigrants. Typically referred to as "Tejanos," many are from families that never migrated at all. The old saying is "I didn't cross the border; the border crossed me," a reference to the 1845 U.S. annexation of Texas and the people who were already living in the separatist northern province of Mexico. It wasn't until the 1848 Treaty of Guadalupe Hidalgo that Mexico ceded all land north of the Rio Grande. Many more Tejanos crossed the border after 1848 and have now resided in the United States for six, seven, and even eight generations—longer than most Italian, German, or Greek American families. These early cohorts were subject to strict assimilationist regimes in Texas schools, and some stopped speaking Spanish. It is easy to understand how Tejanos struggle to relate to the experience of more recent cohorts of fellow Mexican Americans, let alone recent arrivals from the Dominican Republic or Guatemala. As early as the mid-twentieth century, Tejanos were eager to distance themselves from these more recent immigrants but also from the *Chicano* activists politicizing their presence.

While 94 percent of Zapata County residents count their ethnicity as Hispanic/Latino on U.S. census forms today, 98 percent of the population marks their race as white.[9]

"I'm too white to be Mexican, and I'm too Mexican to be white," said lifelong Zapata County resident Cynthia Villarreal to a *Politico* correspondent after the 2020 election. Villareal is a lifelong Democrat who, like many along the Texas border, says that her family history begins with the Spaniards' colonial regime along the Rio Grande. "No soy Mexicana, ni gringa," she said. "Soy Tejana."[10]

Another Zapata resident but ardent Trump supporter, Yvonne Trappe, told *Politico*, "I see myself just as an American. Growing up, I never knew that Hispanics were another race, that we were brown. Everybody just put white—not that it matters. Our culture is one thing, but we were just Americans. . . . Today, the people coming over are not the kind of people who came before, like the *braceros*, who came to work, to educate their children, to better themselves. No, the people coming now are looking for handouts."[11]

Starr County Republican Party chair Ross Barrera told *Politico*, "I think when people say they don't like Mexicans, to me it means a Mexican citizen, or a Mexican national, who has crossed illegally. And then again, not all Mexicans look alike. So when they say they don't like Mexicans, I don't think it means me. . . . It means a Mexican national who has broken the law."[12]

Thus, many Tejanos experienced Trump's nativism as natives. If anything, they approach the issue of immigration from a border control perspective; much like New York's Irish, many Tejanos work in law enforcement and did not appreciate some Democrats' calls to defund police departments and abolish immigration and customs officers.[13]

For all of this book's concern with inclusive and exclusive institutions, Tejanos demonstrate why we must consider not only how governments and leaders draw social boundaries but how people understand those social boundaries and position themselves amid their subjectivities. This 2020 election subplot illuminates the fluidity of racial identity—in particular, whiteness in America. Tejanos—clearly Latino in the context of broader American demography—understand themselves locally and personally as "white" and behave accordingly in their choices at the national political level. If such a trend extended to Latino populations or other long-settled ethnic minorities beyond the banks of the Rio Grande to New York, Chicago, or Los Angeles, it would realign American politics and effectively postpone the country's majority minority milestone altogether. In this chapter, I show how the vagaries of "whiteness" already postponed the United States' first majority minority milestone, and I report the results of survey research that evaluates the likelihood that it will happen again.

Majority Minority America: Part 1

The racial basis for the American nation has contradicted the country's race-blind civic ideals throughout the course of U.S. history. The Constitution endorsed the enslavement of Africans in southern states, and it was encoded in a key 1790 law limiting naturalization to "free white persons."[14] Although modified after the Civil War, this law remained in force until 1952, evidence that America's designation as a "white" republic survived African American emancipation by almost a hundred years.[15]

For a nation so conscious of racial differences, however, the definition of "whiteness" has been fluctuating since the inception of the country's independence. Early on, most agreed that whiteness was limited to people of Anglo-Saxon backgrounds, but the construction of whiteness evolved to suit the needs of America's westward expansion. One of the earliest examples of this evolution of convenience took place in Texas, where President James Polk initially supported the annexation of Mexico because he believed that Mexicans' Spanish blood qualified them as "white."[16] However, as the Mexican-American War sent U.S. soldiers south of Texas and into contact with more

Mexican people, officials decided that the country was not white enough to merit annexation beyond the Rio Grande.[17] About a decade later, Tejanos were conscripted to fight for the Confederacy in the Civil War.

Such contact with other ethnic groups was always what made Anglo-Saxons confront the vagaries of the social construction upon which American social relations and plantation capitalism was built. New states on the American frontier offered citizenship and land rights to the French in Louisiana, the Spanish in Florida and Mississippi, Germans in Wisconsin and Minnesota, and the Spanish of New Mexico for their whiteness alone rather than any allegiance to the nascent United States.[18] When the Oregon Territory disbursed land donations to citizens, Asian and Hawaiian immigrants were not eligible, but the mixed children of white men and Native American women were.[19] When the California Supreme Court blocked Chinese immigrants from giving evidence in court in the 1850s, it used legislative language that previously made the same distinction for Indians, concluding that both groups were of the same "Mongolian type."[20]

Even though late-nineteenth-century outgroups like the Irish, Italians, and Eastern Europeans were subjected to severe exclusion and discrimination in northern cities, the "white" majority began to relax these prejudices when large numbers of African Americans arrived as part of the Great Migration in the early twentieth century. For every standard deviation increase in the Black population of a given city, intermarriage rates increased by 0.54 percentage points, and naturalization rates increased by 1.5 percentage points.[21] However, other processes also motivated this reimagination of whiteness.

Around the turn of the twentieth century, American leaders began to recognize the accumulating effects of immigration and emancipation. Millions of Irish Catholic families arrived in New York and all over the East Coast between 1846 and 1856. In 1870, the Fifteenth Amendment declared that no man shall be denied the right to vote on account of race, color, or previous condition of servitude—enfranchising millions of African American men who just a decade before were thought undeserving of a say in public affairs. In subsequent decades, the United States admitted millions of Italians, Eastern Europeans, Chinese, and Japanese with their foreign languages, religions, and complexions.

The diversification of the American population took place as global migration was also transforming the colonial and settler populations of the Caribbean, East Africa, and Oceania. As people experienced more cross-cultural contact, eugenicist theories of racial hierarchy were popularized to justify why certain groups were being subordinated: put simply, nonwhite people were thought to be genetically incapable of self-governance. The word "race" came to mean more than just the national character.[22]

Inside the United States, as elsewhere, it became clear that nativist movements like the Know Nothings and the Ku Klux Klan did little to halt the onward diversification of the citizenry. There was a gradual realization that the Protestant, Northern European orientation of "whiteness" was unlikely to sustain a dominant majority.[23]

Indeed, if late-nineteenth-century understandings of whiteness were applied to the current moment in the United States, nonwhite minorities would comprise approximately 61 percent of the national population today. According to 2018 estimates by the U.S. Census Bureau, Latinos (including Tejanos) today comprise about 18 percent of the 2018 population, African Americans make up 12 percent, and Asians and Pacific Islanders 5 percent. People with predominantly Irish heritage make up 11 percent, people of Slavic descent 6 percent, Italians and Greeks 6 percent, and Jews, Arabs, and other Middle Easterners about 3 percent. Through nineteenth-century spectacles, the United States reached its majority minority milestone decades ago.

National Life and Character

During the late nineteenth century, the supremacy of the white race—as it was then constructed—was beginning to be questioned. In 1893, Australian academic Charles Pearson published *National Life and Character*, a book that prophesied decolonization and the ascendance of the "black and yellow" races. He cited the power of differential fertility rates and the way that state socialism was keeping white populations "stationary." He closed his work on race with an ominous prediction:

> We shall wake to find ourselves elbowed and hustled, and perhaps even thrust aside by peoples whom we looked down upon as servile, and thought of as bound always to minister to our needs. The solitary consolation will be, that the changes have been inevitable. It has been our work to organise and create, to carry peace and law and order over the world, that others may enter in and enjoy.[24]

Soon to win the White House, Theodore Roosevelt found these developments alarming. In 1894 writings, Roosevelt blamed rapacious "trans-oceanic aristocracies" like Britain and Spain for the way the trade of slaves and indentured servants altered the fragile demographics of their colonies in a manner "fatal to the white race." In contrast, he took solace from the fact that the United States and other new democratic settler states, "with the clear instinct of race selfishness, saw the race foe, and kept out the dangerous alien" by oppressing those in their midst.[25]

In an 1894 letter to Pearson, Roosevelt reassured him:

What occurs in our own Southern States at the least sign of a race war between the blacks and the whites seems to me to foreshadow what would occur on a much bigger scale if any black or yellow people should really menace the whites. An insurrectionary movement of blacks in any one of our Southern States is always abortive, and rarely takes place at all; but any manifestation of it is apt to be accompanied by some atrocity [in] the same way an Indian outbreak on the frontier would to this day mean something approaching to a war of extermination.[26]

With much of the "competition between the races reducing itself to the warfare of the cradle," Roosevelt wrote in 1897, "no race has any chance to win a great place unless it consists of good breeders as well as of good fighters." Wary of the persistent proliferation and civilizational development of the darker races, Roosevelt concluded then that there was a need to consolidate a broader white identity and guard the temperate zones of the earth as a "heritage for the white people."[27]

Though Roosevelt recognized the power of restrictive immigration regulations,[28] the only way to sustain this heritage against what was being called "race suicide"[29] would be to incrementally admit other races into the fellowship of whiteness—to assimilate them into the American creed. In his writings, Roosevelt described "the transmission of acquired characters" as not only possible but a strong feature "in every civilized State."[30]

Despite his susceptibility to eugenics and racial theories of supremacy, Roosevelt's nationalism was always defiantly civic rather than ethnic in nature. In his narrative histories published between 1885 and 1894, he argued that as European immigrants were assimilated, their bloodlines were being absorbed into the national body, fusing Americans into a single, pure people forged in the crucible of the frontier. The acts of claiming and holding land, developing it into something greater than it had been, and defending it against the forces of nature all constituted rites of passage that transformed foreigners into Americans. In Roosevelt's understanding, Americans were born through no document; they were made by their encounters with the wilderness and their development of strength, individualism, and democratic community. For Roosevelt, the white ethnicities admitted into the United States were not entitled to their American identity; that identity was earned.

The effort thereafter to redraw the color line took decades to develop in the United States but ultimately led to contemporary American conceptions of whiteness. It was a way to broaden the definition of white people enough to maintain power over what Roosevelt called the "black and yellow people," without having to incorporate the least "assimilable" among them.

The Chinese Exclusion Act of 1882 made Chinese people ineligible for citizenship and effectively prohibited future entry, but the eligibility of Armenians, East Indians, Syrians, and the Japanese was borderline. Were they white enough, like the Irish or the Italians? The answer ultimately came from the judiciary. Between 1887 and 1923, federal courts heard twenty-five cases contesting the legal status of immigrants seeking citizenship.[31] In the 1922 Supreme Court decision of *Takao Ozawa v. United States*, justices ruled that a Japanese-born man who had lived in the United States for twenty years was ineligible for naturalization because he did not qualify as a "free white person" as required under the Naturalization Act of 1906. In *United States v. Bhagat Singh Thind*, a 1923 Supreme Court decision ruled that an Indian Sikh man who identified himself as a "high caste aryan, of full Indian blood," was also racially ineligible. Neither Ozawa nor Thind challenged the constitutionality of the Naturalization Act's racial restrictions; what they wanted was to be recognized as white, not to end the legal superiority extended to white people.

Were Ozawa and Thind today's Tejano Trump voters? Independent of how one may feel about the racial identification choices of those born on its ambiguous borderlines, changes in the way people classify themselves hold downstream effects for American demography because the Census Bureau relies only on self-reporting, not objective racial criteria. There are none.

Past and Future

The story of the Tejanos, who acknowledge their Hispanic/Latino ancestry but identify as white and increasingly vote in solidarity with white Americans, is entirely predictable to sociologist Richard Alba from City University of New York. One of the United States' most prolific scholars of immigrant assimilation, Alba has been attempting to lead a counternarrative about America's majority-minority milestone for several years. In public commentary, academic articles, and a 2020 book, he argues that a combination of bad census data and the overlooked power of assimilation means that the prospect of a racially divided majority-minority country is vastly overstated and has unnecessarily left many white Americans feeling vulnerable to the numerical power of minorities.[32]

Even though the Census Bureau classifies individuals who report mixed or Hispanic ancestries as "not white" in its public presentations, Alba shows that this does not correspond with "the social realities of the lives of most mixed individuals, who are integrated with whites at least as much as with minorities." He points to the significant share of Hispanics who—like Tejanos—identify as white but are not included in the Bureau's tally of white Americans. If these white Hispanics were counted as white, white people would be projected to remain a near two-thirds majority in 2060.[33] The projected number of non-Hispanics who report part-white racial backgrounds and the estimated number of Hispanics with Anglo ancestry drops by just 5 percentage points between 2018 and 2060—when white and partly white newborns are still projected to make up a majority.[34]

Alba also notes that the predominant form of intermarriage in the United States unites minority and white partners. Marriages between Hispanics and non-Hispanic whites make up more than 40 percent of all recent interracial marriages, while marriages between whites and Asians comprise 15 percent. Altogether, intermarriages with one non-Hispanic white partner constitute more than 80 percent of the whole.[35] According to 2010 census data, the children of such marriages tend to marry white people. Seventy percent of white American Indian and white Asian individuals marry white partners, and a majority of white-Black individuals does as well.[36] The census data, Alba thus argues, distort demographic change by seemingly accelerating the decline of the white population and presenting as certain something that is no more than speculative.[37]

To the scholar of assimilation, the absorption of millions of people once vilified and excluded as inferior into the "white mainstream" is a triumph of American social relations. Alba expects America's more diverse regions to develop an incrementally adjusted mainstream drawn from a visibly wide set of origins and perceived in new multiracial and multicultural terms.[38] "Instead of a society riven along ethno-racial lines, between whites and nonwhites," he envisions, "we could see a society divided between an increasingly multi-hued majority and others whose lives are more determined by their minority status."[39]

The problem is the persistence of lives "determined by their minority status." Assimilation is not a racial justice movement. The mainstream expansion that crosses ethnoracial divisions "to envision a new kind of 'us,'" which Alba touts, is available only to those Hispanics pale enough to pass as white and people who possess some degree of white ancestry. This connects directly with the "boundary problem" inherent in democracies, which I discussed in chapter 2. Because "the people" are thought to precede the state, "the people" are identified according to undemocratic principles that marginalize specific members of the population and sacrifice components of democracy.

Alba's conclusions would suggest that today's anxious nativists take comfort in the inclination of immigrants to adopt the American creed. "This," Alba writes, "calls up echoes of the canonical experience of assimilation—the inclusion of the second and third generations of white ethnics after World War II."[40] However, any such inclusion—whether of the Irish, Italians, Jews, Tejanos, or people of mixed racial backgrounds—merely admits the newest entrants to whiteness in order to sustain the previous white majority and reinforce whiteness itself as the gateway to status and power. It is a marginal promotion that sustains a history of subjugation of Blacks, Asians, and Latinos too dark to qualify.

Today's Tejanos may forget that a 1935 Supreme Court decision ruled that Mexicans were not white, that their ancestors were forced into racially segregated platoons in both world wars. Biracial individuals were once subject to discrimination according to the "one-drop rule" of minority status. Italians, Jews, and Slavs were long excluded from employment, educational institutions, and social clubs, and their admission into the "mainstream" around the 1960s did not produce racial harmony anyway. Alba makes a concerted effort to draw attention to America's persisting social inequities, but he does not connect these inequities as they are experienced by some minorities (principally African, Latino, and, in many settings, Asian Americans) with the selective assimilation of other minorities (white ethnics).

A further risk of such a perspective is that it perceives little value in the maintenance of any cultural differences. Rather, it validates a social environment that incentivizes, if not pressures, the shedding or whitewashing of ethnic distinctions. Would America not be better off if the Irish, Italians, and Jews never forgot their earlier exclusion, never came to think of themselves as white, and instead found common purpose with African Americans, Asians, and Latinos in a country where all people are equal? This counterfactual could be a multiculturalist vision of a population mosaic, but also a story of assimilation into a cross-cutting civic ideal. The truth is that America's "canonical experience of assimilation" only reimagined "whiteness"; it did not reimagine America itself.

Any new embrace of minorities into a "white"-turned-"multihued" mainstream is part of a calculation—conscious or not—that consolidates whiteness around the next most assimilable group of ethnic minorities in the interest of distinguishing, if not excluding, those deemed still too different. Alba is correct to foresee the expansion of whiteness. But ultimately, it is the persistent whiteness of America's national identity that is the problem. By continuing to interpret America's heritage and mainstream as "white" rather than something far more civic, we reinforce the myth that this whiteness always included all those who now identify with it. If the United States is to broaden the mainstream, maintaining a standard of "whiteness" cannot be the price of entry into it.

From One, Many

The "ethnic fluidity" Alba observes in Americans' self-labeling is the driver of the future he foresees, but it is also untested and not well understood. We have seen how Tejanos felt unthreatened by Trump's anti-immigrant and anti-Latino rhetoric. Does this suggest that those Hispanics who *do* feel targeted by this rhetorical environment will behave differently?

Approached another way, multiracialism and racial pluralism offer a middle ground between the warring factions in America's tribalized politics. For all their differences, nativists and multiculturalists ironically share an assumption that people are stuck within singular identities primordially ascribed to them and must engage the political system from within those groups. The rising recognition and embrace of Americans with multiple racial backgrounds and identities contradicts this assumption. Individuals who identify simultaneously with different groups are more likely to engage and empathize across group boundaries and less likely to view politics through the lens of zero-sum racial competition.[41] At the same time, political tribalism reimposes the barriers that identity pluralism works to permeate. We know little about the racial identity and group consciousness of borderline white people in this rhetorical environment.

Still, countless political pundits have popularized two prominent arguments. First, many political observers predicted that the same inflammatory rhetoric would produce an electoral wave of Hispanic voters in favor of Democrats in the 2020 election.[42] And second, conventional wisdom suggested that Trump raised the salience of white identity with his anti-immigrant, nationalist rhetoric and racist innuendo during the course of his 2015–2016 campaign and presidency between 2017 and 2021.[43] Using survey research, political scientist Morris Levy and I assessed both possibilities.

To explore the effect of racially polarizing rhetoric on Hispanics' ethnoracial and national identities, we fielded an online survey to a nationally representative sample of ten thousand Americans of Hispanic origins in May 2021. After participants answered a few warm-up questions about their general state and the state of the country, we divided them into two control groups and two different treatment groups. The first treatment group was exposed to a report of "comments a politician in Washington recently made."

The anonymized comments actually derived from a May 2018 National Public Radio (NPR) interview of Gen. John F. Kelly, President Trump's chief of staff between July 31, 2017, and January 2, 2019. During the course of the interview, NPR correspondent John Burnett asked Kelly, "Are you in favor of this new move announced by the attorney general early this week that if you cross the border illegally even if you're a mother with your children [we're going] to arrest you? We're going to prosecute you, we're going to send your kids to a juvenile shelter?" Respondents read only the following excerpt of General Kelly's answer:

> Immigration is one of the most pressing issues before us. It needs to be addressed with good sense and compassion, and above all without further delay.
>
> The vast majority of the people that move into the United States from Latin America are not bad people.
>
> But they're also not people that would easily assimilate into the United States, into our modern society. They don't speak English; obviously that's a big thing. They don't integrate well; they don't have skills.[44]

Respondents were not informed who made these marginalizing, microaggressive statements. The objective was to communicate a rhetorical environment generally hostile to people of Hispanic immigrant origins, such as the environment created by the Trump White House during the previous four years. (Preceding excerpts and the transcript, NPR admonished readers in an Editor's Note, "*This post contains language some may find offensive.*")

While one subset of our respondents was exposed to the marginalizing language and nothing else, another subset received the marginalizing language and an inclusive rejoinder: "The politician's comments were widely criticized as inaccurate and insulting. Some noted that previous generations of immigrants to America were unfairly criticized in similar ways, including the politician's own Irish and Italian ancestors." The rejoinder simulated a more contested public sphere and tested whether a more balanced rhetorical environment—where such marginalizing statements, while present and prominent, were also publicly condemned and where Hispanic immigrants were defended—negated any effects of the original microaggression.

What was the effect of the marginalizing rhetoric from an elite public official on Hispanic Americans' identity? Could such rhetoric have the opposite effect, pressuring these borderline individuals to "drift" toward whiteness and conform to the traditional mainstream while eschewing their minority background and heritage? Or would it cause borderline white Americans to identify more exclusively as members of minority groups and to see politics primarily through the lens of minority identity? Both reactions are defensive in nature: the former defends a stigmatized minority group; the latter defends the individual from stigma.

The results suggest that, despite being disturbed by the marginalizing statement,[45] Hispanic-origin Americans feel no more and no less "white," but slightly less "American" and slightly less "Hispanic." The treatments have no effect on white identity or its perceived importance among those who identify as white, and reduce the importance of Hispanic identity and American identity to respondents in a small but significant way. The rejoinder did not hold a significant effect either way.

Social identity researchers have found that people downplay marginalized identities to shore up their own individual centrality to the broader society. Confronted with microaggressive statements about them, Hispanics do indeed identify less with their polarizing ethnicity and yet feel as though the door has closed to their being "fully American." As a result, respondents are turning to other group identities or individual identities to maintain self-esteem and a sense of place in their society.[46]

These findings are corroborated when we examine results from the American National Election Studies. In our analysis, the importance of being "white" to Americans who identify as white dropped between 2012 and 2016, but also while President Trump was in office between 2016 and 2020. To be fair, the 2012–2016 drop in white identity was driven by non-Hispanic white Democrats (a 0.07 decrease on a 0-to-1 scale), who have grown warier of white identity amid greater awareness of racial injustice. However, it is noteworthy that white Republicans' views about the importance of white identity did not change during the same period. More interestingly, Hispanic and non-Hispanic white Americans—both Democrats and Republicans—reported a *weaker* sense of white identity between 2016 and 2020.

Taken together, these studies show that Hispanic Americans appear to be defaulting toward a political identity that neither defends nor ignores their stigmatized ethnic background. We are clearly not witnessing—at least in aggregate—an extraordinary reinforcement of white identity in the United States in light of increasingly nativist and nationalist rhetoric at the highest levels. However, we are also not witnessing a reinvigoration of Hispanic identity among those most implicated by such rhetoric. The implication is that even while many Hispanics are wary of the current political atmosphere, Democrats cannot rely on identity politics to mobilize them and Republicans cannot rely on identity politics to assimilate them. It will likely require many nuanced and subgroup-specific appeals in different regions and across diverse Hispanic constituencies.

When Party Is Race

To discredit the most politicized visions of a majority-minority future, Alba points to the state of California, where white people are already a minority of the population. California, Alba writes, "does not suggest an upheaval in the established ethno-racial order."[47] Such a fear "ignores internal diversity and assumes far too much coherence on the part of the minority bloc." Minorities are "too diverse in their histories, experiences, and social situations for anyone to assume that they could act politically in a unified way."[48]

However, the histories of earlier majority-minority societies suggest that the domination of coherent coalitions of ethnic groups is an oversimplified scenario. The political parties of Mauritius, Trinidad and Tobago, and historic New York—the three democratic cases I study—were not that coherent, but they were sufficiently racialized. Under these circumstances, ethnic and religious affinities overshadow the greater national interest. Identity politics undercuts people's capacity to empathize with other races or religions they view as existential threats. Voters then value political power more than democratic institutions, making them more willing to break the rules to win.

In short, the most likely upheaval we'll see in the United States will merely build on the upheaval of the four years Trump was in the White House. Already today, most Republican voters identify as white, vast majorities of nonwhite racial and religious minorities support Democrats, and American politics regularly devolves into a competition between ethnic constituencies that duel over resources and symbols of cultural power.

It wasn't always like this. Even when they bloc-voted, different ethnic groups once supported different parties. About 70 percent of Asian Americans voted for George H. W. Bush in 1992; about 70 percent of Muslim Americans voted for George W. Bush in 2000, and he also won nearly half the Latino vote. But today, 66 percent of Latinos and 66 percent of Asians regularly back Democrats, along with 90 percent of Muslims and African Americans. Elections are now turning into existential competitions over which party can anger or scare their constituents the most about their racial or cultural counterparts. Once-nonpartisan organizations, civic associations, and guilds have started to split along identity-based lines. This upheaval produced an insurrection in 2021 when Trump attempted to leverage these identity politics to support his attempts to invalidate the election results.

It is reasonable to assume that Trump's Republican successors will see in the aspiring whiteness of borderline white people a path to victory in this era of identity politics. In this view, Trump's primary mistake was not widening his vision of "white" America enough. Indeed, this is not so different from the strategy Republicans were prepared to pursue before the party's platform was swept away by anti-immigrant fervor.

In advance of the 2000 presidential election, when George W. Bush was governor of Texas, his chief strategist, Karl Rove, famously calculated that, given American (and Texan) demographics, the path to future Republican majorities was to better incorporate Latino leaders and voters into the party's caucus. The party was becoming increasingly older, whiter, and nonurban, while new voters were increasingly diverse and urban.

With their devout religiosity, conservative social values, and propensity to identify as white, Latinos, he predicted, would be predisposed to Republican politics if it weren't for the party's saber-rattling over immigration and Latinos. Bush pitched himself as a "compassionate conservative" who cultivated Latino votes, and he would win 44 percent of them against Vice President Al Gore. However, Rove and the Republican Party would ultimately compromise this long-term strategy for the short-term voter mobilization provided by nativist politics in the post-9/11 era—alienating not only many Latinos but also many Muslim and Asian voters as well.

When President Barack Obama entered the White House in 2009 on the back of an electoral coalition of white urban liberals and diverse ethnic minorities, a number of Democratic consultants giddily pointed to projections that reliably Republican voters comprised a dwindling share of the American electorate. "Demography is destiny," they taunted then. ("Demography is destiny," they comforted themselves after Trump's 2016 victory.)

Such a simplistic philosophy assumes that political coalitions do not change over time with the nature of new public challenges. Worse, the hubristic implication is that the left can be complacent and take their coalition for granted; its ultimate victory is imminent (in twenty-five years), the "destiny" coalition believed, regardless of the evolution of people's changing attitudes and changing identities.

Ultimately, both political parties are clinging to current understandings of whiteness to justify their brinkmanship, when the future of identity politics really depends on the new ways people come to understand themselves and their country.

13
Reimagined Communities

Connectedness as a Criterion for Governance

Reimagined Communities

Demographic change poses a unique challenge for any political community. It asks the nation—which has long explained its persistence with the creed of a specific ethnoreligious people—to endure when its ethnoreligious composition changes. The contemporary political tensions inside the United States and other diversifying countries are therefore best understood as the conflict between exigent demands to maintain a sense of its traditional social structure and broader long-term pressures to reconsider that structure altogether.

In chapter 2, I identified and addressed the "gravitational pull" of nationalism under conditions of demographic change. I argued that states undergoing transformational demographic change have struggled to escape the seemingly magnetic pull of nationalism precisely because they have failed to reimagine their respective nations and peoples. Instead, they have sought to institutionalize the boundaries of the current (and likely temporary) majority as the boundaries of the enduring "people"—which has made the definition of the nation and its public identity a primary source of conflict as the population evolves.

In my portraits of majority minority societies thereafter, we encountered dozens of individuals, organizations, and political movements devoted to protecting static, exclusive, or nostalgic concepts of the nation. Despite Carnival's potential to transcend Trinidad and Tobago's racial divide, Culture Minister Nyan Gadsby-Dolly cannot conceive of her Indian-origin countrymen equally as "people determined to be free." Despite Native Hawaiians' dwindling numbers and need for a broader alliance, the *kumu hula* Hui Hui Kanahele-Mossman insists that some elements of indigenous culture cannot be shared, that some boundaries should not be crossed. Despite his popularity and qualification to serve as Singapore's first non-Chinese head of state, Deputy Prime Minister Tharman Shamugaratnam justifies his own glass ceiling by insisting, "You cannot have too many changes in cultural identity at the same time." And despite its overwhelming

Majority Minority. Justin Gest, Oxford University Press. © Justin Gest 2022. DOI: 10.1093/oso/9780197641798.003.0013

diversity, New York has produced the xenophobia of moralizing Whigs, furtive Know Nothings, and eventually the rise of Donald Trump, who nostalgically promised to "make America great again." While it would be wrong to equate the conservationism of Kanahele-Mossman with the bigotry of Trump, or the conservatism of Tharman with the narrowness of Gadsby-Dolly, these are still different expressions of the nationalism upon which modern states have been built.

Across the cases I discussed in the book, I emphasized the constructed nature of these national imaginaries—the sense of "we." In many countries, nationalism was built toward the end of colonialism to justify independence and the founding of a new country. But its implicit adoption of colonial racial tropes also made it divisive. In Mauritius and Trinidad, people of Indian origin embraced Indian and Hindu nationalism while African Creoles tightened their connections with a pan-African diaspora. Despite Singapore's Malay roots and predominantly Chinese population, the city-state fashioned itself as a race-blind meritocratic nation. Under a sense of existential threat, initially from irredentist Shia and later as part of the 2011 Arab Spring, Bahrain has oriented nationalism around fealty to the Crown and populated its citizenry with new, carefully selected members whose allegiance would supersede that of the native-born.

These constructions and contradictions aside, nationalism has experienced a rebirth in the twenty-first century. In the face of destabilizing demographic change and the uncertainties of globalization, nationalism is a reassuringly familiar security blanket. In democracies particularly, nationalism asserts precisely what demographic change threatens: a specific ethnoreligious people's social dominance and entitlement to the state. The integrity of this threadbare blanket is sustained through all sorts of questionable patchworks: the notion of racial "balance" in Singapore, legends of the maroons in Mauritius, the African ownership of Carnival in Trinidad, the contortions of whiteness in the United States. It is not surprising, therefore, that in societies subject to great tension or conflict with newcomers, nationalism begets nationalism. Recall the competition for UNESCO World Heritage Site designation between Le Morne and the Aapravasi Ghat in Mauritius, or the divisive Hindu nationalism of Trinidad's Sat Maharaj.

But as chapter 2 concludes, connectedness also begets connectedness. And while this book has shown the way in which cultural spaces are often the venues of contestation, they are also the venues for connection. Cultural media and practices are more prone than politics to experimentation, hybridity, and intimacy. In art, sport, music, food, and festival, the stakes are lower, but the symbolic meaning can be higher. Cultural spaces have the freedom to engage in the reimagination of national identities and the reach to influence people across ethnic or racial boundaries. With fewer barriers to entry, freely expressed forms of culture may be cacophonous, but they are also collaborative, deliberative, and ultimately a democratic antidote to state-sponsored nationalism.

A Gravity Assist

Over the course of this book, I have showed how progress toward greater connectedness and more successful coexistence is not made by denying the power of an imaginary as alluring as nationalism. For so many citizens, nationalism is a "sacred truth," the violation of which would end any boundary-crossing conversation before it started. Nationalism is the turf on which progress must be made. Perhaps this is the best way to interpret the motivations behind philosopher Michael Walzer's Princeton University lecture in which he endorsed the politics of feeling "at home." Philosophers like Walzer are inclined to seek, however fruitlessly, a logical, grounded rationalization for nativism because there is an inherent sense that it is intractable. As I have stated metaphorically, nationalism and its imaginaries have a sort of gravitational pull.

To reimagine a nation, gravity is not something to be resisted or escaped but rather something to be leveraged. In orbital mechanics, a gravity assist takes place when a rocket uses the relative movement and gravity of a planet to alter the spacecraft's path and speed. In engaging the planet's gravity, the rocket acquires some of the planet's orbital energy in the process. This helps visualize the success of the experiments in chapter 11, which nudge people toward incrementally more open immigration policies by leveraging the logic of national survival and the credibility of fellow nationalists. It also shows how the political institutions I underscore in chapter 10 must honor heritage if they are to successfully include more diverse populations, cultivate a more civic understanding of the nation, and unify the population behind a reimagined understanding of the "people."

When one invokes "heritage," there is a natural concern among some observers that it may produce retrogressive results or that it may validate a derogatory prior state of affairs. And indeed, many heritage-based appeals do so. However, conservatives and nativists should not hold a monopoly on the use of nostalgia and heritage. (And one glimpse of the commercial marketplace will show that nostalgia is regularly used to sell a variety of very modern, progressive products and ideas.) So it is worth distinguishing how heritage may be honored without reproducing historic inequities.[1] I envision three ways, with some contemporary American examples:

1. Underscore the themes and artifacts of heritage that exemplify inclusivity and justify the evolution of the nation.

Not all components of heritage are retrogressive. And so it is worth underscoring the antecedents of contemporary attempts to craft a civic ideal. One American example recently comes from the West Virginia Can't Wait political movement, a progressive coalition of 2020 political candidates who took inspiration from "rednecks." Contrary to common understandings of the term, "rednecks" originally described the motley militia of Black and white native-born Americans and foreign-born immigrants who fought against federal troops in 1919 for the right to organize for better working conditions in the state's coal mines, battles referred to as the Mine Wars.[2] Without uniforms, they tied red kerchiefs to their necks to distinguish themselves in the fog of battle. A predecessor to unions and their pan-ethnic solidarity, West Virginia Can't Wait leveraged a key milestone in the state's history and the irony of rednecks' recent association with many white nationalists today to reach out to a predominantly white state largely supportive of former president Trump.

2. Rather than compete for vulnerability, victimhood, or supremacy, identify occasions in which the historic struggle has been shared or the landmark success was cooperative.

Too often, debates center on questions about who qualifies as a legitimate member of "the people" or the legitimacy of grievances, when all citizens share a concern for inclusion and recognition. As an example, #BelongingBeginsWithUs is a US mass-media campaign that was initiated in 2020 to sensitize Americans to the shared humanity of recent immigrant arrivals.[3] Independent of how Americans may feel about policy matters or the moral worthiness of immigrants, exclusion is an experience that is universal. The campaign leverages the fact that most Americans believe they and their country are inherently welcoming. Designed by the Ad Council and sponsored by the American Immigration Council, Walmart, and the YMCA, among numerous others with broad reach, the campaign not only communicates ways that Americans can extend a sense of belonging to newcomers; it also seeks to create opportunities to extend a sense of belonging in practice at the local level.

3. To the extent that there is a concern to reflect population diversity in organizations or conversations, symbolic presence should extend to members of the historic majority to acknowledge the equal weight of their voices and value.

The White House under President Joe Biden made news when it promised to designate staff inside its Office of Public Engagement for outreach to conservatives. The Office has always been oriented to outreach, but historically with an emphasis on the key constituencies that are inclined to support the current officeholder. However, at the *Wall Street Journal*'s CEO Council in December 2020, Biden appointee Rep. Cedric Richmond (D-Louisiana) said, "We're not elected just to help Democrats or urban cities or minorities. We were elected to help this entire country and that means reaching out to conservatives, that means reaching out to rural areas, reaching out to people who didn't vote for us."[4] The office then hired aides to promote outreach to traditionally Republican groups like rural, white Evangelical Christians and the business community.

Even though these initiatives are nascent with uncertain effects in future years, they exemplify how to acknowledge the value of national heritage without unquestioningly validating it. And each demonstrates a concern for the historic nation—or those who might be most invested in it—and harnesses its gravity to assist in the cultivation of a more connected society. In this way, the nation may be reimagined:

The White House has always served country, not party.
Americans have always been welcoming.
Rednecks were always inclusive.

A Criterion for Governance

Tactics are important, but they must be complemented by strategy.

What should be the goal of government institutions? Ultimately, the goal is to expand the sense of who "we" are. This goes far beyond who holds citizenship; it is a question of the people with whom we share a perceived common experience, such that we may identify them as an extension of ourselves, that we may empathize with their plight, and that we may expect them to listen to our own. Over the decades, the share of society with whom people feel this connection has dwindled with the closure of houses of worship, the shuttering of neighborhood bars, and the bankruptcy and consolidation of local newspapers. The internet has atomized associational life into ever more nuanced subcultures, narrowing the groups of people with whom people co-identify and converse. This separation was deepened when the world lived through a pandemic.

At its core, national unity must be a criterion for leadership, much as environmental sustainability has now become. Policymakers, business executives, and civic leaders routinely ask: What is the environmental impact of our actions? To what extent are our actions sustainable? How can we modify existing actions to make them more sustainable?

These same leaders must ask three analogous questions related to the cohesion that binds people together:

1. Does our action reinforce or break down social boundaries between people?
2. How can our action be adjusted to strengthen the sense of connection between people?
3. After our action, will the people trust this institution more and participate in its efforts?

Unity—a broad sense of "we"—is foundational to everyday life, so the ideal venues for its cultivation are the places people frequent, like schools and workplaces, parks and grocery stores, houses of worship and healthcare providers. The government administers many of these venues or influences their operation and can reorient elements of their work to broaden our sense of "we." And across all of its institutions, the government could cultivate a sense of shared moral purpose that crosses social, economic, and partisan boundaries in its lifetime work over multiple generations.

While the cultivation of a reimagined nation is a multidecade endeavor that cannot be the initiative of a single government, individual leaders nevertheless possess unique power. As we saw in chapter 11, leaders set norms like few others—a key instrument in the cultivation of cross-boundary connections. Executives can also coordinate and reinforce efforts to build inclusivity with the resources of large national foundations, philanthropists, and corporations. This can stimulate similar initiatives at the municipal and provincial levels.

Alas, it is also often the executive who has succumbed to the gravitational pull of ethnoreligious nationalism across all our cases and pivoted the trajectories of these societies away from connectedness at key historical junctures. The Chinese orientation of Lee Kuan Yew and Lee Hsien Loong in Singapore. King Hamad's use of citizenship in Bahrain. Eric Williams's skepticism of

Indians in Trinidad and Tobago. Seewoosagur Ramgoolam's dismissal of Creoles in Mauritius. The anti-Catholic orientation of Whigs and Know Nothings in New York. The concessions of King Kalākaua in Hawaiʻi.

The spotty history of political leaders, elected or otherwise, to cultivate an inclusive civic identity amid great demographic change reveals the way their rhetoric and governance can cut both ways—to increase or decrease the social distance between ethnic or religious subgroups. However, it also reveals the inherent risk of relying exclusively on political leaders (or even governments more broadly) to unify a nation; they are typically associated with a political or ethnoreligious faction—drivers of division in majority minority societies. When President Biden made cross-partisan, cross-racial unity the hallmark of his 2021 inaugural address, it was swiftly dismissed by his Republican opponents as a cheap attempt to gain political favor rather than a genuine appeal for solidarity after a divisive period in American history. While the executive retains the pivotal power exhibited throughout this book, other leaders and organizations may be better situated to cross boundaries.

Even though they have variable reach and limited power, artists, musicians, chefs, professional athletes, teachers, religious leaders, and businesses can more fluidly cross social boundaries outside of overtly political spaces. Indeed, they interact with people in the world of culture, the school, and the workplace. And because they cultivate the admiration and trust of their followers, they can reach the minds of listeners otherwise closed to the appeals of politicians. It is in these covertly political spaces where the nation can be reframed, where culture change is more likely to occur—the museums of Singapore, soca music in Trinidad and Tobago, the organic farms of Hawaiʻi.

The American Prospect

The six cases explored in this book cannot predict what the future holds for the United States, which anticipates the world's next majority minority milestone. Rather, they offer microcosmic glimpses of America's alternative futures, depending on the way its leaders navigate demographic change and social relations. Already, US leaders are falling into the same short-term thinking that has plunged earlier majority minority societies into social conflict. Rather than inspire new, broad-church forms of nationhood that cross population boundaries and leverage nationalism toward inclusion, civic leaders are seeking to intensify support among their political or ethnoreligious "base." This is a strategy that goes "deep" rather than "broad," much like the approach of Trinidad and Tobago's racialized political factions. And unless America's political, business, and civil society leaders change course, it is reasonable to predict that the United States will remain just as divided and politically paralyzed as these islands in the East Caribbean.

A far worse scenario in the United States would be if social division drives Americans to embrace illiberal forms of governance that seek to undemocratically entrench the dominance of one population subgroup. While it is unlikely that the United States will adopt an autocracy like those observed in Singapore or Bahrain, today's political polarization and negative partisanship are producing a growing appetite for illiberalism if it secures the power of one political or ethnoreligious faction over the other. Early indications of this appetite abounded when Trump sought to overturn the 2020 presidential election result and pursued various other abuses of power, all tolerated and often defended by his supporters. Such are the risks when people place their ethnoreligious subgroup over country.

At a minimum, we are already seeing early evidence of what took place in New York and the United States at the time of its earlier majority minority milestone: the expansion of whiteness to secure the continued supremacy of "white" people in American society. As chapter 12 details, it is possible that Americans are now in the process of similarly altering their conception of whiteness again. Many Hispanics and mixed-race individuals identify as white. And marriages between Hispanics and non-Hispanic whites make up more than 40 percent of recent interracial marriages, having increased nearly threefold between 2010 and 2020. That may be enough to artificially postpone America's majority minority milestone again and reassure the millions of "white" Americans who feel threatened by the increasing status and power of today's ethnic minorities. Doing so may secure enough support for maneuvers that manipulate American institutions—whether through racialized gerrymandering or voter suppression—to "white" people's advantage. The result can only be deeper division and conflict.

Stoking fears of white decline reinforces the myth that "white" America always included all who now identify with it—as if the Irish had never been demonized, as if Italians had never endured discrimination, as if Jews had never been excluded. As my historical analysis shows, America's demographic boundaries evolve with the country's composition. No group goes extinct or disappears; it just gets absorbed into new ways that people define community and feel belonging.

The most hopeful prospects for the United States rely upon a Hawai'i-style reconsideration of what it means to be American, a community reimagined. And it is worth acknowledging that the United States has a number of qualities that differentiate it from the historical cases this book explores. These qualities give the United States distinct structural advantages in reimagining its sense of community, particularly without someone like Trump in the White House.

First, American minorities do not share a singular background. Indeed, they are from hundreds of countries, hundreds of religions, hundreds of ethnicities, and speak hundreds of languages. This almost infinite number of combinations complicates any division of the people. Though the binary of whiteness has been present throughout American history, as we see in chapter 12, even whiteness has been complicated by the country's diversity. Can Americans see past this ahistorical and monolithic conceptualization of what it means to be "white" to reveal all the ways their identities and experiences intersect?

Second, American immigrants have continuously arrived individually and voluntarily rather than en masse and at the coordination of external forces. This has given the United States a degree of agency in the composition of its population. With the exception of the undocumented and some asylum seekers, the government has endorsed the arrival and settlement of all immigrants. This limits resentment and fosters an American heritage and tradition of immigration on all sides. Can the US government communicate a sense of management and control over immigration and the demographic change it produces?

Third, as chapter 12 elaborates, the United States has already reached a majority minority milestone once, before whiteness was reinterpreted to imagine a new national majority. It is not discussed in everyday conversation, but once it is, this legacy can be a resource—an immediate national point of reference—that contextualizes the approaching majority minority milestone destabilizing contemporary politics and social relations. In discussing this history alongside those of other societies that have confronted similar challenges, this book anticipates the experience of multiethnic societies more broadly in the hope that new paths may be charted. Can leaders place the imminent majority minority milestone in historical context?

And fourth, after centuries of institutionalized segregation and decades of self-segregation into diverse cities and a more homogeneous countryside, ethnoreligiously diverse people are penetrating all US regions. Just over 96 percent of all US counties experienced an increase in their population diversity between 2010 and 2020.[5] Per the data discussed in chapter 12, the rate of interethnic and interreligious marriage—and therefore the population of multiethnic and mixed-religion children—in the United States is also now growing. An effectively ungovernable phenomenon, these families and their children are perhaps the most effective way to defuse the politics of ethnoreligious nationalism because they defy the boundaries nationalism

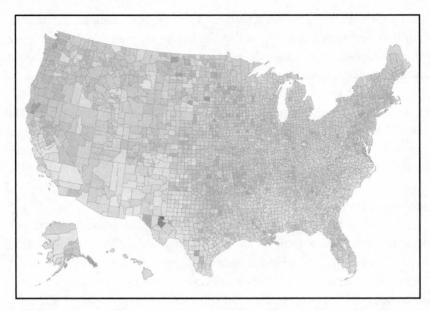

Figure 13.1 A county-by-county look at the US Census Bureau's Diversity Index, which shows the likelihood that two residents chosen at random in a given area will be of different races and/or ethnicities.

Source: New American Economy, "The United States Is More Diverse Than Ever, in More Places Than Ever," September 23, 2021, https://data.newamericaneconomy.org/en/census2020/.

seeks to enforce. Even when the government and its leaders will not, multiethnic people reimagine the nation because, in their own identity, they complicate and redefine its categories. Will they reject established labels and bridge the social boundaries that historically divided their countrymen?

Immigrants thus arrive as a source of instability but evolve into a resource for reimagining and reconciling the people. For if there is one thing that all immigrants know, it is that no nation is an island.

Appendix

Nineteen-Country European Study

Our data comes from an experiment embedded in national surveys of adults across nineteen European countries: Austria, Bulgaria, Czechia, Denmark, Estonia, France, Germany, Hungary, Italy, Latvia, Lithuania, the Netherlands, Poland, Romania, Slovakia, Slovenia, Spain, Sweden, and the United Kingdom. These were fielded online via Ipsos in August 2020. We collected a large sample, N = 20,896, benchmarked to be representative of the national population of adults in each country (descriptive statistics can be found in Table A.1) to ensure we had large enough groups to precisely estimate relatively small treatment effects as well as investigate subgroup treatment effects across moderators of interest.[1]

Survey Design and Treatment Conditions

Respondents began by answering pretreatment covariates, including basic demographics, views toward democracy and populism, relative deprivation, ethnocentrism, self-reported contact with out-groups, and political variables (partisan preferences, voting record, ideology, importance of various multilevel elections).

After passing an attention check to ensure they were carefully reading the text, respondents were randomized into one of three conditions: a control group, a group that was asked to read two paragraphs explaining the need for more immigrants in order to maintain the current national population, and a group that was asked to read an additional paragraph with the Orbán-inspired rebuttal. Treatments and cell sizes are summarized in Table A.1.

Results are described in chapter 11, but figures follow here.

Elite Influence Experiment

Our data comes from an experiment embedded in a national survey of American adults fielded online via Lucid Theorem in August 2020. When appropriate data quality checks are in place, Lucid has been shown to provide high-quality data.[2] We collected a large sample, N = 9,393, benchmarked to be representative of the national population of American adults to ensure we had large enough groups to precisely estimate relatively small treatment effects as well as investigate subgroup treatment effects across moderators of interest, particularly among self-identified Republicans who are our primary subjects of theoretical interest in this study.[3]

Survey Design and Treatment Conditions

Respondents began by answering pretreatment covariates, including basic demographics, political variables (partisanship, ideology, strength of partisan identity), self-reported contact with out-groups, self-monitoring, and feeling thermometers toward a variety of groups.

Table A.1 Treatments

Condition	Treatment	N
0	Control	6,937
T1	News Article	6,983
T2	News Article + Nativist Rebuttal	6,976

Table A.2 Treatments

Condition	Treatment	N
A	Generic Republican + Prime	1,478
B	Generic Republican – Prime	1,514
C	Generic Democrat + Prime	1,554
D	Generic Democrat – Prime	1,553
E	Sean Hannity + Prime	1,548
F	Control	1,746

After passing an attention and technology check (respondents had to be able to play video and hear audio), respondents were randomized (via Qualtrics's simple randomization) into one of six conditions: a fullycrossed 2x2 factorial design varying the party of fictional speaker (Democrat or Republican) and an identity prime (prime present or absent), a Sean Hannity treatment which will be used for a robustness check. Treatments and cell sizes are summarized in Table A.2.

In the 2x2 conditions (A, B, C, and D), respondents first were asked to read introductory text on a page before proceeding to the treatment video: "Yesterday, John Wagner, co-chairman of the [Republican/Democratic] National Committee ([RNC/DNC]), spoke at a meeting of [Republican/Democratic] Party officials and volunteers. Click the video on the next page to listen to a clip of these remarks." Respondents then proceeded to the next page, which introduced the video: "In a moment, you will be shown a short video clip. Please pay close attention when you watch it, as you'll be asked detailed questions about it shortly afterward."

Respondents then watched a video that had an image of the speaker, high-quality voice-over audio recorded by a professional voice actor, and scrolling text that accompanied the voice-over.[4]

For dependent variables, respondents were asked a series of questions intended to measure immigration policy attitudes. This includes a set of five policy items measuring support for expansive immigration policy (7-point Likert scales), including support for deportation, legalization programs, job training programs for immigrants, granting immigrants broader access to public benefits, and establishing a Hispanic Heritage Month. We combined these items into an additive scale of immigration policy support (mean = 0.38, min = 0, max = 1, a = 0.76).[5] In order to see if our treatment spills over into attitudes toward immigrants themselves, respondents were then asked a series of questions about immigrants (7-point Likert scale): whether they are doing enough to assimilate, whether they strengthen the country, whether they are a burden on the economy, and whether they increase the risk of terrorist attacks in the United States. These items were combined into an additive scale of immigration attitudes (mean = 0.41, min = 0, max = 1, a = 0.73). Finally, respondents were asked a behavioral question about whether they would be willing to send a publicly identifiable message (4), zip code–identifiable message (3), anonymous message (2), or no message at all (1) to their member of Congress expressing support for a pathway to citizenship (min = 1, max = 4, mean = 2.87) before answering a manipulation check, and then a question about their affect toward the speaker portrayed in the video to measure the RINO-effect (min = –2 (much cooler), max = 2 (much warmer), mean = 0.40).

As outlined in our preregistration, we report means and difference-in-means treatment effects calculated using OLS with heteroskedastic-robust standard errors.

While our experiment includes Democratic and Independent respondents as well as Democratic messengers to assess how treatment effects might work on different groups and with different messengers, our motivation with this study is to assess how theoretical targets of persuasion, Republicans, respond to messages from in-group elites. For this reason, we focus primarily on how self-identified Republican respondents[6] respond to Republican messengers.[7]

We might expect that those who have higher levels of Republican identity would be more likely to "follow the leader" than those who may see themselves as Republicans but do not have strong levels of Republican partisan identity.[8] We might expect those who are more "self-monitoring"—the extent to which individuals regulate the image they present to others in social situations—to be more likely to conform to the norms that a leader sets.[9] Finally, we may expect an adjustment among those Republicans who already feel warmer toward immigrants compared to those who entered our experiment with strongly anti-immigrant attitudes.[10] But we see little variation across the board.

In Figure A.5, those with higher and lower Republican identities, self-monitoring habits, and pretreatment anti-immigrant animus all move in a liberal direction following exposure to John Wagner, so long as he primes his Republican identity. While there appears to also be no major difference between people who are more strongly or weakly partisan, the findings on the far-left side of Figure A.5 are not statistically significant.

Notes

Chapter 1

1. Sandra Colby and Jennifer Ortman, "Projections of the Size and Composition of the U.S. Population: 2014 to 2060," US Census Bureau, 2015, https://www.census.gov/content/dam/Census/library/publications/2015/demo/p25-1143.pdf. The Census Bureau had previously released a report stating that the majority minority milestone would take place in 2042. This earlier report was released in August 2008 but garnered less public attention, likely because the milestone was still thirty-four years away and the political context was far more concerned by the global financial crisis and recession. The 2015 announcement came in the midst of the second term of the Obama administration and the early days of the 2016 election campaign, which was dominated by conversations about immigration and cultural politics.
2. Author interview, August 10, 2020.
3. Richard Alba, *The Great Demographic Illusion: Majority, Minority, and the Changing American Mainstream* (Princeton, NJ: Princeton University Press, 2020); Eric Kaufmann, *Rise and Fall of Anglo-America* (Cambridge, MA: Harvard University Press, 2004).
4. Daniel Hopkins, John Sides, and Jack Citrin, "The Muted Consequences of Correct Information about Immigration," *Journal of Politics* 81, no. 1 (2019): 315–320; Brian Guay et al., "Bayesian Origins of Demographic Misperceptions," unpublished working paper, Department of Political Science, Duke University, 2020.
5. John Sides, Michael Tesler, and Lynn Vavreck, *Identity Crisis: The 2016 Presidential Campaign and the Battle for the Meaning of America* (Princeton, NJ: Princeton University Press, 2018).
6. Justin Gest, *The New Minority: White Working Class Politics in an Age of Immigration and Inequality* (New York: Oxford University Press, 2016).
7. See Bill Schneider, *Standoff: How America Became Ungovernable* (New York: Simon & Schuster, 2019).
8. Barrett A. Lee et al., "State-Level Changes in US Racial and Ethnic Diversity, 1980 to 2015: A Universal Trend?," *Demographic Research* 37 (2017): 1031.
9. See US Census Bureau, "2020 Census Statistics Highlight Local Population Changes and Nation's Racial and Ethnic Diversity," Release Number CB21-CN.55, August 12, 2021, https://www.census.gov/newsroom/press-releases/2021/population-changes-nations-diversity.html.
10. Ariela Schachter, "From 'Different' to 'Similar': An Experimental Approach to Understanding Assimilation," *American Sociological Review* 81, no. 5 (2016): 981–1013.
11. Robert Outten et al., "Feeling Threatened about the Future: Whites' Emotional Reactions to Anticipated Ethnic Demographic Changes," *Personality and Social Psychology Bulletin* 38, no. 1 (2012): 14–25. More recently, an experiment by political scientist Morris Levy and demographer Dowell Myers found that exposure to information about "white decline"

drove respondents to express more anxiety and anger, anticipate more discrimination against white people, and show more willingness to invest in public goods than those exposed to information about interracial marriage. See Morris Levy and Dowell Myers, "Racial Projections in Perspective: Public Reactions to Narratives about Rising Diversity," *Perspectives on Politics* (2021): 1–18, https://www.cambridge.org/core/journals/perspecti ves-on-politics/article/abs/racial-projections-in-perspective-public-reactions-to-narrati ves-about-rising-diversity/E9D8F620367A68C3267301F342232A1B.

12. Maria Abascal, "Us and Them: Black-White Relations in the Wake of Hispanic Population Growth," *American Sociological Review* 80, no. 4 (2015): 789–813.

13. Maureen Craig and Jennifer Richeson, "More Diverse yet Less Tolerant? How the Increasingly Diverse Racial Landscape Affects White Americans' Racial Attitudes," *Personality and Social Psychology Bulletin* 40, no. 6 (2014): 750–761.

14. Ryan Enos, "The Causal Effect of Intergroup Contact on Exclusionary Attitudes," *Proceedings of the National Academy of Sciences of the United States of America* 111, no. 10 (2014): 3699–3704.

15. See findings in Eric Kaufmann and Matthew J. Goodwin, "The Diversity Wave: A Meta-analysis of the Native-Born White Response to Ethnic Diversity," *Social Science Research* 76 (2018): 120–131.

16. Myron Weiner, *Sons of the Soil: Migration and Ethnic Conflict in India* (Princeton, NJ: Princeton University Press, 1978), 371.

17. See Jack Goldstone, Eric Kaufmann, and Monica Toft, *Political Demography: How Population Changes Are Reshaping International Security and National Politics* (New York: Oxford University Press, 2011).

18. Eric Kaufmann and Oded Haklai, "Dominant Ethnicity: From Minority to Majority," *Nations and Nationalism* 14, no. 4 (2008): 743–767.

19. Tatu Vanhanen, "Domestic Ethnic Conflict and Ethnic Nepotism: A Comparative Analysis," *Journal of Peace Research* 36, no. 1 (1999): 55–73; Eric Kaufmann, "Dominant Ethnicity: Background to Foreground," in *Rethinking Ethnicity Majority Groups and Dominant Minorities*, ed. Eric Kaufmann (London: Routledge, 2004), 1–12.

20. Isabelle Côté, Matthew Mitchell, and Monica Toft, *People Changing Places: New Perspectives on Demography, Migration, Conflict, and the State* (London: Routledge, 2018); see Dru Gladney, *Making Majorities: Constituting the Nation in Japan, Korea, China, Malaysia, Fiji, Turkey, and the United States* (Palo Alto, CA: Stanford University Press, 1998).

21. Please see chapter 3 and its notes for a fuller discussion of the case selection.

22. See David Fitzgerald and David Cook-Martin, *Culling the Masses: The Democratic Origins of Racist Immigration Policy in the Americas* (London: Harvard University Press, 2014); Daniel Tichenor, *Dividing Lines: The Politics of Immigration Control in America* (Princeton, NJ: Princeton University Press, 2002); Adam McKeown, *Melancholy Order: Asian Migration and the Globalization of Borders* (New York: Columbia University Press, 2008); Marilyn Lake and Henry Reynolds, *Drawing the Global Colour Line: White Men's Countries and the International Challenge of Racial Equality* (Cambridge: Cambridge University Press, 2008).

23. Tim Edensor, *National Identity, Public Culture, and Everyday Life* (Oxford: Berg, 2002), 20.

24. Eric Hobsbawm, *Nations and Nationalism Since 1780: Programme, Myth, Reality* (Cambridge: Cambridge University Press, 1990), 10.

25. Brian F. Harrison and Melissa R. Michelson, *Listen, We Need to Talk: How to Change Attitudes about LGBT Rights* (New York: Oxford University Press, 2017).

26. Richard Alba, Brenden Beck, and Duygu Basaran Sahin, "The Rise of Mixed Parentage: A Sociological and Demographic Phenomenon to Be Reckoned With," *Annals of the American Academy of Political and Social Science* 677, no. 1 (2018): 26–38.

27. Richard Alba and Victor Nee, *Remaking the American Mainstream: Assimilation and Contemporary Immigration* (Cambridge, MA: Harvard University Press, 2003).

Chapter 2

1. For example, see Rogers Smith, *Civic Ideals: Conflicting Visions of Citizenship in U.S. History* (New Haven, CT: Yale University Press, 1997), 6 and throughout.

2. David Bateman, "The Dilemmas of Democratic Peoplehood," Working Paper, Ithaca, NY: Cornell University, 2018.

3. Frederick G. Whelan, "Democratic Theory and the Boundary Problem," in *Liberal Democracy*, ed. J.R. Pennock and J. W. Chapman (New York: NYU Press, 1983), 13–47.

4. Bateman, "The Dilemmas of Democratic Peoplehood."

5. Hobsbawm, *Nations and Nationalism since 1780*, 163–170.

6. Hobsbawm, *Nations and Nationalism since 1780*, 168. It is also notable that, earlier, social theorist Max Weber thought that "primordial phenomena" like ethnicity and nationalism would decrease in importance and eventually vanish as a result of modernization, industrialization, and individualism. See Thomas Hylland Eriksen, *Ethnicity and Nationalism: Anthropological Perspectives*, 3rd ed. (London: Pluto Press, 1994), 2.

7. Robert Kagan, "The Strongmen Strike Back," *Washington Post*, March 14, 2019, https://www.washingtonpost.com/news/opinions/wp/2019/03/14/feature/the-strongmen-strike-back/.

8. Vanhanen, "Domestic Ethnic Conflict and Ethnic Nepotism," 57.

9. Eric Kaufmann, *Whiteshift: Populism, Immigration, and the Future of White Majorities* (New York: Abrams, 2018), 203–204.

10. Neil Howe and Richard Jackson, "Demography and Geopolitics: Understanding Today's Debate in Its Historical and Intellectual Context," in *Political Demography: How Population Changes Are Reshaping International Security and National Politics*, ed. Jack Goldstone, Eric Kaufmann, and Monica Toft (Boulder, CO: Paradigm, 2011), 32–33.

11. Côté, Mitchell, and Toft, *People Changing Places*, 87–88. See also Paul Morland, *Demographic Engineering: Population Strategies in Ethnic Conflict* (London: Routledge, 2014), 4.

12. Nadav Shelef, "Lessons from the Experience of Two Israeli Nationalist Movements," in *People Changing Places: New Perspectives on Demography, Migration, Conflict, and the State*, ed. Isabelle Côté, Matthew Mitchell, and Monica Toft (London: Routledge, 2018), 130, 145–146.

13. Howe and Jackson, "Demography and Geopolitics," 35; Elliott Green, "Demographic Change and Conflict in Contemporary Africa," in *Political Demography: How Population Changes Are Reshaping International Security and National Politics*, ed. Jack Goldstone, Eric Kaufmann, and Monica Toft (Boulder, CO: Paradigm, 2011), 241–242.

14. Hobsbawm, *Nations and Nationalism since 1780*, 133–134.

15. Vanhanen, "Domestic Ethnic Conflict and Ethnic Nepotism," 64.

16. Rogers Brubaker, "The Manichean Myth: Rethinking the Distinction between 'Civic' and 'Ethnic' Nationalism," in *Nations and National Identity: The European Experience*

in Perspective, ed. Hanspeter Kriesi, Klaus Armington, Hannes Siegrist, and Andreas Wimmer (Zurich: Verlag Ruegger, 1999), 55–71; Maxim Tabachnik, "Untangling Liberal Democracy from Territoriality: From Ethnic/Civic to Ethnic/Territorial Nationalism," *Nations and Nationalism* 25, no. 1 (2019): 191–207; David Miller, *Citizenship and National Identity* (Cambridge, UK: Polity Press, 2000); Yael Tamir, *Liberal Nationalism* (Princeton, NJ: Princeton University Press, 1993).

17. David Held, *Democracy and the Global Order: From the Modern State to Cosmopolitan Governance* (Stanford, CA: Stanford University Press, 1995); Will Kymlicka, *Politics in the Vernacular: Nationalism, Multiculturalism, and Citizenship* (Oxford: Oxford University Press, 2001); Martha Nussbaum and Joshua Cohen, *For Love of Country: Debating the Limits of Patriotism* (Boston: Beacon Press, 1996).

18. Will Kymlicka, *States, Nations and Cultures* (Assen: Van Gorcum, 1997), 40.

19. "Blunkett Names 'Britishness' Chief," BBC News, September 10, 2002, http://news.bbc.co.uk/2/hi/uk_news/politics/2248319.stm.

20. Kagan, "The Strongmen Strike Back"; Judith Shklar, "The Liberalism of Fear," in *Liberalism and the Moral Life,* ed. Nancy Rosenblum (Cambridge, MA: Harvard University Press, 1989), 21–37; Francis Fukuyama, "Identity, Immigration, and Liberal Democracy," *Journal of Democracy* 17, no. 2 (2006): 5–20.

21. "Blair Defines 'British Values,'" BBC News, March 28, 2000, http://news.bbc.co.uk/2/hi/uk_news/politics/693591.stm.

22. Goldstone, Kaufmann, and Toft, *Political Demography,* 268–275.

23. This all sets aside the irony that these politics emerge in settler states, where nativists' ancestors were wholly unconcerned with the extent to which indigenous peoples felt "at home."

24. Hobsbawm, *Nations and Nationalism since 1780,* 45.

25. See John Higham, *Strangers in the Land: Patterns of American Nativism, 1860–1925* (New Brunswick, NJ: Rutgers University Press, 1955), 3–4.

26. Andreas Wimmer, "Dominant Ethnicity and Dominant Nationhood," in *Rethinking Ethnicity Majority Groups and Dominant Minorities,* ed. Eric Kaufmann (London: Routledge, 2004), 37.

27. Wimmer, "Dominant Ethnicity and Dominant Nationhood," 37–38.

28. Daniel Ziblatt, *Conservative Parties and the Birth of Democracy* (Cambridge: Cambridge University Press, 2017). Also see Bateman, "The Dilemmas of Democratic Peoplehood."

29. Michael Tesler, "How Anti-Immigrant Attitudes Are Fueling Support for Donald Trump," *Monkey Cage,* November 24, 2015, https://www.washingtonpost.com/news/monkey-cage/wp/2015/11/24/how-anti-immigrant-attitudes-are-fueling-support-for-donald-trump/.

30. Kerem Kalkan, "What Differentiates Trump Supporters from Other Republicans? Ethnocentrism," *Monkey Cage,* February 28, 2016, https://www.washingtonpost.com/news/monkey-cage/wp/2016/02/28/what-differentiates-trump-supporters-from-other-republicans-ethnocentrism/.

31. John Sides, "Race, Religion, and Immigration in 2017: How the Debate over American Identity Shaped the Election and What It Means for a Trump Presidency," Voter Study Group, June 2017, https://www.voterstudygroup.org/publications/2016-elections/race-religion-immigration-2016.

32. Hans-George Betz, "The New Politics of Resentment: Radical Right Wing Populist Parties in Western Europe," *Comparative Politics* 25 (1993): 413–427; Paul Sniderman, Louk Hagendoorn, and Markus Prior, "Predisposing Factors and Situational

Triggers: Exclusionary Reactions to Immigrant Minorities," *American Political Science Review* 98, no. 1 (2004): 35–49; Ruud Koopmans et al., *Contested Citizenship: Immigration and Cultural Diversity in Europe* (Minneapolis: University of Minnesota Press, 2005); Elizabeth Ivarsflaten, "What Unites Right-Wing Populists in Western Europe?," *Comparative Political Studies* 41 (2008): 3–23.

33. In *Civic Ideals* (6), Smith writes that "virtually all successful American political actors have not been pure liberals, democratic republicans, or ascriptive Americanists, but have instead combined politically potent elements of all three views." Also see discussion on 10–11.

34. However, for an extensive discussion of how states attempt to do so, see Morland, *Demographic Engineering*. See also Myron Weiner and Michael Teitelbaum, *Political Demography, Demographic Engineering* (New York: Berghahn Books, 2001).

35. José Alemán and Dwayne Woods, "No Way Out: Travel Restrictions and Authoritarian Regimes," *Migration and Development* 3, no. 2 (2014): 285–305. However, see John Torpey, *The Invention of the Passport Surveillance, Citizenship and the State* (New York: Cambridge University Press, 1999).

36. Lamenting that philosophy titans like Robert Dahl and John Rawls sidestepped the challenges of such connectedness in multiethnic and multireligious societies, political theorist Rogers Smith writes that such ethnic and religious communities are "ineradicably political human creations, crafted to govern and assist some people more than others. They are capable of performing vital human services, and, indeed, efforts to do without them have thus far been failures. Still, they are likely to behave in unduly partisan ways. In light of the good that they do, we may rightly value them highly and feel great loyalty toward them; but in light of their dangerous tendencies, we should understand them to be imperfect human instruments and not take them as the proper objects of our full trust or ultimate allegiance" (*Civic Ideals*, 11).

37. Michael Lind, *The Next American Nation: The New Nationalism and the Fourth American Revolution* (New York: Free Press, 1995), 1–14.

38. Danielle Allen, "Toward a Connected Society," in *Our Compelling Interests: The Value of Diversity for Democracy and a Prosperous Society*, ed. Earl Lewis and Nancy Cantor (Princeton, NJ: Princeton University Press, 2016), 71–105.

39. Benedict Anderson, *Imagined Communities: Reflections on the Origin and Spread of Nationalism* (New York: Verso, 1983), 6–7.

Chapter 3

1. Danielle Allen, "Charlottesville Is Not the Continuation of an Old Fight: It Is Something New," *Washington Post*, August 14, 2017, https://www.washingtonpost.com/opinions/charlottesville-is-not-the-continuation-of-an-old-fight-it-is-something-new/2017/08/13/971812f6-8029-11e7-b359-15a3617c767b_story.html.

2. See Fitzgerald and Cook-Martin, *Culling the Masses*; Tichenor, *Dividing Lines*; McKeown, *Melancholy Order*; Lake and Reynolds, *Drawing the Global Colour Line*.

3. Although the British established settlements in Suriname in the mid-seventeenth century, these were transferred in the Treaty of Breda to the Dutch, who went on to colonize Suriname thereafter. Interestingly, that same treaty also transferred power from the Dutch to the British over New Amsterdam, which was thereafter known as New York. The British never colonized Hawai'i, but Capt. James Cook is thought to be the earliest imperialist

explorer to visit the islands, in 1778. And in the years after, as this book will elaborate, British and European military technology allowed Kamehameha I to conquer and unite the entire archipelago as the Hawaiian Kingdom by 1795. European and American officials, missionaries, and planters would remain influential in the governance of Hawai'i thereafter.

4. See Mark Frost, "An Unsettled Majority: Immigration and the Racial 'Balance' in Multicultural Singapore," *Journal of Ethnic and Migration Studies*, July 22, 2020, https://www.tandfonline.com/doi/full/10.1080/1369183X.2020.1774112.

5. Anderzej Kapiszewski, "Arab versus Asian Migrant Workers in the GCC Countries," paper presented at United Nations Expert Group Meeting on International Migration and Development in the Arab Region, Beirut, May 15–17, 2006.

6. See Raymond Ramcharitar, "Ethnic Anxiety and Competing Citizenships in Trinidad and Tobago," *Journal of Ethnic and Migration Studies*, July 22, 2020, https://www.tandfonline.com/doi/full/10.1080/1369183X.2020.1774116.

7. This influx also included a fair number of Germans.

8. See Hidetaka Hirota, "Limits of Intolerance: Nativism and Immigration Control in Nineteenth-Century New York," *Journal of Ethnic and Migration Studies*, July 22, 2020, https://www.tandfonline.com/doi/full/10.1080/1369183X.2020.1774114.

9. It is worth noting that a share of the population loss was due to the emigration of Hawaiian sailors.

10. See Mariko Iijima, "'Nonwhiteness' in Nineteenth-Century Hawai'i: Sovereignty, White Settlers, and Japanese Migrants," *Journal of Ethnic and Migration Studies*, July 22, 2020, https://www.tandfonline.com/doi/full/10.1080/1369183X.2020.1774115.

11. Kaufmann, *Whiteshift*.

12. Pew Research Center, "Shifting Public Views on Legal Immigration into the U.S.," June 28, 2018, http://www.people-press.org/2018/06/28/shifting-public-views-on-legal-immigration-into-the-u-s/.

13. Act of June 28, 1847; Act to Abolish the Disabilities of Aliens to Acquire and Convey Lands in Fee Simple.

14. See Benjamin Klebaner, "The Myth of Foreign Pauper Dumping in the United States," *Social Service Review* 35 (1961): 302–309; Tyler Anbinder, "From Famine to Five Points: Lord Lansdowne's Irish Tenants Encounter North America's Most Notorious Slum," *American Historical Review* 107, no. 2 (2002): 350–387; Gerard Moran, *Sending Out Ireland's Poor: Assisted Emigration to North America in the Nineteenth Century* (Dublin: Four Court Press, 2004); Patrick Duffy, *To and from Ireland: Planned Migration Schemes c. 1600–2000* (Dublin: Geography Publications, 2004); Hidetaka Hirota, note to author, 2018.

15. William Greene, *British Slave Emancipation: The Sugar Colonies and the Great Experiment 1830–1865* (Oxford: Oxford University Press, 1976), 261–262.

16. Greene, *British Slave Emancipation*, 261–262.

17. Min Zhou and Gregor Benton, "Intra-Asian Chinese Migrations: A Historical Overview," in *Contemporary Chinese Diasporas*, ed. Min Zhou (Singapore: Palgrave Macmillan, 2017), 1–25.

18. Mark Frost and Yu-Mei Balasinghamchow, *Singapore: A Biography* (Singapore: Hong Kong University Press, 2009), 91–97.

19. John Crawfurd, *Journal of an Embassy from the Governor-General of India to the Courts of Siam and Cochin China* (London: Colburn and Bentley, 1830), 23–24, 29–32.

20. Ralph Kuykendal, *The Hawaiian Kingdom*, vol. 3: *1874–1893: The Kalakaua Dynasty* (Honolulu: University of Hawai'i Press, 1967).

21. Davianna McGregor-Alegado, note to author, 2018.

22. Amitava Chowdhury, "Narratives of Home: Diaspora Formations among the Indian Indentured Labourers," in *Between Dispersion and Belonging: Global Approaches to Diaspora in Practice*, ed. Amitava Chowdhury and D. H. Akenson (Montreal: McGill-Queen's University Press, 2016), 240–253; Amitava Chowdhury, note to author, 2018.

23. K. O. Laurence, *A Question of Labour: Indian Indentured Emigration into Trinidad and British Guiana, 1875–1917* (Kingston: Ian Randle/James Currey, 1994), 525.

24. Kelvin Singh, *Race and Class Struggles in a Colonial State: Trinidad 1917–1945* (Calgary: University of Calgary Press, 1994), 124–157.

25. Kevin Yelvington, "The War in Ethiopia and Trinidad, 1935–36," in *The Colonial Caribbean in Transition: Essays on Postemancipation and Cultural History*, ed. Bridget Brereton and Kevin Yelvington (Kingston: The Press, University of the West Indies, 1999), 189–225.

26. See C. L. R. James, *The Life of Captain Cipriani, an Account of British Government in the West Indies, with the Pamphlet the West Indian Case for Self-Government* (Durham, NC: Duke University Press, 2014).

27. Kuykendal, *The Hawaiian Kingdom*, 227–241.

28. "Ke Kumukānāwai o ka Makahiki 1839" (The 1839 Constitution), Naʻi Aupuni, accessed March 14, 2021, www.naiaupuni.org/docs/pres/dm/1839_1840%20Constitution.pdf.

29. Act of June 28, 1847; Act of July 10, 1850.

30. Imani Altemus-Williams and Marie Eriel Hobro, "Hawaiʻi Is Not the Multicultural Paradise Some Say It Is," *National Geographic*, May 17, 2021. https://www.nationalgeographic.com/culture/article/hawaii-not-multicultural-paradise-some-say-it-is.

31. Frost and Balasinghamchow, *Singapore*.

32. Tichenor, *Dividing Lines*, 48–59.

33. Robert Ernst, *Immigrant Life in New York City, 1825–1863* (Syracuse, NY: Syracuse University Press, 1994); Eric Foner, *The Story of American Freedom* (New York: Norton, 1998); Eric Foner, *Free Soil, Free Labor, Free Men: The Ideology of the Republican Party before the Civil War* (Oxford: Oxford University Press, 1995); Thomas O'Connor, *The Boston Irish: A Political History* (Cambridge, MA: Back Bay Books, 1997).

34. See Ramcharitar, "Ethnic Anxiety and Competing Citizenships."

35. Davianna McGregor-Alegado, "Hawaiian Resistance: 1887–1889" (master's thesis, University of Hawaii, Manoa, 1979).

36. See Iijima, "'Nonwhiteness' in Nineteenth-Century Hawaiʻi."

37. "Singapore Opposition Makes 'Landmark' Election Gains," BBC News, May 9, 2011, https://www.bbc.com/news/world-asia-pacific-13313695.

38. See Frost, "An Unsettled Majority."

39. Anna Boucher and Justin Gest, *Crossroads: Comparative Immigration Regimes in a World of Demographic Change* (Cambridge: Cambridge University Press, 2018).

40. Jay Dolan, *The Irish Americans: A History* (New York: Bloomsbury Press, 2008).

41. Hidetaka Hirota, *Expelling the Poor: Atlantic Seaboard States and the Nineteenth-Century Origins of American Immigration Policy* (New York: Oxford University Press, 2017); Ernst, *Immigrant Life in New York City*.

42. See Hirota "Limits of Intolerance."

43. Terry Golway, *Machine Made: Tammany Hall and the Creation of Modern American Politics* (New York: Liveright, 2014); Steven Erie, *Rainbow's End: Irish-Americans and the Dilemmas of Urban Machine Politics, 1840–1985* (Oakland: University of California Press, 1990).

44. Edensor, *National Identity, Public Culture, and Everyday Life*, 20.

45. Edensor, *National Identity, Public Culture, and Everyday Life*, 16–17.

46. Ernest Renan, "What Is a Nation?," trans. M. Thom, in *Nation and Narration*, ed. Homi Bhabha (Abington: Routledge, 2013), 8–23.

47. For example, in the United States, white Christian cultural and religious bodies were informally charged with oversight of education, television, film, and the arts for decades. See Michael Lind, *The New Class War: Saving Democracy from the Managerial Elite* (New York: Portfolio/Penguin, 2020).

Chapter 4

1. Belinda Yuen, "Creating the Garden City: The Singapore Experience," *Urban Studies* 33, no. 6 (1996): 955–970.

2. Irene Tham, "Maintaining Harmony Here a 'Daily Struggle,'" *Straits Times*, March 16, 2011, quoted in Kamaludeen Mohammed Nasir and Bryan S. Turner, "Governing as Gardening: Reflections on Soft Authoritarianism in Singapore," *Citizenship Studies* 17, nos. 3–4 (2013): 339–352.

3. Tham, "Maintaining Harmony Here a 'Daily Struggle,'" 349.

4. T. Harper, "Communists, Leftists and Populists: The Social and Ideological Roots of Postwar Left-Wing Politics," paper presented at Symposium on Paths Not Taken: Political Pluralism in Postwar Singapore, organized by the Asia Research Institute, National University of Singapore, and Centre for Social Change Research, Singapore, 2005, quoted in Tai-Yong Tan, "Port Cities and Hinterlands: A Comparative Study of Singapore and Calcutta," *Political Geography* 26 (2007): 851–865.

5. Michael Barr and Zlatko Skrbis, *Constructing Singapore: Elitism, Ethnicity, and the Nation-Building Project* (Copenhagen: Nordic Institute of Asian Studies, 2008), 40.

6. Tan, "Port Cities and Hinterlands," 856. However, it is important to note that the Chinese were excluded or subject to severe discrimination in Malaya outside of Singapore.

7. Barr and Skrbis, *Constructing Singapore*, 43.

8. Nasir and Turner, "Governing as Gardening," 340.

9. Barr and Skrbis, *Constructing Singapore*, 6.

10. Tan, "Port Cities and Hinterlands," 857.

11. William Case, *Politics in Southeast Asia: Democracy or Less* (London: Routledge Curzon, 2002).

12. Steven Levitsky and Lucan Way, "The Rise of Competitive Authoritarianism," *Journal of Democracy* 13, no. 2 (2002): 51–65.

13. Stephen McCarthy, *The Political Theory of Tyranny in Singapore and Burma: Aristotle and the Rhetoric of Benevolent Despotism* (Abingdon: Routledge, 2006).

14. Nasir and Turner, "Governing as Gardening," 341.

15. Li-Ann Thio, "Rule of Law within a Non-liberal 'Communitarian' Democracy: The Singapore Experience," in *Asian Discourses of Rule of Law: Theories and Implementation of Rule of Law in Twelve Asian Countries, France, and the U.S.*, ed. Randall Peerenboom (London: Routledge, 2004), 183–224.

16. Garry Rodan, *Transparency and Authoritarian Rule in Southeast Asia: Malaysia and Singapore* (London: Routledge Curzon Press, 2004), quoted in Nasir and Turner, "Governing as Gardening," 341–342.

17. Garry Rodan and K. Jarasuriya, "Capitalist Development: Regime Transitions and New Forms of Authoritarianism in Asia," *Pacific Review* 22, no. 1 (2009): 23–47, quoted in in Nasir and Turner, "Governing as Gardening," 342.

18. Barr and Skrbis, *Constructing Singapore*, 6.

19. Ping Tijn Thum, *The History of Singapore*, podcast, episode 1, 2015.

20. Pang Eng Fong, "Foreign Talent and Development in Singapore," in *Competing for Global Talent*, ed. Christiane Kuptsch and Pang Eng Fong (Geneva: International Labour Office, 2006), 158–159.

21. Singapore Ministry of Manpower, "Quota and Levy for S Pass," accessed 11 June 2012, http://www.mom.gov.sg/foreign-manpower/foreign-worker-levies/Pages/levies-quotas-for-hiring-foreign-workers.aspx.

22. Boucher and Gest, *Crossroads*.

23. Ministry of Manpower, "Quota and Levy for S Pass." See also Fong, "Foreign Talent and Development in Singapore," 167.

24. Mui Teng Yap, "The Singapore State's Responses to Migration," *SOJOURN* 14, no. 1 (1999): 198–211; Nicola Piper, *Migrant Labor in Southeast Asia: Country Study: Singapore* (Singapore: Asian Research Institute Friedrich Ebert Stiftung Project on Migrant Labor in South East Asia, 2005);.See also Singapore National Population and Talent Division, "Our Population Our Future," 2012.

25. Brenda S. A. Yeoh, "Bifurcated Labour: The Unequal Incorporation of Transmigrants in Singapore," *Tijdschrift voor Economische en Sociale Geografie* 97, no. 1 (2006): 26–37.

26. Brenda S. A. Yeoh and Weiqiang Lin, "Rapid Growth in Singapore's Immigration Population Brings Policy Challenges," Migration Information Source, 2012, http://www.migrationinformation.org/feature/display.cfm?ID=887.

27. Yeoh and Lin, "Rapid Growth in Singapore's Immigration Population"; Fong, "Foreign Talent and Development in Singapore," 158–159.

28. Barr and Skrbis, *Constructing Singapore*, 47.

29. Barr and Skrbis, *Constructing Singapore*, 47; Michael Barr, *Lee Kuan Yew: The Beliefs Behind the Man* (Richmond, UK: Curzon, 2000), 196–197.

30. Geraldine Heng and Janadas Devan, "State Fatherhood: The Politics of Nationalism, Sexuality, and Race in Singapore," in *Nationalism and Sexualities*, ed. Andrew Parker et al. (London: Routledge, 1992), 345.

31. "The Coffee Shop Divide," *Straits Times*, May 2008, quoted in Brenda S. A. Yeoh and Weiqiang Lin, "Chinese Migration to Singapore: Discourses and Discontents in a Globalizing Nation-State," *Asian and Pacific Migration Journal* 22, no. 1 (2013): 35.

32. Wang Gungwu, *The Nanhai Trade: Early Chinese Trade in the South China Sea* (Singapore: Times Media, 2003). Also see Zhou and Benton, "Intra-Asian Chinese Migrations."

33. Yeoh and Lin, "Chinese Migration to Singapore," 37. Also see Min Zhou and Hong Liu, "Homeland Engagement and Host-Society Integration: A Comparative Study of New Chinese Immigrants in the United States and Singapore," *International Journal of Comparative Sociology* 57 nos. 1–2 (2016): 30–52.

34. Yeoh and Lin, "Chinese Migration to Singapore," 39; Ai Yun Hing et al., "Mainland Chinese 'Foreign Talents' in Singapore," *Asian Journal of Social Science* 37, no. 5 (2009): 757–777.

35. Brenda S. A. Yeoh, "'Upwards' or 'Sideways' Cosmopolitanism? Talent/Labour/Marriage Migrations in the Globalising City-State of Singapore," *Migration Studies* 1, no. 1 (2013): 96–116.

36. Yeoh and Lin, "Chinese Migration to Singapore," 39–42.

37. Yeoh and Lin, "Chinese Migration to Singapore," 42; "The Coffee Shop Divide."

38. Palash Ghosh, "Singapore Seeks to Cut Quota on Foreign Workers amid Worries over Immigration, Rising Labor Costs," *International Business Times*, February 26, 2013, www.ibtimes.com/singapore-seeks-cut-quota-foreign-workers-amid-worries-over-immigration-rising-labor-costs-1103229.

39. Crystal Neo, "Singaporeans and the Question of Immigration," *Morningside Post*, June 2012, www.themorningsidepost.com/2012/06/06/singaporeans-and-the-question-of-immigration/.

40. Sylvia Ang, "The 'New Chinatown': The Racialization of Newly Arrived Chinese Migrants in Singapore," *Journal of Ethnic and Migration Studies* 44, no. 7 (2018): 1177–1194.

41. John Furnivall, *Colonial Policy and Practice: A Comparative Study of Burma and Netherlands India* (Cambridge: Cambridge University Press, 1948), 123.

42. Lily Zubaidah Rahim, *The Singapore Dilemma: The Political and Educational Marginality of the Mala Community* (Kuala Lumpur: Oxford University Press, 1998), 49.

43. Barr and Skrbis, *Constructing Singapore*, 88–89.

44. C. Hirschman, "The Meaning and Measurement of Ethnicity in Malaysia: An Analysis of Census Classifications," *Journal of Asian Studies* 46 (1987): 555–582.

45. C. A. Vlieland, quoted in Hirschman, "The Meaning and Measurement of Ethnicity in Malaysia," 565.

46. Barr and Skrbis, *Constructing Singapore*, 31.

47. Ping Tijn Thum, *The History of Singapore*, podcast, episode 17, 2016.

48. Barr and Skrbis, *Constructing Singapore*, 92.

49. Beng Huat Chua, "Multiculturalism in Singapore: An Instrument of Social Control," *Race and Class* 44, no. 3 (2003): 58–77.

50. Daniel Goh and Philip Holden, "Introduction: Postcoloniality, Race, and Multiculturalism," in *Race and Multiculturalism in Malaysia and Singapore*, ed. Daniel Goh et al. (New York: Routledge, 2009), 1–16. See also Partha Chatterjee, *The Nation and Its Fragments: Colonial and Postcolonial Histories* (Princeton, NJ: Princeton University Press, 1993).

51. Barr, *Lee Kuan Yew*, 191.

52. Barr and Skrbis, *Constructing Singapore*, 51.

53. Rahim, *The Singapore Dilemma*.

54. Beng Huat Chua, "Culture, Multi-racialism, and National Identity in Singapore," in *Trajectories: Inter-Asia Cultural Studies,* ed. Kuan-Hsing Chen et al. (London: Routledge, 1998), 191.

55. Barr, *Lee Kuan Yew*, 158.

56. Teik Soon Lau, *Majority-Minority Situation in Singapore*, Occasional Paper Number 7, Department of Political Science, National University of Singapore, 1974. Also see Nasir and Turner, "Governing as Gardening," 344.

57. Barr and Skrbis, *Constructing Singapore*, 96.

58. Han Fook Kwang, Warren Fernandez, and Sumiko Tan, *Lee Kuan Yew: The Man and His Ideas* (Singapore: Singapore Press Holdings and Times Editions, 1998), 184.

59. Barr and Skrbis, *Constructing Singapore*, 11.

60. Jalil Aaron, "Some Facts about Singapore," in *Development and Commemoration of National Day* (Singapore: Usaha Enterprises, 1967).

61. Raj Vasil, *Asianising Singapore: The PAP's Management of Ethnicity* (Singapore: Heinemann, 1995).

62. Christine Lee et al., "Children's Experiences of Multiracial Relationships in Informal Primary School Settings," in *Beyond Rituals and Riots: Ethnic Pluralism and Social Cohesion in Singapore*, ed. A. E. Lai (Singapore: Marshall Cavendish, 2004), 114–145.

63. Amanda Rajah, "Making and Managing Tradition in Singapore: The National Day Parade," in *Our Place in Time: Exploring Heritage and Memory in Singapore*, ed. K. W. Kwok et al. (Singapore: Singapore Historical Society, 1999), 66–75.

64. Barr and Skrbis, *Constructing Singapore*, 107.

65. Yeoh and Lin, "Chinese Migration to Singapore," 46.

66. Clifford Geertz, *The Interpretation of Cultures* (London: Fontana, 1973).

67. Kathleen F., "Activist Sangeetha Thanapal Receives Stern Warning from Authorities after Calling Singapore 'a Terribly Racist Country,'" *Online Citizen*, January 30, 2019, https://www.straitstimes.com/singapore/courts-crime/activist-sangeetha-thanapal-issued-stern-warning-for-facebook-post-that

68. Shamim Adam, "Singapore Curry Protest Heats Up Vote with Facebook Campaign," *Bloomberg*, August 18, 2011, http://www.bloomberg.com/news/2011-08-18/singapore-curry-protest-heats-up-vote.html.

69. Tan, "Port Cities and Hinterlands."

70. Ng Huiwen, "More Marriages Took Place in 2017, with Nearly a Quarter of Them Inter-ethnic," *Straits Times*, July 10, 2018, https://www.straitstimes.com/singapore/more-marria ges-took-place-in-2017-of-which-nearly-a-quarter-were-inter-ethnic.

71. Lee said, "My expectations are that there will always be a small group of the adventurous in all the ethnic groups, perhaps those who are less egotistical, who marry across ethnic lines. But they will probably be in the minority. Therefore, the chances are that if you come back to Singapore a century from now, you would find a people more or less the same." Quoted in Sharon Siddique, "The Phenomenon of Ethnicity: A Singapore Case Study," in *Understanding Singapore Society*, ed. Ong Jin Hue et al. (Singapore: Times Academic Press, 1997), 108.

72. Jewel Stolarchuk, "Whopping 92% of Singaporeans in Viral Poll Vote for Tharman to Become Next PM," *The Independent*, April 1, 2019, http://theindependent.sg/whopping-92-of-singaporeans-in-viral-poll-vote-for-tharman-to-become-next-pm/.

73. Barr and Skrbis, *Constructing Singapore*, 107.

74. "Up Close with Tharman Shanmugaratnam," Channel NewsAsia, April 14, 2005.

75. Barr and Skrbis, *Constructing Singapore*, 108.

76. Eugene K. B. Tan, "'We, the Citizens of Singapore': Multiethnicity, Its Evolution, and Its Aberrations," in *Beyond Rituals and Riots: Ethnic Pluralism and Social Cohesion in Singapore*, ed. Lai Ah Eng (Singapore: Eastern Universities Press, 2004), 1–40.

77. Garry Rodan, "Embracing Electronic Media but Suppressing Civil Society: Authoritarian Consolidation in Singapore," *Pacific Review* 16, no. 4 (2011): 503–524.

78. Ernest Renan, "What Is a Nation?," trans. M. Thom, in *Nation and Narration*, ed. Homi Bhabha (Abington: Routledge, 2013), 8–23.

79. Laura Hein and Mark Selden, "Learning Citizenship from the Past: Textbook Nationalism, Global Context, and Social Change," *Bulletin of Concerned Asian Scholars* 30, no. 2 (1998): 3–15.

80. Ram Haggay, "The Immemorial Iranian Nation? School Textbooks and Historical Memory in Post-revolutionary Iran," *Nations and Nationalism* 6, no. 1 (2000): 67–90; Charles

Jelavich, "Serbian Textbooks: Toward Greater Serbia or Yugoslavia?," *Slavic Review* 42, no. 4 (1983): 601–619.

81. "The PM's Address to the Historical Society, Nanyang University, February 10," in *Bilingualism in Our Society*, ed. Ministry of Culture (Singapore: Singapore National Printers, 1978); Theophilus Kwek, "Full Colour Illustrations: Presentations of Race in Singapore's History Textbooks, 1965–2000," in *Southeast Asian Education in Modern History Schools, Manipulation, and Contest*, ed. Pia Maria Jolliffe and Thomas Richard Bruce (London: Routledge, 2018), 158–177.

82. "Text of a Discussion on TV with Mr. Lee Yuan Kew," in *Bilingualism in Our Society*, ed. Ministry of Culture (Singapore: Singapore National Printers, 1978).

83. Singapore Ministry of Information and the Arts, "National Day Rally 1993," August 15, 1993.

84. Adeline Low, "The Past in the Present: Memories of the 1964 'Racial Riots' in Singapore," *Asian Journal of Social Sciences* 23L3 (2001): 431–455.

85. Singapore Ministry of Information and the Arts, "National Day Rally 1996," August 18, 1996.

86. Singapore Ministry of Information and the Arts, "National Day Rally 1996."

87. Singapore Ministry of Education, "Speech by Brigadier-General Lee Hsien Loong, at the Launch of National Education on 17 May 1997," www.moe.gov.sg/media/speeches/1997/170597.htm.

88. Koun Chin Kok, *Malaysia and Singapore 1400–1963: A Comprehensive History* (Singapore: Oxford University, 1988).

89. Kwek, "Full Colour Illustrations," 168.

90. Kwek, "Full Colour Illustrations," 170.

91. See also Anderson, *Imagined Communities*, 178–183.

92. Allen, "Charlottesville Is Not the Continuation of an Old Fight."

Chapter 5

1. Robert A. Carter, *Sea of Pearls: Arabia, Persia, and the Industry That Shaped the Gulf* (London: Arabian, 2012), chapter 7.

2. Carter, *Sea of Pearls*, chapter 7.

3. Bahrain Authority for Culture and Antiquities Cultural and National Heritage, "Pearling Path: The Seashore," 2020, https://pearlingpath.bh/en/location/the-seashore/.

4. Carter, *Sea of Pearls*, 134.

5. Carter, *Sea of Pearls*, 152.

6. Carter, *Sea of Pearls*, 212.

7. Lubna Selaibeekh, "Citizenship Education in Bahrain: An Investigation of the Perceptions and Understandings of Policymakers, Teachers and Pupils" (PhD thesis, Surrey University, 2017), 28.

8. Nelida Fuccaro, "Pearl Towns and Early Oil Cities: Migration and Integration in the Arab Coast of the Persian Gulf," in *The City in the Ottoman Empire: Migration and the Making of Urban Modernity*, ed. Ulrike Freitag et al. (Abingdon: Routledge, 2011), 103.

9. See Emile Nakhleh, *Bahrain* (Lexington, KY: Lexington Books, 1976), 176, quoted in Andrew Gardner, *City of Strangers: Gulf Migration and the Indian Community in Bahrain* (Ithaca, NY: ILR Press, 2010), 145.

10. Fuccaro, "Pearl Towns and Early Oil Cities," 101.

11. Fuccaro, "Pearl Towns and Early Oil Cities," 101–102.

12. Fuccaro, "Pearl Towns and Early Oil Cities," 106.

13. Fuccaro, "Pearl Towns and Early Oil Cities," 102.

14. Laurence Louër, "The Political Impact of Labor Migration in Bahrain," *City & Society* 20, no. 1 (2008): 34.

15. I. J. Seccombe and R. I. Lawless, "Foreign Worker Dependence in the Gulf, and the International Oil Companies: 1910–50," *International Migration Review* 20, no. 3 (1986): 548–574.

16. Omar Hesham Alshehabi, "Radical Transformations and Radical Contestations: Bahrain's Spatial-Demographic Revolution," *Middle East Critique* 23, no. 1 (2014): 38.

17. Carter, *Sea of Pearls*, 132–137.

18. Fuccaro, "Pearl Towns and Early Oil Cities," 107.

19. Nelida Fuccaro, *Histories of City and State in the Persian Gulf: Manama since 1800* (Cambridge: Cambridge University Press, 2009), 93.

20. Fuccaro, "Pearl Towns and Early Oil Cities," 105.

21. The royal court continues to host a weekly *majlis*, which the government says demonstrates its "commitment to rooted traditions and values that are underpinned by His Majesty's aspirations to maintain a strong bond amongst Bahrain's society." See "HRH the Crown Prince Holds Weekly Majlis," Bahrain News Agency, November 6, 2019, https://www.bna.bh/en/HRHtheCrownPrinceholdsweeklyMajlis.aspx?cms=q8FmFJgiscL2fwIz ON1%2BDscKMJ0f7wV80tMHxDh13HY%3D.

22. Fuccaro, "Pearl Towns and Early Oil Cities," 105.

23. Fuccaro, "Pearl Towns and Early Oil Cities," 109–110.

24. Fuccaro, "Pearl Towns and Early Oil Cities," 109–110.

25. Fuccaro, "Pearl Towns and Early Oil Cities," 110.

26. Fuccaro, "Pearl Towns and Early Oil Cities," 111. When Sheikh Isa resisted the imperial reforms, British agents forced him to abdicate in 1923, and then exiled his nationalist supporters to India. See Khaldoun Nassan Al-Naqeeb et al., *Society and State in the Gulf and Arab Peninsula: A Different Perspective*, vol. 4 (London: Routledge, 2013), 75.

27. Fuccaro, "Pearl Towns and Early Oil Cities," 111.

28. Fuccaro, "Pearl Towns and Early Oil Cities," 112.

29. Fuccaro, "Pearl Towns and Early Oil Cities," 112.

30. Alshehabi, "Radical Transformations and Radical Contestations," 37.

31. Ralph Magnus, "Societies and Social Change in the Persian Gulf," in *The Persian Gulf States*, ed. Alvin Cottrell (London: Johns Hopkins University Press, 1980), 369–413; Al-Naqeeb et al., *Society and State in the Gulf*, 2013.

32. Fuad Khuri, *Tribe and State in Bahrain: The Transformation of Social and Political Authority in an Arab State* (Chicago: University of Chicago Press, 1980), 198, quoted in John Chalcraft, "Monarchy, Migration and Hegemony in the Arabian Peninsula," London School of Economics and Political Science, Kuwait Programme on Development, Governance and Globalisation in the Gulf States, Paper 12, 2010.

33. Khuri, *Tribe and State in Bahrain*, 196, quoted in Louër, "The Political Impact of Labor Migration in Bahrain," 38.

34. Louër, "The Political Impact of Labor Migration in Bahrain," 35.

35. Selaibeekh, "Citizenship Education in Bahrain," 33–34.

36. Selaibeekh, "Citizenship Education in Bahrain," 30.

37. Selaibeekh, "Citizenship Education in Bahrain," 30.

38. Angela Clarke, *The Islands of Bahrain: An Illustrated Guide to Their Heritage* (Manama: Bahrain Historical and Archaeological Society, 1981), 69, quoted in Gardner, *City of Strangers*, 41.

39. Gardner, *City of Strangers*, 27.

40. Abdulhadi Khalaf, "Labor Movements in Bahrain," *Middle East Report Online*, May 4, 1985, https://merip.org/1985/05/labor-movements-in-bahrain/.

41. Gardner, *City of Strangers*, 41.

42. See Daryl Champion, "The Kingdom of Saudi Arabia: Elements of Instability within Stability," *Meria* 3, no. 4 (1999): 1–23; Anh Nga Longva, *Walls Built on Sand: Migration, Exclusion and Society in Kuwait* (Boulder, CO: Westview Press, 1997), 46–52; Andrzej Kapiszewski, *Nationals and Expatriates: Population and Labour Dilemmas of the Gulf Cooperation Council States* (Ithaca, NY: Ithaca Press, 2001), 5–9.

43. About 92 percent of the national (as opposed to noncitizen) workforce is employed in the public sector—the highest percentage in the world. These jobs also encompass much of the petroleum industry, the aluminum industry, and telecommunications (see Gardner, *City of Strangers*, 144).

44. Boucher and Gest, *Crossroads*, 72.

45. Anh Nga Longva, "Keeping Migrant Workers in Check: The Kafala System in the Gulf," *Middle East Report* 211 (1999): 22.

46. Philippe Fargues, "Immigration without Inclusion: Non-nationals in Nation-Building in the Gulf States," *Asian and Pacific Migration Journal* 20, nos. 3–4 (2011): 287.

47. Gardner, *City of Strangers*, 59.

48. Gardner, *City of Strangers*, 46.

49. Jane Kinninmont, "Bahrain's Contentious Politics," Working Paper, London: The Elders, 2018, 9.

50. Kinninmont, "Bahrain's Contentious Politics," 9. This is consistent with the citizenship laws of other Arab emirates in the Gulf region. Among these other states, however, Bahrain's citizenship regime is distinct for its frequent application of the law for the purpose of revocation and naturalization.

51. Louër, "The Political Impact of Labor Migration in Bahrain," 41–42.

52. Selaibeekh, "Citizenship Education in Bahrain," 30–31.

53. Justin Gengler, *Group Conflict and Political Mobilization in Bahrain and the Arab Gulf: Rethinking the Rentier State* (Bloomington: Indiana University Press, 2015), 26. See also Justin Gengler, "Segregation and Sectarianism: Geography, Economic Distribution, and Sectarian Resilience in Bahrain," in *Countering Sectarianism in the Middle East*, ed. Jeffry Martini, Dalia Dassa Kaye, and Becca Wasser (Santa Monica, CA: RAND, 2019), 41–63.

54. Kinninmont, "Bahrain's Contentious Politics," 9.

55. Bahrain Institute of Human Rights and Democracy, "Bahraini Court Revokes 138 Individuals of Their Citizenship and Sentences 69 to Life in a Mass Trial," April 16, 2019, http://birdbh.org/2019/04/bahraini-court-revokes-138-individuals-of-their-citizenship-in-a-mass-trial/.

56. David Trimbach and Nicole Reiz, "Unmaking Citizens: The Expansion of Citizenship Revocation in Response to Terrorism," Center for Migration Studies, 2018, https://cmsny.org/publications/unmaking-citizens/.

57. "Bahrain Revokes Top Shii Cleric Isa Qassim's Citizenship," BBC News, June 20, 2016, https://www.bbc.com/news/world-middle-east-36578000.

58. Zahra Babar, "The 'Enemy Within': Citizenship-Stripping in the Post–Arab Spring GCC," *Middle East Journal* 71, no. 4 (Autumn, 2017): 543.

59. Justin Gengler, "Bahrain: A Special Case," in *What Does the Gulf Think about the Arab Awakening?*, ed. Fatima Ayub (London: European Council on Foreign Relations, 2013), 16–17.

60. See Boucher and Gest, *Crossroads.*

61. Gengler, *Group Conflict and Political Mobilization in Bahrain and the Arab Gulf,* 176.

62. Gengler, *Group Conflict and Political Mobilization in Bahrain and the Arab Gulf,* 48.

63. Gengler, *Group Conflict and Political Mobilization in Bahrain and the Arab Gulf,* 96.

64. Gengler, *Group Conflict and Political Mobilization in Bahrain and the Arab Gulf,* 96.

65. Jane Kinninmont and Omar Sirri, "Bahrain: Civil Society and Political Imagination," Chatham House, October 2014, www.chathamhouse.org/sites/default/files/publications/research/20141028BahrainKinninmontSirri.pdf.

66. International Crisis Group, "Bahrain's Sectarian Challenge," Middle East/North Africa Report Number 40, May 6, 2005, 7–8, https://d2071andvip0wj.cloudfront.net/40-bahrain-s-sectarian-challenge.pdf.

67. Gardner, *City of Strangers,* 87, 114. A number of foreign families who have been in Bahrain since the 1950s possess a certificate of residence, which exempts them from *kafala* sponsorship without enfranchisement.

68. International Crisis Group, "Bahrain's Sectarian Challenge," 8.

69. "Citizenship as a Bahraini Government Tool," *Stratfor Worldview,* September 21, 2012, https://worldview.stratfor.com/article/citizenship-bahraini-government-tool.

70. "Naturalization of Displaced Syrians . . . King of Bahrain Manipulates Demography," *Al Masalah,* March 3, 2016, http://almasalah.com/ar/NewsDetails.aspx?NewsID=27990.

71. Catherine Shakdam, "Bahrain Using Targeted Immigration to Quell Political Dissent," *Mint Press News,* December 3, 2014, https://www.mintpressnews.com/bahrain-is-using-targeted-immigration-to-quell-political-dissent/199527/.

72. Gardner, *City of Strangers,* 147.

73. Mazen Mahdi, "Leading Bahrainis Call for Halt to Naturalization," *The National,* May 11, 2009; Kinninmont, "Bahrain's Contentious Politics."

74. Shakdam, ""Bahrain Using Targeted Immigration."

75. Selaibeekh, "Citizenship Education in Bahrain," 38.

76. Gengler, "Segregation and Sectarianism," 49.

77. Frank Gardner, "Bahrain Brothers Describe Shock at Losing Nationality," BBC, November 9, 2012, https://www.bbc.com/news/world-middle-east-20271933.

78. Gardner, "Bahrain Brothers Describe Shock at Losing Nationality."

79. Justin Gengler, "Royal Factionalism, the Khawalid, and the Securitization of 'the Shī'a Problem' in Bahrain," *Journal of Arabian Studies* 3, no. 1 (2013): 70–71.

80. Khuri, *Tribe and State in Bahrain,* 48, quoted in Gengler, "Royal Factionalism," 69.

81. Khalaf, "Labor Movements in Bahrain."

82. Louay Bahry, "The Socioeconomic Foundations of the Shiite Opposition in Bahrain," *Mediterranean Quarterly* 11 (2000): 129–43, quoted in Gengler, "Royal Factionalism," 69.

83. Gengler, *Group Conflict and Political Mobilization in Bahrain and the Arab Gulf,* 111. See also Gengler, "Segregation and Sectarianism," 53–54.

84. International Crisis Group, "Bahrain's Sectarian Challenge," 7.

85. Gengler, *Group Conflict and Political Mobilization in Bahrain and the Arab Gulf,* 42–43.

86. Clive Holes, "Dialect and National Identity: The Cultural Politics of Self-Representation in Bahraini Musalsalat," in *Monarchies and Nations: Globalization and Identity in the Arab States of the Gulf,* ed. Paul Dreschand and James Piscatori (London: I. B. Tauris, 2005), 60.

87. Gengler, *Group Conflict and Political Mobilization in Bahrain and the Arab Gulf,* 143. Sunnis who dared to break ranks to join demonstrators at the Pearl Roundabout during the 2011 uprising were singled out for swift retribution.

88. Gengler, *Group Conflict and Political Mobilization in Bahrain and the Arab Gulf,* 81–82.

89. Gengler, *Group Conflict and Political Mobilization in Bahrain and the Arab Gulf,* 81–82.

90. Justin Gengler, "Electoral Rules (and Threats) Cure Bahrain's Sectarian Parliament," *Monkey Cage,* December 1, 2014, https://www.washingtonpost.com/news/monkey-cage/wp/2014/12/01/electoral-rules-and-threats-cure-bahrains-sectarian-parliament/.

91. Alshehabi, "Radical Transformations and Radical Contestations," 41.

92. Kinninmont, "Bahrain's Contentious Politics," 15.

93. Sheikh was later imprisoned after authoring an article that questioned the capacity of Saudi-led coalition forces in Yemen. See Ibrahim Sheikh, "Naturalization and the Missing Link," *Akhbar Akhaleej,* accessed March 12, 2021, http://www.akhbar-alkhaleej.com/13543/article/18790.html.

94. Kinninmont, "Bahrain's Contentious Politics," 15. Even the Saudi Arabian government, Bahrain's closest ally, has criticized the Al-Khalifa naturalization regime because naturalized Yemenis thereafter have access to Saudi labor markets as legal citizens of the a fellow GCC state. See "Saudis to Bahrain . . . Stop Naturalization of Yemenis," *Al Hurra,* January 10, 2018, https://www.alhurra.com/a/saudi-bahrian-yemen/413113.html.

95. Selaibeekh, "Citizenship Education in Bahrain," 33.

96. Gardner, *City of Strangers,* 28–29.

97. Gardner, *City of Strangers,* 87–88.

98. Gardner, *City of Strangers,* 77.

99. Guy Petherbridge, "Vernacular Architecture: The House and Society," in *Architecture of the Islamic World: Its History and Social Meaning,* ed. George Michell (London: Thames and Hudson, 1978), 195.

100. Thomas Fibiger, "Global Display—Local Dismay: Debating 'Globalized Heritage' in Bahrain," *History and Anthropology* 22, no. 2 (2011): 187–202.

101. Thomas Fibiger, "Heritage Erasure and Heritage Transformation: How Heritage Is Created by Destruction in Bahrain," *International Journal of Heritage Studies* 21, no. 4 (2015): 390–404.

102. Fibiger, "Global Display—Local Dismay," 197.

103. Fibiger, "Heritage Erasure and Heritage Transformation," 395.

104. Fibiger, "Heritage Erasure and Heritage Transformation," 395.

105. "Bahrain Bans Newspaper for 'Sowing Division,'" *Yahoo News,* 4 June 2017, https://www.yahoo.com/news/bahrain-bans-newspaper-sowing-division-153554750.

106. "H.E. Dr. Shaikh Khalid Bin Khalifa Al Khalifa, Statement of the Chairman of the Board of Trustees," King Hamad Global Centre for Peaceful Coexistence, accessed October 12, 2021, https://kinghamadglobalcentre.com/.

107. Claire Beaugrand, "Deconstructing Minorities/Majorities in Parliamentary Gulf States (Kuwait and Bahrain)," *British Journal of Middle Eastern Studies* 43, no. 2 (2016): 234–249.

108. Justin Gengler, "The Political Economy of Sectarianism in the Gulf," Carnegie Endowment for International Peace, August 2016, https://carnegieendowment.org/files/Gengler_Sectarianism_Final.pdf.

Chapter 6

1. Patricia De Freitas, "'Playing Mas': The Construction and Deconstruction of National Identity in the Trinidad Carnival" (PhD thesis, McMaster University, 1994), 63.
2. Milla Cozart Riggio, "Carnival Crossings: From Here to There, Arkansas to Harvard to Trinidad," Carnival Crossroads Distinguished Lecture, University of the West Indies, St. Augustine, February 3, 2014, https://sta.uwi.edu/news/releases/release.asp?id=1217, quoted in Raymond Ramcharitar, "The Invention of Trinidad Carnival: The New World Gleichschaltung," *Caribbean Quarterly*, 2020.
3. James Millette, "The Wage Problem in Trinidad and Tobago 1838–1938," in *The Colonial Caribbean in Transition: Essays on Postemancipation and Cultural History*, ed. Bridget Brereton and Kevin Yelvington (Kingston: The Press, University of the West Indies, 1999), 59–60.
4. Carl Campbell, "Black Testators: Fragments of the Lives of Free Africans and Free Creole Blacks in Trinidad 1813–1877," in *The Colonial Caribbean in Transition: Essays on Postemancipation and Cultural History*, ed. Bridget Brereton and Kevin Yelvington (Kingston: The Press, University of the West Indies, 1999), 50.
5. Campbell, "Black Testators," 50.
6. Lloyd Braithwaite, "Social Stratification in Trinidad: A Preliminary Analysis," *Social and Economic Studies* 2, nos. 2–3 (1953): 9.
7. Millette, "The Wage Problem in Trinidad and Tobago," 61.
8. Bridget Brereton, *Race Relations in Colonial Trinidad 1870–1900* (Cambridge: Cambridge University Press, 1979), 176–177.
9. Brereton, *Race Relations in Colonial Trinidad*, 176–177.
10. Brereton, *Race Relations in Colonial Trinidad*, 180.
11. Brereton, *Race Relations in Colonial Trinidad*, 181.
12. Brereton, *Race Relations in Colonial Trinidad*, 174.
13. Brereton, *Race Relations in Colonial Trinidad*, 177.
14. Yelvington, "The War in Ethiopia and Trinidad," 217.
15. Tejaswini Niranjana, *Mobilizing India: Women, Music and Migration between India and Trinidad* (Durham, NC: Duke University Press, 2006), 169–189.
16. Shameen Ali, "Indian Diaspora and Renaissance, 1941–1946," in *Calcutta to Caroni and the Indian Diaspora*, ed. John La Guerre and Ann Marie Bissessar (St. Augustine: UWI School for Continuing Studies, 2005), 485–486; See also Braithwaite, "Social Stratification in Trinidad," 9.
17. Braithwaite, "Social Stratification in Trinidad," 37–38.
18. Braithwaite, "Social Stratification in Trinidad," 15.
19. Braithwaite, "Social Stratification in Trinidad," 13.
20. Eric Eustace Williams, *History of the People of Trinidad and Tobago* (Brooklyn, NY: A&B, 1962), 132, 151.
21. Ramcharitar, "Ethnic Anxiety and Competing Citizenships in Trinidad and Tobago," 6.

22. Selwyn Ryan, *Race and Nationalism in Trinidad* (Toronto: University of Toronto Press, 1972), 109.
23. Ramcharitar, "Ethnic Anxiety and Competing Citizenships in Trinidad and Tobago," 7.
24. Ramcharitar, "Ethnic Anxiety and Competing Citizenships in Trinidad and Tobago," 13. Citing *The Guardian*, April 2, 1958.
25. Ralph Premdas, "The Ascendance of an Indian Prime Minister in Trinidad: The Election of 1995," in *Identity, Ethnicity and Culture in the Caribbean*, ed. Ralph Premdas (St. Augustine: UWI School of Continuing Studies, 2003), 323–358: 324.
26. Roy McCree, "Ethnicity and Involvement in Cultural Festivals in Trinidad and Tobago," in *Identity, Ethnicity and Culture in the Caribbean*, ed. Ralph Premdas (St. Augustine: UWI School of Continuing Studies, 2003), 116–117.
27. B. C. Pires, "The Slim Lady Sings," *Newsday*, April 19, 2021, 21, quoting Glenda Collins: "Williams promised the 'small islanders' their own land and a better life in return for their votes." See also Raymond Ramcharitar, *A History of Creole Trinidad, 1956–2016* (New York: Palgrave, 2021), chapter 6.
28. An audit of Trinidadian police services revealed that, in 1970, people of Indian origin made up only 6 of 149 police sergeants, and only 9 of 274 police officers. A decade later, Indo-Trinidadians comprised 180 out of 1,282 police officers, 22 of 244 sergeants, 1 assistant superintendent out of 47, and 1 of 9 assistant commissioners of police. Despite being largely excluded from such law enforcement and other government positions, Indo-Trinidadians nevertheless grew more educated and prosperous. See "UWI Study: Ethnic Imbalance in T&T Police Service Spans Decades," *Guyana News*, April 3, 2011.
29. Ufot Inamete, "Politics and Governance in Trinidad and Tobago: Major Issues and Developments," *Caribbean Studies* 25, nos. 3–4 (1992): 305–324.
30. For further discussion of the West Indian diaspora, see Nancy Foner, *Islands in the City: West Indian Migration to New York* (Berkeley: University of California Press, 2001).
31. Ramcharitar, *A History of Creole Trinidad*, citing *Sandesh*, January 2, 1987.
32. For a detailed discussion of the "substate" that Abu Bakr and Jamaat represented, see Ramcharitar, *A History of Creole Trinidad*.
33. Premdas, "The Ascendance of an Indian Prime Minister in Trinidad," 324, 342.
34. Selwyn Ryan, *Deadlock: Ethnicity and Electoral Competition in Trinidad, 1995–2002* (St. Augustine: Institute for Social and Economic Studies, 2003), 17.
35. Peter Koningsbruggen, *Trinidad Carnival: A Quest for National Identity* (London: Macmillan Education, 1997), 14. Ramcharitar writes that the Canboulay parody began with criminal immigrants shipped to Trinidad from other islands. They were incited to riot by the middle class. Posters had appeared in Port of Spain days before and merchants knew to expect a disturbance. One newspaper reported a white man in a mask directing rioters to kill the police commandant. See Ramcharitar, "The Invention of Trinidad Carnival."
36. Brereton, *Race Relations in Colonial Trinidad*, 148.
37. Brereton, *Race Relations in Colonial Trinidad*, 148.
38. Brereton, *Race Relations in Colonial Trinidad*, 170.
39. Gordon Rohlehr, *Calypso and Society in Pre-Independence Trinidad* (Port of Spain: Gordon Rohlehr, 1990), 27.
40. Koningsbruggen, *Trinidad Carnival*, 15–16.
41. Koningsbruggen, *Trinidad Carnival*, 20.

42. Koningsbruggen, *Trinidad Carnival*, 62–63.
43. Brereton, *Race Relations in Colonial Trinidad*, 170.
44. Brereton, *Race Relations in Colonial Trinidad*, 172.
45. Brereton, *Race Relations in Colonial Trinidad*, 173.
46. Errol Hill, *The Trinidad Carnival: Mandate for a National Theatre* (Austin: University of Texas Press, 1972), 85, quoted in Koningsbruggen, *Trinidad Carnival*, 77.
47. Rohlehr, *Calypso and Society*, 494.
48. Rohlehr, *Calypso and Society*, 253.
49. Gordon Rohlehr, "Apocalypso and the Soca Fires of 1990," in *The Shape of That Hurt* (Port of Spain: Lexicon, 1992), 322–323.
50. Ramcharitar, *A History of Creole Trinidad*.
51. Ramcharitar, *A History of Creole Trinidad*, 220, citing *The Guardian*, February 31, 1991.
52. Ramcharitar, *A History of Creole Trinidad*, 221, citing *The Guardian*, February 12, 1995.
53. Larry Rohter, "High-Level Name-Calling across the Racial Fence," *New York Times*, August 20, 1997.
54. Rohter, "High-Level Name-Calling across the Racial Fence."
55. Isaac Fergusson, "Carnival's Controversies: Tensions Underscore Island Fest," *Billboard*, March 29, 1997, 1.
56. Fergusson, "Carnival's Controversies," 14.
57. Kathianne Hingwan, "Identity and Carnival in Trinidad" (PhD thesis, Goldsmiths College, University of London, September 2002), 118.
58. Anton Allahar, "Popular Culture and Racialisation of Political Consciousness in Trinidad and Tobago," in *Identity, Ethnicity and Culture in the Caribbean*, ed. Ralph Premdas (St. Augustine: UWI School of Continuing Studies, 2003), 254.
59. Rohter, "High-Level Name-Calling across the Racial Fence."
60. Gordon Rohlehr, "The State of Calypso Today," in *Identity, Ethnicity and Culture in the Caribbean*, ed. Ralph Premdas (St. Augustine: UWI School of Continuing Studies, 2003), 40–41.
61. Buron Sankeralli, "Indian Presence in Carnival," in *Carnival: Culture in Action—The Trinidad Experience*, ed. Milla Cozart Riggio (New York: Routledge, 2004), 77–78.
62. Earl Lovelace, *Salt* (New York: Persea Books, 1979), 66.
63. Lovelace, *Salt*, 49–50.
64. Gerard Aching, *Masking and Power: Carnival and Popular Culture in the Caribbean* (Minneapolis: University of Minnesota Press, 2002), 59.
65. Earl Lovelace, *The Dragon Can't Dance* (Alexandria, VA: Alexander Street Press, 1989), 26.
66. Rohter, "High-Level Name-Calling across the Racial Fence."
67. Christopher Ballengee, "From Indian to Indo-Creole: Tassa Drumming, Creolization, and Indo-Caribbean Nationalism in Trinidad and Tobago" (PhD dissertation, University of Florida, 2013).
68. Peter Manuel, "Chutney and Indo-Trinidadian Cultural Identity," *Popular Music* 17, no. 1 (1998): 38.
69. Sankeralli, "Indian Presence in Carnival," 81.
70. Satnarine Balkaransingh, "Chutney Crosses over into Chutney Soca in Trinidad and Tobago Carnival," in *Identity, Ethnicity and Culture in the Caribbean*, ed. Ralph Premdas (St. Augustine: UWI School of Continuing Studies, 2003), 50.
71. Manuel, "Chutney and Indo-Trinidadian Cultural Identity," 25.

Chapter 7

1. Jacques David, *Mauritius: The Slave Legacy* (India: Ajanta Offset and Packagings, 2010), 436–437.

2. Amitava Chowdhury, "Maroon Archaeological Research in Mauritius and Its Possible Implications in a Global Context," in *The Archaeology of Slavery: Toward a Comparative Global Framework*, ed. Lydia Wilson Marshall (Carbondale: Southern Illinois University Press, 2014), 270.

3. Chowdhury, "Maroon Archaeological Research in Mauritius," 257–258.

4. Richard Blair Allen, *Slaves, Freedmen, and Indentured Laborers in Colonial Mauritius* (Cambridge: Cambridge University Press, 1999), 14.

5. Allen, *Slaves, Freedmen, and Indentured Laborers*, 14.

6. David, *Mauritius*, 3.

7. Allen, *Slaves, Freedmen, and Indentured Laborers*, 16–17.

8. Allen, *Slaves, Freedmen, and Indentured Laborers*, 16–17.

9. Chowdhury, "Maroon Archaeological Research in Mauritius," 257; David, *Mauritius*, xii.

10. David, *Mauritius*, 179–181.

11. David, *Mauritius*, 418.

12. David, *Mauritius*, 424.

13. Allen, *Slaves, Freedmen, and Indentured Laborers*, 36.

14. Chowdhury, "Maroon Archaeological Research in Mauritius," 270. Allen (*Slaves, Freedmen, and Indentured Laborers*, 46) reports a number of examples. On June 19, 1767, the Bureau de Police recorded the capture of Sylvestre, La Rose, and Thérése, all Malagasy slaves who had each been free for at least a year and a half. In 1804, the Bureau du Marronage recorded the capture of Philippe, another Malagasy slave, who had fled from his master six years earlier. The following year, the Bureau reported that Jupiter, a Mozambican slave, had been killed after having reportedly been free for twelve to fifteen years.

15. David, *Mauritius*, 424.

16. David, *Mauritius*, 121.

17. Chowdhury, "Maroon Archaeological Research in Mauritius," 259–263.

18. Chowdhury, "Maroon Archaeological Research in Mauritius," 262.

19. Allen, *Slaves, Freedmen, and Indentured Laborers*, 51.

20. Allen, *Slaves, Freedmen, and Indentured Laborers*, 15.

21. Moses Nwulia, "The 'Apprenticeship' System in Mauritius: Its Character and Its Impact on Race Relations in the Immediate Post-Emancipation Period, 1839–1879," *African Studies Review* 21, no. 1 (1978): 90–93.

22. Allen, *Slaves, Freedmen, and Indentured Laborers*, 53.

23. Nicolay to Glenelg, May 4, 1839, Public Record Office, C.O. 167/210, quoted in Nwulia, "The 'Apprenticeship' System in Mauritius," 99. In fact, Allen (*Slaves, Freedmen, and Indentured Laborers*, 121–128) notes that large numbers of ex-apprentices Large numbers of ex-apprentices occupied vacant land after emancipation, often near estates where their presence was perceived to be a threat not only to public order but also to the estate's economic viability. Some landowners responded by leasing the land in question or entering into informal sharecropping agreements that helped sustain an agricultural workforce at a time when their ability to coerce laborers was circumscribed. The census of 1846 reported the presence of 4,116 "independent proprietors" in Mauritius, 58 percent of whom were former apprentices.

24. Allen, *Slaves, Freedmen, and Indentured Laborers*, 50, 82.
25. See Allen, *Slaves, Freedmen, and Indentured Laborers*, 353. Early in the 1770s, the colonial government established several camps on Port Louis's outskirts where *gens de couleur* of the appropriate cultural or ethnic background were expected to reside. A 1791 map of the city noted the existence of five such camps: *des malabars et lascars* (Indians and sailors), *des iolofs* (Wolofs), *des malgaches* (Malagasy), *des bambaras* (West Africans), and *des noirs libres* (free Black people).
26. Allen, *Slaves, Freedmen, and Indentured Laborers*, 98.
27. Allen, *Slaves, Freedmen, and Indentured Laborers*, 85, 93.
28. David, *Mauritius*, 172.
29. Allen, *Slaves, Freedmen, and Indentured Laborers*, 109.
30. Allen, *Slaves, Freedmen, and Indentured Laborers*, 104.
31. David, *Mauritius*, 177.
32. Allen, *Slaves, Freedmen, and Indentured Laborers*, 16.
33. Allen, *Slaves, Freedmen, and Indentured Laborers*, 16–17.
34. Allen, *Slaves, Freedmen, and Indentured Laborers*, 56. Much of the planters' anxiety related to ex-slaves' reluctance to return to the fields and otherwise their expectations of higher wages to fill the void.
35. "In 19th Century Mauritius: The Resistance and Struggle of the Indian Workers," *Le Mauricien*, April 30, 2013, https://www.lemauricien.com/article/19th-century-mauritius-resistance-and-struggle-indian-workers/.
36. Allen, *Slaves, Freedmen, and Indentured Laborers*, 37.
37. Allen, *Slaves, Freedmen, and Indentured Laborers*, 134.
38. Allen, *Slaves, Freedmen, and Indentured Laborers*, 73, 143–144.
39. David, *Mauritius*, 265.
40. See Oddvar Hollup, "The Disintegration of Caste and Changing Concepts of Indian Ethnic Identity in Mauritius," *Ethnology* 33, no. 4 (1994): 299.
41. Allen, *Slaves, Freedmen, and Indentured Laborers*, 168.
42. Lance Brennan, John Mcdonald, and Ralph Shlomowitz, "The Geographic and Social Origins of Indian Indentured Labourers in Mauritius, Natal, Fiji, Guyana and Jamaica," *South Asia: Journal of South Asian Studies* 21 (1998): 55; See also Hollup, "The Disintegration of Caste," 306.
43. Chowdhury, "Narratives of Home," 247–248.
44. Hollup, "The Disintegration of Caste," 208.
45. Chowdhury, "Narratives of Home," 249–250.
46. Chowdhury, "Narratives of Home," 249–250.
47. Eleanor Nicole Thornton, "Negotiating Race, Ethnicity and Nation: Diasporic Multiculturalism and the Politics of Language in Mauritius" (PhD dissertation, Johns Hopkins University, 2017), 165.
48. Thornton, "Negotiating Race, Ethnicity and Nation," 86.
49. Rosabelle Boswell, "Can Justice Be Achieved for Slave Descendents in Mauritius?," *International Journal of Law, Crime and Justice* 42, no. 2 (2014): 153.
50. Thornton, "Negotiating Race, Ethnicity and Nation," 164.
51. Thornton, "Negotiating Race, Ethnicity and Nation," 61, 166, 187.
52. Thornton, "Negotiating Race, Ethnicity and Nation," 175–176.
53. Boswell, "Can Justice Be Achieved," 153; Thornton, "Negotiating Race, Ethnicity and Nation," 176.

54. Thornton, "Negotiating Race, Ethnicity and Nation," 169–170. The names of counterpart movements that followed communicated this concern with establishing an Afro-Creole identity: Rassemblement des Organisations Créoles, Muvman Morisyen Kreol Afrikain, Mouvement Authentique Mauricien, L'Association Socio-Culturelle Afro-Mauricienne, and L'Organisation Culturelle Afro-Malagasy.

55. Rosabelle Boswell, "Heritage Tourism and Identity in the Mauritian Villages of Chamarel and Le Morne," *Journal of Southern African Studies* 31, no. 2 (2005): 287; Thornton, "Negotiating Race, Ethnicity and Nation," 171–172.

56. Thornton, "Negotiating Race, Ethnicity and Nation," 195.

57. Thornton, "Negotiating Race, Ethnicity and Nation," 171.

58. Clifford Vellien, "Rioting in Mauritius Set Off by Jail Death of Singer," *The Guardian*, February 24, 1999, https://www.theguardian.com/world/1999/feb/25/7 .

59. Thornton, "Negotiating Race, Ethnicity and Nation," 201.

60. Vijaya Teelock, Mauritius Truth and Justice Commission Report, vol. 1, doi:10.13140/RG.2.1.2699.2801, November 2011, https://www.researchgate.net/publication/278496497_Truth_and_Justice_Commission_report_Volume_I.

61. Chowdhury, "Maroon Archaeological Research in Mauritius," 263–264.

62. "Mauritius: Contribution of Travel and Tourism to GDP as a Share of GDP," Knoema, 2018, https://knoema.com/atlas/Mauritius/topics/Tourism/Travel-and-Tourism-Total-Contribution-to-GDP/Contribution-of-travel-and-tourism-to-GDP-percent-of-GDP.

63. Jean-Clément Cangy, *Le Séga, des origines . . . à nos jours* (Port Louis: Makanbo, 2012). "Le Séga est né dans la douleur, dans les souffrances de l'esclavage, des humiliations et des privations . . . mais aussi dans la révolte devant l'horreur, le crime contre l'humanité, dans le marronage."

Chapter 8

1. This streak effectively was halted by the 2020 coronavirus pandemic. However, despite the city's cancellation and lockdown, a small contingent defiantly marched up Fifth Avenue in the early morning hours of March 17, 2020, to continue the tradition.

2. Golway, *Machine Made*, xxi.

3. Golway, *Machine Made*, xxi.

4. Golway, *Machine Made*, 48, citing *New York Times*, June 22, 1887.

5. Golway, *Machine Made*, 47.

6. Peter Quinn, "The Future of Irish America," in *Making the Irish American: History and Heritage of the Irish in the United States*, ed. J. J. Lee and Marion Casey (New York: New York University Press, 2006), 682.

7. Roger Waldinger and Claudia Der-Martirosian, "The Immigrant Niche: Pervasive, Persistent, Diverse," in *Strangers at the Gates: New Immigrants in Urban America*, ed. Roger Waldinger (Berkeley: University of California Press, 2001), 228–271.

8. Tyler Anbinder, *City of Dreams: The 400-Year Epic History of Immigrant New York* (Boston: Houghton Mifflin Harcourt, 2016), 111.

9. Hirota, *Expelling the Poor*, 48.

10. Hirota, *Expelling the Poor*, 48.

11. James Lardner and Thomas Reppetto, *NYPD: A City and Its Police* (New York: Henry Holt, 2000), 26.

12. David Noel Doyle, "The Irish in North America, 1776–1845," in *Making the Irish American: History and Heritage of the Irish in the United States*, ed. J. J. Lee and Marion Casey (New York: New York University Press, 2006), 182.

13. Higham, *Strangers in the Land*, 5–6.

14. Theodore Parker, *The Material Condition of the People of Massachusetts* (Boston: Geo. C. Rand & Avery, 1860), 43, quoted in Hirota, *Expelling the Poor*, 122–123; Theodore Parker Papers, From Theodore Parker to Francis Jackson, August 21, 1859, roll 1, vol. 3, Massachusetts Historical Society, Boston.

15. Golway, *Machine Made*, xxii.

16. Golway, *Machine Made*, 24.

17. Kerby Miller, *Emigrants and Exiles: Ireland and the Irish Exodus to North America* (New York: Oxford University Press, 1985), 278.

18. Miller, *Emigrants and Exiles*, 188–189.

19. Hirota, *Expelling the Poor*, 69.

20. David Noel Doyle, "The Remaking of Irish America, 1845–1880," in *Making the Irish American: History and Heritage of the Irish in the United States*, ed. J. J. Lee and Marion Casey (New York: New York University Press, 2006), 215.

21. Golway, *Machine Made*, 30.

22. Golway, *Machine Made*, 30.

23. Richard Shaw, *Dagger John: The Unquiet Life and Times of Archbishop John Hughes of New York* (New York: Paulist Press, 1977), quoted in Golway, *Machine Made*, 36–37.

24. Golway, *Machine Made*, xxii.

25. Lardner and Reppetto, *NYPD*, 26.

26. James Donnelly, *The Great Irish Potato Famine* (Phoenix Mill: Sutton, 2001), 181–82, quoted in Golway, *Machine Made*, 45; Miller, *Emigrants and Exiles*, 195–196, 297. For further discussion on successive waves of immigration, see Nancy Foner, *From Ellis Island to JFK: New York's Two Great Waves of Immigration* (New Haven, CT: Yale University Press, 2000).

27. Lardner and Reppetto, *NYPD*, 26.

28. Anbinder, *City of Dreams*, 117.

29. Anbinder, *City of Dreams*, 117.

30. Miller, *Emigrants and Exiles*, 326–327.

31. Miller, *Emigrants and Exiles*, 326–327.

32. Miller, *Emigrants and Exiles*, 327.

33. Golway, *Machine Made*, 40–41, citing *Census of the State of New York for 1855* (Albany: 1857).

34. Golway, *Machine Made*, 40–41, citing *Census of the State of New York for 1855*.

35. Doyle, "The Remaking of Irish America," 216–217, 230.

36. Miller, *Emigrants and Exiles*, 329.

37. Anbinder, *City of Dreams*, 189.

38. Anbinder, *City of Dreams*, 192.

39. Miller, *Emigrants and Exiles*, 330.

40. Lardner and Reppetto, *NYPD*, 3.

41. Lardner and Reppetto, *NYPD*, 16.

42. Lardner and Reppetto, *NYPD*, 23. The fire department was made into a permanent, state-employed force by 1865.

43. Anbinder, *City of Dreams*, 193.

44. Lardner and Reppetto, *NYPD*, 37.

45. Miller, *Emigrants and Exiles*, 495.

46. Miller, *Emigrants and Exiles*, 525–526.

47. Lardner and Reppetto, *NYPD*, 38.

48. Golway, *Machine Made*, 90, citing *New York Times*, November 6, 1856.

49. Lardner and Reppetto, *NYPD*, 37.

50. Adrian Cook, *The Armies of the Street: The New York City Draft Riots of 1863* (Lexington: University Press of Kentucky, 1982), 43, quoted in Golway, *Machine Made*, 50–51; Ronald Bayor and Timothy Meagher, *The New York Irish* (Baltimore, MD: Johns Hopkins University Press. 1996), 95.

51. Anbinder, *City of Dreams*, 292–293.

52. Anbinder, *City of Dreams*, 292–293.

53. Kevin Kenny, "Labor and Labor Organizations," in *Making the Irish American: History and Heritage of the Irish in the United States*, ed. J. J. Lee and Marion Casey (New York: New York University Press, 2006), 360.

54. Irene Whelan, "Religious Rivalry and the Making of Irish-American Identity," in *Making the Irish American: History and Heritage of the Irish in the United States*, ed. J. J. Lee and Marion Casey (New York: New York University Press, 2006), 276; Golway, *Machine Made*, 158. For a fuller discussion of the integration of Catholics into American political life, see Richard Alba and Nancy Foner, *Strangers No More: Immigration and the Challenges of Integration in North America and Western Europe* (Princeton, NJ: Princeton University Press, 2006).

55. Miller, *Emigrants and Exiles*, 526–527.

56. Miller, *Emigrants and Exiles*, 526–527.

57. Golway, *Machine Made*, 74.

58. Lardner and Reppetto, *NYPD*, xiii.

59. Lardner and Reppetto, *NYPD*, xiii.

60. Golway, *Machine Made*, 50–51.

61. Daniel Patrick Moynihan, "The Irish (1963, 1970)," in *Making the Irish American: History and Heritage of the Irish in the United States*, ed. J. J. Lee and Marion Casey (New York: New York University Press, 2006), 503.

62. Golway, *Machine Made*, 33–34, citing *Freeman's Journal*, August 7, 1841.

63. Golway, *Machine Made*, 33–34.

64. Lawrence Kehoe, *Complete Works of the Most Rev. John Hughes, DD* (New York: Lawrence Kehoe, 1866), quoted in Golway, *Machine Made*, 33–34.

Chapter 9

1. Seth Archer, *Sharks upon the Land: Colonialism, Indigenous Health, and Culture in Hawai'i, 1778–1855* (New York: Cambridge University Press, 2018).

2. Ronald Takaki, *Pau Hana: Plantation Life and Labor in Hawaii, 1835–1920* (Honolulu: University of Hawai'i Press, 1984), 28.

3. Takaki, *Pau Hana*, 73.

4. Takaki, *Pau Hana*, 73.

5. Samuel King and Randall Roth, *Broken Trust: Greed, Mismanagement, and Political Manipulation at America's Largest Charitable Trust* (Honolulu: University of Hawai'i Press, 2006), 288.

6. Carol MacLennan, *Sovereign Sugar: Industry and Environment in Hawai'i* (Honolulu: University of Hawai'i Press, 2014), 238.

7. MacLennan, *Sovereign Sugar*, 238.

8. MacLennan, *Sovereign Sugar*, 170–171, 197.

9. Altemus-Williams and Eriel Hobro, "Hawai'i Is Not the Multicultural Paradise Some Say It Is." According to these authors, "Some planters even tried to revive Southern-style cotton plantations on O'ahu. Laborers were whipped, stripped of their names, and only referred to by their 'bango' identification tags. 'Much like slave patrols in the South, police officers hunted plantation workers who tried to escape the islands and their indentured servitude, overstayed their contracts, or became unruly according to plantation standards,' says Michael Miranda, chair of the Filipino American National Historical Society, Kaua'i Committee. Katsu Goto, a Japanese merchant and interpreter, was lynched in 1889 for overstaying his contract, establishing a business, and translating documents from English to Japanese for colleagues."

10. MacLennan, *Sovereign Sugar*, 197.

11. According to Mariko Iijima (personal note, 2020), the Hawaiian term *haole* is not an equivalent to "white," as is used in the continental United States. Not all Europeans and Americans are considered *haole*. For example, Portuguese migrants, who came to Hawai'i from the islands of Madeira and the Azores between 1878 and 1887 and 1906 and 1913, were not subsumed as *haole* despite their European origins. The reason was that many of them were from peasant classes with low literacy in their homeland, and they worked alongside Asian immigrants for Euro-American bosses and managers on sugar plantations. See John McDermott and Naleen Naupaka Andrade, *People and Cultures of Hawai'i: The Evolution of Culture and Ethnicity* (Honolulu: University of Hawai'i Press, 2011), 33; Jonathan Okamura, *Raced to Death in 1920s Hawai'i: Injustice and Revenge in the Fukunaga Case* (Urbana: University of Illinoi Press, 2019), 5. In the Hawaiian census, until 1930, Portuguese along with Spanish and Puerto Rican people were counted separately from "other Caucasians (Haole)," even though they constituted the largest number of Europeans in Hawai'i. Eleanor Nordyke, *The Peopling of Hawai'i*, 2nd ed (Honolulu: University of Hawai'i Press, 1989), 180. Therefore, *haole* is a concept that considers both race and class.

12. Jacqueline Lasky, "Waiahole-Waikane," in *A Nation Rising: Hawaiian Movements for Life, Land, and Sovereignty*, ed. Noelani Goodyear-Ka'opua et al. (Durham, NC: Duke University Press, 2014), 51–54.

13. Lasky, "Waiahole-Waikane," 53.

14. Franklin Odo, *A Pictorial History of the Japanese in Hawaii: 1885-1924—Commemorating the Centennial of the First Arrival of Government Contracted Japanese Laborers in Hawai'i* (Honolulu: Hawai'i Immigrant Heritage Preservation Center, 1985). MacLennan, *Sovereign Sugar*, 170–171 says that the Japanese made up almost 53 percent of the population by 1900.

15. MacLennan, *Sovereign Sugar*, 170–171.

16. By virtue of its status as a US territory until 1945, the Philippines was exempted and was able to continue to send workers.

17. MacLennan, *Sovereign Sugar*, 193.

18. MacLennan, *Sovereign Sugar*, 193.

19. Takaki, *Pau Hana*, 115.

20. Takaki, *Pau Hana*, 125–126.

21. King and Roth, *Broken Trust*, 288.

22. King and Roth, *Broken Trust*, 288.

23. Takaki, *Pau Hana*, 174.

24. Davianna McGregor, *Nā Kuaʻāina: Living Hawaiian Culture* (Honolulu: University of Hawaiʻi Press, 2007), 249.

25. Lasky, "Waiahole-Waikane," 60–61.

26. King and Roth, *Broken Trust*, 53–54.

27. King and Roth, *Broken Trust*, 287–288.

28. J. Kehaulani Kauanui, "Resisting the Akaka Bill," in *A Nation Rising: Hawaiian Movements for Life, Land, and Sovereignty*, ed. Noelani Goodyear-Kaʻopua et al. (Durham, NC: Duke University Press, 2014), 315–316.

29. Troy Yoshino, "Ua Mau Ke Ea O Ka Aina I Ka Pono: Voting Rights and the Native Hawaiian Sovereignty Plebiscite," *Michigan Journal of Race and Law* 3, no. 2 (1998): 475–522.

30. Haunani-Kay Trask, *From a Native Daughter: Colonialism and Sovereignty in Hawaiʻi* (Honolulu: University of Hawaiʻi Press, 1999), 6–7.

31. Darin Arsenault, "Rhetorical Vision of the Independent and Sovereign Nation of Hawaiʻi: A Fantasy Theme Analysis," *Journal of Critical Postmodern Organization Science* 3, no. 2 (2005): 57–73.

32. Linda Hosek, "Qhana Council Builds Nation a Step at a Time," *Honolulu Star-Bulletin*, August 6, 1994; Shannon Tongonan, "State Wants Makapuʻu Campers Moved to Waimanalo," *Honolulu Advertiser*, September 24, 1993.

33. Christopher Neil, "A Year of Controversy at Beach Park," *Honolulu Advertiser*, May 21, 1994.

34. Hosek, "Qhana Council Builds Nation a Step at a Time."

35. US Congress, "S.1783: A Bill Expressing the Policy of the United States regarding the United States Relationship with Native Hawaiians and to Provide a Process for the Recognition by the United States of the Native Hawaiian Governing Entity, and of Other Purposes," 107th Congress (2001–2002), 2001, https://www.congress.gov/bill/107th-congress/senate-bill/1783/text.

36. Daniel Wood, "Hawaii's Search for Sovereignty," *Christian Science Monitor*, October 17, 1994; Arsenault, "Rhetorical Vision of the Independent and Sovereign Nation of Hawaiʻi."

37. Noelani Goodyear-Kaʻopua, *The Seeds We Planted: Portraits of a Native Hawaiian Charter School* (Minneapolis: University of Minnesota Press, 2013), 7.

38. Goodyear-Kaʻopua, *The Seeds We Planted*, 7.

39. Constance Hale, "Is the Hawaiian Language Dead or Alive," *Honolulu Magazine*, November 14, 2013, www.honolulumagazine.com/Honolulu-Magazine/November-2013/Hawaiian-Dead-or-Alive/index.php?cparticle=2&siarticle=1#artanc.

40. University of Hawaiʻi Foundation, "Saving the Hawaiian Language: The Great Work of Saving the Hawaiian Language," accessed March 12, 2021, http://uhfoundation.org/saving-hawaiian-language.

41. Kristin Pauker et al., "Race Essentialism and Social Contextual Differences in Children's Racial Stereotyping," *Child Development* 87, no. 5 (2016): 1409–1422.

42. Kristin Pauker et al., "The Role of Diversity Exposure in Whites' Reduction in Race Essentialism over Time," *Social Psychological and Personality Science* 9, no. 8 (2018): 944–952.

43. Poka Laenui, "Poka Laenui (Hayden F. Burgess)," Kalihi Palama Hawaiian Civic Club.

44. Kekoa Catherine Enomoto, "Name Change: Different Paths to a New Beginning," *Star-Bulletin*, March 31, 1998, archives.starbulletin.com/98/03/31/features/story2.html.

45. Some modern scholars, such as Jonathan Okamura, ascribe early intermarriage rates to a sex imbalance among the Hawaiian population rather than any special tolerance. See Altemus-Williams and Eriel Hobro, "Hawai'i Is Not the Multicultural Paradise Some Say It Is." But Native Hawaiians were not reportedly subject to such a sex imbalance before 1893; this was common among plantation workers, who were disproportionately non-Native Hawaiian.

Chapter 10

1. John Sides and Jack Citrin, "European Opinion about Immigration: The Role of Identities, Interests, and Information," *British Journal of Political Science* 37, no. 3 (2007): 477–504.
2. Sides, "Race, Religion, and Immigration in 2017."
3. M. D. Berzonsky, "A Social-Cognitive Perspective on Identity Construction," in *Handbook of Identity Theory and Research*, ed. Seth Schwartz, Koen Luyckx, and Vivian Vignoles (New York: Springer, 2011), 55–76.
4. Vanhanen, "Domestic Ethnic Conflict and Ethnic Nepotism," 57.
5. See Kaufmann, *Whiteshift*, 203–204.
6. Tracking news stories from the 1800s to 2010, Howe and Jackson ("Demography and Geopolitics," 32–33) find far more mentions of the phrase "population decline" linked with "nation" or "power" between 2000 and 2010 than in any earlier decade on record.
7. Kaufmann and Haklai, "Dominant Ethnicity," 743.
8. Kaufmann and Haklai, "Dominant Ethnicity," 746.
9. Côté, Mitchell, and Toft, *People Changing Places*, 87–88.
10. Côté, Mitchell, and Toft, *People Changing Places*, 88–89.
11. See Higham, *Strangers in the Land*, 3–4.
12. Hidetaka Hirota, note to author, 2018; D. Bennett, *The Party of Fear: From Nativist Movements to the New Right in American History* (New York: Vintage Books, 1995), 39.
13. Edwin Burrows and Mike Wallace, *Gotham: A History of New York City to 1898* (New York: Oxford University Press, 1999); Anbinder, *City of Dreams*.
14. Alshehabi, "Radical Transformations and Radical Contestations."
15. See Ramcharitar, "Ethnic Anxiety and Competing Citizenships in Trinidad and Tobago."
16. See Iijima, "'Nonwhiteness' in Nineteenth-Century Hawai'i."
17. See Morland, *Demographic Engineering*; Weiner and Teitelbaum, *Political Demography*.
18. Benjamin Newman, "Acculturating Contexts and Anglo Opposition to Immigration in the U.S.," *American Journal of Political Science* 57, no. 2 (2013): 374–390; Benjamin Newman and Yamil Velez, "Group Size vs. Change? Assessing Americans' Perception of Local Immigration," *Political Research Quarterly* 67, no. 2 (2014): 293–303. See also Janet Adamy and Paul Overberg, "Counties That Experienced Rapid Diversification Voted Heavily for Donald Trump," *Wall Street Journal*, November 9, 2016; Janet Adamy and Paul Overberg, "Places Most Unsettled by Rapid Demographic Change Are Drawn to Donald Trump," *Wall Street Journal*, November 1, 2016.
19. Kaufmann and Goodwin, "The Diversity Wave."
20. Kaufmann and Goodwin, "The Diversity Wave," 120, 121.
21. Seth Hill, Daniel Hopkins, and Gregory Huber, "Local Demographic Changes and US presidential voting, 2012 to 2016," *Proceedings of the National Academy of Sciences* 116, no. 50 (December 10, 2019): 25023–25028.

22. Anna Maria Mayda, Giovanni Peri, and Walter Steingress, "The Political Impact of Immigration: Evidence from the United States," National Bureau of Economic Research, Working Paper 24510, April 2018, https://www.nber.org/papers/w24510.pdf.

23. Elizabeth Paluck, Seth Green, and Donald Green, "The Contact Hypothesis Re-evaluated," *Behavioural Public Policy* 3, no. 2 (2019): 129–158.

24. Pauker et al., "Race Essentialism and Social Contextual Differences in Children's Racial Stereotyping"; Pauker et al., "The Role of Diversity Exposure in Whites' Reduction in Race Essentialism over Time."

25. Karen Alter and Michael Zürn, "Conceptualising Backlash Politics: Introduction to a Special Issue on Backlash Politics in Comparison," *British Journal of Politics and International Relations* 22, no. 4 (202): 563–584.

26. Gest, *The New Minority*; Justin Gest and Sean Gray, "Silent Citizenship: The Politics of Marginality in Unequal Democracies," *Citizenship Studies* 19, no. 5 (2015): 465–473.

27. Hirota, *Expelling the Poor.*

28. Agnes Quigg, "Kalakaua's Hawaiian Studies Abroad Program," *Hawaiian Journal of History* 22 (1988): 170–208; Stacy Kamehiro, *The Arts of Kingship: Hawaiian Art and National Culture of the Kalākaua Era* (Honolulu: University of Hawai'i Press, 2009).

29. In Singapore, it is noteworthy that, since Lee Kuan Yew and his deputies founded the People's Action Party in 1954, its core principle has been that the "multiracial" city-state belonged equally to "one united people regardless of race, religion or language."

30. Pauker et al., "Race Essentialism and Social Contextual Differences in Children's Racial Stereotyping."

31. Pauker et al., "The Role of Diversity Exposure in Whites' Reduction in Race Essentialism over Time."

32. Gordon Rohlehr, "The Culture of Williams: Context, Performance, Legacy," in *A Scuffling of Islands: Essays on Calypso*, ed. Gordon Rohlehr (Port of Spain: Lexicon, 2004), 131–139.

33. Anbinder, "From Famine to Five Points"; Anbinder, *City of Dreams.*

34. Arend Lijphart, *Democracy in Plural Societies: A Comparative Exploration* (New Haven, CT: Yale University Press, 1977); Arend Lijphart, *Patterns of Democracy: Government Forms and Performance in Thirty-Six Countries* (New Haven, CT: Yale University Press, 1999).

Chapter 11

1. Chris Jackson and Annaleise Azevedo Lohr, "2019 US Politics: Immigration Is a Much More Salient Issue for 34% of Republicans," Ipsos Public Affairs, January 16, 2019, https://www.ipsos.com/en/2019-us-politics-immigration-much-more-salient-issue-34-republicans; Edgar Grande, Tobias Schwarzbözl, and Matthias Fatke, "Politicizing Immigration in Western Europe," *Journal of European Public Policy* 26, no. 10 (2019): 1444–1463.

2. James Dennison, "How Issue Salience Explains the Rise of the Populist Right in Western Europe," *International Journal of Public Opinion Research* 32, no. 3 (2020): 397–420.

3. Philip Converse and Gregory Markus, "'Plus ça Change . . .': The New CPS Election Study Panel," *American Political Science Review* 73 (1979): 2–49; Donald Kinder and Lynn Sanders, *Divided by Color: Racial Politics and Democratic Ideals* (Chicago: University of Chicago Press, 1996); Tesler, "How Anti-immigrant Attitudes Are Fueling Support for Donald Trump."

4. Daniel Bartels, "Principled Moral Sentiment and the Flexibility of Moral Judgment and Decision Making," *Cognition* 108 (2008): 381–417; Jon Krosnick, "The Role of Attitude Importance in Social Evaluation: A Study of Policy Preferences, Presidential Candidate Evaluations, and Voting Behavior," *Journal of Personality and Social Psychology* 55, no. 2 (1988): 196–210; Jon Krosnick and Richard Petty, "Attitude Strength: An Overview," in *Ohio State University Series on Attitudes and Persuasion*, vol. 4: *Attitude Strength: Antecedents and Consequences*, ed. Jon Krosnick and Richard Petty (East Sussex: Psychology Press, 1995), 1–24; David Sears, "Symbolic Politics: A Socio-psychological Theory," in *Explorations in Political Psychology: Duke Studies in Political Psychology*, ed. Shanto Iyengar and William McGuire (Durham, NC: Duke University Press, 1993), 113–149; John Zaller, *The Nature and Origins of Mass Opinion* (Cambridge: Cambridge University Press, 1992).

5. Alexander Kustov, Dillon Laaker, and Cassidy Reller, "The Stability of Immigration Attitudes: Evidence and Implications," *Journal of Politics* 83, no. 4 (2019): 1478–1494. This material is derived from a working paper submitted to the annual meeting of the American Political Science Association: Tyler Reny and Justin Gest, "Viewers Like You: How Elite Co-Identity Reinforcement Primes Facilitate Persuasion," October 1, 2021.

6. Terry Golway, *Frank and Al: FDR, Al Smith, and the Unlikely Alliance That Created the Modern Democratic Party* (New York: St. Martin's Press, 2018), 43.

7. See Marisa Abrajano and Zoltan L. Hajnal, *White Backlash: Immigration, Race, and American Politics* (Princeton, NJ: Princeton University Press, 2015); Michael Tesler, *Post-Racial or Most Racial? Politics and Race in the Obama Era* (Chicago: University of Chicago Press, 2016); Sides, Tesler, and Vavreck, *Identity Crisis*; Andrew Geddes and Peter Scholten, *The Politics of Migration and Immigration in Europe*, 2nd ed. (London: SAGE, 2016); Robert Ford and Will Jennings, "The Changing Cleavage Politics of Western Europe," *Annual Review of Political Science* 23, no. 1 (2020): 295–314.

8. Tyler Reny, Loren Collingwood, and Ali Valenzuela, "Vote Switching in the 2016 Election: How Racial and Immigration Attitudes, Not Economics, Explain Shifts in White Voting," *Public Opinion Quarterly* 83, no. 1 (2019) 91–113; Sides, Tesler, and Vavreck, *Identity Crisis*; Ivarsflaten, "What Unites Right-Wing Populists in Western Europe?"

9. Abrajano and Hajnal, *White Backlash*; Gest, *The New Minority*.

10. Harrison and Michelson, *Listen, We Need to Talks*. See Reny and Gest, "Viewers Like You."

11. Frank Luntz, *Words That Work: It's Not What You Say, It's What People Hear* (New York: Hyperion, 2007).

12. Gary Freeman, "Modes of Immigration Policies in Liberal Democratic States," *International Migration Review* 29, no. 4 (1995): 885.

13. Grace Yukich, "Constructing the Model Immigrant: Movement Strategy and Immigrant Deservingness in the New Sanctuary Movement," *Social Problems* 60, no. 3 (August 2013): 302–320; Irene Bloemraad, Michèle Lamont, Will Kymlicka, and Leanne Son Hing, "Membership without Social Citizenship? Deservingness and Redistribution as Grounds for Equality," Daedalus: Journal of the American Academy of Arts and Science 148, no. 3 (2019): 73–104.

14. Beyond those discussed, also see Suzette Brooks Masters, "Change Is Hard: Managing Fear and Anxiety about Demographic Change and Immigration in Polarized Times," *Welcoming America*, January 2020, https://www.welcomingamerica.org/sites/default/files/Changei shard_FINAL.pdf.

15. Bobby Clark, Jeff Krehely, and David Winkler, "What the Numbers Don't Tell Us: An Evaluation of Messaging and Communications Capacity in the Pro-Immigrant Movement," Four Freedoms Fund, August 2017.
16. See Patrick Ruffini, "Far from Settled: Varied and Changing Attitudes on Immigration in America," Democracy Fund, Voter Study Group, October 2018, https://www.voterstudygr oup.org/publication/far-from-settled.
17. Ryan Senser and Eleanor Morison, "New Insights: Winning on Immigration Research Findings and Analysis," Unbound Philanthropy, October 2018.
18. The information in the next two paragraphs also appears in Justin Gest, *The White Working Class: What Everyone Needs to Know* (New York: Oxford University Press, 2018).
19. Haw. Rev. Stat. §10—2 (1993).
20. Alexander Kustov, Dillon Laaker, and Cassidy Reller, "The Stability of Immigration Attitudes: Evidence and Implications," *Journal of Politics* (2019).
21. These are the raw results; they do not filter out respondents who fail attention or comprehension checks.
22. Chris Haynes, Jennifer Merolla, and S. Karthick Ramakrishnan, *Framing Immigrants: News Coverage, Public Opinion, and Policy* (New York: Russell Sage Foundation, 2016).
23. Paul Sniderman and Sean Theriault, "The Structure of Political Argument and the Logic of Issue Framing," in *Studies in Public Opinion*, ed. Willem Saris and Paul Sniderman (Princeton, NJ: Princeton University Press, 2004), 133–165; Dennis Chong and James Druckman, "Framing Public Opinion in Competitive Democracies," *American Political Science Review* 101, no. 4 (2007): 637–655. While most attempts to reduce prejudice or exclusionary attitudes have proved unsuccessful in rigorous experimental settings (Elizabeth Paluck and Donald Green, "Prejudice Reduction: What Works? A Review and Assessment of Research and Practice," *Annual Review of Psychology* 60 [2009]: 339–367; Paluck, Green, and Green, "The Contact Hypothesis Re-evaluated"), several methods have shown promise. These include long-term interpersonal contact with outgroups (Henning Finseraas and Andreas Kotsadam, "Does Personal Contact with Ethnic Minorities Affect Anti-immigrant Sentiments? Evidence from a Field Experiment," *European Journal of Political Research* 56, no. 3 [2017]: 703–722), perspective-taking exercises via surveys and online games (Gábor Simonovits, Gábor Kézdi, and Péter Kardos, "Seeing the World through the Other's Eye: An Online Intervention Reducing Ethnic Prejudice," *American Political Science Review* 112, no. 1 [2018]: 186–193; David Broockman and Joshua Kalla, "Durably Reducing Transphobia: A Field Experiment on Door-to-Door Canvassing," *Science* 352, no. 6282 [2016]: 220–224; Joshua Kalla and David Broockman, "Reducing Exclusionary Attitudes through Interpersonal Conversation: Evidence from Three Field Experiments," *American Political Science Review* 114, no. 2 [2020]: 410–425; though see Claire Adida, Adeline Lo, and Melina Platas, "Perspective Taking Can Promote Short-Term Inclusionary Behavior toward Syrian Refugees," *Proceedings of the National Academy of Sciences* 115, no. 38 [2018]: 9521–9526) and door-to-door canvassing (Broockman and Kalla, "Durably Reducing Transphobia"), as well as through the exchange of interpersonal narratives (Kalla and Broockman, "Reducing Exclusionary Attitudes"). While these approaches are promising, they are prohibitively expensive or logistically impossible to scale up in order to reach an entire population.
24. Thomas Leeper and Rune Slothuus, "Political Parties, Motivated Reasoning, and Public Opinion Formation," *Political Psychology* 35 (2014): 129–156; Charles Taber and Milton Lodge, "Motivated Skepticism in the Evaluation of Political Beliefs," *American Journal of Political Science* 50, no. 3 (2006): 755–769.

25. Claude Steele, "The Psychology of Self-Affirmation: Sustaining the Integrity of the Self," in *Advances in Experimental Social Psychology*, vol. 21: *Social Psychological Studies of the Self: Perspectives and Programs*, ed. Leonard Berkowitz (Cambridge, MA: Academic Press, 1988), 261–302; Geoffrey Cohen, Joshua Aronson, and Claude Steele, "When Beliefs Yield to Evidence: Reducing Biased Evaluation by Affirming the Self," *Personality and Social Psychology Bulletin* 26, no. 9 (2000): 1151–1164.

26. Alex Theodoridis, "Me, Myself, and (I), (D), or (R)? Partisanship and Political Cognition through the Lens of Implicit Identity," *Journal of Politics* 79, no. 4 (2017): 1253–1267.

27. Michael Slater and Donna Rouner, "Entertainment-Education and Elaboration Likelihood: Understanding the Processing of Narrative Persuasion," *Communication Theory* 12, no. 2 (2002): 173–191. This material is derived from Reny and Gest, "Viewers Like You." Also see a larger review in Broockman and Kalla, "Durably Reducing Transphobia"; Kalla and Broockman, "Reducing Exclusionary Attitudes."

28. Michael Barber and Jeremy Pope, "Does Party Trump Ideology? Disentangling Party and Ideology in America," *American Political Science Review* 113 (2018): 1–17.

29. See Brian F. Harrison and Melissa R. Michelson, "God and Marriage: The Impact of Religious Identity Priming on Attitudes toward Same-Sex Marriage," *Social Science Quarterly* 96 no. 5 (2015): 1411–1423. See also Betina Cutaia Wilkinson, Melissa R. Michelson, and Alexis Webster, "Sports Elites, Counter-stereotypical Statements, and Immigration Attitudes," *Social Science Quarterly* (2021), published online ahead of print.

30. Mackenzie Weinger, "Hannity: I've 'Evolved' on Immigration and Support a 'Pathway to Citizenship,'" *Politico*, November 8, 2012, https://www.politico.com/blogs/media/2012/11/hannity-ive-evolved-on-immigration-and-support-a-pathway-to-citizenship-149078.

31. And because Wagner's audio was a replica of the impersonation a voice actor had recorded for the Pence impression, we know that Wagner's appeal is not unique to his linguistic cadence or style.

32. We find that the message is most likely to move respondents' attitudes about a pathway to citizenship, job-training programs, welfare benefits, and establishing a Hispanic heritage month, all policies aimed at accommodation. It did not, however, change attitudes about deportation.

33. Henri Tajfel and John Turner, "An Integrative Theory of Inter-group Conflict," in *The Social Psychology of Inter-group Relations*, ed. W. G. Austin and S. Worchel (Monterey, CA: Brooks/Cole, 1979), 33–47; Leonie Huddy and Alexa Bankert, "Political Partisanship as a Social Identity: Groups and Identities, Political Psychology," *Oxford Research Encyclopedia of Politics*, May 2017.

34. Taber and Lodge, "Motivated Skepticism in the Evaluation of Political Beliefs."

35. Andrew Guess and Alexander Coppock, "Does Counter-Attitudinal Information Cause Backlash? Results from Three Large Survey Experiments," *British Journal of Political Science* 50, no. 4 (2020): 1497–1515.

36. The study summarized in this section is from Reny and Gest, "Viewers Like You."

Chapter 12

1. Yocelin Gallardo, "Zapata County Turns Red for 2020 Election," KGNS TV, November 4, 2020, https://www.kgns.tv/2020/11/05/zapata-county-turns-red-for-2020-election/.

2. Branda Camacho, "Webb County Republicans Double Turnout in 2020 Election," KGNS TV, November 5, 2020, https://www.kgns.tv/2020/11/06/webb-county-republicans-dou ble-turnout-in-2020-election/.

3. Molly Hennessy-Fiske, "'We've Only Started': How Latino Support for Trump Grew in Texas Borderlands," *Los Angeles Times*, November 12, 2020, https://www.latimes.com/ world-nation/story/2020-11-12/latino-support-grew-for-trump-on-the-texas-border.

4. Jack Herrera, "Trump Didn't Win the Latino Vote in Texas: He Won the Tejano Vote," *Politico*, November 17, 2020, https://www.politico.com/news/magazine/2020/11/17/ trump-latinos-south-texas-tejanos-437027.

5. Hennessy-Fiske, "'We've Only Started.'"

6. Herrera, "Trump Didn't Win the Latino Vote in Texas."

7. Hennessy-Fiske, "'We've Only Started'"; Mitchell Ferman, "Donald Trump Made Inroads in South Texas This Year: These Voters Explain Why," *Texas Tribune*, November 13, 2020, https://www.texastribune.org/2020/11/13/south-texas-voters-donald-trump/; Michael Powell, Cecilia Ballí, and Betsabeth Monica Lugo, "Real Talk: Understanding Texas Latino Voters through Meaningful Conversation," Texas Organizing Project Education Fund, 2020, https://drive.google.com/file/d/12yQDyRxZiYg7Wzvm6c19pewM70jjBwxd/view.

8. Elizabeth Findell, "Why Democrats Lost So Many South Texas Latinos—The Economy," *Wall Street Journal*, November 8, 2020, https://www.wsj.com/articles/how-democrats-lost-so-many-south-texas-latinosthe-economy-11604871650.

9. Herrera, "Trump Didn't Win the Latino Vote in Texas."

10. Herrera, "Trump Didn't Win the Latino Vote in Texas."

11. Herrera, "Trump Didn't Win the Latino Vote in Texas."

12. Herrera, "Trump Didn't Win the Latino Vote in Texas."

13. Cat Cardenas, "Why Did Joe Biden Lose Ground with Latinos in South Texas?," *Texas Monthly*, November 11, 2020, https://www.texasmonthly.com/politics/latinos-biden-trump-south-texas/.

14. Gary Gerstle, *American Crucible: Race and Nation in the Twentieth Century* (Princeton, NJ: Princeton University Press, 2017), 4.

15. Gerstle, *American Crucible*, 4.

16. Paul Frymer, *Building an American Empire: The Era of Territorial and Political Expansion* (Princeton, NJ: Princeton University Press, 2019), 19–20.

17. Frymer, *Building an American Empire*, 194.

18. Frymer, *Building an American Empire*, 18.

19. Frymer, *Building an American Empire*, 139.

20. Lake and Reynolds, *Drawing the Global Colour Line*, 19.

21. Vasiliki Fouka, Soumyajit Mazumder, and Marco Tabellini, "From Immigrants to Americans: Race and Assimilation during the Great Migration," IDEAS Working Paper Series from RePEc, May 2018, 23–24, https://economics.mit.edu/files/15100.

22. Higham, *Strangers in the Land*, 11.

23. See Kaufmann, *Rise and Fall of Anglo-America*, 2–5.

24. Charles Pearson, *National Life and Character: A Forecast* (London: Macmillan, 1894), 90.

25. Theodore Roosevelt, "National Life and Character," *Sewanee Review* 2, no. 3 (1894): 353–376.

26. Theodore Roosevelt to Charles Pearson, May 11, 1894, Pearson Papers, Bodleian Library, MS English letters, folio pages 187–191, d. 190, cited in Lake and Reynolds, *Drawing the Global Colour Line*, 103.

27. Theodore Roosevelt, "National Life and Character," in *American Ideals and Other Essays Social and Political* (New York, Putnam's Sons, 1897), 293–294.

28. Roosevelt, "National Life and Character," 277.

29. Edward Ross, "The Causes of Race Superiority," *Annals of the American Academy of Political and Social Science* 18 (July 1901): 88.

30. Roosevelt, "National Life and Character," 282–283.

31. The information in this paragraph was elaborated at some length by Lake and Reynolds, *Drawing the Global Colour Line*, 266–267.

32. Richard Alba, *The Great Demographic Illusion: Majority, Minority, and the Expanding American Mainstream* (Princeton, NJ: Princeton University Press, 2020), chapter 1.

33. Alba, *The Great Demographic Illusion*, 64–66.

34. Alba, *The Great Demographic Illusion*, 85.

35. Alba, *The Great Demographic Illusion*, 73–74.

36. Alba, *The Great Demographic Illusion*, 120–121.

37. Alba, *The Great Demographic Illusion*, 4–5.

38. Alba, *The Great Demographic Illusion*, 8.

39. Alba, *The Great Demographic Illusion*, 257–258.

40. Alba, *The Great Demographic Illusion*, 261–262.

41. Pauker et al., "Race Essentialism"; Alba et al., "The Rise of Mixed Parentage."

42. For example, see Jens Manuel Krogstad and Mark Hugo Lopez, "Latino Voters Have Growing Confidence in Biden on Key Issues, While Confidence in Trump Remains Low," Pew Research Center, October 16, 2020, https://www.pewresearch.org/fact-tank/2020/10/16/latino-voters-have-growing-confidence-in-biden-on-key-issues-while-confidence-in-trump-remains-low/; Matt Lavietes, "There Will Be a Record Number of Hispanic Voters in 2020, and That Could Have a Major Impact on Trump's Political Fate," CNBC, February 7, 2019, https://www.cnbc.com/2019/02/07/surge-in-hispanic-voters-could-have-major-impact-on-trump-re-election-bid.html; Andres Oppenheimer, "Commentary: The Hispanic Vote Has Been a Sleeping Giant, but There Are Signs That It Will Wake in 2020," *Morning Call*, September 17, 2019, https://www.mcall.com/opinion/mc-opi-hispanic-voting-2020-registered-20190917-x3jbwpor4ff3fl7bt7pexeg62a-story.html; Suzanne Gamboa, "Latinos Downgrade Trump on Coronavirus Response, Kick Up Biden Support, Poll Shows," NBC News, August 17, 2020, https://www.nbcnews.com/news/latino/latinos-downgrade-trump-coronavirus-response-kick-biden-support-poll-shows-n1236963.

43. For example, see Benjamin Newman et al., "The Trump Effect: An Experimental Investigation of the Emboldening Effect of Racially Inflammatory Elite Communication," *British Journal of Political Science* 51, no. 3 (2021): 1138–1159; Eric Knowles and Linda Tropp, "Donald Trump and the Rise of White Identity in Politics," *The Conversation*, October 20, 2016, https://theconversation.com/donald-trump-and-the-rise-of-white-identity-in-politics-67037; T. Lopez Bunyasi, "The Role of Whiteness in the 2016 Presidential Primaries," *Perspectives on Politics* 17, no. 3 (2019): 679–698.

44. John Burnett, "Transcript: White House Chief of Staff John Kelly's Interview with NPR," NPR, May 11, 2018, https://www.npr.org/2018/05/11/610116389/transcript-white-house-chief-of-staff-john-kellys-interview-with-npr. Kelly's full response: "The name of the game to a large degree. Let me step back and tell you that the vast majority of the people that move illegally into United States are not bad people. They're not criminals. They're not MS-13. Some of them are not. But they're also not people that would easily assimilate into the United States into our modern society. They're overwhelmingly rural people in the

countries they come from—fourth, fifth, sixth grade educations are kind of the norm. They don't speak English, obviously that's a big thing. They don't speak English. They don't integrate well, they don't have skills. They're not bad people. They're coming here for a reason. And I sympathize with the reason. But the laws are the laws. But a big name of the game is deterrence."

45. It is clear that the treatments registered. Those in the two treatment groups reported feeling nearly twice as "angry," "unhappy," and "less hopeful" after reading the marginalizing statements.

46. Remarkably, the marginalizing rhetoric *increased* respondents' perceived centrality to society. Even if it's not clear what these alternative sources of belonging may be—it's clearly not as fellow Americans or as Hispanics—they are sufficient to reinforce Hispanic respondents' sense of status.

47. Alba, *The Great Demographic Illusion*, 244.

48. Alba, *The Great Demographic Illusion*, 244.

Chapter 13

1. Kaufmann, *Whiteshift*.

2. Stephen Smith, Wilma Lee Steele, and Tina Russell, "We Are Proud to Be 'Rednecks': It's Time to Reclaim That Term," *The Guardian*, April 14, 2018, https://www.theguardian.com/us-news/2018/apr/14/redneck-pride-west-virginia-protests-strikes.

3. "Ad Council Launches 'Belonging Begins with Us' Campaign Featuring Exclusive New Music from Lake Street Dive," *PR Newswire*, December 3, 2020, https://www.prnewswire.com/news-releases/ad-council-launches-belonging-begins-with-us-campaign-featuring-exclusive-new-music-from-lake-street-dive-301185344.html.

4. Jennifer Jacobs, "Biden Administration Will Create Position to Reach Conservatives," *Bloomberg News*, December 7, 2020, https://www.bloomberg.com/news/articles/2020-12-08/biden-administration-will-create-position-to-reach-conservatives.

5. This is based on an analysis by New American Economy, which examines change in the Census Bureau's Diversity Index from 2010 to 2020. The Diversity Index shows the likelihood that two residents chosen at random in a given area will be of different races and/or ethnicities. See New American Economy, "The United States Is More Diverse Than Ever, in More Places Than Ever," September 23, 2021, https://data.newamericaneconomy.org/en/census2020/.

Appendix

1. We preregistered our design and analyses with OSF.io before full data collection commenced. IRB approval was acquired for the full survey experiment.

2. C. Tausanovitch, L. Vavreck, T. Reny, A. Rossell Hayes, and A. Rudkin, "Democracy Fund + UCLA Nationscape Methodology and Representativeness Assessment," Democracy Fund + UCLA Nationscape Project, 2019, https://www.voterstudygroup.org/uploads/reports/Data/Nationscape-Methodology-RepresentativenessAssessment.pdf; Alexander Coppock and Oliver A. McClellan, "Validating the Demographic, Political, Psychological, and Experimental Results Obtained from a New Source of Online Survey Respondents,"

Research & Politics 6, no. 1 (2019), https://journals.sagepub.com/doi/10.1177/205316801
8822174.

3. We preregistered our design and analyses with OSF.io before full data collection commenced. IRB approval was acquired for all pilot tests and the full survey experiment.

4. We ensured compliance with the treatment in a few different ways. First, we ensured that respondents had working speakers and could watch video on their device by having them pass a video and audio check (picture of a cow and audio of a dog barking) before they could proceed to the video. The video itself was hosted on YouTube to maximize compatibility across mobile devices and browsers and minimize streaming issues with slow internet. We set a timer for the duration of the video so that respondents couldn't skip the video without waiting for twenty seconds, removed the scroll bar from the video so they had to watch the entire thing, and embedded a code at the end of the video that respondents had to enter into a text box correctly before proceeding.

5. We measured but did not include an item on English-language-only policy because the reverse-coding was clearly confusing for respondents and does not correlate with other immigration policy attitudes. While the inclusion of the item, a departure from our pre-analysis plan, does not change substantive findings of the study, we have omitted it from all analyses.

6. We further probe this relationship by breaking Republicans into strong versus weak partisanship (as measured by branching partisan identity question), those with stronger versus weaker partisan identity, and those high or low in self-monitoring. See Leonie Huddy, Liliana Mason, and Lene Aaroe, "Expressive Partisanship: Campaign Involvement, Political Emotion, and Partisan Identity," *American Political Science Review* 109, no. 1 (2015): 1–17; Elizabeth Connors, "The Social Dimension of Political Values," *Political Behavior* 42 (2020): 961–982.

7. By examining partisan subgroups separately, we are theoretically assuming, of course, that respondent partisanship is moderating the treatment effects we observe in each, though we acknowledge that making a causal moderation claim here requires randomly assigning respondent partisanship, which is infeasible (Kam and Trussler 2017).

8. Henri Tajfel and John Turner, "An Integrative Theory of Inter-Group Conflict," in *The Social Psychology of Inter-Group Relations*, ed. W. G. Austin and S. Worchel (Monterey, CA: Brooks/Cole, 1979), 33–47; Leonie Huddy and Alexa Bankert, "Political Partisanship as a Social Identity: Groups and Identities, Political Psychology," *Oxford Research Encyclopedia of Politics*, May 2017.

9. See Connors, "The Social Dimension of Political Values."

10. Charles Taber and Milton Lodge, "Motivated Skepticism in the Evaluation of Political Beliefs," *American Journal of Political Science* 50, no. 3 (2006): 755–769.

Bibliography

Aaron, Jalil. "Some Facts about Singapore." In *Development and Commemoration of National Day*. Singapore: Usaha Enterprises, 1967.

Abascal, Maria. "Us and Them: Black-White Relations in the Wake of Hispanic Population Growth." *American Sociological Review* 80, no. 4 (2015): 789–813.

Abrajano, Marisa, and Zoltan L. Hajnal. *White Backlash: Immigration, Race, and American Politics*. Princeton, NJ: Princeton University Press, 2015.

Aching, Gerard. *Masking and Power: Carnival and Popular Culture in the Caribbean*. Minneapolis: University of Minnesota Press, 2002.

Adam, Shamim. "Singapore Curry Protest Heats Up Vote with Facebook Campaign." *Bloomberg*, August 18, 2011. http://www.bloomberg.com/news/2011-08-18/singapore-curry-protest-heats-up-vote.html.

Adamy, Janet, and Paul Overberg. "Counties That Experienced Rapid Diversification Voted Heavily for Donald Trump." *Wall Street Journal*, November 9, 2016.

Adamy, Janet, and Paul Overberg. "Places Most Unsettled by Rapid Demographic Change Are Drawn to Donald Trump." *Wall Street Journal*, November 1, 2016.

"Ad Council Launches 'Belonging Begins with Us' Campaign Featuring Exclusive New Music from Lake Street Dive." *PR Newswire*, December 3, 2020. https://www.prnewswire.com/news-releases/ad-council-launches-belonging-begins-with-us-campaign-featuring-exclusive-new-music-from-lake-street-dive-301185344.html.

Adida, Claire, Adeline Lo, and Melina Platas. "Perspective Taking Can Promote Short-Term Inclusionary Behavior toward Syrian Refugees." *Proceedings of the National Academy of Sciences* 115, no. 38 (2018): 9521–9526.

Alba, Richard. *The Great Demographic Illusion: Majority, Minority, and the Changing American Mainstream*. Princeton, NJ: Princeton University Press, 2020.

Alba, Richard, Brenden Beck, and Duygu Basaran Sahin. "The Rise of Mixed Parentage: A Sociological and Demographic Phenomenon to Be Reckoned With." *Annals of the American Academy of Political and Social Science* 677, no. 1 (2018): 26–38.

Alba, Richard, and Nancy Foner. *Strangers No More: Immigration and the Challenges of Integration in North America and Western Europe*. Princeton, NJ: Princeton University Press, 2006.

Alba, Richard, and Victor Nee. *Remaking the American Mainstream: Assimilation and Contemporary Immigration*. Cambridge, MA: Harvard University Press, 2003.

Alemán, José, and Dwayne Woods. "No Way Out: Travel Restrictions and Authoritarian Regimes." *Migration and Development* 3, no. 2 (2014): 285–305.

Ali, Shameen. "Indian Diaspora and Renaissance, 1941–1946." In *Calcutta to Caroni and the Indian Diaspora*, edited by John La Guerre and Ann Marie Bissessar, 480–498. St. Augustine: UWI School for Continuing Studies, 2005.

Allahar, Anton. "Popular Culture and Racialisation of Political Consciousness in Trinidad and Tobago." In *Identity, Ethnicity and Culture in the Caribbean*, edited by Ralph Premdas, 246–281. St. Augustine: UWI School of Continuing Studies, 2003.

Allen, Danielle. "Charlottesville Is Not the Continuation of an Old Fight: It Is Something New." *Washington Post*, August 14, 2017. https://www.washingtonpost.com/opinions/charlottesvi

lle-is-not-the-continuation-of-an-old-fight-it-is-something-new/2017/08/13/971812f6-8029-11e7-b359-15a3617c767b_story.html.

Allen, Danielle. "Toward a Connected Society." In *Our Compelling Interests: The Value of Diversity for Democracy and a Prosperous Society*, edited by Earl Lewis and Nancy Cantor, 71–105. Princeton, NJ: Princeton University Press, 2016.

Allen, Richard Blair. *Slaves, Freedmen, and Indentured Laborers in Colonial Mauritius.* Cambridge: Cambridge University Press, 1999.

Al-Naqeeb, Khaldoun Nassan, et al. *Society and State in the Gulf and Arab Peninsula: A Different Perspective.* Vol. 4. London: Routledge, 2013.

Alshehabi, Omar Hesham. "Radical Transformations and Radical Contestations: Bahrain's Spatial-Demographic Revolution." *Middle East Critique* 23, no. 1 (2014): 29–51.

Altemus-Williams, Imani, and Marie Eriel Hobro. "Hawai'i Is Not the Multicultural Paradise Some Say It Is." *National Geographic*, May 17, 2021. https://www.nationalgeographic.com/culture/article/hawaii-not-multicultural-paradise-some-say-it-is.

Alter, Karen, and Michael Zürn. "Conceptualising Backlash Politics: Introduction to a Special Issue on Backlash Politics in Comparison." *British Journal of Politics and International Relations* 22, no. 4 (2020): 563–584.

Anbinder, Tyler. *City of Dreams: The 400-Year Epic History of Immigrant New York.* Boston: Houghton Mifflin Harcourt, 2016.

Anbinder, Tyler. "From Famine to Five Points: Lord Lansdowne's Irish Tenants Encounter North America's Most Notorious Slum." *American Historical Review* 107, no. 2 (2002): 350–387.

Anderson, Benedict. *Imagined Communities: Reflections on the Origin and Spread of Nationalism.* New York: Verso, 1983.

Ang, Sylvia. "The 'New Chinatown': The Racialization of Newly Arrived Chinese Migrants in Singapore." *Journal of Ethnic and Migration Studies* 44, no. 7 (2018): 1177–1194.

Archer, Seth. *Sharks upon the Land: Colonialism, Indigenous Health, and Culture in Hawai'i, 1778–1855.* New York: Cambridge University Press, 2018.

Arsenault, Darin. "Rhetorical Vision of the Independent and Sovereign Nation of Hawai'i: A Fantasy Theme Analysis." *Journal of Critical Postmodern Organization Science* 3, no. 2 (2005): 57–73.

Babar, Zahra. "The 'Enemy Within': Citizenship-Stripping in the Post–Arab Spring GCC." *Middle East Journal* 71, no. 4 (Autumn, 2017): 525–543.

Bahrain Authority for Culture and Antiquities Cultural and National Heritage. "Pearling Path: The Seashore." 2020. https://pearlingpath.bh/en/location/the-seashore/.

"Bahrain Bans Newspaper for 'Sowing Division.'" *Yahoo News*, June 4, 2017. https://www.yahoo.com/news/bahrain-bans-newspaper-sowing-division-153554750.

Bahrain Institute of Human Rights and Democracy. "Bahraini Court Revokes 138 Individuals of Their Citizenship and Sentences 69 to Life in a Mass Trial." April 16, 2019. http://birdbh.org/2019/04/bahraini-court-revokes-138-individuals-of-their-citizenship-in-a-mass-trial/.

"Bahrain Revokes Top Shii Cleric Isa Qassim's Citizenship." BBC News, June 20, 2016. https://www.bbc.com/news/world-middle-east-36578000.

Bahry, Louay. "The Socioeconomic Foundations of the Shiite Opposition in Bahrain." *Mediterranean Quarterly* 11 (2000): 129–143.

Balkaransingh, Satnarine. "Chutney Crosses over into Chutney Soca in Trinidad and Tobago Carnival." In *Identity, Ethnicity and Culture in the Caribbean*, edited by Ralph Premdas, 47–53. St. Augustine: UWI School of Continuing Studies, 2003.

Ballengee, Christopher. "From Indian to Indo-Creole: Tassa Drumming, Creolization, and Indo-Caribbean Nationalism in Trinidad and Tobago." PhD dissertation, University of Florida, 2013.

Barber, Michael, and Pope, Jeremy. "Does Party Trump Ideology? Disentangling Party and Ideology in America." *American Political Science Review* 113 (2018): 1–17.

Barr, Michael. *Lee Kuan Yew: The Beliefs Behind the Man.* Richmond, UK: Curzon, 2000.

Barr, Michael D., and Zlatko Skrbis. *Constructing Singapore: Elitism, Ethnicity, and the Nation Building Project.* Copenhagen: Nordic Institute of Asian Studies, 2008.

Bartels, Daniel. "Principled Moral Sentiment and the Flexibility of Moral Judgment and Decision Making." *Cognition* 108 (2008): 381–417.

Bateman, David. "The Dilemmas of Democratic Peoplehood." Working Paper, Cornell University, Ithaca, NY. 2018.

Bayor, Ronald, and Timothy Meagher. *The New York Irish.* Baltimore, MD: Johns Hopkins University Press, 1996.

Beaugrand, Claire. "Deconstructing Minorities/Majorities in Parliamentary Gulf States (Kuwait and Bahrain)." *British Journal of Middle Eastern Studies* 43, no. 2 (2016): 234–249.

Bennett, D. *The Party of Fear: From Nativist Movements to the New Right in American History.* New York: Vintage Books, 1995.

Berzonsky, M. D. "A Social-Cognitive Perspective on Identity Construction." In *Handbook of Identity Theory and Research,* edited by Seth Schwartz, Koen Luyckx, and Vivian Vignoles, 55–76. New York: Springer, 2011.

Betz, Hans-George. "The New Politics of Resentment: Radical Right Wing Populist Parties in Western Europe." *Comparative Politics* 25 (1993): 413–427.

"Blair Defines 'British Values.'" BBC News, March 28, 2000. http://news.bbc.co.uk/2/hi/uk_n ews/politics/693591.stm.

Bloemraad, Irene, Michèle Lamont, Will Kymlicka, and Leanne Son Hing. "Membership without Social Citizenship? Deservingness and Redistribution as Grounds for Equality." *Daedalus: Journal of the American Academy of Arts and Science* 148, no. 3 (2019): 73–104.

"Blunkett Names 'Britishness' Chief." BBC News, September 10, 2002. http://news.bbc.co.uk/2/ hi/uk_news/politics/2248319.stm.

Boswell, Rosabelle. "Can Justice Be Achieved for Slave Descendents in Mauritius?" *International Journal of Law, Crime and Justice* 42, no. 2 (2014): 146–161.

Boswell, Rosabelle. "Heritage Tourism and Identity in the Mauritian Villages of Chamarel and Le Morne." *Journal of Southern African Studies* 31, no. 2 (2005): 283–295.

Boucher, Anna, and Justin Gest. *Crossroads: Comparative Immigration Regimes in a World of Demographic Change.* New York: Cambridge University Press, 2018.

Braithwaite, Lloyd. "Social Stratification in Trinidad: A Preliminary Analysis." *Social and Economic Studies* 2, nos. 2–3 (1953): 5–175.

Brennan, Lance, John Mcdonald, and Ralph Shlomowitz. "The Geographic and Social Origins of Indian Indentured Labourers in Mauritius, Natal, Fiji, Guyana and Jamaica." *South Asia: Journal of South Asian Studies* 21 (1998): 39–71.

Brereton, Bridget. *Race Relations in Colonial Trinidad 1870–1900.* Cambridge: Cambridge University Press, 1979.

Broockman, David, and Joshua Kalla. "Durably Reducing Transphobia: A Field Experiment on Door-to-Door Canvassing." *Science* 352, no. 6282 (2016): 220–224.

Brubaker, Rogers. "The Manichean Myth: Rethinking the Distinction between 'Civic' and 'Ethnic' Nationalism." In *Nations and National Identity: The European Experience in Perspective,* edited by Hanspeter Kriesi, Klaus Armington, Hannes Siegrist, and Andreas Wimmer, 55–71. Zurich: Verlag Ruegger, 1999.

Burnett, John. "Transcript: White House Chief of Staff John Kelly's Interview with NPR." NPR, May 11, 2018. https://www.npr.org/2018/05/11/610116389/transcript-white-house-chief-of-staff-john-kellys-interview-with-npr.

Burrows, Edwin, and Mike Wallace. *Gotham: A History of New York City to 1898.* New York: Oxford University Press, 1999.

Camacho, Brenda. "Webb County Republicans Double Turnout in 2020 Election." KGNS TV, November 5, 2020. https://www.kgns.tv/2020/11/06/webb-county-republicans-double-turnout-in-2020-election/.

Campbell, Carl. "Black Testators: Fragments of the Lives of Free Africans and Free Creole Blacks in Trinidad 1813–1877." In *The Colonial Caribbean in Transition: Essays on Postemancipation and Cultural History*, edited by Bridget Brereton and Kevin Yelvington, 43–54. Kingston: The Press, University of the West Indies, 1999.

Cangy, Jean-Clément. *Le Séga, des origines . . . à nos jours*. Port Louis, Mauritius: Makanbo, 2012.

Cardenas, Cat. "Why Did Joe Biden Lose Ground with Latinos in South Texas?" *Texas Monthly*, November 11, 2020. https://www.texasmonthly.com/politics/latinos-biden-trump-south-texas/.

Carter, Robert A. *Sea of Pearls: Arabia, Persia, and the Industry That Shaped the Gulf*. London: Arabian, 2012.

Case, William. *Politics in Southeast Asia: Democracy or Less*. London: Routledge Curzon, 2002.

Census of the State of New York for 1855. Albany, NY: 1857.

Chalcraft, John. "Monarchy, Migration and Hegemony in the Arabian Peninsula." London School of Economics and Political Science, Kuwait Programme on Development, Governance and Globalisation in the Gulf States, Paper 12. 2010.

Champion, Daryl. "The Kingdom of Saudi Arabia: Elements of Instability within Stability." *Meria* 3, no. 4 (1999): 1–23.

Chatterjee, Partha. *The Nation and Its Fragments: Colonial and Postcolonial Histories*. Princeton, NJ: Princeton University Press, 1993.

Chong, Dennis, and James Druckman. "Framing Public Opinion in Competitive Democracies." *American Political Science Review* 101, no. 4 (2007): 637–655.

Chowdhury, Amitava. "Maroon Archaeological Research in Mauritius and Its Possible Implications in a Global Context." In *The Archaeology of Slavery: Toward a Comparative Global Framework*, edited by Lydia Wilson Marshall, 255–275. Carbondale: Southern Illinois University Press, 2014.

Chowdhury, Amitava. "Narratives of Home: Diaspora Formations among the Indian Indentured Labourers." In *Between Dispersion and Belonging: Global Approaches to Diaspora in Practice*, edited by Amitava Chowdhury and Donald H. Akenson, 240–253. Montreal: McGill-Queen's University Press, 2016.

Chua, Beng Huat. "Culture, Multi-Racialism, and National Identity in Singapore." In *Trajectories: Inter Asia Cultural Studies*, edited by Kuan-Hsing Chen et al., 186–205. London: Routledge, 1998.

Chua, Beng Huat. "Multiculturalism in Singapore: An Instrument of Social Control." *Race and Class* 44, no. 3 (2003): 58–77.

"Citizenship as a Bahraini Government Tool." *Stratfor Worldview*, September 21, 2012. https://worldview.stratfor.com/article/citizenship-bahraini-government-tool.

Clark, Bobby, Jeff Krehely, and David Winkler. "What the Numbers Don't Tell Us: An Evaluation of Messaging and Communications Capacity in the Pro-Immigrant Movement." Four Freedoms Fund, August 2017. New York, NY.

Clarke, Angela. *The Islands of Bahrain: An Illustrated Guide to Their Heritage*. Manama: Bahrain Historical and Archaeological Society, 1981.

"The Coffee Shop Divide." *Straits Times*, April 25, 2008.

Cohen, Geoffrey, Joshua Aronson, and Claude Steele. "When Beliefs Yield to Evidence: Reducing Biased Evaluation by Affirming the Self." *Personality and Social Psychology Bulletin* 26, no. 9 (2000): 1151–1164.

Colby, Sandra, and Jennifer Ortman. "Projections of the Size and Composition of the U.S. Population: 2014 to 2060." US Census Bureau, 2015. https://www.census.gov/content/dam/Census/library/publications/2015/demo/p25-1143.pdf.

Connors, Elizabeth. "The Social Dimension of Political Values." *Political Behavior* 42 (2020): 961–982.

Converse, Philip, and Gregory Markus. "'Plus ça Change . . .': The New CPS Election Study Panel." *American Political Science Review* 73 (1979): 2–49.

Cook, Adrian. *The Armies of the Street: The New York City Draft Riots of 1863*. Lexington: University Press of Kentucky, 1982.

Coppock, Alexander, and Oliver A. McClellan. "Validating the Demographic, Political, Psychological, and Experimental Results Obtained from a New Source of Online Survey Respondents." *Research & Politics* 6, no. 1 (2019). https://journals.sagepub.com/doi/10.1177/2053168018822174.

Côté, Isabelle, Matthew Mitchell, and Monica Toft. *People Changing Places: New Perspectives on Demography, Migration, Conflict, and the State*. London: Routledge, 2018.

Craig, Maureen, and Richeson, Jennifer. "More Diverse yet Less Tolerant? How the Increasingly Diverse Racial Landscape Affects White Americans' Racial Attitudes." *Personality and Social Psychology Bulletin* 40, no. 6 (2014): 750–761.

Crawfurd, John. *Journal of an Embassy from the Governor-General of India to the Courts of Siam and Cochin China*. London: Colburn and Bentley, 1830.

David, Jacques. *Mauritius: The Slave Legacy*. New Delhi, India: Ajanta Offset and Packagings, 2010.

De Freitas, Patricia. "Playing Mas': The Construction and Deconstruction of National Identity in the Trinidad Carnival." PhD thesis. McMaster University, 1994.

Dennison, James. "How Issue Salience Explains the Rise of the Populist Right in Western Europe." *International Journal of Public Opinion Research* 32, no. 3 (2020): 397–420.

Dolan, Jay. *The Irish Americans: A History*. New York: Bloomsbury Press, 2008.

Donnelly, James. *The Great Irish Potato Famine*. Phoenix Mill: Sutton, 2001.

Doyle, David Noel. "The Irish in North America, 1776–1845." In *Making the Irish American: History and Heritage of the Irish in the United States*, edited by J. J. Lee and Marion Casey, 171–212. New York: New York University Press, 2006.

Doyle, David Noel. "The Remaking of Irish America, 1845–1880." In *Making the Irish American: History and Heritage of the Irish in the United States*, edited by J. J. Lee and Marion Casey, 213–252. New York: New York University Press, 2006.

Duffy, Patrick. *To and from Ireland: Planned Migration Schemes c. 1600–2000*. Dublin: Geography Publications, 2004.

Edensor, Tim. *National Identity, Public Culture, and Everyday Life*. Oxford: Berg, 2002.

Enomoto, Kekoa Catherine. "Name Change: Different Paths to a New Beginning." *Star-Bulletin*, March 31, 1998. archives.starbulletin.com/98/03/31/features/story2.html.

Enos, Ryan. "The Causal Effect of Intergroup Contact on Exclusionary Attitudes." *Proceedings of the National Academy of Sciences of the United States of America* 111, no. 10 (2014): 3699–3704.

Erie, Steven. *Rainbow's End: Irish-Americans and the Dilemmas of Urban Machine Politics, 1840–1985*. Oakland: University of California Press, 1990.

Eriksen, Thomas Hyland. *Ethnicity and Nationalism: Anthropological Perspectives*. 3rd ed. London: Pluto Press, 1994.

Ernst, Robert. *Immigrant Life in New York City, 1825–1863*. Syracuse, NY: Syracuse University Press, 1994.

F., Kathleen. "Activist Sangeetha Thanapal Receives Stern Warning from Authorities after Calling Singapore 'a Terribly Racist Country.'" *Online Citizen*, January 30, 2019. https://www.straitstimes.com/singapore/courts-crime/activist-sangeetha-thanapal-issued-stern-warning-for-facebook-post-that.

Fargues, Philippe. "Immigration without Inclusion: Non-Nationals in Nation-Building in the Gulf States." *Asian and Pacific Migration Journal* 20, nos. 3–4 (2011): 273–292.

Fergusson, Isaac. "Carnival's Controversies: Tensions Underscore Island Fest." *Billboard*, March 29, 1997.

Ferman, Mitchell. "Donald Trump Made Inroads in South Texas This Year: These Voters Explain Why." *Texas Tribune*, November 13, 2020. https://www.texastribune.org/2020/11/13/south-texas-voters-donald-trump/.

Fibiger, Thomas. "Global Display—Local Dismay: Debating 'Globalized Heritage' in Bahrain." *History and Anthropology* 22, no. 2 (2011): 187–202.

Fibiger, Thomas. "Heritage Erasure and Heritage Transformation: How Heritage Is Created by Destruction in Bahrain." *International Journal of Heritage Studies* 21, no. 4 (2015): 390–404.

Findell, Elizabeth. "Why Democrats Lost So Many South Texas Latinos—The Economy." *Wall Street Journal*, November 8, 2020. https://www.wsj.com/articles/how-democrats-lost-so-many-south-texas-latinosthe-economy-11604871650.

Finseraas, Henning, and Andreas Kotsadam. "Does Personal Contact with Ethnic Minorities Affect Anti-immigrant Sentiments? Evidence from a Field Experiment." *European Journal of Political Research* 56, no. 3 (2017): 703–722.

Fitzgerald, David, and David Cook-Martin. *Culling the Masses: The Democratic Origins of Racist Immigration Policy in the Americas*. London: Harvard University Press, 2014.

Foner, Eric. *Free Soil, Free Labor, Free Men: The Ideology of the Republican Party before the Civil War*. Oxford: Oxford University Press, 1995.

Foner, Eric. *The Story of American Freedom*. New York: Norton, 1998.

Foner, Nancy. *From Ellis Island to JFK: New York's Two Great Waves of Immigration*. New Haven, CT: Yale University Press, 2000.

Foner, Nancy. *Islands in the City: West Indian Migration to New York*. Berkeley: University of California Press, 2001.

Fong, Pang Eng. "Foreign Talent and Development in Singapore." In *Competing for Global Talent*, edited by Christiane Kuptsch and Pang Eng Fong, 155–168. Geneva: International Labour Office, 2006.

Ford, Robert, and Will Jennings. "The Changing Cleavage Politics of Western Europe." *Annual Review of Political Science* 23, no. 1 (2020): 295–314.

Fouka, Vasiliki, Soumyajit Mazumder, and Marco Tabellini. "From Immigrants to Americans: Race and Assimilation during the Great Migration." IDEAS Working Paper Series from RePEc. May 2018. https://economics.mit.edu/files/15100.

Freeman, Gary. "Modes of Immigration Policies in Liberal Democratic States." *International Migration Review* 29, no. 4 (1995): 881–902.

Frost, Mark. "An Unsettled Majority: Immigration and the Racial 'Balance' in Multicultural Singapore." *Journal of Ethnic and Migration Studies*, July 22, 2020. https://www.tandfonline.com/doi/full/10.1080/1369183X.2020.1774112.

Frost, Mark, and Yu-Mei Balasinghamchow. *Singapore: A Biography*. Singapore: Hong Kong University Press, 2009.

Frymer, Paul. *Building an American Empire: The Era of Territorial and Political Expansion*. Princeton, NJ: Princeton University Press, 2019.

Fuccaro, Nelida. *Histories of City and State in the Persian Gulf: Manama since 1800*. Cambridge: Cambridge University Press, 2009.

Fuccaro, Nelida. "Pearl Towns and Early Oil Cities: Migration and Integration in the Arab Coast of the Persian Gulf." In *The City in the Ottoman Empire: Migration and the Making of Urban Modernity*, edited by Ulrike Freitag et al., 99–116. Abingdon: Routledge, 2011.

Fukuyama, Francis. "Identity, Immigration, and Liberal Democracy." *Journal of Democracy* 17, no. 2 (2006): 5–20.

Furnivall, John. *Colonial Policy and Practice: A Comparative Study of Burma and Netherlands India*. Cambridge: Cambridge University Press, 1948.

Gallardo, Yocelin. "Zapata County Turns Red for 2020 Election." KGNS TV, November 4, 2020. https://www.kgns.tv/2020/11/05/zapata-county-turns-red-for-2020-election/.

Gardner, Frank. "Bahrain Brothers Describe Shock at Losing Nationality." BBC, November 9, 2012. https://www.bbc.com/news/world-middle-east-20271933.

Gamboa, Suzanne. "Latinos Downgrade Trump on Coronavirus Response, Kick Up Biden Support, Poll Shows." NBC News, August 17, 2020. https://www.nbcnews.com/news/lat ino/latinos-downgrade-trump-coronavirus-response-kick-biden-support-poll-shows-n1236963.

Gardner, Andrew. *City of Strangers: Gulf Migration and the Indian Community in Bahrain*. Ithaca, NY: ILR Press, 2010.

Geddes, Andrew, and Peter Scholten. *The Politics of Migration and Immigration in Europe*. 2nd ed. London: SAGE, 2016.

Geertz, Clifford. *The Interpretation of Cultures*. London: Fontana, 1973.

Gengler, Justin. "Bahrain: A Special Case." In *What Does the Gulf Think about the Arab Awakening?*, edited by Fatima Ayub, 1–20. London: European Council on Foreign Relations, 2013.

Gengler, Justin. "Electoral Rules (and Threats) Cure Bahrain's Sectarian Parliament." *Monkey Cage*, December 1, 2014. https://www.washingtonpost.com/news/monkey-cage/wp/2014/12/01/electoral-rules-and-threats-cure-bahrains-sectarian-parliament/.

Gengler, Justin. *Group Conflict and Political Mobilization in Bahrain and the Arab Gulf: Rethinking the Rentier State*. Bloomington: Indiana University Press, 2015.

Gengler, Justin. "The Political Economy of Sectarianism in the Gulf." Carnegie Endowment for International Peace, August 2016. https://carnegieendowment.org/files/Gengler_Sectari anism_Final.pdf.

Gengler, Justin. "Royal Factionalism, the Khawalid, and the Securitization of 'the Shiʿa Problem' in Bahrain." *Journal of Arabian Studies* 3, no. 1 (2013): 53–79.

Gengler, Justin. "Segregation and Sectarianism: Geography, Economic Distribution, and Sectarian Resilience in Bahrain." In *Countering Sectarianism in the Middle East*, edited by Jeffrey Martini, Dalia Dassa Kaye, and Becca Wasser, 41–63. Santa Monica, CA: RAND, 2019.

Gerstle, Gary. *American Crucible: Race and Nation in the Twentieth Century*. Princeton, NJ: Princeton University Press, 2017.

Gest, Justin. *The New Minority: White Working Class Politics in an Age of Immigration and Inequality*. New York: Oxford University Press, 2016.

Gest, Justin. *The White Working Class: What Everyone Needs to Know*. New York: Oxford University Press, 2018.

Gest, Justin, and Sean Gray. "Silent Citizenship: The Politics of Marginality in Unequal Democracies." *Citizenship Studies* 19, no. 5 (2015): 465–473.

Ghosh, Palash. "Singapore Seeks to Cut Quota on Foreign Workers amid Worries over Immigration, Rising Labor Costs." *International Business Times*, February 26, 2013. www.ibtimes.com/singapore-seeks-cut-quota-foreign-workers-amid-worries-over-immigration-rising-labor-costs-1103229.

Gladney, Dru. *Making Majorities: Constituting the Nation in Japan, Korea, China, Malaysia, Fiji, Turkey, and the United States*. Palo Alto, CA: Stanford University Press, 1998.

Goh, Daniel, and Philip Holden. "Introduction: Postcoloniality, Race, and Multiculturalism." In *Race and Multiculturalism in Malaysia and Singapore*, edited by Daniel Goh et al., 1–16. New York: Routledge, 2009.

Goldstone, Jack, Eric Kaufmann, and Monica Toft. *Political Demography: How Population Changes Are Reshaping International Security and National Politics*. New York: Oxford University Press, 2011.

Golway, Terry. *Frank and Al: FDR, Al Smith, and the Unlikely Alliance That Created the Modern Democratic Party*. New York: St. Martin's Press, 2018.

Golway, Terry. *Machine Made: Tammany Hall and the Creation of Modern American Politics*. New York: Liveright, 2014.

Goodyear-Kaʻopua, Noelani. *The Seeds We Planted: Portraits of a Native Hawaiian Charter School*. Minneapolis: University of Minnesota Press, 2013.

Grande, Edgar, Tobias Schwarzbözl, and Matthias Fatke. "Politicizing Immigration in Western Europe." *Journal of European Public Policy* 26, no. 10 (2019): 1444–1463.

Green, Elliott. "Demographic Change and Conflict in Contemporary Africa." In *Political Demography: How Population Changes Are Reshaping International Security and National Politics*, edited by Jack Goldstone, Eric Kaufmann, and Monica Toft, 238–251. Boulder, CO: Paradigm, 2011.

Greene, William. *British Slave Emancipation: The Sugar Colonies and the Great Experiment 1830–1865*. Oxford: Oxford University Press, 1976.

Guay, Brian, et al. "Bayesian Origins of Demographic Misperceptions." Unpublished working paper, Department of Political Science, Duke University, 2020.

Guess, Andrew, and Alexander Coppock. "Does Counter-Attitudinal Information Cause Backlash? Results from Three Large Survey Experiments." *British Journal of Political Science* 50, no. 4 (2020): 1497–1515.

Gungwu, Wang. *The Nanhai Trade: Early Chinese Trade in the South China Sea*. Singapore: Times Media, 2003.

Haggay, Ram. "The Immemorial Iranian Nation? School Textbooks and Historical Memory in Post-revolutionary Iran." *Nations and Nationalism* 6, no. 1 (2000): 67–90.

Hale, Constance. "Is the Hawaiian Language Dead or Alive." *Honolulu Magazine*, November 14, 2013. www.honolulumagazine.com/Honolulu-Magazine/November-2013/Hawaiian-Dead-or-Alive/index.php?cparticle=2&siarticle=1#artanc.

Harewood, Jack. "The Population of Trinidad and Tobago, 1974." C.I.C.R.E.D. Series, Austin: University of Texas, 1975.

Harper, T. "Communists, Leftists and Populists: The Social and Ideological Roots of Postwar Left-Wing Politics." Paper presented at Symposium on Paths Not Taken: Political Pluralism in Postwar Singapore, organized by the Asia Research Institute, National University of Singapore, and Centre for Social Change Research, Singapore, 2005.

Harrison, Brian F., and Melissa R. Michelson. "God and Marriage: The Impact of Religious Identity Priming on Attitudes toward Same-Sex Marriage." *Social Science Quarterly* 96 no. 5 (2015): 1411–1423.

Harrison, Brian F., and Melissa R. Michelson. *Listen, We Need to Talk: How to Change Attitudes about LGBT Rights*. New York: Oxford University Press, 2017.

Haynes, Chris, Jennifer Merolla, and S. Karthick Ramakrishnan. *Framing Immigrants: News Coverage, Public Opinion, and Policy*. New York: Russell Sage Foundation, 2016.

"H.E. Dr. Shaikh Khalid Bin Khalifa Al Khalifa, Chairman of the Board of Trustees." King Hamad Global Centre for Peaceful Coexistence. Accessed October 12, 2021. https://kingha madglobalcentre.com/.

Hein, Laura, and Mark Selden. "Learning Citizenship from the Past: Textbook Nationalism, Global Context, and Social Change." *Bulletin of Concerned Asian Scholars* 30, no. 2 (1998): 3–15.

Held, David. *Democracy and the Global Order: From the Modern State to Cosmopolitan Governance*. Stanford, CA: Stanford University Press, 1995.

Heng, Geraldine, and Janadas Devan. "State Fatherhood: The Politics of Nationalism, Sexuality, and Race in Singapore." In *Nationalism and Sexualities*, edited by Andrew Parker et al., 343–364. London: Routledge, 1992.

Hennessy-Fiske, Molly. "'We've Only Started': How Latino Support for Trump Grew in Texas Borderlands." *Los Angeles Times*, November 12, 2020. https://www.latimes.com/world-nat ion/story/2020-11-12/latino-support-grew-for-trump-on-the-texas-border.

Herrera, Jack. "Trump Didn't Win the Latino Vote in Texas: He Won the Tejano Vote." *Politico*, November 17, 2020. https://www.politico.com/news/magazine/2020/11/17/trump-latinos-south-texas-tejanos-437027.

Higham, John. *Strangers in the Land: Patterns of American Nativism, 1860–1925*. New Brunswick, NJ: Rutgers University Press, 1955.

Hill, Errol. *The Trinidad Carnival: Mandate for a National Theatre*. Austin: University of Texas Press, 1972.

Hill, Seth, Daniel Hopkins, and Gregory Huber. "Local Demographic Changes and US Presidential Voting, 2012 to 2016." *Proceedings of the National Academy of Sciences* 116, no. 50 (December 10, 2019): 25023–25028.

Hing, Ai Yun, et al. "Mainland Chinese 'Foreign Talents' in Singapore." *Asian Journal of Social Science* 37, no. 5 (2009): 757–777.

Hingwan, Kathianne. "Identity and Carnival in Trinidad." PhD thesis, Goldsmiths College, University of London, September 2002.

Hirota, Hidetaka. *Expelling the Poor: Atlantic Seaboard States and the Nineteenth-Century Origins of American Immigration Policy*. New York: Oxford University Press, 2017.

Hirota, Hidetaka. "Limits of Intolerance: Nativism and Immigration Control in Nineteenth-Century New York." *Journal of Ethnic and Migration Studies*, July 22, 2020. https://www.tandfonline.com/doi/full/10.1080/1369183X.2020.1774114.

Hirschman, C. "The Meaning and Measurement of Ethnicity in Malaysia: An Analysis of Census Classifications." *Journal of Asian Studies* 46 (1987): 555–582.

Hobsbawm, Eric. *Nations and Nationalism Since 1780: Programme, Myth, Reality*. Cambridge: Cambridge University Press, 1990.

Holes, Clive. "Dialect and National Identity: The Cultural Politics of Self-Representation in Bahraini Musalsalat." In *Monarchies and Nations: Globalization and Identity in the Arab States of the Gulf*, edited by Paul Dreschand and James Piscatori, 52–72. London: I. B. Tauris, 2005.

Hollup, Oddvar. "The Disintegration of Caste and Changing Concepts of Indian Ethnic Identity in Mauritius." *Ethnology* 33, no. 4 (1994): 297–316.

Hopkins, Daniel, John Sides, and Jack Citrin. "The Muted Consequences of Correct Information about Immigration." *Journal of Politics* 81, no. 1 (2019): 315–320.

Hosek, Linda. "Qhana Council Builds Nation a Step at a Time." *Honolulu Star-Bulletin*, August 6, 1994.

Howe, Neil, and Richard Jackson. "Demography and Geopolitics: Understanding Today's Debate in Its Historical and intellectual Context." In *Political Demography: How Population Changes Are Reshaping International Security and National Politics*, edited by Jack Goldstone, Eric Kaufmann, and Monica Toft, 31–48. Boulder, CO: Paradigm, 2011.

"HRH the Crown Prince Holds Weekly Majlis." Bahrain News Agency, November 6, 2019. https://www.bna.bh/en/HRHtheCrownPrinceholdsweeklyMajlis.aspx?cms=q8FmFJgiscL2fwIzON1%2BDscKMJ0f7wV80tMHxDh13HY%3D.

Huddy, Leonie, and Alexa Bankert. "Political Partisanship as a Social Identity: Groups and Identities, Political Psychology." *Oxford Research Encyclopedia of Politics*, May 2017, 1–31.

Huddy, Leonie, Liliana Mason, and Lene Aaroe. "Expressive Partisanship: Campaign Involvement, Political Emotion, and Partisan Identity." *American Political Science Review* 109, no. 1 (2015): 1–17.

Huiwen, Ng. "More Marriages Took Place in 2017, with Nearly a Quarter of Them Inter-Ethnic." *Straits Times*, July 10, 2018. https://www.straitstimes.com/singapore/more-marriages-took-place-in-2017-of-which-nearly-a-quarter-were-inter-ethnic.

Iijima, Mariko. "'Nonwhiteness' in Nineteenth-Century Hawai'i: Sovereignty, White Settlers, and Japanese Migrants." *Journal of Ethnic and Migration Studies*, July 22, 2020. https://www.tandfonline.com/doi/full/10.1080/1369183X.2020.1774115.

"In 19th Century Mauritius: The Resistance and Struggle of the Indian Workers." *Le Mauricien*, April 30, 2013. https://www.lemauricien.com/article/19th-century-mauritius-resistance-and-struggle-indian-workers/.

Inamete, Ufot. "Politics and Governance in Trinidad and Tobago: Major Issues and Developments." *Caribbean Studies* 25, nos. 3–4 (1992): 305–324.

International Crisis Group. "Bahrain's Sectarian Challenge." Middle East/North Africa Report Number 40. May 6, 2005. https://d2071andvip0wj.cloudfront.net/40-bahrain-s-sectarian-challenge.pdf.

Ivarsflaten, Elisabeth. "What Unites Right-Wing Populists in Western Europe?" *Comparative Political Studies* 41 (2008): 3–23.

Jackson, Chris, and Annaleise Azevedo Lohr. "2019 US Politics: Immigration Is a Much More Salient Issue for 34% of Republicans." Ipsos Public Affairs, January 16, 2019. https://www.ipsos.com/en/2019-us-politics-immigration-much-more-salient-issue-34-republicans.

Jacobs, Jennifer. "Biden Administration Will Create Position to Reach Conservatives." *Bloomberg News*, December 7, 2020. https://www.bloomberg.com/news/articles/2020-12-08/biden-administration-will-create-position-to-reach-conservatives.

James, C. L. R. *The Life of Captain Cipriani, an Account of British Government in the West Indies, with the Pamphlet the West Indian Case for Self-Government.* Durham, NC: Duke University Press, 2014.

Jelavich, Charles. "Serbian Textbooks: Toward Greater Serbia or Yugoslavia?" *Slavic Review* 42, no. 4 (1983): 601–619.

Kagan, Robert. "The Strongmen Strike Back." *Washington Post*, March 14, 2019. https://www.washingtonpost.com/news/opinions/wp/2019/03/14/feature/the-strongmen-strike-back/.

Kalkan, Kerem. "What Differentiates Trump Supporters from Other Republicans? Ethnocentrism." *Monkey Cage*, February 28, 2016. https://www.washingtonpost.com/news/monkey cage/wp/2016/02/28/what-differentiates-trump-supporters-from-other-republicans- ethnocentrism/.

Kalla, Joshua, and David Broockman. "Reducing Exclusionary Attitudes through Interpersonal Conversation: Evidence from Three Field Experiments." *American Political Science Review* 114, no. 2 (2020): 410–425.

Kamehiro, Stacy. *The Arts of Kingship: Hawaiian Art and National Culture of the Kalākaua Era.* Honolulu: University of Hawai'i Press, 2009.

Kapiszewski, Anderzej. "Arab versus Asian Migrant Workers in the GCC Countries." Paper presented at United Nations Expert Group Meeting on International Migration and Development in the Arab Region, Beirut, May 15–17, 2006.

Kapiszewski, Andrzej. *Nationals and Expatriates: Population and Labour Dilemmas of the Gulf Cooperation Council States.* Ithaca, NY: Ithaca Press, 2001.

Kauanui, J. Kehaulani. "Resisting the Akaka Bill." In *A Nation Rising: Hawaiian Movements for Life, Land, and Sovereignty*, edited by Noelani Goodyear-Ka'ōpua et al., 312–330. Durham, NC: Duke University Press, 2014.

Kaufmann, Eric. "Dominant Ethnicity: Background to Foreground." In *Rethinking Ethnicity: Majority Groups and Dominant Minorities*, edited by Eric Kaufmann, 1–12. London: Routledge, 2004.

Kaufmann, Eric. *Rise and Fall of Anglo-America.* Cambridge, MA: Harvard University Press, 2004.

Kaufmann, Eric. *Whiteshift: Populism, Immigration, and the Future of White Majorities.* New York: Abrams, 2018.

Kaufmann, Eric, and Matthew J. Goodwin. "The Diversity Wave: A Meta-Analysis of the Native-Born White Response to Ethnic Diversity." *Social Science Research* 76 (2018): 120–131.

Kaufmann, Eric, and Oded Haklai. "Dominant Ethnicity: From Minority to Majority." *Nations and Nationalism* 14, no. 4 (2008): 743–767.

"Ke Kumukānāwai o ka Makahiki 1839" (The 1839 Constitution). Na'i Aupuni. Accessed March 14, 2021. www.naiaupuni.org/docs/pres/dm/1839_1840%20Constitution.pdf.

Kehoe, Lawrence. *Complete Works of the Most Rev. John Hughes, DD*. New York: Lawrence Kehoe, 1866.

Kenny, Kevin. "Labor and Labor Organizations." In *Making the Irish American: History and Heritage of the Irish in the United States*, edited by J. J. Lee and Marion Casey, 354–363. New York: New York University Press, 2006.

Khalaf, Abdulhadi. "Labor Movements in Bahrain." *Middle East Report Online*, May 4, 1985. https://merip.org/1985/05/labor-movements-in-bahrain/.

Khuri, Fuad. *Tribe and State in Bahrain: The Transformation of Social and Political Authority in an Arab State*. Chicago: University of Chicago Press, 1980.

Kinder, Donald, and Lynn Sanders. *Divided by Color: Racial Politics and Democratic Ideals*. Chicago: University of Chicago Press, 1996.

King, Samuel, and Randall Roth. *Broken Trust: Greed, Mismanagement, and Political Manipulation at America's Largest Charitable Trust*. Honolulu: University of Hawai'i Press, 2006.

Kinninmont, Jane. "Bahrain's Contentious Politics." Working Paper, The Elders, London, 2018.

Kinninmont, Jane, and Omar Sirri. "Bahrain: Civil Society and Political Imagination." Chatham House, October 2014. www.chathamhouse.org/sites/default/files/publications/research/20141028BahrainKinninmontSirri.pdf.

Klebaner, Benjamin. "The Myth of Foreign Pauper Dumping in the United States." *Social Service Review* 35 (1961): 302–309.

Knowles, Eric, and Linda Tropp. "Donald Trump and the Rise of White Identity in Politics." *The Conversation*, October 20, 2016. https://theconversation.com/donald-trump-and-the-rise-of-white-identity-in-politics-67037.

Kok, Koun Chin. *Malaysia and Singapore 1400–1963: A Comprehensive History*. Singapore: Oxford University Press, 1988.

Koningsbruggen, Peter. *Trinidad Carnival: A Quest for National Identity*. London: Macmillan Education, 1997.

Koopmans, Ruud, et al. *Contested Citizenship: Immigration and Cultural Diversity in Europe*. Minneapolis: University of Minnesota Press, 2005.

Krogstad, Jens Manuel, and Mark Hugo Lopez. "Latino Voters Have Growing Confidence in Biden on Key Issues, While Confidence in Trump Remains Low." Pew Research Center, October 16, 2020. https://www.pewresearch.org/fact-tank/2020/10/16/latino-voters-have-growing-confidence-in-biden-on-key-issues-while-confidence-in-trump-remains-low/.

Krosnick, Jon. "The Role of Attitude Importance in Social Evaluation: A Study of Policy Preferences, Presidential Candidate Evaluations, and Voting Behavior." *Journal of Personality and Social Psychology* 55, no. 2 (1988): 196–210.

Krosnick, Jon, and Richard Petty. "Attitude Strength: An Overview." In *Ohio State University Series on Attitudes and Persuasion*. Vol. 4: *Attitude Strength: Antecedents and Consequences*, edited by Jon Krosnick and Richard Petty, 1–24. East Sussex, UK: Psychology Press, 1995.

Kustov, Alexander, Dillon Laaker, and Cassidy Reller. "The Stability of Immigration Attitudes: Evidence and Implications." *Journal of Politics* 83, no. 4 (2019): 1478–1494.

Kuykendal, Ralph. *The Hawaiian Kingdom*. Vol. 3: *1874–1893: The Kalakaua Dynasty*. Honolulu: University of Hawai'i Press, 1967.

Kwang, Han Fook, Warren Fernandez, and Sumiko Tan. *Lee Kuan Yew: The Man and His Ideas*. Singapore: Singapore Press Holdings and Times Editions, 1998.

Kwek, Theophilus. "Full Colour Illustrations: Presentations of Race in Singapore's History Textbooks, 1965–2000." In *Southeast Asian Education in Modern History Schools, Manipulation, and Contest*, edited by Pia Maria Jolliffe and Thomas Richard Bruce, 158–177. London: Routledge, 2018.

Kymlicka, Will. *Politics in the Vernacular: Nationalism, Multiculturalism, and Citizenship.* Oxford: Oxford University Press, 2001.

Kymlicka, Will. *States, Nations and Cultures.* Assen: Van Gorcum, 1997.

Laenui, Poka. "Poka Laenui (Hayden F. Burgess)." Kalihi Palama Hawaiian Civic Club. www.nativehawaiian.org/candidates/oahu/poka-laenui/.

Lake, Marilyn, and Henry Reynolds. *Drawing the Global Colour Line: White Men's Countries and the International Challenge of Racial Equality.* Cambridge: Cambridge University Press, 2008.

Lardner, James, and Thomas Reppetto. *NYPD: A City and Its Police.* New York: Henry Holt, 2000.

Lasky, Jacqueline. "Waiahole-Waikane." In *A Nation Rising: Hawaiian Movements for Life, Land, and Sovereignty,* edited by Noelani Goodyear-Kaʻopua et al., 48–65. Durham, NC: Duke University Press, 2014.

Lau, Teik Soon. *Majority-Minority Situation in Singapore.* Occasional Paper Number 7. Department of Political Science, National University of Singapore, 1974.

Laurence, K. O. *A Question of Labour: Indian Indentured Emigration into Trinidad and British Guiana, 1875–1917.* Kingston: Ian Randle/James Currey, 1994.

Lavietes, Matt. "There Will Be a Record Number of Hispanic Voters in 2020, and That Could Have a Major Impact on Trump's Political Fate." CNBC, February 7, 2019. https://www.cnbc.com/2019/02/07/surge-in-hispanic-voters-could-have-major-impact-on-trump-re-election-bid.html.

Lee, Barrett A., et al. "State-Level Changes in US Racial and Ethnic Diversity, 1980 to 2015: A Universal Trend?" *Demographic Research* 37 (2017): 1031–1048.

Lee, Christine, et al. "Children's Experiences of Multiracial Relationships in Informal Primary School Settings." In *Beyond Rituals and Riots: Ethnic Pluralism and Social Cohesion in Singapore,* edited by A. E. Lai, 114–145. Singapore: Marshall Cavendish, 2004.

Leeper, Thomas, and Rune Slothuus. "Political Parties, Motivated Reasoning, and Public Opinion Formation." *Political Psychology* 35 (2014): 129–156.

Levitsky, Steven, and Lucan Way. "The Rise of Competitive Authoritarianism." *Journal of Democracy* 13, no. 2 (2002): 51–65.

Levy, Morris, and Dowell Myers. "Racial Projections in Perspective: Public Reactions to Narratives about Rising Diversity." *Perspectives on Politics* (2021): 1–18. https://www.cambridge.org/core/journals/perspectives-on-politics/article/abs/racial-projections-in-perspective-public-reactions-to-narratives-about-rising-diversity/E9D8F620367A68C3267301F342232A1B.

Lijphart, Arend. *Democracy in Plural Societies: A Comparative Exploration.* New Haven, CT: Yale University Press, 1977.

Lijphart, Arend. *Patterns of Democracy: Government Forms and Performance in Thirty-Six Countries.* New Haven, CT: Yale University Press, 1999.

Lind, Michael. *The New Class War: Saving Democracy from the Managerial Elite.* New York: Portfolio/Penguin, 2020.

Lind, Michael. *The Next American Nation: The New Nationalism and the Fourth American Revolution.* New York: Free Press, 1995.

Longva, Anh Nga. "Keeping Migrant Workers in Check: The Kafala System in the Gulf." *Middle East Report* 211 (1999): 20–22.

Longva, Anh Nga. *Walls Built on Sand: Migration, Exclusion and Society in Kuwait.* Boulder, CO: Westview Press, 1997.

Lopez Bunyasi, T. "The Role of Whiteness in the 2016 Presidential Primaries." *Perspectives on Politics* 17, no. 3 (2019): 679–698.

Louër, Laurence. "The Political Impact of Labor Migration in Bahrain." *City & Society* 20, no. 1 (2008): 32–53.

Lovelace, Earl. *The Dragon Can't Dance*. Alexandria, VA: Alexander Street Press, 1989.

Lovelace, Earl. *Salt*. New York: Persea Books, 1979.

Low, Adeline. "The Past in the Present: Memories of the 1964 'Racial Riots' in Singapore." *Asian Journal of Social Sciences* 23L3 (2001): 431–455.

Luntz, Frank. *Words That Work: It's Not What You Say, It's What People Hear*. New York: Hyperion, 2007.

MacLennan, Carol. *Sovereign Sugar: Industry and Environment in Hawai'i*. Honolulu: University of Hawai'i Press, 2014.

Magnus, Ralph. "Societies and Social Change in the Persian Gulf." In *The Persian Gulf States: A General Survey*, edited by Alvin Cottrell, 369–413. London: Johns Hopkins University Press, 1980.

Mahdi, Mazen. "Leading Bahrainis Call for Halt to Naturalization." *The National*, May 11, 2009.

Manuel, Peter. "Chutney and Indo-Trinidadian Cultural Identity." *Popular Music* 17, no. 1 (1998): 21–43.

"Maps of the World." In *Encyclopedia Britannica*, August 17, 2011. https://www.britannica.com/topic/Maps-of-the-World-1788586.

Masters, Suzette Brooks. "Change Is Hard: Managing Fear and Anxiety about Demographic Change and Immigration in Polarized Times." *Welcoming America*, January 2020. https://www.welcomingamerica.org/sites/default/files/Changeishard_FINAL.pdf.

Matthews, Mathew. "CNA-IPS Survey on Race Relations." Institute of Policy Studies and Channel NewsAsia, August 2016.

"Mauritius: Contribution of Travel and Tourism to GDP as a Share of GDP." Knoema, 2018. https://knoema.com/atlas/Mauritius/topics/Tourism/Travel-and-Tourism-Total-Contribution-to-GDP/Contribution-of-travel-and-tourism-to-GDP-percent-of-GDP.

Mayda, Anna Maria, Giovanni Peri, and Walter Steingress. "The Political Impact of Immigration: Evidence from the United States." National Bureau of Economic Research. Working Paper 24510. April 2018. https://www.nber.org/papers/w24510.pdf.

McCarthy, Stephen. *The Political Theory of Tyranny in Singapore and Burma: Aristotle and the Rhetoric of Benevolent Despotism*. Abingdon: Routledge, 2006.

McCree, Roy. "Ethnicity and Involvement in Cultural Festivals in Trinidad and Tobago." In *Identity, Ethnicity and Culture in the Caribbean*, edited by Ralph Premdas, 115–142. St. Augustine: UWI School of Continuing Studies, 2003.

McDermott, John, and Naleen Naupaka Andrade. *People and Cultures of Hawai'i: The Evolution of Culture and Ethnicity*. Honolulu: University of Hawai'i Press, 2011.

McGregor, Davianna. *Nā Kua'āina: Living Hawaiian Culture*. Honolulu: University of Hawai'i Press, 2007.

McGregor-Alegado, Davianna. "Hawaiian Resistance: 1887–1889." Master's thesis, University of Hawaii, Manoa, 1979.

McKeown, Adam. *Melancholy Order: Asian Migration and the Globalization of Borders*. New York: Columbia University Press, 2008.

Miller, David. *Citizenship and National Identity*. Cambridge, UK: Polity Press, 2000.

Miller, Kerby. *Emigrants and Exiles: Ireland and the Irish Exodus to North America*. New York: Oxford University Press, 1985.

Millette, James. "The Wage Problem in Trinidad and Tobago 1838–1938." In *The Colonial Caribbean in Transition: Essays on Postemancipation and Cultural History*, edited by Bridget Brereton and Kevin Yelvington, 55–76. Kingston: The Press, University of the West Indies, 1999.

Moran, Gerard. *Sending Out Ireland's Poor: Assisted Emigration to North America in the Nineteenth Century*. Dublin: Four Court Press, 2004.

Morland, Paul. *Demographic Engineering: Population Strategies in Ethnic Conflict*. London: Routledge, 2014.

Moynihan, Daniel Patrick. "The Irish (1963, 1970)." In *Making the Irish American: History and Heritage of the Irish in the United States*, edited by J. J. Lee and Marion Casey, 475–525. New York: New York University Press, 2006.

Nakhleh, Emile. *Bahrain*. Lexington, KY: Lexington Books, 1976.

Nasir, Kamaludeen Mohammed, and Bryan S. Turner. "Governing as Gardening: Reflections on Soft Authoritarianism in Singapore." *Citizenship Studies* 17, nos. 3–4 (2013): 339–352.

"Naturalization of Displaced Syrians . . . King of Bahrain Manipulates Demography." *Al Masalah*, March 3, 2016. http://almasalah.com/ar/NewsDetails.aspx?NewsID=27990.

Neil, Christopher. "A Year of Controversy at Beach Park." *Honolulu Advertiser*, May 21, 1994.

Neo, Crystal. "Singaporeans and the Question of Immigration." *Morningside Post*, June 2012. www.themorningsidepost.com/2012/06/06/singaporeans-and-the-question-of-immigration/.

New American Economy. "The United States Is More Diverse Than Ever, in More Places Than Ever," September 23, 2021, https://data.newamericaneconomy.org/en/census2020/.

Newman, Benjamin. "Acculturating Contexts and Anglo Opposition to Immigration in the U.S." *American Journal of Political Science* 57, no. 2 (2013): 374–390.

Newman, Benjamin, and Yamil Velez. "Group Size vs. Change? Assessing Americans' Perception of Local Immigration." *Political Research Quarterly* 67, no. 2 (2014): 293–303.

Newman, Benjamin, et al. "The Trump Effect: An Experimental Investigation of the Emboldening Effect of Racially Inflammatory Elite Communication." *British Journal of Political Science* 51, no. 3 (2021): 1138–1159.

Niranjana, Tejaswini. *Mobilizing India: Women, Music and Migration between India and Trinidad*. Durham, NC: Duke University Press, 2006.

Nordyke, Eleanor. *The Peopling of Hawai'i*. 2nd ed. Honolulu: University of Hawai'i Press, 1989.

Nussbaum, Martha, and Joshua Cohen. *For Love of Country: Debating the Limits of Patriotism*. Boston: Beacon Press, 1996.

Nwulia, Moses. "The 'Apprenticeship' System in Mauritius: Its Character and Its Impact on Race Relations in the Immediate Post-Emancipation Period, 1839–1879." *African Studies Review* 21, no. 1 (1978): 89–101.

O'Connor, Thomas. *The Boston Irish: A Political History*. Cambridge, MA: Back Bay Books, 1997.

Odo, Franklin. *A Pictorial History of the Japanese in Hawaii: 1885–1924—Commemorating the Centennial of the First Arrival of Government Contracted Japanese Laborers in Hawai'i*. Honolulu: Hawai'i Immigrant Heritage Preservation Center, 1985.

Okamura, Jonathan. *Raced to Death in 1920s Hawai'i: Injustice and Revenge in the Fukunaga Case*. Urbana: University of Illinois Press, 2019.

Oppenheimer, Andres. "Commentary: The Hispanic Vote Has Been a Sleeping Giant, but There Are Signs That It Will Wake in 2020." *Morning Call*, September 17, 2019. https://www.mcall.com/opinion/mc-opi-hispanic-voting-2020-registered-20190917-x3jbwpor4ff3fl7bt7pexeg62a-story.html.

Outten, H. Robert, et al. "Feeling Threatened about the Future: Whites' Emotional Reactions to Anticipated Ethnic Demographic Changes." *Personality and Social Psychology Bulletin* 38, no. 1 (2012): 14–25.

Paluck, Elizabeth, and Donald Green. "Prejudice Reduction: What Works? A Review and Assessment of Research and Practice." *Annual Review of Psychology* 60 (2009): 339–367.

Paluck, Elizabeth, Seth Green, and Donald Green. "The Contact Hypothesis Re-Evaluated." *Behavioural Public Policy* 3, no. 2 (2019): 129–158.

Parker, Theodore. *The Material Condition of the People of Massachusetts*. Boston: Geo. C. Rand & Avery, 1860.

Parliament of the Republic of Trinidad and Tobago. "Sixth Report of the Joint Select Committee on Ministries, Statutory Authorities and State Enterprises." 2014. ttparliament.org/reports/p10-20130308-s4-HOUS-R6.pdf.

Parliament of the Republic of Trinidad and Tobago, Divisions and Projects Financial Scrutiny Unit. "Head 62: Ministry of Community Development, Culture and the Arts." 2020. http://ttparliament.org/documents/2895.pdf.

Pauker, Kristin, et al. "Race Essentialism and Social Contextual Differences in Children's Racial Stereotyping." *Child Development* 87, no. 5 (2016): 1409–1422.

Pauker, Kristin, et al. "The Role of Diversity Exposure in Whites' Reduction in Race Essentialism over Time." *Social Psychological and Personality Science* 9, no. 8 (2018): 944–952.

Pearson, Charles. *National Life and Character: A Forecast*. London: Macmillan, 1894.

Petherbridge, Guy T. "Vernacular Architecture: The House and Society." In *Architecture of the Islamic World: Its History and Social Meaning*, edited by George Michell, 176–208. London: Thames and Hudson, 1978.

Pew Research Center. "Shifting Public Views on Legal Immigration into the U.S." June 28, 2018. http://www.people-press.org/2018/06/28/shifting-public-views-on-legal-immigration-into-the-u-s/.

Piper, Nicola. *Migrant Labor in Southeast Asia: Country Study: Singapore*. Singapore: Asian Research Institute Friedrich Ebert Stiftung Project on Migrant Labor in South East Asia, 2005.

Pires, B. C. "The Slim Lady Sings." Newsday, April 19, 2021.

"The PM's Address to the Historical Society, Nanyang University, February 10." In *Bilingualism in Our Society*, edited by Ministry of Culture. Singapore: Singapore National Printers, 1978.

Powell, Michael, Cecilia Ballí, and Betsabeth Monica Lugo. "Real Talk: Understanding Texas Latino Voters through Meaningful Conversation." Texas Organizing Project Education Fund, 2020. https://drive.google.com/file/d/12yQDyRxZiYg7Wzvm6c19pewM70jjBwxd/view.

Premdas, Ralph. "The Ascendance of an Indian Prime Minister in Trinidad: The Election of 1995." In *Identity, Ethnicity and Culture in the Caribbean*, edited by Ralph Premdas, 323–358. St. Augustine: UWI School of Continuing Studies, 2003.

Quigg, Agnes. "Kalakaua's Hawaiian Studies Abroad Program." *Hawaiian Journal of History* 22 (1988): 170–208.

Quinn, Peter. "The Future of Irish America." In *Making the Irish American: History and Heritage of the Irish in the United States*, ed. J. J. Lee and Marion Casey, 680–685. New York: New York University Press, 2006.

Rahim, Lily Zubaidah. *The Singapore Dilemma: The Political and Educational Marginality of the Mala Community*. Kuala Lumpur: Oxford University Press, 1998.

Rajah, Ananda. "Making and Managing Tradition in Singapore: The National Day Parade." In *Our Place in Time: Exploring Heritage and Memory in Singapore*, edited by K. W. Kwok et al., 66–75. Singapore: Singapore Historical Society, 1999.

Ramcharitar, Raymond. "The Carnival Bubble." *The Guardian*, February 8, 2017.

Ramcharitar, Raymond. "Ethnic Anxiety and Competing Citizenships in Trinidad and Tobago." *Journal of Ethnic and Migration Studies*, July 22, 2020. https://www.tandfonline.com/doi/full/10.1080/1369183X.2020.1774116.

Ramcharitar, Raymond. *A History of Creole Trinidad, 1956–2016*. New York: Palgrave, 2021.

Ramcharitar, Raymond. "The Invention of Trinidad Carnival: The New World Gleichschaltung." *Caribbean Quarterly*, 66, no. 1 (2020): 7–28.

Region One Education Service Center. "Region One ESC." Accessed October 25, 2021. https://www.esc1.net/Page/2948.

Renan, Ernest. "What Is a Nation?" Translated by M. Thom. In *Nation and Narration*, edited by Homi Bhabha, 8–23. Abington: Routledge, 2013.

Reny, Tyler, Loren Collingwood, and Ali Valenzuela. "Vote Switching in the 2016 Election: How Racial and Immigration Attitudes, Not Economics, Explain Shifts in White Voting." *Public Opinion Quarterly* 83, no. 1 (2019): 91–113.

Reny, Tyler, and Justin Gest. "Viewers Like You: How Elite Co-Identity Reinforcement Primes Facilitate Persuasion." Paper submitted to the annual meeting of the American Political Science Association, October 1, 2021.

Riggio, Milla Cozart. "Carnival Crossings: From Here to There, Arkansas to Harvard to Trinidad." Carnival Crossroads Distinguished Lecture, University of the West Indies, St. Augustine, February 3, 2014. www.trinidadexpress.com/news/local/unique-take-on-t-t/article_55e62ae8-fyco-52ec-adb-79fa704beoer.html.

Rodan, Garry. "Embracing Electronic Media but Suppressing Civil Society: Authoritarian Consolidation in Singapore." *Pacific Review* 16, no. 4 (2011): 503–524.

Rodan, Garry. *Transparency and Authoritarian Rule in Southeast Asia: Malaysia and Singapore.* London: Routledge Curzon Press, 2004.

Rodan, Garry, and K. Jarasuriya. "Capitalist Development: Regime Transitions and New Forms of Authoritarianism in Asia." *Pacific Review* 22, no. 1 (2009): 23–47.

Rohlehr, Gordon. "Apocalypso and the Soca Fires of 1990." In Gordon Rohlehr, *The Shape of That Hurt and Other Essays*, 305–371. Port of Spain: Lexicon, 1992.

Rohlehr, Gordon. *Calypso and Society in Pre-Independence Trinidad.* Port of Spain: Gordon Rohlehr, 1990.

Rohlehr, Gordon. "The Culture of Williams: Context, Performance, Legacy." In *A Scuffling of Islands: Essays on Calypso*, edited by Gordon Rohlehr, 102–163. Port of Spain: Lexicon, 2004.

Rohlehr, Gordon. "The State of Calypso Today." In *Identity, Ethnicity and Culture in the Caribbean*, edited by Ralph Premdas, 29–46. St. Augustine: UWI School of Continuing Studies, 2003.

Rohter, Larry. "High-Level Name-Calling across the Racial Fence." *New York Times*, August 20, 1997.

Roosevelt, Theodore. "National Life and Character." *Sewanee Review* 2, no. 3 (1894): 353–376.

Roosevelt, Theodore. "National Life and Character." In Theodore Roosevelt, *American Ideals and Other Essays Social and Political.* New York: Putnam's Sons, 1897.

Ross, Edward. "The Causes of Race Superiority." *Annals of the American Academy of Political and Social Science* 18 (July 1901): 67–89.

Ruffini, Patrick. "Far from Settled: Varied and Changing Attitudes on Immigration in America." Democracy Fund, Voter Study Group, October 2018. https://www.voterstudygroup.org/publication/far-from-settled.

Ryan, Selwyn. *Deadlock: Ethnicity and Electoral Competition in Trinidad, 1995–2002.* St. Augustine: Institute for Social and Economic Studies, 2003.

Ryan, Selwyn. *Race and Nationalism in Trinidad.* Toronto: University of Toronto Press, 1972.

Sankeralli, Burton. "Indian Presence in Carnival." In *Carnival: Culture in Action—The Trinidad Experience*, edited by Milla Cozart Riggio, 76–84. New York: Routledge, 2004.

"Saudis to Bahrain . . . Stop Naturalization of Yemenis." *Al Hurra*, January 10, 2018. https://www.alhurra.com/a/saudi-bahrian-yemen/413113.html.

Schachter, Ariela. "From 'Different' to 'Similar': An Experimental Approach to Understanding Assimilation." *American Sociological Review* 81, no. 5 (2016): 981–1013.

Schneider, Bill. *Standoff: How America Became Ungovernable.* New York: Simon & Schuster, 2019.

Sears, David. "Symbolic Politics: A Socio-Psychological Theory." In *Explorations in Political Psychology: Duke Studies in Political Psychology*, edited by Shanto Iyengar and William McGuire, 113–149. Durham, NC: Duke University Press, 1993.

Seccombe, I. J., and R. I. Lawless. "Foreign Worker Dependence in the Gulf, and the International Oil Companies: 1910–50." *International Migration Review* 20, no. 3 (1986): 548–574.

Selaibeekh, Lubna. "Citizenship Education in Bahrain: An Investigation of the Perceptions and Understandings of Policymakers, Teachers and Pupils." PhD thesis, Surrey University, 2017.

Senser, Ryan, and Eleanor Morison. "New Insights: Winning on Immigration Research Findings and Analysis." Unbound Philanthropy, October 2018.

Shakdam, Catherine. "Bahrain Using Targeted Immigration to Quell Political Dissent." *Mint Press News*, December 3, 2014. https://www.mintpressnews.com/bahrain-is-using-targeted-immigration-to-quell-political-dissent/199527/.

Shaw, Richard. *Dagger John: The Unquiet Life and Times of Archbishop John Hughes of New York.* New York: Paulist Press, 1977.

Sheikh, Ibrahim. "Naturalization and the Missing Link." *Akhbar Akhaleej*. Accessed March 12, 2021. http://www.akhbar-alkhaleej.com/13543/article/18790.html.

Shelef, Nadav. "Lessons from the Experience of Two Israeli Nationalist Movements." In *People Changing Places: New Perspectives on Demography, Migration, Conflict, and the State*, edited by Isabelle Côté, Matthew Mitchell, Monica Toft, 128–149. London: Routledge, 2018.

Shklar, Judith. "The Liberalism of Fear." In *Liberalism and the Moral Life*, edited by Nancy Rosenblum, 21–37. Cambridge, MA: Harvard University Press, 1989.

Siddique, Sharon. "The Phenomenon of Ethnicity: A Singapore Case Study." In *Understanding Singapore Society*, edited by Ong Jin Hue et al., 108. Singapore: Times Academic Press, 1997.

Sides, John. "Race, Religion, and Immigration in 2017: How the Debate over American Identity Shaped the Election and What It Means for a Trump Presidency." Voter Study Group, June 2017. https://www.voterstudygroup.org/publications/2016-elections/race-religion-immigration-2016.

Sides, John, and Jack Citrin. "European Opinion about Immigration: The Role of Identities, Interests, and Information." *British Journal of Political Science* 37, no. 3 (2007): 477–504.

Sides, John, Michael Tesler, and Lynn Vavreck. *Identity Crisis: The 2016 Presidential Campaign and the Battle for the Meaning of America*. Princeton, NJ: Princeton University Press, 2018.

Simonovits, Gábor, Gábor Kézdi, and Péter Kardos. "Seeing the World through the Other's Eye: An Online Intervention Reducing Ethnic Prejudice." *American Political Science Review* 112, no. 1 (2018): 186–193.

Singapore Department of Statistics. "Census of Population 2010 Advance Census Release." Accessed March 15, 2021. https://www.singstat.gov.sg/-/media/files/publications/cop2010/census_2010_advance_census_release/c2010acr.pdf.

Singapore Ministry of Education. "Speech by Brigadier-General Lee Hsien Loong, at the Launch of National Education on 17 May 1997." www.moe.gov.sg/media/speeches/1997/170597.htm.

Singapore Ministry of Information and the Arts. "National Day Rally 1993." August 15, 1993.

Singapore Ministry of Information and the Arts. "National Day Rally 1996." August 18, 1996.

Singapore Ministry of Manpower. "Quota and Levy for S Pass." Accessed 11 June 2012. http://www.mom.gov.sg/foreign-manpower/foreign-worker-levies/Pages/levies-quotas-for-hiring-foreign-workers.aspx.

Singapore National Population and Talent Division. "Our Population Our Future." 2012.

"Singapore Opposition Makes 'Landmark' Election Gains." BBC, May 9, 2011. https://www.bbc.com/news/world-asia-pacific-13313695.

Singh, Kelvin. *Race and Class Struggles in a Colonial State: Trinidad 1917–1945.* Calgary: University of Calgary Press, 1994.

Slater, Michael, and Donna Rouner. "Entertainment-Education and Elaboration Likelihood: Understanding the Processing of Narrative Persuasion." *Communication Theory* 12, no. 2 (2002): 173–191.

Smith, Rogers. *Civic Ideals: Conflicting Visions of Citizenship in U.S. History.* New Haven, CT: Yale University Press, 1999.

Smith, Stephen, Wilma Lee Steele, and Tina Russell. "We Are Proud to Be 'Rednecks': It's Time to Reclaim That Term." *The Guardian*, April 14, 2018. https://www.theguardian.com/us-news/2018/apr/14/redneck-pride-west-virginia-protests-strikes.

Sniderman, Paul, Louk Hagendoorn, and Markus Prior. "Predisposing Factors and Situational Triggers: Exclusionary Reactions to Immigrant Minorities." *American Political Science Review* 98, no. 1 (2004): 35–49.

Sniderman Paul, and Sean Theriault. "The Structure of Political Argument and the Logic of Issue Framing." In *Studies in Public Opinion*, edited by Willem Saris and Paul Sniderman, 133–165. Princeton, NJ: Princeton University Press, 2004.

Steele, Claude. "The Psychology of Self-Affirmation: Sustaining the Integrity of the Self." In *Advances in Experimental Social Psychology*. Vol. 21: *Social Psychological Studies of the Self: Perspectives and Programs*, edited by Leonard Berkowitz, 261–302. Cambridge, MA: Academic Press, 1988.

Stolarchuk, Jewel. "Whopping 92% of Singaporeans in Viral Poll Vote for Tharman to Become Next PM." *The Independent*, April 1, 2019. http://theindependent.sg/whopping-92-of-singaporeans-in-viral-poll-vote-for-tharman-to-become-next-pm/.

Tabachnik, Maxim. "Untangling Liberal Democracy from Territoriality: From Ethnic/Civic to Ethnic/Territorial Nationalism." *Nations and Nationalism* 25, no. 1 (2019): 191–207.

Taber, Charles, and Milton Lodge. "Motivated Skepticism in the Evaluation of Political Beliefs." *American Journal of Political Science* 50, no. 3 (2006): 755–769.

Tajfel, Henri, and John Turner. "An Integrative Theory of Inter-Group Conflict." In *The Social Psychology of Inter-Group Relations*, edited by W. G. Austin and S. Worchel, 33–47. Monterey, CA: Brooks/Cole, 1979.

Takaki, Ronald. *Pau Hana: Plantation Life and Labor in Hawaii, 1835–1920*. Honolulu: University of Hawai'i Press, 1984.

Tamir, Yael. *Liberal Nationalism*. Princeton, NJ: Princeton University Press, 1993.

Tan, Eugene K. B. "'We, the Citizens of Singapore': Multiethnicity, Its Evolution, and Its Aberrations." In *Beyond Rituals and Riots: Ethnic Pluralism and Social Cohesion in Singapore*, edited by Lai Ah Eng, 1–40. Singapore: Eastern Universities Press, 2004.

Tan, Tai-Yong. "Port Cities and Hinterlands: A Comparative Study of Singapore and Calcutta." *Political Geography* 26 (2007): 851–865.

Tausanovitch, C., L. Vavreck, T. Reny, A. Rossell Hayes, and A. Rudkin. "Democracy Fund + UCLA Nationscape Methodology and Representativeness Assessment." Democracy Fund + UCLA Nationscape Project, 2019. https://www.voterstudygroup.org/uploads/reports/Data/NS-Methodology-Representativeness-Assessment.pdf.

Teelock, Vijaya. Mauritius Truth and Justice Commission Report. Vol. 1. doi:10.13140/RG.2.1.2699.2801. November 2011. https://www.researchgate.net/publication/278496497_Truth_and_Justice_Commission_report_Volume_I.

Tesler, Michael. "How Anti-Immigrant Attitudes Are Fueling Support for Donald Trump." *Monkey Cage*, November 24, 2015. https://www.washingtonpost.com/news/monkeycage/wp/2015/11/24/how-anti-immigrant-attitudes-are-fueling-support-for-donald-trump/?utm_term=.082085031a4e.

Tesler, Michael. *Post-Racial or Most Racial? Politics and Race in the Obama Era*. Chicago: University of Chicago Press, 2016.

"Text of a Discussion on TV with Mr. Lee Yuan Kew." In *Bilingualism in Our Society*, edited by Ministry of Culture. Singapore: Singapore National Printers, 1978.

Tham, Irene. "Maintaining Harmony Here a 'Daily Struggle.'" *Straits Times*, March 16, 2011.

Theodoridis, Alex. "Me, Myself, and (I), (D), or (R)? Partisanship and Political Cognition through the Lens of Implicit Identity." *Journal of Politics* 79, no. 4 (2017): 1253–1267.

Thio, Li-Ann. "Rule of Law within a Non-Liberal 'Communitarian' Democracy: The Singapore Experience." In *Asian Discourses of Rule of Law: Theories and Implementation of Rule of Law in Twelve Asian Countries, France, and the U.S.*, edited by Randall Peerenboom, 183–224. London: Routledge, 2004.

Thornton, Eleanor Nicole. "Negotiating Race, Ethnicity and Nation: Diasporic Multiculturalism and the Politics of Language in Mauritius." PhD dissertation, Johns Hopkins University, 2017.

Thum, Ping Tijn. *The History of Singapore*. Podcast. Episode 1. 2015.

Thum, Ping Tijn. *The History of Singapore*. Podcast. Episode 17. 2016.

Tichenor, Daniel. *Dividing Lines: The Politics of Immigration Control in America*. Princeton, NJ: Princeton University Press, 2002.

Tongonan, Shannon. "State Wants Makapu'u Campers Moved to Waimanalo." *Honolulu Advertiser*, September 24, 1993.

Torpey, John. *The Invention of the Passport Surveillance, Citizenship and the State*. New York: Cambridge University Press, 1999.

Trask, Haunani-Kay. *From a Native Daughter: Colonialism and Sovereignty in Hawai'i*. Honolulu: University of Hawai'i Press, 1999.

Trimbach, David, and Nicole Reiz. "Unmaking Citizens: The Expansion of Citizenship Revocation in Response to Terrorism." Center for Migration Studies, 2018. https://cmsny.org/publications/unmaking-citizens/.

"Trinidad and Tobago Demographics Profile 2019." Index Mundi, December 7, 2019. https://www.indexmundi.com/trinidad_and_tobago/demographics_profile.html.

Trinidad and Tobago Ministry of Planning and Sustainable Development, Central Statistical Office. "Trinidad and Tobago 2011 Population and Housing Census Demographic Report." 2012. https://www.undp.org/content/dam/trinidad_tobago/docs/DemocraticGovernance/Publications/TandT_Demographic_Report_2011.pdf.

Trinidad and Tobago National Carnival Commission. "Unaudited Statement of Receipts and Payments for the Year Ended September 30, 2014." October 13, 2014. http://www.ncctt.org/new/images/pdf/NCCs_Income_and_Expenditure_Statement_201314.pdf.

"2016 Time Series Study." American National Election Studies. Accessed March 15, 2021. https:// electionstudies.org/data-center/2016-time-series-study/.

United Kingdom Department for Transport. "British Social Attitudes Survey: 2013." July 3, 2014. https://www.gov.uk/government/statistics/british-social-attitudes-survey-2013.

United Nations Population Division. "International Migration Stock 2013: Migrants by Destination and Origin." 2013. https://www.un.org/en/development/desa/population/migration/data/estimates2/estimatesorigin.asp.

United Nations Population Division. "Trends in International Migration Stock: The 2015 Revision." December 2015. https://reliefweb.int/sites/reliefweb.int/files/resources/MigrationStockDocumentation_2015.pdf.

United Nations Statistics Division. "Demographic and Social Statistics." Accessed October 3, 2017. Unstats.un.org.

University of Hawai'i Foundation. "Saving the Hawaiian Language: The Great Work of Saving the Hawaiian Language." Accessed March 12, 2021. http://uhfoundation.org/saving-hawaiian-language.

"Up Close with Tharman Shanmugaratnam." Channel NewsAsia, April 14, 2005.

US Census Bureau. "2020 Census Statistics Highlight Local Population Changes and Nation's Racial and Ethnic Diversity." August 12, 2021. Release Number CB21-CN.55. https://www.census.gov/newsroom/press-releases/2021/population-changes-nations-diversity.html.

US Congress. "S.1783: A Bill Expressing the Policy of the United States regarding the United States Relationship with Native Hawaiians and to Provide a Process for the Recognition by the United States of the Native Hawaiian Governing Entity, and of Other Purposes." 107th Congress (2001–2002). 2001. https://www.congress.gov/bill/107th-congress/senate-bill/1783/text.

"UWI Study: Ethnic Imbalance in T&T Police Service Spans Decades." *Guyana News*, April 3, 2011.

Vanhanen, Tatu. "Domestic Ethnic Conflict and Ethnic Nepotism: A Comparative Analysis." *Journal of Peace Research* 36, no. 1 (1999): 55–73.

Vasil, Raj. *Asianising Singapore: The PAP's Management of Ethnicity*. Singapore: Heinemann, 1995.

Vellien, Clifford. "Rioting in Mauritius Set Off by Jail Death of Singer." *The Guardian*, February 24, 1999. https://www.theguardian.com/world/1999/feb/25/7.

Vespa, Jonathan, Lauren Medina, and David Armstrong. "Demographic Turning Points for the United States: Population Projections for 2020 to 2060." U.S. Census Bureau, March 2018. https://www.census.gov/content/dam/Census/library/publications/2020/demo/p25-1144.pdf.

Waldinger, Roger, and Claudia Der-Martirosian. "The Immigrant Niche: Pervasive, Persistent, Diverse." In *Strangers at the Gates: New Immigrants in Urban America*, edited by Roger Waldinger, 228–271. Berkeley: University of California Press, 2001.

Weiner, Myron. *Sons of the Soil: Migration and Ethnic Conflict in India*. Princeton, NJ: Princeton University Press, 1978.

Weiner, Myron, and Michael Teitelbaum. *Political Demography, Demographic Engineering*. New York: Berghahn Books, 2001.

Weinger, Mackenzie. "Hannity: I've 'Evolved' on Immigration and Support a 'Pathway to Citizenship.'" *Politico*, November 8, 2012. https://www.politico.com/blogs/media/2012/11/hannity-ive-evolved-on-immigration-and-support-a-pathway-to-citizenship-149078.

Whelan, Frederick G. "Democratic Theory and the Boundary Problem." In *Liberal Democracy*, edited by J. R. Pennock and J. W. Chapman, 13–47. New York: NYU Press, 1983.

Whelan, Irene. "Religious Rivalry and the Making of Irish-American Identity." In *Making the Irish American: History and Heritage of the Irish in the United States*, edited by J. J. Lee and Marion Casey, 271–285. New York: New York University Press, 2006.

Wilkinson, Batine Cutaia, Melissa R. Michelson, and Alexis Webster. "Sports Elites, Counter-Stereotypical Statements, and Immigration Attitudes." *Social Science Quarterly* (2021), published online ahead of print.

Williams, Eric Eustace. *History of the People of Trinidad and Tobago*. Brooklyn, NY: A&B, 1962.

Wimmer, Andreas. "Dominant Ethnicity and Dominant Nationhood." In *Rethinking Ethnicity Majority Groups and Dominant Minorities*, edited by Eric Kaufmann, 35–51. London: Routledge, 2004.

Wood, Daniel. "Hawaii's Search for Sovereignty." *Christian Science Monitor*, October 17, 1994.

Yap, Mui Teng. "The Singapore State's Responses to Migration." *SOJOURN* 14, no. 1 (1999): 198–211.

Yelvington, Kevin. "The War in Ethiopia and Trinidad, 1935–36." In *The Colonial Caribbean in Transition: Essays on Postemancipation and Cultural History*, edited by Bridget Brereton and Kevin Yelvington, 189–225. Kingston: The Press, University of the West Indies, 1999.

Yeoh, Brenda S. A. "Bifurcated Labour: The Unequal Incorporation of Transmigrants in Singapore." *Tijdschrift voor Economische en Sociale Geografie* 97, no. 1 (2006): 26–37.

Yeoh, Brenda S. A. "'Upwards' or 'Sideways' Cosmopolitanism? Talent/Labour/Marriage Migrations in the Globalising City-State of Singapore." i 1, no. 1 (2013): 96–116.

Yeoh, Brenda S. A., and Weiqiang Lin. "Chinese Migration to Singapore: Discourses and Discontents in a Globalizing Nation-State." *Asian and Pacific Migration Journal* 22, no. 1 (2013): 31–54.

Yeoh, Brenda S. A., and Weiqiang Lin. "Rapid Growth in Singapore's Immigration Population Brings Policy Challenges." Migration Information Source, 2012. http://www.migrationinformation.org/feature/display.cfm?ID=887.

Yoshino, Troy. "Ua Mau Ke Ea O Ka Aina I Ka Pono: Voting Rights and the Native Hawaiian Sovereignty Plebiscite." *Michigan Journal of Race and Law* 3, no. 2 (1998): 475–522.

Yuen, Belinda. "Creating the Garden City: The Singapore Experience." *Urban Studies* 33, no. 6 (1996): 955–970.

Yukich, Grace. "Constructing the Model Immigrant: Movement Strategy and Immigrant Deservingness in the New Sanctuary Movement." *Social Problems* 60, no. 3 (August 2013): 302–320.

Zaller, John. *The Nature and Origins of Mass Opinion*. Cambridge: Cambridge University Press, 1992.

Zhou, Min, and Gregor Benton. 2017. "Intra-Asian Chinese Migrations: A Historical Overview." In *Contemporary Chinese Diasporas*, edited by Min Zhou, 1–25. Singapore: Palgrave Macmillan, 2017.

Zhou, Min, and Hong Liu. "Homeland Engagement and Host-Society Integration: A Comparative Study of New Chinese Immigrants in the United States and Singapore." *International Journal of Comparative Sociology* 57, nos. 1–2 (2016): 30–52.

Ziblatt, Daniel. *Conservative Parties and the Birth of Democracy*. Cambridge: Cambridge University Press, 2017.

Index

For the benefit of digital users, indexed terms that span two pages (e.g., 52–53) may, on occasion, appear on only one of those pages.

Tables and figures are indicated by *t* and *f* following the page number